12.95
D3-5

ESSAYS IN PROCESS THEOLOGY

ESSAYS IN PROCESS THEOLOGY

Daniel Day Williams

Edited by
Perry LeFevre

Exploration Press, Chicago

Printed in the United States of America

Exploration Press
Chicago Theological Seminary
5757 University Avenue
Chicago, Illinois 60637

ISBN: Cloth: 0–913552–25–9
Paper: 0–913552–26–7

Library of Congress Catalog Card Number 84–82337

Contents

Editor's Preface

Daniel Day Williams was one of the great theological teachers of the last generation. In his years at Chicago and at Union he helped to shape the minds and thought of many who now give leadership to the churches and who work at the tasks of theological reconstruction. His major work, *The Spirit and the Forms of Love,* continues to be one of the most significant formulations of process theology, while his earlier works helped to interpret the relevance of process theology for a broader public. Much of William's work, however, took the form of essays published in theological journals or of contributions to books. This literature is in danger of being lost to the present generation of students and scholars by being scattered in many different publications. It seemed important to the Editors of Exploration Press to bring together many of these essays for the contemporary theological community. As we began this enterprise we were pleased to discover that another of Williams' students, Tony Wolfe, was embarked on a similar project. We have therefore divided the task of gathering the Williams' material. Wolfe's volume will include essays not reprinted in this volume and some previously unpublished lectures.

The organization of this volume of essays is broadly chronological. We have, however, divided Williams' papers into two groups, those which are primarily constructive, developing his own form of process theology, and those which are primarily critical dialogues with other theologians. It has seemed useful to introduce the volume with one of Williams' last papers (1970) "A Philosophical Outlook" in which he gives a synoptic view of his theological position. The volume concludes with a reprinting of the Williams bibliography originally published in the *Union Seminary Quarterly Review* with some additions which escaped the first compilation.

Perry LeFevre

A PHILOSOPHICAL OUTLOOK

1

DANIEL DAY WILLIAMS

Philosophical concerns are an integral part of my work in Christian theology. The Christian faith has always been articulated in relation to philosophical outlooks. The process begins in the New Testament with the Greek and gnostic background of the Logos doctrine, the theme of incarnation, and the stoic elements in Paul's ethical outlook. To be a philosophical theologian is to carry on the task of seeking that understanding which arises from faith and which is coherent with the data of human experience and the rational intelligibility which philosophy seeks.

The service of theology and philosophy to each other must arise from the common search for a truth which lies beyond any particular achievement of either mode of inquiry. Philosophy which is merely the handmaiden of theology is philosophy exploited and divorced from its proper function. Theology which is only philosophical thought in the guise of traditional language is theology divorced from its responsibility to the community of faith. The problem of the proper relationship of the two disciplines has concerned me for many years. I have concluded that there is no single methodological answer. We must tackle our problems of faith and truth in the cultural and philosophic situation in which we find ourselves. Theology may work in various ways in relation to philosophic inquiry and in relation to a particular philosophical outlook. In my own case I have found a new possibility for theology in the philosophy of Alfred North Whitehead and the general point of view of process philosophy and it is with this point of view that I am concerned here.

Critical issues have always arisen for theology and religion on the question of the nature of God and our knowledge of God. The modern questions are those raised by the critical analysis of empirical knowledge beginning with David Hume, and pressed in our time through an analysis of the possible range of language about 'God'. There are also the issues concerning the relevance of any meaning of God to the values and decisions which press upon us in the twentieth century. This latter point was put forcefully by

Professor Alisdair Macintyre in his Bampton lectures in Columbia University in 1966. He argued that whereas questions about God were relevant to the world-view of the eighteenth century and the nineteenth with the new sciences of Newton and of Darwin, in our time the problems posed by the scientific aspect of nature do not involve issues which are resolvable by appeal to God. The pressing issues of our time concern the achievement of viable human modes of living together, and to these issues traditional meanings of God are not relevant.

Theology in my view must meet the philosophical issues which are thus posed for any belief in God. This is not primarily for apologetic reasons. It is for the sake of the self-understanding within faith itself. Believers in God are also contemporary men who live in the same world which scientists, social strategists, and logicians inhabit. We are all responsible for engaging with human problems. I reject the view that theology can be satisfied with a private and parochial truth which bears on no concern for the common life.

Two theses about God will be defended here.

First, the critique by positivism of assertions about God is directed against the traditional conceptions of God. As a criticism of traditional doctrine it has validity. What is required is the reconception of the metaphysical aspect of traditional theology and the development of a concept of God in which his transcendence and immanence, his being and becoming, his power and his participation in the world's life are held together. Theology which holds the traditional conception of God's being is not able to interpret the world's life as a continuing evolutionary activity, and the life of man as a realm of limited freedom and originality within which man has power to shape his environment and his existence.

Second, God conceived as metaphysically creative activity, as becoming, does enter into the processes of human society, and his being lends its structure and value to the forms of human relatedness. The task is to show how the actuality of God does qualify and give both judgment and hope to the quest for social justice.

It is astonishing in the discussion about God among the philosophical critics of traditional theology how little attention has been paid to the conception of God in process philosophy even though that conception has had such major contributions as those of C. Lloyd Morgan, Henri Bergson, S. Alexander, Alfred North Whitehead, Henry Nelson Wieman, and Charles Hartshorne. So far as I can tell, practically the entire discussion about religious language has gone on as if the only conception of God which can be offered is that of traditional Christian theism especially in the form it takes in Anglican orthodoxy. Paul Tillich's theology is suggestive on the side of metaphysical doctrine; but on every crucial question such as God's relation to time, his impassibility, and his relation to the ontological categories Tillich sides with the tradition.[1]

It is my purpose here to state the theistic philosophic outlook which I find developed in process thought, especially that of Alfred North Whitehead and Charles Hartshorne, and to explore one way upon which this point of view may be fruitfully developed as a philosophy directly relevant to the task of living together and achieving a tolerable environment for significant human living.

What Whitehead has made possible in his metaphysics is the statement of an authentically social doctrine of reality. It is perhaps the first truly social doctrine of being ever stated. I perfer the term social to organic in speaking of metaphysical structure, for organism suggests a monistic view which Whitehead explicitly disavows though there is a type of organic relatedness of all actualities to each other in his doctrine. Whitehead proposes his metaphysics as a way of unifying an intelligible world view based on the data of modern science, and as a critical instrument for appraising traditional ethical and religious systems, including the Christian doctrine of God. His critique of Christian theology is profoundly important and I have elsewhere analysed it at length.[2]

I shall here state my own philosophical convictions about this view of reality and the theory of metaphysical knowledge which it involves.

The statement of a metaphysical outlook involves a twofold requirement. There is the establishment of the basis on which metaphysical assertions can be made and justified. That is the epistemological and methodological problem. Second, there is the elaboration of the metaphysical doctrine. It is a cardinal tenet of my position that these two tasks are inseparable. Our understanding of the way we know cannot be separated from our view of what we know, and what we know involves judgments about what things, and minds, and statements are. These are metaphysical judgments,

[1] I have elaborated this critique in 'Tillich's Doctrine of God,' *The Philosophical Forum*, Vol. xviii, 1960–1.

[2] Daniel D. Williams, 'Deity, Monarchy, and Metaphysics; Whitehead's Critique of the Theological Tradition', in Ivor Leclerc, ed. *The Relevance of Whitehead*, New York, Macmillan, 1961.

or at least they have metaphysical aspects. Bertrand Russell certainly cannot be accused of any strong bias toward metaphysics, but he says in *An Inquiry into Meaning and Truth:*

'. . . Complete metaphysical agnosticism is not compatible with the maintenance of linguistic propositions. Some modern philosophers hold that we know much about language, but nothing about anything else. This view forgets that language is an empirical phenomenon like another, and that a man who is metaphysically agnostic must deny that he knows when he uses a word. For my part, I believe that, partly by means of the study of syntax, we can arrive at considerable knowledge concerning the structure of the world.'[1]

Since one thing must be said before another, I will state first the conception of knowledge which I hold and then outline the main points in a social doctrine of reality.

The epistemological doctrine might be called an organic empiricism. It has affinities with the idealist's rendering of experience, and with American pragmatism. We know through the grasping of our environment by the psychophysical organism which displays for mental reflection its patterns, qualities, and interactions. The experience from which we derive knowledge is not in the first instance the sense-data. They are important but superficial elements in the organic process. The experience is the concretely felt bodily being-in-the-world and grasping the aliveness, the becoming, the give and take with a real world in the total complex functioning of the animal body and its conceptual apparatus. The flow of experience is the stream of qualities coming into our bodily perceiving. We 'cut up' the world through the functioning of our perceptive apparatus. We screen out much of it. Our bodies take in more than our consciousness ever grasps. But we really perceive the world of things which have their life, their qualities, their impingement upon our receptive organism.

There are two modes of perception; presentational immediacy and causal efficacy, as Whitehead calls them. The first is the end-product of the total bodily functioning as it produces the sharp specific qualities on the sense-data. The second is the deep organic bodily process of 'non-sensuous intuition' through which we feel our being in the world in interaction with other real things. Hume

[1] Bertrand Russell, *An Inquiry Into Meaning and Truth*, New York, W. W. Norton, 1940, pp. 437–8.

attends only to presentational immediacy and can find no relations there, but Whitehead denies that the flow of atomic sensations is the only mode of experience. There is an organic flow of feeling from the past into the present. Each new occasion of experience grasps the immediate past as now efficacious in its conditioning of the new occasion of experience. Hence causality is directly experienced when we attend to the ground stream of becoming.

Each occasion of experience involves the grasp of the structure of possibility in the form of aim at a new pattern of completed satisfaction. Hence into our knowing there enters always some laying hold of the realm of possible structures as qualifying present experience, and luring us towards a future where possibilities become realized. Hence our knowledge of the world has its 'conceptual pole', our feeling of the realm of structures which may or may not come to be exemplified in spatio-temporal realities. By calling this 'conceptual' we do not say that we always consciously attend to it. The body-mind organism may grasp the structure of the future more clearly than does the conscious mind in particular moments. Psychological clinics give abundant evidence here.

Our knowledge of the world is a knowledge of the structures exemplified in the actual world as we take it in through its structures for definition, analysis, and logical development. The fundamental process of knowing is the bringing of abstract structures to concrete experience for verification. There are degrees of precision, of course, and there are kinds of questions we can ask which concern the possibility of conceiving the most general characteristics of the world. Here we come to the possibility of metaphysical knowledge; but one further point about the epistemological doctrine must be made.

All knowing is evaluation. There is no knowledge without selection, affirmation, and negation of specific possibilities in our relations to the world. Our bodies select and our minds select. We give attention or we refuse it. We judge importance and triviality.

Every formulation of an hypothesis involves judgments of relevance and precision which have an aspect of evaluation. Some human adjustment to an on-going process is involved in all knowing. This is what the pragmatists have clearly taught us. All the implications of this view cannot be developed here, but it is worth while pointing to its significance for ethics, since the question of ethical judgments is raised anew by contemporary analytic philosophy.

The problem of value judgments viewed from this perspective is not a special problem involved in some types of judgments. It is involved in all judgments whatsoever. To be is to value, and to judge is to value some mode of thought and form of expression over others. To be sure all value judgments are not ethical. They may be aesthetic, organic, or purely utilitarian. Ethical judgments arise where a value judgment involves the principles of valuation which a responsible person accepts as relevant to his use of his freedom, and in which his relationships to the significance of other persons and their needs is involved.

METAPHYSICAL KNOWLEDGE

Of course we know something; but do we have knowledge of 'reality', the kind of knowledge which philosophy has sought in metaphysical inquiry? There are types of metaphysics which it seems to me cannot be brought within the scope of the kind of knowledge I have been pointing to. What we can know is the generic traits of existence. The position I take is that metaphysical inquiry depends upon the relating of conceptual structure to experience just as does scientific inquiry, but what marks off metaphysical inquiry is that it must treat all experience as evidence. This generality of aim gives metaphysical inquiry its special character and constitutes its central problems. My position concerning metaphysical method is as follows.

The question of what constitutes evidence for any assertion has received intense discussion in contemporary philosophy. Empirical theories of verifiability hold that evidence consists of specific observations of the behaviour of things as that behaviour is predicted in hypotheses. General theories contain elements not directly confirmable in this way; but they are indirectly confirmed in so far as they are logically related to hypotheses which involve specific predictions. Evidence derived from observations can justify the claim to knowledge, at least to probable knowledge, in so far as experience yields specific confirmations or disconfirmations. While there is a necessary caution in holding that what has taken place in a certain way will do so in the future, science proceeds with a pragmatic expectation that prediction is possible.

Metaphysical statements have a different character from scientific statements because they refer to structures which are found in everything, or they may refer to the 'whole'. The object of metaphysical inquiry has been differentiy understood in philosophy.

Broadly speaking the three possibilities are to define metaphysics as the search for 'being itself', or for the 'whole', or for the most general structures which characterize everything that is. The question of what constitutes evidence cannot be satisfactorily answered apart from a clear position on the object of the metaphysical inquiry. For the purpose of the present discussion we can acknowledge that these three views of metaphysical inquiry have this in common, they seek evidence which will justify assertions about what is real which go beyond the description of any particular area of experience. Metaphysics seeks the characterization of everything that is. This holds whether the reality is conceived as 'being-itself' beyond existence, or the 'whole', or the generic traits of all processes. In each case the question of the logic of validity involves the question of how a limited experience can justify statements about what characterizes every experience. How can we go from some experience to 'every possible experience'?

It is understandable that metaphysicians and their critics sometimes take the position that metaphysical doctrines appeal to intuitions which cannot be justified by anything beyond themselves. They must be accepted on faith or as visions which satisfy, guide, and enrich life, but which are not subject to confirmation or disconfirmation as scientific statements.

Against this view I argue that there is evidence which may count for or against every metaphysical assertion because every statement about what is 'real' or about the traits of all experience is a statement about some part of reality. All experience is potentially evidential with regard to metaphysical statements. We say 'potentially' because for something to function as evidence it must be related to an hypothesis and to some prescribed mode of investigation, so that the statement to be confirmed is logically related to the resolution of the inquiry which is going on. The metaphysician does not simply stare at the world, or turn his gaze inward. He inquires in relation to a set of concepts and their logical and existential implications. What he is seeking is a structure of interrelated categories which in principle can be verifiable in every experience, and in every type of datum yielded by human investigation. He seeks the structures which are involved in the description of everything that is, and in the way things go together to make up one world.

It may seem trivial to stress that for the metaphysician everything gives evidence of the structures which characterize everything; but the real point now becomes clear that the difficulty in metaphysics does not lie in the absence of evidence but rather in the wealth of evidence. Concepts such as those of space, time, cause, freedom, value, possibility, structure, process, matter, mind appear in every metaphysical doctrine in some form. The problem is to clarify their meaning and their relationships and therefore to gain some knowledge about the way the world is. We experience a common world or at least a world which has some traits in common. Whitehead says, 'Metaphysics is nothing but the description of the generalities which apply to all the details of practice'.[1] Metaphysical systems vary greatly because there is so much evidence and it is subject to alternative types of analysis.

Are there, then, criteria for the validity of metaphysical doctrines? Whitehead states three: consistency, which is defined in logical terms; applicability, that is, the metaphysical scheme must be exemplified in some area of experience; and adequacy, that is, it must express and illuminate what is found in its extension to every possible area of experience. Whitehead recognizes, of course, that completeness in any of these aspects is a limit to guide inquiry and is never attained. He pleads for the widest possible understanding of the range of experience:

'Nothing can be omitted, experience drunk, and experience sober, experience sleeping and experience waking . . . experience anticipatory and experience retrospective . . . experience normal and experience abnormal.

And he then comments:

'The main sources of evidence respecting this width of human experience are language, social institutions, and action, including thereby the fusion of the three which is language interpreting action and social institutions.'[2]

Every doctrine of the nature of being is in some sense a synthesis of concepts which taken together are asserted to characterize what is really there presented to us in experience. Traditionally metaphysical systems have not only sought this synthesis but have made

[1] Alfred North Whitehead, *Process and Reality*, New York, Macmillan, 1936 p. 19.

[2] Alfred North Whitehead, *Adventures of Ideas*, New York, Macmillan, 1933, pp. 290–1.

extravagant claims for their completeness and finality. Sometimes they have appealed to a special kind of experience for the ultimate knowledge which unites the whole, as in mystical neo-Platonism. Sometimes they have held that the rational structure which embraces the whole of reality can be philosophically exhibited as in Hegel's unguarded claims. Often religious apologetics have been constructed to show that the religious conception of the divine being provides an adequate unifying principle for metaphysics.

Against any claim for metaphysical omniscience a cautious assessment of the nature of metaphysical knowledge is in order. Rather than treat metaphysical systems as having a special privilege in access to knowledge of reality, they should be recognized as explorations of an infinitely complex reality, and the attempt to reach an adequate system of categories for interpreting it. All systems are abstractions. While religious experience and valuations have their rightful place in the inquiry, they cannot claim some privileged access to final truth apart from the general justification which they sustain in the inquiry as a whole. Evidence is present in abundance which confirms or disconfirms metaphysical statements, but there is always a limit on the process of verification, and therefore on the claim we should make for the adequacy of the conclusions.

Such a metaphysical method does not rule out reference to religious experience. There is no *a priori* reason why religious experience should not count towards our ultimate judgment about what things are. But the method does not permit the use of metaphysical argument to reach conclusions congenial to a particular religious outlook regardless of what the range of evidence in human experience will sustain.

There are always commitments and valuations in the perspective of every inquirer. These elements do not arise from the evidence alone apart from personal response, and cultural conditioning. There is no metaphysical inquiry without some implicit valuations which arise in the faith or the personal commitment of the inquirer. But the evidence which justifies a conclusion must be what is gathered from as faithful a discrimination of the whole range of experience as possible. And if it be said that the evidence for a metaphysical outlook cannot be conclusive since differences of interpretation are possible, it needs to be pointed out that in that respect scientific theories are in no different situation.

From this point of view the metaphysical inquiry after God is no longer a search for a cause outside the world, but for that reality which is involved in the structure and becoming of everything that is, and which is necessary to give coherence, relatedness, and an ultimate valuation to each occasion of experience. Either God is immanent in the metaphysical situation as its supreme and necessary participant, or rational experiential knowledge of him is impossible. I agree entirely with contemporary humanists and atheists that the problem of knowledge of God requires us to ask what difference God as an actual entity makes in the flow of events and our understanding of their structure. Traditional metaphysics has generally looked for God as an external 'cause' of the world and has therefore been baffled about how to apply the term cause to this relationship, and has required God as responsible for everything that happens. Hume's critique stands clearly justified.

In process metaphysics we require God not as external cause but as the immanent structure-giving actuality, participating in all becoming, and moving from actuality to new possibilities with the life of the world.

There has developed among Whiteheadians an issue concerning the relation of the ontological argument to the kind of metaphysical description which we can give of that supreme actual entity which is God in his primordial nature as the structure of all possibility and in his consequent nature as the supreme experiencer of the objective outcome of every actual occasion. Charles Hartshorne has taken the position that the only argument for God is the ontological argument.[1] While he once found the traditional arguments in various forms in Whitehead, he now rejects all forms of empiricism in the knowledge of God. The ontological idea is the statement of what is required for a rational understanding of anything; for the standards of perfection must be accessible to reason, and the absolute standard of perfection implies its own existence. To be sure the perfection of God is that of a continually creative and 'self-surpassing' perfection. Hartshorne holds to the doctrine of God's continual becoming as process theologians hold it. But he believes that all reliance on experiential knowledge for affirmation of God's existence is futile.

The ontological argument stands as the permanent challenge of conceptual rationality to a metaphysical system. I am one of those

[1] Charles Hartshorne, *The Logic of Perfection*, LaSalle, Open Court, 1962; *Anselm's Discovery*, LaSalle, Ill., Open Court; and *A Natural Theology for our Time*, LaSalle, Open Court, 1967.

who hold that affirmations of existence require some kind of experience of what exists. I cannot see what use the ontological argument is to our understanding of God and the world apart from our experience of that 'most perfect being' which enters into every thought. Is the idea of God equatable with an experience of God? William Ernest Hocking put it this way in *The Meaning of God in Human Experience*. But if this be so then the ontological argument does not move simply from concept to actuality but from a concept which involves experience to a description of what is experienced.

The service of reason to metaphysical understanding involves the clarification of what is involved in understanding God as that being whose actuality is necessary to the existence of every other actuality. But I keep my reliance for the reality of our knowledge of God on the conviction that in every experience we are, however dimly, aware of the sustaining, value-producing, goal-ordering reality at work in all things. I am not sure I am saying something different from Charles Hartshorne here. He continually refers to experience in giving concrete content to the idea of perfection. I am concerned only that preoccupation with the ontological argument does not deprive empirical theism of its claim that God is experienced. What Hartshorne has done is to show that the logic of perfection can apply to God in a way which undercuts the traditional monarchial absolutism in the doctrine of God, and this is an achievement of epic proportions in the history of man's vision of deity.

Process metaphysics proposes to elaborate an authentic doctrine of the *social* character of reality. The elaboration of the structure of sociality is one of the pressing requirements for metaphysics and theology relevant to contemporary man's experience. Here surely the issue about the significance of God for human relationships must be met. In the concluding part of this article I outline the point of view which I am trying to elaborate, and indicate some main lines along which further work in process philosophy may go on.

THE LOGIC OF SOCIALITY

One way of exhibiting the meaning of a position is to identify the kinds of problems to which it leads. For process philosophy the metaphysical task is the elaboration of the social doctrine of the world and of God. We have had an implicit monarchianism in the metaphysical tradition in which all meaning is finally determined by one omnipotent source whether that be God, or the scientific method, or reason, or sense data. It has been opposed by a nominalism in which nothing is necessarily related to anything else, and relations are merely names for accidental arrangements of items in experience. These two poles offered as exclusive alternatives have dominated and I believe corrupted much of the philosophical discussion of being.

There are ethical implications of this monarchianism. The source of responsibility is either some supreme and external law given before whom there is no response save that of an absolute obedience which adds nothing creative to the universe, or there is anarchy without any basis of responsible relatedness. A social doctrine of reality in its ethical dimension would be one in which individual creativity and significance has its place in the context of a social process, with means and ends, conditions and consequences, freedom and responsibility, in some organic mutual interaction.

Such a statement can, of course, be more easily made than expounded. But it indicates the overall direction. The task which is imposed upon us is elaborating such a conception of how the world and its possibilities, God and the creatures are together in an ongoing process. From this point of view we can explore the nature of man's relation both to the natural order and to God who enters into every relationship as the supreme member of the society of being. God functions in his eternal primordial aspect as the structure of possibility, and in his concrete consequent aspect as participant in the society of free creative beings. The entire society depends upon him in a way which does not apply to the creatures. He is necessary to them, but no particular creature is essential to him for his being. Charles Hartshorne has suggested the analogy here of the human personality, which is in Whiteheadian terms a society with a dominant member. A route of actual occasions of experience forms the ruling thread of continuity which mobilizes, informs, and sustains the integrity of the person. This is only an analogy when used to describe God's relationship to the world, but it does point towards that kind of structure which we shall have to describe if we are to have a theistic account of the pattern of the social. Every relationship of things to each other in the world will reflect their participation in a structural order and a supreme experience which is in the actual process in which both participate. For one being to respond to another is to create a new situation to which God must respond, and the divine response enters into the qualification of each new occasion of experience between the finite members of the society.

Two persons, A and B, are in conflict with one another. Each asserts himself in the relationship, and communicates his interests, his feelings, his indignation. What A does creates a new situation for B, and B's response to A reconstitutes the situation for A. But neither A nor B has the meaning of his action solely within himself. Each appeals to standards of judgment, meaning, right and wrong, which he asserts as the true meaning of the conflict. Each tries to change the other, or destroy the other according to an image which he holds, not only of himself but of life and being. So the meaning of the relationship brings each to the boundary of that which gives shape to the being of both, which holds before each a structured future with certain delimited possibilities, including, perhaps, the possibility of reconciliation. The appeal to a good which embraces both, or to a possibility beyond the present state of either A or B is, metaphysically speaking, an appeal to recognize the larger context in which the conflict takes place. It is, though it may be mute and unrecognized, an appeal to God.

God is present in the relationship first as the order of possibility which gives logical structure to every element in the experience. Without God there would be no conflict. Chaos leads to no decision. Only where there are meanings to be appealed to, satisfactions to be derived can there be a clash. The conflict may be over the meanings of words and their interpretation. It may be over the appropriation of items of value, property, ideas, or institutions. It may be the dark background of hostile feeling which arises out of past history and resentments and colours the present perception of each by the other. In every case there is the immanent structure of the order of valuation of which each participant must be aware in order to discover the meaning of his relationship to the other.

God is also present as the supreme appropriation in a unity of experience of the actual feelings and decisions of the participants. No human experience is self-contained. It has depths of awareness of the issues of truth and error, fact and illusion of which we are not the standard but for which a standard must exist. Being known by another has within it a tangent which reflects an awareness of what being fully known by another would mean. 'God knows', we say, piously or profanely, giving linguistic testimony to our sense that what is actual must be known as actual in some experience, and that ours is fragmentary.

In this doctrine the conflict between A and B means something for them, but it also means something for God. It presents to God new data to be brought into his experience of the world with its suffering, its becoming and its possibilities. The meaning of the conflict, therefore, is not only what A and B find it to be for themselves, but what it is for the larger society of which they are a part and that society includes the divine experience. What we are for ourselves and one another is both judged and adjusted by what we are for God. The meaning of any life is not complete in itself, it is what it is for the society of being. 'For the love of God', we say, appealing in agony or pity or joy to our sense that what we are and do has a destiny in something beyond this present enjoyment or suffering.

Professor Findlay has recently written that the idea of God 'has unique logical properties'.[1] From the process point of view, those properties have to do with God's unique metaphysical status; but they do not require the complete separation of God's being or the content of the divine experience and its value from what happens in the world. The use of the phrase 'acts of God' for 'inexplicable catastrophes' reflects the implicit monarchianism in much of our religious language. The affirmation 'God with us' fully interpreted has profound implications for a more adequate language of value judgments. The good society is not the society beyond all struggle, suffering and incompleteness, but the society most open to the widening creative life which moves through it, which reaches toward a good it can never fully embody, but with a confidence in its ultimate worth because it involves the life of every member, and this includes the life of God which appreciates, judges, and is enriched by every finite good.

A social metaphysics will ultimately lead to the transformation of religious language because every language includes the adumbration of modes of metaphysical thought.

It is to the elaboration of the implications of the social vision of reality that process philosophy can address itself. Metaphysics, ethics, aesthetics, and religion are all aspects of the total task. My own thought has turned towards the logical formulation of the structure of social relationship. Can we set forth the complex of interrelationships which is invloved in the way in which things come into being in relation to their own past, to other entities, to future possibilities? Can we formulate the structural relationship which holds

[1] J. N. Findlay, *Language, Mind, and Value*, London, Allen & Unwin, 1963, p. 9.

between God as the supreme member of the society of being and all the finite members? The simple logic of one and many will not suffice for this, nor will the traditional notion of God as being itself which absorbs all particular beings into one transcendent unity. A society is both one and many, it compromises individual members with their freedom and spontaneity, yet each individual participates in the ground of all possibility and is related to the supreme participant, God. It is the problems involved in stating the abstract aspects of such a view which I have called the logic of sociality. The use of the term 'logic' here may produce some perplexity. How far can we identify the analysis of forms of existential relationships as a 'logical' problem? Carnap seems to believe this is possible. He indicates that Russell and Whitehead began the application of logic to existential relations, but did not carry it very far.[1]

I shall here summarily set forth what would seem to be some requirements of an adequate logic of our speech about social relationships.

A first requirement would be that all existential relations would involve both the freedom and individuality of each member of the society as well as the participation of each member in the life of the others, drawing upon them and contributing to them. To be is to become, but to become is to draw upon the achieved becoming of other things, including the events in one's own past, the becoming of other things. It is also to draw upon the structure of possibility which embraces all becoming. In Whitehead's universe to some extent 'we are one another'. Absolute individuality is as meaningless as the absolute unity of all things. What each appropriates from another never exhausts the uniqueness of the other, but uniqueness is always a contribution of value or disvalue to a society.

But in a society where there is a supreme participant necessary to every other member, to be related to other individuals is to be related to that structural order which enters into every individual determination. In personal terms, to be related to another person is to be related to that person as he is related to other persons and to God. To value another person is not only to appreciate his being in itself but his being as it contributes to every other experience including the value of the unifying experience of all things which is the experience of God. From this point of view we can state in clear if abstract terms the answer to Professor Macintyre's chal-

[1] Rudolf Carnap, *The Logical Structure of the World*, Chicago, University of Chicago Press, 1967, p. 8.

lenge as to whether the idea of God is relevant to contemporary social problems. The problem of our time is the problem of how men can find a free, humane, just relationship to one another. The issues of what kind of being and value men assign to one another, the sources of ultimate human valuation of life, and the kind of freedom which belong to persons are all questions to which theism contributes an answer. The discovery of God is the discovery of a metaphysical order which binds life to life, in a dynamic community and that surely is relevant to every social issue.

A second requirement of the logic of sociality is the working out of the insight that all action involves being acted upon. Monarchianism again dominates much of our language here. To be 'free', we say, is to dispose of the other, to be invulnerable, to brush aside all obstacles. But metaphysically this is false. Nothing acts effectively without being conformed to the world. To act toward another is to enter into a mutual interaction. What the employer does toward his employees remakes the employer. What the revolutionary does to the established power reshapes the mind and being of the revolutionary. This is not a moralistic prescription that we ought to take account of consequences. It is a metaphysical analysis which reveals that all action is self-transformation through relationship to the other. Much moralizing actually overlooks this metaphysical insight. It forgets that the moral stance itself remakes the being of the person who holds it, for better or for worse. One remembers Kierkegaard's astute analysis of the puritanical conscience. Being afraid of falling into guilt, we fall into guilt.[1] The art of self-control is always the art of discovering the conditions of self-transformation.

The third requirement is the elaboration of the logic of value judgments in the context of social relatedness in which values occur. Contextualism in ethics and value theory is one of the pervasive movements of thought in our time and process philosophy agrees to a considerable measure with the contextualist thesis. Things are good in so far as they serve the increase of a certain kind of being and creativity in the context in which they occur. What is relevant, releasing and effective for the increase of social communion in one situation may become obstructive habit in another context. Every present good must be appraised in relation to what is now given, but also in relation to the continuum of means and ends, conditions

[1] S. Kierkegaard, *The Concept of Dread*. Eng. trans. by Walter Lowrie. Princeton University Press, 1946, Ch. 11.

and consequences, which stretches into the future. Morality which is simply the imposition of abstract law without this concrete responsibility for the future consequences of acts is truncated and legalistic. It becomes destructive.

The logic of value judgments thus becomes involved in the pattern of social relationship. And again we are brought to the question of an ultimate standard of value judgment which is not outside of but pervasive in every particular context. It is the question of God raised at the point of value judgments. I must mention here the important contribution of Henry Nelson Wieman, who points out that the problem of value judgment in the context of a genuinely social metaphysics leads to a distinction between two kinds of good: *created goods*, which are achieved desirable things or situations, and *creative good* which is the living process of creativity, the creative event bringing new structures of meaning and value into existence. Wieman's doctrine is a major contribution to value theory.[1] It suggests a new problem in the logical analysis of value judgments. *Creative* good is good because it produces new *created* goods, but *created* goods are good as they serve the working of creative good. Here is significant dialectic in value judgments. Clearly the supreme standard of value, God, must value both kinds of good, but in different ways. For Wieman God is identified with the *creative* good, but the creative good must seek and value the created results of its activity.

We see here again that the theistic outlook is relevant to the question of human commitment within social processes and conflicts. The creative good can claim absolute commitment, but it is not identical with our human ideals and structures of value as we now hold them. All present judgments are held subject to the working of the creative good which they serve.

Finally, the logic of a genuinely social relationship must include the logic of an ever-enlarging experience. It must embrace past, present, and future. A society requires new being, freedom, spontaneity of the members bringing new value into the increasing life of the whole. Perfection identified with static completeness is the apotheosis of monarchical values and culture. The logic of perfection needs to be radically restated so that the conception of perfection itself, that is the aim of all striving, includes the continual search for new good beyond present actua-

[1] Henry Nelson Wieman, *The Source of Human Good*, Chicago, The University of Chicago Press, 1946, Ch. III.

lity. The adventure of life is involved in the meaning of fulfillment.

Such a doctrine of perfection does not in one sense solve the problem of evil. There is no answer to the question why the world is the way it is, why goods and evils are mixed as they are. But the doctrine of social relatedness does not impute the cause of all imperfection to the creator of the society. To create a society (and we speak of God as the creator, for without him there is no society) is to create creators with their spontaneity and freedom. It is to make even the creator vulnerable to the accidents, the distortions, and the perversities of free and finite beings. If God is to have a world in which love has any meaning, he must have a world where evil is risked. Thus far the logic of social relatedness can take us. It is not an explanation of how the world came to be what it is; but a discovery of what is required if the supreme value of communion among things is intelligible at all.

Abstractions have just as much meaning as comes from their power to illuminate the concrete realities of human experience. The search for a new logic of sociality, abstracted from the complex of relations of God and the world seems to me a necessary and revolutionary philosophical task. It would contribute to the illumination of the human struggle to find viable forms of social existence. It is not a substitute for empirical social analysis, for historical understanding, or artistic sensitivity. Logic and metaphysics are not the climax of the search for reality, but only indispensable modes of analysis of the concrete.

The logic of sociality needs therefore to be put alongside other modes of interpretation of human experience. I am concerned with the possibility of a phenomenological understanding of human experience. Such studies of man as those of Paul Ricoeur from a phenomenological point of view surely supplement metaphysical analysis, and I have attempted one such analysis of suffering.[1]

Phenomenology without a metaphysical doctrine of being, however, seems to me to fall short of what phenomenologists are seeking, that is, the meaning of the forms of human experience. For the meaning is not only in intuited essences. Man is in a world, and his meanings arise between him and his world. The question of what is real is ultimately a metaphysical question. Hence the abstrac-

[1] Cf. Paul Ricoeur, *Philosophie de la Volonté* I, II, Paris, Aubier, 1950, 1960. My analysis is in a paper on 'Suffering and Being in Empirical Theology' to be published by the Divinity School of the University of Chicago in a volume of essays on empirical theology.

tions of metaphysical inquity are instruments for detecting the ground patterns in the real world and thus illuminating experience.

The question of how the logic of sociality can enter into Christian theology is a separate topic; but it is not hard to see that when the Christian faith has affirmed that God is love, and has seen the divine life as a self-giving redemption of the world through suffering, it has anticipated the social view of reality which has all too often been obscured by the failure of traditional metaphysics to see that God must share the life of the world and its becoming if he is to be relevant to it.

THEOLOGY AND TRUTH 2

DANIEL DAY WILLIAMS

CHRISTIAN theology, the systematic expression in verbal symbols of Christian belief, arises within the Christian movement and has a function within that movement. No one has shown more clearly than Shailer Mathews the organic relation between Christian thought and the life of the Christian community. But what is the central function of theology? Does it exist primarily to maintain the loyalty of Christians and the vitality of the movement, or is its primary function the inquiry for and the expression of truth about those objects with which Christianity as a religion is concerned?

Some recent interpretations of theology deny that its aim can be the inquiry after truth. These interpretations are of two quite different kinds. The first, usually held by those who do not call themselves theologians, denies that theology has any concern with truth at all. Its function is to maintain the traditional symbolism of religion in such a way that the devotion of believers is kept strong and undisturbed. The second interpretation, advanced by many theologians, is that theology's function is the exposition of a truth which in essence is known or possessed by faith before the work of theology begins. Theology aims at unfolding or interpreting a truth which is given as the presupposition of theology itself.

Definition of the term "theology" is arbitrary, and undoubtedly theologies of both these types exist. This paper does not quarrel with the definitions, except at the point where they become exclusive. It seeks to inquire whether there may not be a legitimate type of Christian theology arising within the Christian movement, using Christian symbols, and yet having as its primary aim and function the inquiry after and disclosure of truth about the objects of Christian concern: that is, God, Christ, man, sin, salvation, the church.

I

The possibility of such a theology may be disclosed through an examination of the two current ways of denying that theology is inquiry after truth.

Professor E. R. Walker holds that theology has no interest in truth. In a paper, "Philosophy of Religion and Theology," read at the American Philosophical Society in April, 1940, he said:

> The question: is this idea Christian? indicates the nature and function of theology. The question: is this idea true? indicates the character of philosophy of religion.
>
> Theology is concerned to preserve the tradition as it expresses itself in ideational symbols.

It may not be amiss to remark immediately that such a theology must find itself in the peculiar position of having to conceal its real nature from those to whom it is addressed; for religion always is concerned with the truth of its beliefs, and the effectiveness of belief depends in large part upon its being held as true.

The central question raised by Walker's definition is: Can truth about the objects of Christian concern be adequately sought for and expressed in the traditional symbols? Professor Walker's answer, in the paper referred to, is "No"; hence his denial that theology can be concerned with truth. He holds that the inherited symbols of religion produce primarily emotional or "biotic" responses and therefore tend to obscure the truth rather than to reveal it.

> It is usually the case that biotically rich symbols are semantically obscure, indefinite, or ambiguous. . . . . A symbol that is weighted with pragmatic significance is a handicap rather than an asset in philosophic inquiry.

Admitting that the problem of symbolism in relation to truth is crucial for theology, we may at once state a thesis in sharp opposition to Professor Walker's. Not only is it the case that the use of an inherited symbolism does not necessarily hinder the search for truth, but the truth about the objects of religion can never be adequately discovered or expressed apart from such symbolism, with its freight of aesthetic, emotional, and qualitative content.

Christianity is concerned with objects and events which have as their most important characteristics values and qualities. Values and qualities, whether of aesthetic, moral, religious, or any other sort, must always awaken some response of a definite feeling quality in order to be discerned. Stones have no feeling for symphonies, and only persons can appreciate saintliness. But it is precisely this qualitative richness of value in God and in the life related to him which can never be discovered, expressed, or communicated apart from words and other symbols which have the capacity to suggest, express, and illuminate these value-facts.

This truth is so elementary that it is easily overlooked, especially by those overly impressed with the precision of the mathematical sciences. The attempt to express truth about any of the higher realms of value inevitably involves language which is suggestive and qualitative. Any newspaper column of music, painting, or moving-picture criticism will offer abundant illustration.

It is not clear at all that even the most abstract and precise science—logic—can consider itself apart from all qualitative considerations. Logicians are fond of comparing the "elegance" of various demonstrations, and a capacity to respond with some trace of aesthetic sensitivity to elegance in logic is certainly an aid to understanding it.

Let logic, however, stand for the pole of scientific precision apart from any merely suggestive or qualitative considerations. The farther one moves toward the other pole of truth about the values of existence the less absolutely precise the terms can become, and the more they tend to become artistic illuminations of truth. This conclusion is illustrated and defended at length not by a theologian but by a philosopher—Professor Wilbur M. Urban, of Yale, in his *Language and Reality*. The results of his research are stated by Urban with respect to poetry and are also directly applied to religious knowledge:

> The insight symbol, we found, does not merely *describe*, through images drawn from sense, an object otherwise known (conceptually), but finds its importance as a gateway into a "spiritual" world. . . . . Images from the narrower world of sensuous intuition are taken, not merely to picture, but to give us insight into, to enable us to intuit a non-sensuous world of value relations. . . . . These symbols "say something," and what they say may be not only "more valuable than the real values," to use Van Gogh's terms, but more true than the literal truth.[1]

I believe one can accept the fundamental validity of this analysis without being committed to the particular supernaturalistic metaphysical framework in which Urban places it or to the doctrine of an entirely nonsensuous experience.

Professor Charles Hartshorne has sought for the utmost possible precision in the formulation of the results of metaphysical inquiry, yet he also protests against the tendency to exclude from philosophy all meanings which cannot be given precise mathematical formulation:

> Positivism tends almost uniformly to encourage science in its exclusions and to rob philosophy of one of its main functions. The hard dualism between cognitive and emotive meaning is partly responsible for this tendency. Peirce held that the idea of God was more emotional than intellectual. But he did not commit the *non sequitur* of supposing that the idea was therefore not at all descriptive of the universe, but merely of the state of man's mind. If the universe is itself emotional in character—and some parts of it certainly are—the way for us to reflect this character is by paralleling the cosmic emotions in ourselves.[2]

Since he does not do so here, I do not know whether Professor Hartshorne would draw the two conclusions which seem to be implied by this statement: first, that the expression of truth

[1] *Language and Reality* (New York: Macmillan Co., 1939), pp. 484–85; cf. p. 581.

[2] *Beyond Humanism* (Chicago: Willett, Clark & Co., 1937), p. 293.

about those aspects of the universe which are emotional or, I should say, qualitative in character must be made in symbols which can indicate or suggest this qualitative content; and, second, that such expression of truth will inevitably be less precise in meaning than the symbols of pure logic or mathematical physics.

How do symbols become capable of carrying the freight of truth about qualitative values? Primarily, we answer, through being shared within a social group or culture, usually over a considerable period of historic experience. Where is one to find symbols of religious objects and values which have become expressive through such use? Only in the concrete culture of a historic faith. Here then is validation of the claim that the traditional Christian words are indispensable tools in the expression of any truth which Christians may discern.

Significant support for this view may be found in the fact that Professor Wieman, who previously held the interpretation of theology stated by Professor Walker, has now come to regard theology as a legitimate and in a certain sense necessary inquiry for truth. In 1936 Professor Wieman defined the theologian's task as the endeavor "to present the object of religious devotion in a form that is intellectually acceptable to the people of his time and group."[3] The definition was clarified with the use of the following analogy:

> If religion is like eating, then the reality which interests the religious person is analogous to food. In that case the theologian is the one who puts this food into such form that it is palatable and can be most readily eaten. The theologian is a good cook. But the philosopher is a dietician. . . . . The theologian talks about beefsteak and lettuce. The philosopher talks about starches and calories.[4]

Which is to say that the theologian is not concerned about the truth of his theology as long as it nourishes the religious life.

In an article published in July, 1940, Professor Wieman fore-

[3] H. N. Wieman and Bernard E. Meland, *American Philosophies of Religion* (Chicago: Willett, Clark & Co., 1936), p. 15.

[4] *Ibid.*, p. 16.

goes this distinction and concedes that theology, like philosophy of religion, may be a legitimate inquiry for truth. The difference is in the symbols used:

> Theology undertakes to do all its thinking and intellectual seeking in terms that are traditional. Philosophy of religion is free to use any terminology which the best thought of the day may provide or which experts in the field of philosophy of religion may devise for that time or for special problems.[5]

Of first importance is Professor Wieman's claim that religious truth cannot be discovered apart from religious living which makes use of the traditional symbols. Symbols could not even designate realities "if they did not at first shape conduct, for we come to know only by doing and responding."[6] It would be premature to claim that this position has come all the way toward the thesis defended in this paper, that traditional symbolism is a necessary element in the expression of religious truth. Professor Wieman still seems to regard the principal function of religious symbols as the stimulation of particular kinds of religious living, that is, as a preparation for the discovery of truth rather than an expression of truth itself; but he no longer denies that truth can be sought with the Christian words.[7]

Possibly much of Christian truth can be given alternative types of expression. How far this is possible is a matter for inquiry, not for dogmatic prescription. In so far as possible, theologian and philosopher of religion ought to be able to "translate back and forth" from one language to another as Professor Wieman suggests. Before we accept too easily a theory of complete "translation," however, there is another aspect of Christian symbolism to be taken into account.

Any given religion is a historical event or series of events in itself, and it makes claims about the religious significance of certain historical events. Christianity holds that God reveals

[5] Wieman, "On Using Christian Words," *Journal of Religion*, XX, No. 3 (July, 1940), 265.

[6] *Ibid.*, p. 263.

[7] *Ibid.*, p. 268.

himself in history. This characteristic concern of religion with actual empirical events is often overlooked by philosophers who talk abstractly about "religion." But if one is to talk about religion in the only way in which we know anything about it—that is, in its concrete forms—the historical claims of religion cannot be avoided and its historical symbols cannot be overlooked.[8] This means that the theologian who endeavors to express the truth he discovers within Christianity must not only examine, discuss, and speak about those concrete events and symbols; but in some way he will have to use them in expressing the truth which they disclose. The Christian may claim that God has disclosed himself in Jesus Christ or that the church is the Body of Christ or that the Holy Spirit inspires the human soul. These beliefs either mean something that corresponds to fact or they do not. If they do mean something true, then the theologian must point out that truth, and in doing so he cannot avoid using the symbols themselves. While Dean Mathews held that theological symbols must be interpreted through the cultural patterns which they involved, this never implied for him that theology was not concerned with objective fact. The crucial case in point is, of course, that of the event and symbol Jesus Christ. As Professor Aubrey points out, the "Christ figure," however related to the historical person, is itself in history.[9] Whatever truth Christianity discerns there cannot be adequately stated without some reference to the historical symbol itself. When this historical element in Christian faith is given its place in theological method, the really serious problem for consideration is not whether Christian truth can be expressed in Christian words but whether it can be expressed in any other way.

The significance of theology as quest for religious truth may

[8] Cf. Paul Tillich, "The Religious Symbol," *Journal of Liberal Religion*, II, No. 1 (1940), 28–30; Urban, *op. cit.*, pp. 617–19; A. E. Taylor, *The Faith of a Moralist* (London: Macmillan & Co., 1930).

[9] E. E. Aubrey, *Man's Search for Himself* (Nashville: Cokesbury Press, 1940), p. 36.

be further underscored by raising the question whether even philosophy of religion can avoid the traditional symbols. Professor Walker says in the paper referred to that theology speaks of "the Father of our Lord and Savior, Jesus Christ." Philosophy of religion speaks of "the object of religious loyalty." But what is the content of this word "religious," or even of "loyalty"? Does it have no reference to the historic religious experience? And suppose I desire to state and communicate some truth about the object of religious loyalty? What tools are available? If a symbolism is invented, one must still explain the symbols, and ultimately in all probability words out of the common culture will be introduced to clarify the abstract terms. Furthermore, any philosophy of religion, certainly one which makes empirical professions, cannot avoid making statements about and expressing its view of the meaning of the symbols of the empirical religions of mankind. Heaven, Buddha, God, Christ, repentance, the Son of Heaven, Hinayana, and Mahayana—these are the concrete symbols of religion. And philosophy must enter into their meaning before it can decide whether or not they disclose any truth.

None of this is meant to justify uncritical use of symbols or the surrender of the attempt at as much precision as is possible. Philosophy of religion, which seeks to become more critical and precise by escaping traditional words, is a necessary aspect of religious inquiry. On the basis of the facts just stated, however, it may be pointed out that the principal danger of a philosophy of religion speaking in an invented and abstract symbolism is that it will neither discover nor express the concrete reality of religion and its objects. And it may be fairly concluded that the theological attempt to express truth in the symbolism organic to the Christian movement is necessary for the sake of truth itself. Of course, there is danger of ambiguities and misunderstanding; but does philosophy have no difficulties of that kind?

II

After all, theology speaks for a religious movement—yes, even for a specific institution, a church. Is it not committed, therefore, before its work begins, to the dogma, faith, and belief of that church? Does it not thereby become the defense of a tradition rather than a critical inquiry?

This second question about theology assumes especial importance in the light of the fact that the most prominent and vocal of contemporary theological movements stresses and glories in the presupposed commitment of Christian thought to a supernaturally revealed truth appropriated by faith.

In order to specify the position under discussion, a few quotations from its defenders may be introduced. Karl Barth holds that theology is the exposition of a revealed truth known by faith. Dogmatics is "in its substance an act of faith"[10] which seeks to explain and understand itself, that is to "think the content of revelation over again in human thoughts and say it over again in human speech."[11] Barth variously speaks of the Holy Spirit, the Scripture,[12] and the "Word of God whose name is God," as ultimate norms of Christian faith. "It is the Word of God who created the Christian apprehension of revelation. From Him it gains its content, its form and its limit. This is indeed what the adjective 'Christian' implies, and thereby the field under consideration is imperiously defined and all discussion about it is ruled out."[13] More recently Barth places dogmatics entirely within the framework of the confession of the church. "The private character of the professor of Theology—his views and insights as such are matters of no interest. And the same is to be said of his hearers and readers as the future preachers."[14]

[10] *Credo* (Eng. trans.; New York: Scribner's, 1936), p. 3.

[11] *Ibid.*, p. 7.

[12] *Ibid.*

[13] Barth, in *Revelation*, ed. John Baillie and Hugh Martin (Eng. trans.; New York: Macmillan, 1937), pp. 42–43.

[14] *Credo*, p. 4.

Emil Brunner draws together the various factors in the norm of Christian theology and relates them as links in a chain: God, the Logos, Christ, Scripture, the church, the Holy Spirit, faith—this is the channel of mediation of Christian truth. Dogmatics is the exposition of the truth thus received.

> The Word of God and the word of Faith are inseparable. It is not God who believes but I myself who believe; yet I do not believe of myself, but because of God's speech, which is a gift. . . . . In this faith He gives me not only Himself, but He also gives me knowledge of myself. In this faith he decides about my existence, so that I decide for myself. Outside this decision there is no true knowledge, no true knowledge of human existence.[15]

Such concessions to philosophy and science as Brunner makes are in peripheral, not in central, matters.[16] Once the Word is accepted and known in faith, the human language which theology then uses can be criticized and revised. But the fundamental point of view is determined from the beginning in such a way that it cannot be questioned or examined into by theology. Following this general line, Dean David Roberts, of Union Seminary, rejects any attempt even to synthesize the philosophical and theological inquiries.

> Faith undeniably demands that this world be interpreted in the light of unique event wherein God, who transcends the world, has entered it in the Person of Jesus Christ, there disclosing completely, as nowhere else, his will to redeem it . . . . the basic tenets of Christianity can be related to human experience and knowledge in general by philosophy operating within the framework of faith.[17]

Here again we reject only the exclusiveness of these definitions of theology. For each of these three theologians there is no other possible type of genuine Christian theology than the one he defends. They thus at least implicitly classify anyone who raises the question whether another kind of theology may not be

[15] *Man in Revolt* (Eng. trans.; New York: Scribner's, 1939), pp. 67–68.

[16] *Ibid.* "Whatever the claims of philosophy may be, I maintain that faith must never renounce its own ontology" (p. 542).

[17] "Is Christian Philosophy a Contradiction in Terms?" *Journal of Religion*, XIX (1939), 115.

Christian as a heretic or an unbeliever. Any embarrassment which one feels at this classification, however, is relieved when one finds that these theologians are themselves called "heretics" by others.

The problem of Christian theology is the problem of the nature of the relationship of the Christian as thinker or theologian to the Christian movement or church. If the only possible theology is of the type just described, then Professor Walker's claim that theology's sole function is to perpetuate a tradition would appear to be justified, for these theologies in their very essence depend upon the claim that a complete and controlling word from God must be accepted in faith before theology can begin. But if this be the case, then theology cannot be genuine inquiry after truth. The truth is already possessed. Theology is no voyage of discovery, only an excursion from a home port to which it must return and which, indeed, it must always keep well within sight.

What alternative is there? I believe there is another possible relationship of the theologian to the Christian movement. This relationship and the type of theology belonging to it may be characterized as follows:

Christian theology is an inquiry for the correct expression of those truths which are discovered within the Christian movement and which can be expressed in Christian symbols. It arises within the Christian movement and is organically related to it as its frame of reference. Thus it is to the Christian movement as a whole, in all its breadth and depth and ramifications, that theology belongs; but no presuppositions about the absolute or supernatural character of any portion of the beliefs or objects of the movement need be accepted as the starting-point. The theologian may legitimately inquire as to the truth of any proposition which appears within the Christian fold, and the nature and significance of Christianity itself may be a legitimate object of theological inquiry. If this is not the case, why has the history of Christian thought been filled with theological works entitled "What Is Christianity?"

The relation of the individual theologian to the Christian movement would be that of a living participant in this specific religious fellowship—sharing in its work, discussing its beliefs, worshiping in its rituals, and seriously trying to make concrete life-decisions in the light of the values which the fellowship shares, as far as he understands them. Some of these concrete decisions will have an experimental character. Some of them will take on more of the character of decision according to conviction as convictions develop. To be sure, he will have to come to terms with Jesus Christ, with the Trinity, with the doctrines of sin and salvation, with the church. Having come to terms with them, he will have to say something about them, if only in some cases to deny that they have any meaning. Remember that many Christian theologians have specifically denied many of the claims which the Christian movement has made. If that were not possible, there would have been no Reformation. Should one come to the conclusion that nothing in any Christian belief or symbol corresponds in any way to any significant truth, he probably would cease to be Christian or theologian. Participation in the Christian movement would be meaningless. But what is being said is that genuine participation in the Christian movement and genuine inquiry after its truth need not bind one to any specific claim of revelation which must be accepted before Christian thinking can begin at all. The point of the position is that the meanings of Christian words and the ultimately true propositions about the objects of Christian belief are not prescribed from the beginning for the Christian thinker. These are always subject to revision, and different opinions about them may be significantly held within the Christian fellowship.

What would such a theology derive from the movement in whose life it exists, whose symbols it uses, and whose claims to truth it explores? It would derive its impetus, the living experience of a religious fellowship in which alone religious inquiry can very effectively proceed, a symbolism more or less adequate for the expression of truth, and a rich body of concrete historical experience in and through which men believe at least that God has had vital dealings with them.

The question arises: since to participate in a living movement must mean to accept some truth about that movement, how can there be free inquiry on the part of one sharing in a cultural fellowship which has its own symbols, rites, interpretation of events, and standards? A partial answer is that either there can be inquiry on this basis or there can never be any truth discovered at all. Every investigation presupposes a social milieu in which it arises, an inherited symbolism which it uses, and standards of inquiry to which it conforms. Yet this fact does not involve the commitment of the investigator to any absolute and unexaminable truth of any kind.

An illustration may clarify this statement. Modern mathematical physics represents an inquiry into the nature of the physical world. In its present stage it is the culmination of a long history of research, of trial and error, of invention and modification of formulas and symbols. At the present time most of the basic conceptions of the Newtonian physics have been radically modified. The atom, motion, space, time, and energy are all differently conceived. The tools of investigation, both material and theoretical, have been developed and changed in the inquiry itself. The contemporary physicist uses these inherited concepts and tools. He could not possibly do otherwise and make any progress at all. Yet there is no absolute, either within physical theory or in the method, to which the physicist must commit himself from the beginning. Analysis of any quest for truth, from pure logic to theology, discloses that it takes place within a social movement with given concepts, symbols, and attitudes as the milieu of inquiry. This is not to say that theology is not in any way different from other inquiries in method or objects. It is to point out that the fact of belonging to an inherited culture as frame of reference does not invalidate inquiry but makes it possible.[18]

Consider the family as an illustration perhaps closer to the nature of the church. Human life develops in some kind of family relationship. Human thinking about the meaning of "family," the language for expressing this thought, and the philosophy of other aspects of life are all organically related to and colored by the kind of experience within the family which the thinker has had. Yet to share in this experience and to think on the basis of it surely does not commit one to any a priori dogma about how or where the truth about the meaning of "family" is to be discovered.

It will be objected that these analogies miss the point, for the Christian movement is just that kind of fellowship which is characterized by its belief. Surely Christians have always been believers. If one shares in the Christian movement, does not that imply the acceptance of some Christian beliefs? Conceivably one might share in the Christian movement without at first accepting any Christian belief at all; but this is a theoretical limit rather than a genuine possibility. But the propositions which one does accept in deciding to share in the Christian movement are not necessarily of the type prescribed by the "neo-orthodox" theologies. In the position here outlined, what one accepts in participating in the Christian movement are propositions such as these: "The Christian movement offers a significant body of experience and idea related to the objects of religion; it is therefore worthy of exploration"; or "the symbols and beliefs which have arisen within the Christian movement offer a significant realm of inquiry into the nature of the objects of human concern." Perhaps the position is implied: "Somewhere within the Christian movement there are significant clues to truth." This is not to say that these are all the beliefs of Christians. Obviously, they are not. These are simply those

[18] John Dewey, *Logic* (New York: Henry Holt & Co., 1938), chap. i.

most general judgments of importance and relevance which theology, like any inquiry, must make about its subject matter. The common attempt to defend a theory of revelation by saying that science, too, must have faith in its method overlooks entirely the wide difference between accepting an absolute starting-point as the controlling factor in inquiry and the scientific judgments of relevance and use of method which are always subject to revision in the light of new data.

Does not such a loose frame of reference for theology mean the disintegration of the Christian church? The reply is that this view is true to the nature of the church if by the church is meant the only church we actually know in experience. It is just this general frame of reference which the church offers the theologian and nothing more. The plain fact is that there is no one set of propositions about any of the objects of Christian concern or about the method of Christian thinking which all Christian churches are agreed upon. In the creedal churches, apart from Rome, interpretation of the creeds is left to the individual. Further, the basis on which the creed is believed and recited is not prescribed in the creed itself. Christians do arrive at their beliefs by different routes, and their beliefs differ. How then can any one starting-point and any one theological method be prescribed for Christian thought?

Those who affirm that theology can begin only with faith in an event which constitutes an absolute and unique revelation discover that many Christians do not agree with them, and they may even have to conclude that there is no Christian church which fully accepts what they regard as the only Christian truth. This is ironically illustrated in the case of Karl Barth, who now conceives dogmatics as an expression of faith entirely within the context of the church. He recognizes, however, that the actual thought of the church he professes to be speaking for does not agree with his theology. His only alternative he acutely sees and bravely confesses. He understands the church better than the church understands itself, and he will have to be the church in his own way until the true church emerges.[19] It is this dogma of an absolutely given starting-point for theology which is the really anarchistic position. The position of this paper represents a willingness to share in the Christian movement without excommunicating any serious and consecrated participants. Does this destroy Christian fellowship?

A reference to the problem of the place of Jesus Christ in Christian thought may sharpen the issues here raised and help to clarify the position. In every Christian theology there must be some concern with and place for Jesus Christ. In the "final" theology he will have that place which rightfully belongs to him. But the position here taken is that the meaning of this phrase "Jesus Christ" in any or all of its parts is variously interpreted by Christians, that new discoveries have been made about its significance, and that its final place in Christian thought is not yet known. Therefore, there is no one dogmatic statement about Jesus Christ which can be prescribed as determinative for Christian thought. The meaning of the phrase is not given in the phrase itself. Its meaning can be arrived at only through the inquiry which began during Jesus' lifetime and which will continue until the end of all things.

What I have said is in no way intended to justify a lack of conviction about Christian truth. Indeed, precisely the opposite is the case. The beliefs of Christians ought to be convictions, that is, beliefs arrived at through the sharing of common experience and the critical examination of that experience—beliefs by which Christians are willing to live and to die. But no Christian or church can prescribe any dogma which is not open to Christian inquiry and revision in the light of the truth which the Christian movement has always professed to seek.

[19] *The Doctrine of the Word of God: Prolegomena to Church Dogmatics*, I, Part I (Eng. trans.; 2d ed.; New York: Scribner's, 1936), xii–xiii.

Christian Faith and Social Action 3

Daniel D. Williams

Our topic is the theological basis of Christian social action. All theology requires that we risk our being, our minds, and our thoughts in the activities of the Christian church and in Christian action. We cannot get our theology apart from action. There are three special reasons why we need to consider especially the theology of social action.

First, the social gospel movement of which we are grateful heirs, did not have a very thoroughly thought out theological structure. Its theology was of a fairly simple and too exclusively moralistic type. We need to deal much more adequately with the full complexity of the problem of Christian action in society than the social gospel movement did.

Second, there is a kind of Christian social action going on in our society at the present time which has a new theology and which raises for us very serious questions. Movements like Spiritual Mobilization and the groups behind *Christian Economics* have social and economic programs which appear under a Christian guise and which are defended on Biblical and theological grounds. We have to meet them where they are. We can no longer assume that all Christian social action agrees in general with the kind of liberal social program which the social gospel leaders defended. We need to establish our theological ground in dealing with this new theology of a Christian economic program. We ought not to be deceived by the naiveté and superficiality of much of this theological defense of laissez-faire economics. It is naive and superficial if you like, but the problems involved are by no means simple.

Third, there is the difficult problem of the Christian church in social action. If the Christian church is to be the Body of Christ bringing the broken communities of mankind into a new relationship in Christ then the question of how and where that Church can take sides in the arena of social conflict is a difficult one. We will never be done with trying to make plain to ourselves how it is that as church groups we can take sides in social conflict and at the same time remain the Church. My theme is that we have to do it, but it involves a continual and prayerful theological struggle.

I

All human life is social action. Human life is social and to act at all is to act in a social relationship with others. But by social action in its specific sense we mean any voluntary and deliberate effort to try to change the social relationships in which men live. Social action means acting within the social order so to modify or change it in some direction. We are inquiring for the Christian basis for the ground, the ends, and the spirit of such action. I shall state first what I take to be the Christian basis of social action and then relate this basis to three pairs of concepts by which it has to be worked out.

The Christian basis for social action is found in what God has done for us and to us in Jesus Christ. It is the action of God with which we have to deal. That action is God's personal, powerful, living Word expressed in Jesus Christ. In Jesus Christ the meaning of life has been broken open as nowhere else. This act of God is something more than the teaching of Jesus, although it involves a moral teaching which is the summing up of the prophetic moral tradition and the transformation of it. But it is more than a moral teaching. It is a living relationship which God has established with us through a personal life. When we say "Jesus Christ" we do not simply mean something which is bounded by the life of Jesus as we have it testified to in the Bible. Jesus Christ gathers up for us the whole of our experience of God in his dealings with the Hebrew people. It includes the word of his prophets, in their struggle for righteousness, justice, and mercy. This word points forward to its consummation in Jesus Christ who stands at the pinnacle and the center of this history. "Jesus Christ" gathers up for us the history of God's dealing with his people after the life and death and resurrection of Jesus. Jesus Christ for us is the reality whom we know again and again in our experience in the Church where God's Holy Spirit is present to us, renewing our knowledge of who Jesus Christ is. Jesus Christ is the act of God which gathers up and clarifies all human groping after truth and justice. There are fragments of the meaning of life; of man's understanding of God and what he requires of us, everywhere in human experience. When we say God acts in Jesus Christ we do not mean that he is something detached from universal human experience but that Christ is the personal Word in whom God has disclosed who he really is. The universal human quest has had thrown up in it this new and decisive light. This is not an absolutely clear light which answers every question or clarifies every problem immediately, but a light by which now we have to see everything else. Christ is the center from whom now all life is illuminated.

When we look now at three pairs of terms by which Christians have tried to express what God has said to us and done for us in Jesus Christ we find at the center of our faith this personal embodiment of the Word. The three pairs of terms are first, God and man; second, grace and sin; third, the Kingdom of God and vocation.

II

Jesus Christ is the basis of our understanding of God. We understand God as the God who acts, and history as the field of his action. The Christian God is the living Lord of human history. We are absolutely dependent upon him for our being and for the meaning of life. We are called to serve and to act in the history which is the field of his own working.

The God of the Bible acts first in creation. Creation is activity, an assertion of power with purpose. God acts in raising up a people in history who have a special dealing with him in their historical experience. He acts with this people and against them. He raises up prophets by the power of his word to speak for his people and to them, to point to his work in history. He makes and breaks the nations.

God acts in Jesus Christ. Here God asserts his power in history to judge, to break open, to restore the true meaning of life. It is with this God that we have to do in the Christian faith, not merely a "first being", nor an abstract law, or principle, or ideal; but with the primary, sovereign, and inescapable Lord of all creation and all history.

Man as God's creature is made for a life with a certain structure. He is created for a life in community with God and his fellows. Community is not a thin word; it is a word of dimensions. It means a community of worship. Man as bearer of the image of God is created to stand before him in adoration and reverence. It is a community of freedom for man is intended to be a responsible, personal servant of God and his fellows. It is a community of personal, mutual membership so that the meaning of life is to be found in giving and receiving in relations with God and our fellows. Men are not individuals who happen to be gathered together for certain purposes because they prefer it that way. God gathers us together. He has created us members one of another. To be a person then is to be one who has his life only by giving and receiving in a community of life. This is not a statement of an ideal to be achieved. It is a statement of the inescapable character of our existence. So Paul writes to the Corinthians, "What have you that you have not received?" i.e., your very faith, the meaning of your life, is something which you have only as a member of the community of sharing. Paul's image of the Christian church reinforces the point. His favorite image is that of the organism in which if one member suffers all suffer. There is a difference of function but the meaning of life for each member is that he serves the life of the other members.

There is one consequence of this view of God and man of especial significance for our view of social action. When we come to the basic principles of social action, the moral principles which guide the formation of the common life, such as freedom, justice, equality, and brotherhood, we need to see that these terms receive a new and a qualified meaning within the Christian faith which is not identical with the purely rationalistic, legalistic, and idealistic definitions of them. Nearly all men in the world today identify their goal as freedom. Everyone says he is fighting for justice. Equality is somewhat more debatable. Certainly brotherhood is generally accepted as good. All systems of ethics in the great central tradition have affirmed human brotherhood. But Christian understanding of freedom, justice, equality, and brotherhood, while it may begin some agreement with the definition of those terms which it finds in the social body generally, must always be allowed its own definition of these terms.

Take freedom for example. What is freedom? It can be defined in all kinds of ways as a political order or ethical value. It may mean freedom of speech as defined in particular, constitutional arrangements enforced in a legal system. It may mean freedom of economic enterprise as that is actually worked out and established in an economic system, constitutionally guaranteed and legally enforced. But when the Christian speaks of freedom he means the freedom to be a member of the community of mankind. He means freedom to use his life in the give and take with others upon whom he depends and who depend upon him. A Christian definition of freedom should never be equated with an abstract, rationalistic definition of freedom which leaves out of account the conception of man as created to use his freedom in a community of sharing and serving. In the Christian view, if man tries to use his freedom outside his responsibility to the whole social body he only loses it.

So also with justice. Dr. Niebuhr and others have made us see that the rational and legal orders of justice are always something less than what Christians mean when they talk about love. Christian love makes us members one of another. Its spirit sacrificially goes out to serve the neighbor. All human schemes of justice fall short of that spirit.

In the Bible, as Paul Ramsey has made clear, *God's justice, that is his righteousness, is his love, his mercy, and his forgiveness.* When the Christian deals with the standards of justice in society he may find much that is valuable in general definitions of justice as these are worked out in ethical or legal theory and in constitutional structures. But the Christian knows that ultimate justice is something more than any of these human orders. Ultimate justice means life in the one community of membership with one another under God. Justice which is other than love is less than what we ultimately understand God's justice to be.

We can make a similar analysis of equality. Equality can be defined in an abstract and purely rationalistic manner so that it may mean simply equal opportunity for all to assert themselves and let the consequences fall where they may. This conception of equality is that everybody starts equally and the one who runs the fastest wins the prize. Or equality may mean equal membership in one monolithic social body or classless order where there is in theory no special privilege, no distinction, no individual freedom. The Christian conception of equality is opposed to both of these views. The Christian conception means equal access to personal sharing with one another and with God. It means equal opportunity to be a person who gives and shares his life along with all the others in the community. This may very well involve real inequalities of income, or social status, or of power within the social body. The Christian view does not look just for a single monolithic order as does the Marxist, but rather for a "family order", in which equality is a living thing and not an abstract imposition of uniformity.

Our first pair of terms, God and man, has given us the basis for social action. We know whom we serve and what essentially we are to be when we understand God's Word in Christ.

III

The second pair of terms is grace and sin. The Christian account of man is given in the light of the fact that man is not what he is created to be. We take as the theme of this section the late Archbishop Temple's words, "The supreme importance of every man is that he is the brother for whom Christ died." No Christian theory of social action can be arrived at simply by saying what we ought to be and declaring, "Become that." It looks first at what we actually are, at our separation from one another and from God, and asks what we ought to do in our kind of history which is a history of sin and grace. This means that this human history in which God is the supreme actor involves our separation from God. This human community of membership with one another is blighted, thwarted, broken, and we are, all of us, in the brokenness and the estrangement. History has to be seen as the field in which God is acting. But he acts as he does to save men who are estranged from him and from one another.

There are four specific consequences of this way of looking at human history. The first is this: Sin, by which we mean not simply moral wrong doing but estrangement and isolation from community with God and our neighbor, involves us all. The problem of Christian social action is not basically the problem of finding the good men to repair the damage done in history by the bad men. That is a subordinate problem. I will acknowledge its truth in a moment, but that is not where we begin. The problem of Christian social action is not to find the pure moral position from which good men may do good things. It is to discover the way in which we ought to act in a society where all are estranged from one another.

This is a point at which the social gospel theology was not deep enough. If we do not begin here then what we do in Christian social action is to set ourselves up as the righteous against the sinners and thus increase our actual estrangement from others and from God. Some of you know a Presbyterian minister in the South, Charles Jones of North Carolina. He addressed the Inter-Seminary Conference a few years ago about his work in the area of racial prejudice and tension. He said that we who take sides on ethical issues very often give the impression to the people whom we are trying to change that we love the group for whom we are pleading more than we do those to whom we are speaking. That is fatal to our effectiveness and yet it is very common. It is very easy for us, seeing injustice and identifying ourselves with the victims of injustice, to love the victims more than those who have sinned against them. It is not easy to love those who have sinned against the victims of the injustice. We can do this only in grace, but this is where Christ has us begin. And if we do not begin here Christian social action finally falls into a self righteousness which destroys its distinctive power. Every one of us knows some person who has thrown himself fully and even courageously into projects of social action, all of it concealing the fact that he really does not love anyone and is incapable of being loved. We are rightly suspicious of people who "love all mankind" easily. Usually that pose masks a deep resentment against all men or at least against some. We begin then with our common involvement in sin and estrangement, knowing that outward goodness may be the mask of a deep isolation and that a little goodness may conceal from us our real evil.

The second consequence is that every concrete social program has to be determined by the fact that we are sinners as well as good men. Therefore, every concrete social program has to be judged in the light of its actual consequences for our kind of existence. We are not looking for a pure, moral harmony in history. We are not looking for a Christian social program about which no questions can be raised. We are not, I should say, looking for the perfect or ideal Christian social system. We are looking for that kind of social system which will best serve the human community in view of the fact that men are actually sinners. Reinhold Niebuhr's famous word that "man's capacity for justice makes democracy possible; but man's inclination to injustice makes democracy necessary" is exactly appropriate here. Every social program must be examined with an awareness of the relativities involved. Every social program will achieve something less than the full community of men as Christians understand that. This view may help us to avoid what the late Archbishop Temple characterized as "bleating fatuously about love" when the actual problems with which we have to deal are the practical issues of justice and power in a broken and sinful world. At the same time we say that all Christian social action depends upon faith in grace. There are new possibilities of brotherhood in every situation. No situation is absolutely hopeless. There is a new order of life always ready to come into being. As Christians we act in the light of both our knowledge of sin and our faith in grace.

The third consequence is that when Christians act in the world of conflict, it is inevitable that sometimes they will conceal as well as reveal their Christian witness in acting. To take sides in social conflict is something we must do, but to take sides means that from some you will inevitably conceal your Christian motive and your Christian witness. To some you will become the "enemy". We must try in all ways, even in the midst of war, to say and to do the things which will give a Christian witness, but we have to accept the fact that in Christian social action our activities may hide our motives from one another. To many of his time Jesus appeared to be a destructive agitator, threatening the established order of moral standards. He had to risk this.

The fourth consequence is that Christians in social action ought always to be seeking ways to open up new possibilities of reconciliation in the social body. In Christian social action there is a large place for education, pastoral care, recounciling work, holding together the people who are divided in the social, political, or economic struggle. That is not to say that this is the only kind of Christian social action. But social action which does not give a large place to the work of mediation and reconciliation is less than Christian.

We may illustrate the implication of this second pair of terms, sin and grace, with reference to the problem of property. The Christian view of property tends to be one of the great undiscussed problems. It is discussed at a certain level, but too often a certain naive and idealistic moralism betrays us. We have not provided in our churches a basic Christian discussion of the meaning of private property so that we could begin to think in Christian terms about what it means to have a bank account, or not to have one, or to live in a suburb or to live in a blighted area. If at the present time business men are persuaded by the naive theologies of free enterprise, if they are being taken in by the notion that Christian charity means just personal giving by the rich to the poor and that Christian freedom means the freedom to make as much money as one can by legal means, it is partly because we have not provided an adequate Christian, theological, and Biblical interpretation of private property by which we might resist and see through such a superficial theology. If there is an estrangement between those who stand in the social gospel tradition and the business community it may be partly because we who support the welfare state idea have not made plain enough what we are driving toward. We have not made clear what our conception of private property and private enterprise within the welfare state might be. We have not made clear that we are not looking for a monolithic order in which all power, all control, and all property are held by the state alone.

We need a Christian doctrine of private property interpreted within our faith that men are members one of another and interpreted within the history of sin and grace. Can we make it clear that wealth is both a social as well as an individual product and that the Christian meaning of wealth must be that whatever a man's property is, it is his means of relating himself to his neighbor? Wealth in its inner meaning is a sacrament of God's gift to man and of our gifts to one another. In the history of sin and grace our wealth becomes a "sacrament" also of our isolation from one another. "What have you that you have not received?" asks St. Paul. We ought to see how our property is that which separates us from our brother, and to understand that in its essence it should unite us to him.

All life has a sacramental quality in the Christian faith. Because of sin, all the things we call goods are involved in the tragedy of human lovelessness and hate. But all things stand within the sphere of God's redemptive working. Christian social action takes place then in a world where all material and spiritual things are to be brought into the service of the just and loving human community, and yet where sin and its consequences remain stubbornly present. Every social problem itself becomes for the Christian a sacramental sign pointing both to our potentialities as children of God and to our sin with which only his forgiveness can deal.

IV

The third pair of terms is "vocation and the Kingdom". The question of social action is "Now what are we to do?" How do we find precisely how and where as Christians we ought to act to open the way for the community of men under God? Sometimes the demand of God is very plain. This man wounded by the roadside needs help. We are called to help him. Sometimes there is a clear case of ruthless discrimination on some arbitrary basis against another human being, separating God's people from one another. Then the call of God is clear. Denounce the injustice, reconstruct society. There are some social evils that one can identify so clearly as destroying every meaning of human community that one can clearly and simply set himself against them. This is the way that many Christians felt about the Nazi state.

There is however a large area of difficult decisions of risk, of choice between political and social programs which are mixtures of good and bad. Much social action involves taking sides where there isn't any simple clear choice. How does the Christian keep his sanity and his humility and still his resoluteness in a history where there are so many complex problems? The answer lies in the Christian doctrine of vocation. God calls us to be what we are, to act where we are in this kind of a history, to serve him in this kind of a world because he is already acting in it and in Christ has already established a new order within it. We are to do the best we can in the light of our knowledge that often there isn't any purely good way to act. Our "reasonable service" is precisely to give our life up to God in this world where good and evil are strangely mixed. Only such a conception of our Christian vocation can save us from the intolerable pretension of believing that we are "building the Kingdom of God". One really wonders quite how that phrase could possibly have gotten used as widely as it was in the last generation. If anything is clear now, surely it is that we do not build the Kingdom of God. We build social structures, political, legal, and ecclesiastical structures in the light of the Kingdom of God and out of the faith that God's Reign comes through his power. He is establishing his Kingdom in his own way. Our work is to serve God in removing some obstacles so that he may build it in judgment upon us and give it to us by his grace. Only this can pull Christian action out of that moral desperation which finally ends in cynicism. Only this can enable us to offer up our lives resolutely, deliberately, and sacrificially as God gives us strength and grace to do what needs to be done as best we can see it with firmness in the right as he gives us to see the right. Christian social action then is our witness to the Kingdom. It arises in our dependence upon God's grace which transcends all human power.

* * * * * * *

If we are to have a Christian theology of social action it must come out of the struggle of social action itself. The issues of our time are there where history is being made, where the human community is broken, where the future of the lives of the millions of folk is being determined. The only way to a Christian theology of social action is to serve God in Christ as we know him in the midst of the human struggle and not apart from it.

4

MORAL OBLIGATION IN PROCESS PHILOSOPHY

THE purpose of this paper is to examine the nature of moral obligation from the perspective of process philosophy by showing how this philosophy may deal with two specific problems in the moral life: first, the problem of choices which involve the doing of evil; and second, the aspect of temporal spread in the situations which require moral decision. It is an implicit concern of the paper to show that ethics is inseparable from metaphysics. One way a metaphysical perspective may justify itself is to show that it can illuminate problems of moral decision.

I

My presuppositions are the following:

1. Everything actual is a concrete process. That is, every moment of its being involves reference to a past from which there is a route of inheritance, and a future which involves possibilities. Everything actual has a structure which relates it to the past, to other entities, and to the future.

2. God is the supreme actuality by virtue of which there is a world of finite concrete actualities held together in a societal relationship exhibiting order, relatedness, and definiteness.

3. God's essential nature, here called his primordial nature, is the realm of ordered possibilities. It is abstract, and therefore never exhaustive of any achieved actuality or state of God's own being.

4. God's primordial nature involves the integrity of his vision of the Good; that is, it involves an order and gradation of value. God is that function in the world by virtue of which every occasion

is either positively or negatively related to the possibility of increase of value.

5. Increase of value is the enlargement of the scope and depth of community of actualities. It involves depth of feeling-awareness including qualitative richness, ordered harmony, appreciative communion, and creative advance. Creative advance is the bringing of new structures of value to the enrichment of established orders. It may involve displacement of the old.

6. Some creatures have freedom to make decisions which take into account alternative possibilities for future actualization of value, or which involve destruction of value.

II

From the standpoint of these assumptions the following statements follow with respect to the nature of moral obligation:

1. Moral obligation is the claim of possible good upon the free decision of any creature who is able to consider the effect of his action in relation to that good.

2. God is the source of moral obligation since God is the sole reality by virtue of which there is a unified structure of possible good in any situation.

3. There is a double aspect of moral obligation derived from the two aspects of God's being:

(a) There is the absolute obligation derived from the integrity of God's aim for the creatures. This means that freedom should always be used toward the actualization of the wider, more complete creative order of good. This obligation is absolute, eternal, and in its essential nature does not change. It is implied in every moral choice; and it means that principles of moral action cannot be derived from the analysis of particular historical processes alone. Beyond the definable possibilities of any specific historical situation there stretches the inexhaustible possibility of completion in a wider frame of reference, and that frame of reference ultimately lies in the vision of God.

This position agrees with Immanuel Kant that there are absolute moral requirements implied in human freedom, and with the platonists that the Form of the Good gives the final law to all being.

But there is also a radical difference from these philosophies. The structure of the absolute good is abstract. It is an order of possibilities which does not exhaust the nature of its exemplification in any concrete actuality, not even in the being of God.

Therefore, the second aspect (b) of moral obligation is the requirement for the concrete appraisal of the historical situation in which decisions are taken. What we ought to do here and now can never be derived solely from the statement of principles, whether ultimate principles or derivative ones. Moral decision is a response to the concrete working of God in a situation riddled with the ambiguities of historical good and evil, and with the mysteries of as yet unapprehended qualities and possibilities.

Therefore, the nature of moral obligation has to be stated in a somewhat more complex way. It includes the obligation to participate in the present situation by making such decisions as will reflect both basic integrity of aim, and relationship to the concretely given. Thus there is an absolute moral obligation to do more than acknowledge and obey moral principles, though that is never set aside. There is the absolute obligation to make decisions which bring the good into actuality in those present processes within which one stands.

It follows that there is in every moral decision an aspect which transcends all prediction of what, concretely, will be required. Ethical behavior is genuinely creative in that the very act of decision brings into being a concrete good which cannot be wholly predicted or recognized on the basis of any vision of abstract possibilities, not even the divine vision itself, though nothing the creatures can do can affect the ultimate unity and integrity of the divine vision. In the strange words of the book of Genesis: it is after the world is created that God declares it good.

III

There are endless problems in elaborating a moral doctrine (including the relation of "moral" value to other kinds of values). I shall try to show that this position can cope with the problems involved in two special aspects of the moral life. Any moral theory must prove itself by showing its relevance to specific choices. Indeed, one advantage which may be claimed for the present position is that it anticipates an infinite series of situations involving moral choices which have their unpredictable aspects. Moral theorists will always have new problems to solve.

The first problem dealt with here is that which concerns the choices in which acceptance of the doing of positive evil seems necessary in order to preserve any good. The problem is so clearly stated by Dr. Henry N. Wieman from a perspective closely related to the one here developed, that I refer to his analysis in *The Source of Human Good*. In discussing types of evil, Dr. Wieman analyzes the role of "protective hierarchies" in human society.

Hierarchical structures in government, economic life, and systems of status and privilege, including those which make possible the intellectual life, represent an ordering of life "which is a hard necessity, but it is evil" (p. 118). "It is necessary to enable the creative event to produce the richest fulfillment of value with those most capable of engaging in that kind of communication. It is evil because it imposes upon many an undue protection from pain and discomfort; upon some an undue fatigue from hard labor . . . and so on" (pp. 119–120).

The moral problem here is a difficult one; but I do not see how it can be left just where Dr. Wieman leaves it. For he holds that the absolute obligation is to give oneself to the transforming power of the creative event or process (p. 124). Yet the maintenance of the hierarchies is essential to the working of the event itself. How can anything be necessary to the working of the creative process which is not ingredient in that process itself? The obligation which God lays upon the world is the fulfillment of all the conditions necessary to the achievement of his creative aim. If one of those necessities is the device of the protective hierarchy, then surely in a concrete situation there is an obligation to respect that element of value in the hierarchy. It cannot be simply evil. It is certainly ambiguous in relation to good and evil, but not sheer evil. I am not sure but what my conclusion here coincides with Mr. Wieman's regarding the practical obligation to respect the function of the hierarchies; but once this obligation is recognized it seems to me to have implications for the doctrine of how God works in the world. This cannot be restricted to that "high peak of creative transformation [which] will continue to soar far above the mass of people with only a few finding a place there" (p. 124). God is also involved in more humdrum tasks. Whatever constitutes a necessity for man constitutes in some way a necessity for God also insofar as God is involved in promoting human good.

This position does not in any way relieve us of the problem of dealing with moral choices in ambiguous situations. That there are such ambiguities in which, so far as we can see, any choice involves at least the risk of evil and perhaps the certainty of it, is certainly recognized by Mr. Wieman. Some way must be found to assert the absolute element in moral obligation and yet to take account of such ambiguity. Otherwise moral obligation is split up among the conflicting claims of alternative values. Love is torn apart into sacrificial and mutual love; justice and brotherhood are made mutually exclusive opposites.

The doctrine of process philosophy that the absolute obligation to participate in the integrity of God's aim toward the fuller good also involves the obligation to reckon with the concrete possibilities in actual processes, throws some light on the moral problem here.

It may be that actualization is always involved in the ambiguities of good and evil. For one consideration, every advance includes a possible risk of new evil. The most honest moral intention can create a new situation riddled with evil. But we need not point only to cases where the purity of our motives might be assumed. We have to recognize the possibility that every choice we make is tainted with an interest either in self-satisfaction or self-destruction which cannot stand before the claim of God upon us. But if this be the case, then it is our moral obligation to recognize our actual state, to allow for it, and to make our moral choices in the light of our self-knowledge with its confession of the evil that we do. Since our self-knowledge is not complete, our confession of it can never be. But there are degrees. When one who wields power submits his judgments to a wider criticism, he may be acknowledging that his own bias needs such a corrective. We have no moral obligation to act as if we were morally incorruptible. Quite the contrary, we have an absolute obligation to make decisions which take account of our own fallibility.

This is not not to deny but rather to underline the tragic problem of the necessities of our existence such as those imposed by decisions concerning the development of weapons which potentially can destroy the whole human race. But it is to hold that moral obligation is not set aside by these necessities; rather it is a service of the creative event to make decisions in the light of whatever wisdom we can muster about the concrete factors, and to do with them what expresses, however obliquely, the affirmation of the wider and deeper good which God is creating.

IV

A second aspect of the problem of moral obligation has to do with the fact that what we decide about is, in every case, not a static situation, but a process. This becomes clear in the analysis of the dilemmas just discussed; for part of the problem of the "necessities" has to do with questions of the outcome of a historic process. Necessary for what end? for how long? with what result? All these are questions which are pertinent to moral choice.

In the view of process philosophy every moral decision is itself a process and involves a relationship to the "becoming" of other actualities. Here some of the deepest perplexity of moral choice arises, for we cannot see the end of our actions; and we are dealing with realities which do not disclose their full being to us except through the spread of time. Since there are no discernible limits to the future in which our actions may have some relevance, we are obligated to ask about the effects of our acts "in the long run"; but how long is this?

I suggest that we begin the analysis here with some aspects of the effect of the time dimension on specific moral choices where we can within limits take account of the historic route along which our choices lie. A concrete example is at hand in the recent decision of the Supreme Court bearing upon the desegregation of public schools. Professor Edmond Cahn has pointed out the significance of the method of handling the case and its decision. Having made its decision the court allowed time for consideration of means of implementing it. In its second decision, after hearing arguments concerning implementation, the Court revealed a preference for "an effective gradual adjustment"; and took account of possible differences of timing in local situations. It is in this decision that the District Courts are ordered to proceed toward the abolition of racial discrimination in the schools "with all deliberate speed." The qualifying word, "deliberate," surely contains a moral injunction to hold to the goal; but also to move with a certain caution toward the taking of specific steps.

Professor Cahn's comments on the principle involved here are highly pertinent to the analysis of moral problems in the perspective of process philosophy. He points out the important difference between "time when" something is to be done and "time during which." And he says: "the duration or 'time during which' a transaction occurs is one of the critical dimensions of the transaction itself. Frequently its inmost nature is determined by how long it lasts. . . . Duration is a moral dimension." Thus the Supreme Court found that duration could be inserted as a wedge between "either and or."[1]

There are, of course, factors involved in every legal decision which go beyond the range of any moral theory. What "deliberate speed" means in the language of the Supreme Court will have to be argued and determined by lawyers and courts within their frame of reference. But the moral problem here is clear. It is the question of the way in which the timing of any action is related to our obligation to perform it. That moral theory has had so little to say about this problem is a puzzling fact. It is John Dewey preëminently in contemporary philosophy who has pointed out how sterile and irrelevant much traditional discussion of the means-ends relationship has been, precisely because the continuum of concrete process in which means and ends function has been overlooked.

[1] Edmond Cahn, *The Moral Decision*, Indiana University Press, 1955, pp. 274–277.

In the perspective of process philosophy the fact that moral principles are guides to action within processes is a fundamental aspect of the whole viewpoint. To insist on decision according to principle without reference to the historic routes of becoming in the lives of those affected is irresponsible. "Insistence on birth at the wrong season is the trick of evil," says Whitehead (*Process and Reality,* p. 341). In a sense this doctrine lends itself to a certain conservatism in personal and social ethics; "take your time," "don't rush me," "let it work itself out" are homely moral maxims with a wisdom greater than much arbitrary moralizing.

But the principle is equally valid that the concrete nature of process requires action "before it is too late." Historic processes which lead to monstrous evil can be arrested at a certain point, beyond which there is no return. To fail to act at the point where arrest is possible may be the great moral error, no matter how heroic the too late attack may be. It also is clear that there are times and seasons for the beginning of relationships, in individual and social histories, when to fail to seize the right time means to lose all hope for that future good.

There is a further reply to be made to the criticism that this view can become a rationale for an indefinite postponement of deliberate social change. One hears it said: "in another generation we will have public school integration; but not now." But in the view here being defended there is always a question of the integrity of the fundamental aim. Moral obligation means present identification with a line of creative advance, or resistance to an evil tendency. The fundamental decision, made in the core of the personality, may not be observable in overt action at once; but the decision is there. To refuse the basic decision by postponing to some future generation or situation the actual crisis is morally self-destructive.

There will always be some consequences of decision, even if they affect only the inner structure of the personality. In a social universe they also begin to affect the network of relationships in which one stands. It should be pointed out that the view here taken does not exclude the possibility of a situation where nothing whatever can be done except the expression of the integrity of an absolute aim. There are situations created in which it is too late for anyone to do anything to arrest the historic developments which lead to catastrophe. The only moral requirement may be simply recognition of the realities and personal acknowledgment of the absolute will to the good which resides in God.

The recognition of such situations underlies much of the existentialist ethics. The alternatives often seem to be either sheer witness to integrity when no significant moral choice is possible, or reliance on the creativity of the personal decision beyond all rules and norms. We need not deny such situations; but the decisions taken within them are still taken within the context of the historic life of a community and they have their consequences for the new orders of existence as yet unknown.

V

Process philosophy offers a metaphysics and theory of value which holds together absoluteness of moral obligation with acknowledgement of the creative and the tragic factors which attend ethical decision in an unfinished world.

DANIEL D. WILLIAMS
UNION THEOLOGICAL SEMINARY, NEW YORK

DEITY, MONARCHY, AND METAPHYSICS: WHITEHEAD'S CRITIQUE OF THE THEOLOGICAL TRADITION

5

Whitehead believed that the Christian tradition needs a purification of its doctrine, especially of its doctrine of God. This purification, he held, can be accomplished in part through metaphysical speculation which is the work of reason seeking for the notions of widest generality. Yet Whitehead has a complex view of the origin and nature of metaphysical knowledge, and an acute sense of the limitations of all human understanding. He warns, "The speculative methods of metaphysics are dangerous, easily perverted. So is all Adventure; but Adventure belongs to the essence of civilization."[1]

In this paper I propose to examine Whitehead's critique of certain doctrines in Christian theology. He makes specific criticisms of the traditional doctrine of God which he regards as having been determined by the conception of the Divine Monarch or Despot. There is a wider problem underlying Whitehead's consideration of the doctrine of God, since he makes the claim that metaphysical thought can arrive at knowledge of God, and can correct religious doctrines. The problem of the relation of theology to philosophy has become increasingly acute in the twentieth century, and Whitehead's thought offers an important occasion for analysing the problems involved. In this paper we shall consider what Whitehead says about the significance of philosophy for religious knowledge, and raise further questions which are implied by his position.

Out of the many aspects of Whitehead's doctrine of God I have selected one for special emphasis, that is the question of how God acts in or upon the world and the creatures. This is of fundamental importance in Whitehead's proposal of an alternative to the doctrines he criticizes, and furthermore it is a topic of crucial importance for contemporary Christian theology with its emphasis in the biblical perspective upon the action of God in history.

[1] AI 380.

I

There is no idea to which Whitehead returns more frequently in his writings than that Christian thought has fastened upon religious thinking a conception of God which had its barbaric origin in the despotism of early monarchical social organization. From the earlier Hebrew prophets to the Augustinian synthesis, Whitehead says, the decisive period "begins in barbarism and ends in failure. The failure consisted in the fact that barbaric elements and the defects in intellectual comprehension had not been discarded, but remained as essential elements in the various formulations of Christian theology, orthodox and heretical alike. Also, the later Protestant Reformation was, in this respect, an even more complete failure, in no way improving Catholic theology. The Quakers perhaps form a minor exception to this statement."[2]

'Barbarism', I believe, is never defined by Whitehead; but there is no question as to what he identifies with the barbaric in religion. It is the conceiving of God in the image of the arbitrary ruler with no checks upon his power. It is "the fashioning of God in the image of the Egyptian, Persian, and Roman imperial rulers".[3] The Semitic concept of God as a definite, personal, individual entity, "is the rationalization of the tribal gods of the earlier communal religions".[4]

We come then to the specific content of the Christian conception of God. Whitehead finds three strains of thought in the developed Christian doctrine: the imperial ruler, God in the image of the personification of moral energy, and God in the image of an ultimate metaphysical principle. The last is derived from the fusion of Aristotle's Unmoved Mover with the doctrine of God as the Eminently Real which has been favoured in Christian theology.[5]

Since Whitehead is going to argue that metaphysical thought can criticize this doctrine, what is to be said about the metaphysical element which it already contains? One of his criticisms of the traditional doctrine is that "it leaves God completely outside metaphysical rationalization".[6] Whitehead acknowledges that the Alexandrine theologians made a metaphysical discovery in their doctrine of immanence, as applied both in Christology and in the

[2] AI 212. [3] PR 485 [520]. [4] RM [68].
[5] PR 484–5 [519–20]. [6] RM [70].

general notion of God's relation to the world; but "their general concept of the Deity stopped all further generalization. They made no effort to conceive the World in terms of the metaphysical categories by means of which they interpreted God, and they made no effort to conceive God in terms of the metaphysical categories which they applied to the World. For them God was eminently real, and the World was derivatively real." He goes on to object that with this gulf between God and the world there is no way of knowing God, and that unqualified omnipotence must be responsible "for every detail of every happening".[7]

Whitehead's position concerning the function of metaphysics in the religious doctrine he is criticizing is the following: the conception of God as the eminently real exercising an absolute fiat over the world is a "metaphysical sublimation of the doctrine of God as the supreme agency of compulsion" whereby "he is transformed into the one supreme reality, omnipotently disposing a wholly derivative world".[8] Whitehead at least twice uses the term 'sublimation' in this connection. What happened was that the Semitic concept, which is "clear, terrifying and unprovable was supported by an unquestioned religious tradition. . . . It was also supported by the conservative instinct of society, and by a history and a metaphysic, both constructed expressly for that purpose. Moreover to dissent was death." While affirming that the metaphysic was constructed *ad hoc* to support the Semitic concept, Whitehead observes that "to some extent this was justifiable, because both history and metaphysics must presuppose some canons by which to guide themselves".[9]

We are faced then with the question whether there is such a thing as an independent metaphysics. Some observations about this issue may be pertinent here. There are two points which I think Whitehead does not quite sufficiently underline as essential to his argument. Both points are related to his evolutionary perspective and to certain assumptions he makes about the progress of civilization.

First, Whitehead assumes the possibility of progress in metaphysical understanding. He sees in the life of reason an instrument by which man can free himself from false conceptions. In contrast to Bergson, Whitehead sees reason as the supreme instrument of

[7] AI 217.
[8] AI 213; cf. AI 216–7.
[9] RM [75, 79].

creative advance in the universe, at least in that region of it where man lives.

The point to be noted is that while Whitehead acknowledges that every metaphysical doctrine has its origin in some particular human situation and is guided by some specific interests, he avoids complete relativism through the evolutionary assumption that there is a movement in man and in the universe itself toward a more spiritual, valid, and adequate expression of the good and the true. Whitehead clearly holds that there is such a tendency. He sees a factor in the Universe which constitutes a "general drive towards the conformation of Appearance to Reality". He asserts this against the Kantian doctrine that the conformation of appearance to understanding is derived from the structure of the mind without direct knowledge of the ultimately real. Such conformation Whitehead says is not 'necessary'. If it were necessary then "Morality would vanish . . . Art would also be a meaningless term. For it presupposes the efficacy of purpose."[10] The mind may fail in its grasp of the truth, but it has partial successes and these are supported by a function of the universe itself.

It is by this same evolutionary-metaphysical doctrine that Whitehead supports the appeal in metaphysics to the exceptional aspects of experience. He asks us to remember that "the present level of average waking human experience was at one time exceptional among the ancestors of mankind. We are justified therefore in appealing to those modes of experience which in our direct judgment stand above the average level."[11] These include Art and its gradual sublimation into Truth and Beauty, the sense of tragedy, the sense of evil and the persuasion towards Adventure beyond achieved perfection, the sense of Peace.[12]

The second important point to be noted here is that while Whitehead stresses the aesthetic categories, implicit within them is his appeal to moral intuition. It is here that the most important element in his protest against the divine Monarch appears. Whitehead's argument is that theological doctrine has lagged behind the fundamental ethical intuition both of Plato and of the Gospel itself. Plato came to the final conviction "that the divine element in the world is to be conceived as a persuasive agency and not as a a coercive agency". " . . . the power of Christianity lies in its revelation in act, of that which Plato divined in theory".[13]

[10] AI 378. [11] AI 379–80. [12] AI 380. [13] AI 213, 214.

There are several aspects to this moral critique of the divine Monarch. One is that the traditional God as Whitehead sees the matter must be the direct cause of every happening in the world. Therefore he is as responsible for the evil as for the good. He is the direct cause of both. Whitehead accepts Hume's argument here and sees no answer to it in the tradition.

Again, if persuasion, as opposed to coercion, which Whitehead generally identifies with 'brute force', or sheer compulsion, is seen to be the mode of achievement of all high values then God must leave the creatures free in his action upon them or through them. It is not only that God must not be the cause of evil; but he must be conceived as exercising his metaphysical function in such a way that the higher goods are realized only through persuasion. In Whitehead's view the traditional Deity becomes a bulwark of tyranny, for he himself is a tyrant, and he subjugates his people by fear. "The Christian world (in the early period) was composed of terrified populations."[14] He quotes II Thessalonians here, with its announcement of the time when the Lord "in flaming fire will take vengeance on them that know not God, punishing them with everlasting destruction".[15]

It is not only the divine sanction of coercion which calls forth Whitehead's ethical protest, but he believes that it has been the source of the absolutizing of particular moral systems. "Moral codes have suffered from the exaggerated claims made for them. The dogmatic fallacy has here done its worst. Each such code has been put out by a God on a mountain top, or by a Saint in a cave, or by a divine Despot on a throne, or, at the lowest, by ancestors with a wisdom later beyond question. . . . The result is that the world is shocked or amused, by the sight of saintly old people hindering in the name of morality the removal of obvious brutalities from a legal system. Some *Acta Sanctorum* go ill with civilization."[16]

Whitehead extends his criticism not only to the specific content of moral codes but to legalistic religion itself which he believes is exposed by "keener ethical intuitions". "Every great religious teacher has revolted against the presentation of religion as a mere sanction of rules of conduct."[17]

He recognizes that judgment about a particular moral rule for

[14] RM [75]. [15] II Thessalonians i: 8–9.
[16] AI 374. [17] SMW [274].

conduct varies from situation to situation and age to age.[18] But there is no question of the upward line of religion. "Gradually, slowly, steadily the vision recurs in history under nobler form and with clearer expression. It is the one element in human experience which persistently shows an upward trend. It fades and then recurs. . . ." The religious vision "claims nothing but worship".[19]

Whitehead nowhere seems to have taken the position that only persuasion is ever ethically justified. Writing in 1939, he said that "war, even if successful, can only increase the malignant excitement. The remedy is peace, fostering the slow growth of civilized feelings. War may be necessary to guard world civilization. But for Central Europe the effective remedy is peace." In the same essay he gives a realistic appraisal of the motives in modern nationalism none of which he says "is completely evil or completely good".[20] He expressed in 1931 his enthusiasm for the achievement of Lord Irwin and Gandhi in avoiding strife in India. In that year, he wrote: "We stand at a moment when the course of history depends upon the calm reasonableness arising from a religious public opinion." And he asks, "must religion always remain a synonym for hatred?"[21]

We might from one point of view say that Whitehead has declared for an 'ethical theism', resting upon the deepest intuitions both of Christianity and of certain major philosophical figures, especially Plato. We might accept this as a conclusion drawn from the general development of moral insight through the rise of civilization. Or we could regard it as one reflection of the impact of the Christian revelation upon the form of the human conscience, and agree that Whitehead here makes a protest against certain elements in the traditional doctrine of God which can be brought under the judgment of the Gospel itself.

But Whitehead does not leave the matter here. He argues that in metaphysical thought itself the corrective can be found for the errors in the tradition. Reason operating at the level of speculative metaphysics can demonstrate what is wrong with the traditional doctrine, reconstruct the conception of God so as to avoid these errors, and thus throw light on the questions with which Whitehead is left after he has exposed the monarchical Deity. How then is God

[18] AI 375. [19] SMW [275].
[20] "An Appeal to Sanity", in *Essays in Science and Philosophy*, New York: Philosophical Library, 1947, p. 56. [21] AI 221.

related to the actions of his creatures, and especially, how does he act effectively as the persuasive agency amidst the clash of brute force? Such questions must be answered if Whitehead is to justify his position, and they must be answered metaphysically. At least, the general metaphysical position must make the religious answers intelligible. It is this radical and superior role which Whitehead assigns to metaphysics which constitutes the method for his positive critique of the tradition. If Whitehead is right then metaphysics has a religious function which reaches to the centre of the Christian faith. Reason becomes the primary resource for the purification of inherited doctrine.

It is necessary therefore that we examine what Whitehead means by metaphysics, how he asserts his rational critique of the divine Monarch, and what he proposes to put in place of this conception of God.

II

Whitehead's definition of speculative philosophy identifies it with metaphysics. It is the "endeavour to frame a coherent, logical, necessary system of general ideas in terms of which every element of our experience can be interpreted".[22] This definition and its implications could be analysed at length, but for our purpose we may point to four aspects which bear directly on the significance of metaphysics for religious thought.

First, the validity of metaphysical generalization is tested by its adequacy to account for the wide range of evidence. "The chief danger to philosophy", Whitehead says, "is narrowness in the selection of evidence".[23] "The main sources of evidence . . . are language, social institutions, and action, including thereby the fusion of the three which is language interpreting action and social institutions."[24]

The second aspect of metaphysical method is the search for rational coherence. The validity of a system is to be found in its general usefulness not in the peculiar clarity of its first principles, an important point where Whitehead reverses Descartes. Incoherence is "the arbitrary disconnection of first principles".[25] The coherence of the scheme is not simply its lack of logical inconsistency; but the interrelatedness of its concepts displaying the

[22] PR 3 [4]. [23] PR 477 [512]. [24] AI 291. [25] PR 8 [9].

interfusion of the various modes or aspects of existence, with the eternal structures which are exemplified in them.

Third, the metaphysician seeking interpretation of the width of experience, should not neglect the special significance of the higher experiences, including those of religion. "Rational religion must have recourse to metaphysics for a scrutiny of its terms. At the same time it contributes its own independent evidence which metaphysics must take account of in framing its description."[26] When Whitehead elaborates his doctrine of God in *Process and Reality*, he says frankly that here thought depends upon "the elucidation of somewhat exceptional elements in our conscious experience", "those elements which may roughly be classed together as religious and moral intuitions".[27]

This point needs to be underlined as it bears on our main query in this paper. Whitehead is arguing for the possibility of a metaphysical critique of theology, but he does not argue for a metaphysical position which is constructed apart from the special intuitions of religious experience. We ask, Does this not give the whole scheme away to the historical variety of religious experiences? He concedes that all the versions of Christian thought could equally appeal to history. "The conclusion to be drawn from the appeal entirely depends upon the value-judgments guiding your selection, and upon the metaphysical presuppositions dictating your notions of a coherent theology."[28]

I have pointed earlier to the importance of Whitehead's conception of an evolutionary development integral to the nature of the universe as a defence against a purely relativistic answer to the question of the status of metaphysics. There are to be sure different value-judgments, and there may be different metaphysical presuppositions brought into the definition of the nature of coherence. But because we define coherence in a certain way there is no guarantee that we have achieved it. It is precisely the business of reason to raise the questions which necessarily must be raised about any doctrine, and to challenge it to exhibit its capacity to interpret coherently the wide ranges of experience. What persists through every doctrine about the nature of the world or God is the demand that it hold together in the light of all we know. It is the demand for an organically unifying interpretation of experience. If we ask where this demand comes from, and how it is justified, I

[26] RM [79]. [27] PR 486 [521]. [28] AI 211.

think Whitehead must agree that here we are at the faith of rationalism, a faith supported both by religious experience and by the nature of the world, but still a faith which cannot be absolutely justified by any amount of argument.

Once we grant, however, the necessity for coherent interpretation, we are involved in the discussion of what constitutes coherence and evidence, and we are open to the examination of the nature and results of metaphysical thinking.

We come then to the fourth point about metaphysics. Implicit in its search for coherent interpretation there is the requirement that God is not to be treated as an exception to all metaphysical principles; "he is their chief exemplification".[29]

This is a fundamental link in Whitehead's argument. If metaphysical principles are discoverable at all, they are descriptive of the constituent structures in all being. That is what it means to say they are metaphysical. But if they are genuinely so, then God's being cannot be exempt from them, else there is not being which he shares with the creatures, and hence no *analogia entis*, making rational discourse about God possible.

If coherent metaphysical doctrine can be derived at all, it can be shown what is required in a doctrine of God—and shown on the basis of metaphysical reason. This is Whitehead's claim. And it is his charge against the tradition that precisely here, while it had a metaphysical dimension in its doctrine of God, and indeed trembled on the edge of a major revision of the classical *ens realissimum* doctrine, it failed, and thereby fell into incoherence both in its own rational principles and in relation to its deepest religious intuitions.

I have deliberately used the term *analogia entis* here, for it raises the question of whether metaphysical principles are univocally applicable both to God and to creatures. This is a decisive question for Whitehead's thought because it can be shown without serious question that his doctrine of God does allow exceptions in the mode of God's being as distinct from the requirements laid upon the creatures. William Christian has shown this quite clearly with respect to God's experience of time in Whitehead's system.[30] We have therefore the question whether Whitehead can really

[29] PR 486 [521].

[30] William A. Christian, *An Interpretation of Whitehead's Metaphysics*, Yale University Press, 1959, pp. 292–4.

M*

escape some doctrine of *analogia entis*, some way, that is, of qualifying the application of metaphysical principles as applied to God. I will not dwell further on this point here; but reiterate the main thesis that however he qualifies his principle Whitehead intends to find community of being between God and the creatures. They share the ineluctable elements of the metaphysical situation. It is within this intention and its carrying out that he finds his primary means of criticism of the tradition and his clues as to its reconstruction.

There are three fundamental elements in what Whitehead finds in metaphysics to correct the tradition. Two of them are stated in the following quotation from *Adventures of Ideas*:

"What metaphysics requires is a solution exhibiting the plurality of individuals as consistent with the unity of the Universe, and a solution which exhibits the World as requiring its union with God, and God as requiring his union with the World. Sound doctrine also requires an understanding how the Ideals in God's nature, by reason of their status in his nature, are thereby persuasive elements in the creative advance. Plato grounded these derivations from God upon his will; whereas metaphysics requires that the relationships of God to the World should lie beyond the accidents of will, and that they be founded upon the necessities of the nature of God and the nature of the World."[31]

What grips our attention here is that twice Whitehead affirms that metaphysics requires such a solution, and once that "sound doctrine" requires it. That is, metaphysical reason, set free from the need to sublimate or defend the Divine Monarch, and attending strictly to the evidence in its width and depth leads us to a doctrine of God which does two things. First, it reconciles the unity and diversity of beings without denying either aspect.

It is not often observed how strictly Whitehead's metaphysical analysis is concerned with the traditional formulation of the problem of the One and the Many. Both are ineluctably given for metaphysical reason, and any solution which does not preserve and reconcile unity and diversity is false.

Hence, Whitehead is led to the somewhat startling conclusion that both God and the World are One and Many. He finds a reconciliation of unity and diversity in actual occasions which

[31] AI 215.

synthesize many prehensions into one definite unity of feeling. And he finds both unity and diversity in God who experiences the diversity of the world as a unity through his primordial aim, but whose unity of vision requires the absorption of the multiplicity of the world's effort.[32]

The second part of the argument has to do with the doctrine that process is metaphysically inescapable. Conceivably there could be a unity and diversity which was purely static, but Whitehead appeals to the experience of change. "If all things can be together, Why should there be process? . . . How can the unchanging unity of fact generate the delusion of change? Surely, the satisfactory answer must embody an understanding of the interweaving of change and permanence, each required by the other. This interweaving is a primary fact of experience."[33] Here Whitehead appeals beyond diversity and unity as general concepts to an aspect of experience which he finds in all the diversity and unity we encounter.

When it is said then that metaphysics *requires* a certain solution, in what sense are we to take this? I think we have to say that Whitehead is appealing not to metaphysics as a pure and independent discipline which can completely and adequately correct every false notion, but rather to an enlargement of rational insight made possible by the freeing of the mind in certain cultural epochs to take a further look at experience. This freedom involves its escape from the necessity of protecting an inherited doctrine, and its willingness to re-examine experience.

The critical question is whether alternative metaphysical positions are possible. Whitehead, of course, does not deny that there have been alternative constructions. He makes the suggestion in *Modes of Thought* that the wavering of the metaphysical tradition on the reality of change is related to the fact that orthodox philosophic thought expressed the exhaustion following upon the first three thousand years of civilization, and he warns against philosophies which "express the dominant emotions of periods of slow social decay".[34]

There are some difficulties here for Whitehead's view of the purification of religion and ethics through metaphysics, for how does one judge what is a period of social decay and one of advance? Presumably this judgment itself requires a metaphysical insight. How is one to know then which philosophy one should be wary

[32] PR 494–5 [530]. [33] MT 73. [34] MT 110.

of? Is there not a circle here? Perhaps Whitehead's remark about 'exhaustion' is somewhat incidental to his main argument. He does believe in the gradual freeing of metaphysical intuition from origins which stamp it with the necessity of sublimating special and peculiar circumstances.

Anyone reading Whitehead's rational defence of democracy—"the basis of democracy is the common fact of value-experience, as constituting the essential nature of each pulsation of actuality"[35]—may well raise the question of whether the metaphysical requirement is the foundation of democracy or whether in this case the metaphysician's commitment to democracy is the key to his conclusions. I think it is clear that Whitehead must rely upon his more general assumption of an advance of creative reason, freeing itself from the distortions of its barbaric origin, and achieving a purification of insight through rational reflection upon wider and wider ranges of experience. Within this broad faith his argument has cogency. It is hard to deny that reason can expose rationalizations of particular social systems, through an appeal to wider experience. Scientific knowledge has demonstrated its capacity to check the world views in which religious feeling expresses itself, and the metaphysician has scientific knowledge as part of his data. Whitehead's polemic against the tradition then is not based upon an appeal to pure reason, but it is a perspective upon the meaning of experience developed within a particular cultural and historical situation, and appealing beyond this to considerations which are overlooked, concealed, or confused by certain elements in the traditional positions. At the very least one could say he shows the function of reason in opening up alternative ways of construing the world, ways which may have been closed off for centuries by the dogmas either of religion or of philosophy. Often the first step in the advance of insight is the demonstration that possible alternatives have been overlooked. Charles Hartshorne has expanded this thesis significantly.[36]

III

We turn then to the question of what Whitehead proposes in place of the traditional Monarch or Despot. Is a consistent meta-

[35] MT 151.
[36] Charles Hartshorne, *Man's Vision of God*, Chicago, 1941, Chap. 1.

physical doctrine of God possible which avoids the difficulties in these conceptions?

Without seeking here to expound Whitehead's full doctrine of God, I raise two questions about it which must be asked in the light of our major theme. Does Whitehead himself avoid the problem of the divine Despot? Is his God too arbitrary? And second, if he avoids the Despot, is his God too weak? It is necessary to ask both questions partly because of the complexity of Whitehead's doctrine, and partly because of the development of his position from God as the principle of concretion in *Science and the Modern World* to the later position in *Process and Reality.*

In the interpretation of God as the principle of concretion Whitehead proposes a doctrine of how God acts upon the world. There must be a limitation upon creativity antecedent to the course of events which involves conditions, particularization and standards of value. God is that limitation. No reason can be given for his nature, but as the principle of limitation he is the determining factor not only of the *how* of actualization but in regard to the *what* of fact.[37]

In *Process and Reality*, Whitehead keeps the principle of concretion, for God is "that actual entity from which each temporal concrescence receives that initial aim from which its self-causation starts".[38] He is "the principle whereby there is initiated a definite outcome from a situation otherwise riddled with ambiguity".[39]

It is fair to ask whether the Monarch has not reappeared here in another guise. For if God by himself as an ultimate metaphysical fact contributes the initial aim to every creature, and is himself the sole principle by which a definite outcome is achieved in every occasion of experience, then it is possible to construe this as saying that God is another name for the fact that everything happens exactly as it happens. Whitehead, of course, throughout disavows the doctrine that God is the author of evil, but we have still to ask how evil gets into this universe if the sole principle of *whatness* is God's own nature.

Perhaps Whitehead anticipates this objection when he goes on in *Process and Reality* immediately after discussing the principle of concretion to say: "If we prefer the phraseology, we can say that God and the actual world jointly constitute the character of the creativity for the initial phase of the novel concrescence."[40] To

[37] SMW [256]. [38] PR 345 [374]. [39] PR 488 [523]. [40] PR 346 [374].

which we must say, if we are to avoid the monarchical Deity we certainly must prefer this phraseology, for only in this way can that increment of freedom and self-decision for the creature in its relation to God be preserved.

I am not certain that Whitehead ever intended the doctrine of the principle of concretion to mean any more than that God is the ultimate structure which makes the unity of the world and of each creature possible at all. He offers only an ultimate adjustment of harmony as a lure for the creature, without finally determining the precise way in which the creature will respond. God as the principle of concretion is "never force", he says.[41]

We turn then to the developed doctrine of God in *Process and Reality* as having two polar aspects, the primordial nature and the consequent nature. And, we ask, how does this God act upon his world so as to be at once the redemptive agency and yet never the coercive monarch? And further, is this conception of God too weak to allow for the vital redemptive function?

God's primordial nature is his conceptual valuation of the entire realm of possibility with its eternal objects, its gradations of relevance, and its logical coherence.

God's consequent nature "results from his physical prehensions of the derivative actual entities".[42]

If we ask how God acts upon the world the answer is complex because it involves both poles of his being. The primordial nature acts as the lure for feeling. Every creature knows itself and its world through its grasp of the primordial nature of God. It participates in the realm of possibility with its order, and its grades of relevance. In his primordial nature God moves the world without being moved. He is experienced as the wealth of conceptual valuation, as he holds before each occasion its possible fulfilment in relation to all other occasions including that non-temporal actual occasion which is God himself.

So far the aspect of persuasion is carried to the limit by Whitehead, if our interpretation is correct that we allow for freedom in the creature in its concrete response to the initial aim which it derives wholly from God.

The consequent nature might at first view appear to be wholly passive. God derives his physical feeling, that is, his concrete feelings, initially "from the temporal world". In the static

[41] SMW [276]. [42] PR 42 [46].

majesty of his vision God absorbs the "World's multiplicity of effort".[43]

But it would be too simple to say that the consequent nature is constituted wholly by the world's action upon God, for it is, according to Whitehead, the "weaving of God's physical feelings upon his primordial concepts".[44] This means that in God the world's action receives its final unity, its immediacy is retained, and it is transformed by his wisdom.

There is something puzzling in Whitehead's doctrine here. What is it in God that functions to achieve this retention of the past and the transmutation of diversity into unity? Surely it cannot be merely his unconscious conceptual valuation of the realm of possibility, for this in itself has no transforming power except as it is responded to by concrete beings. And no creature in the world or the world as a whole has the power to achieve this retention in full. There must be a concreteness in God's nature which is his own actual feeling prehending the creatures, and lending his subjective and transforming aim to the way in which he experiences the world.

Leaving this objection for the moment, we can answer the question as to how the consequent nature of God is effective in the world. It is effective as it is experienced by the creatures. This occurs in two ways, I take it. First, through the mutual immanence of all occasions the creatures have an experience, however dim, of God's consequent nature as the felt union of immediacy of the world without loss or obstruction.[45] Here the widsom which uses the wreckage in the temporal world, which saves everything which can be saved, and which passes a judgment upon the world is known directly. Thereby the creature's feelings are transformed through participation in the transformation which takes place initially in God.

Second, there is the love of God for the world which passes back into the world, again through our experience of him. It is the particular providence for particular occasions. Here Whitehead's use of the term 'providence' suggests specific divine action. God's love "floods back again into the world".[46] But the divine activity is interpreted by Whitehead as the holding before the creature of the ultimate possibility of transmutation of present evil into some real good. In *Religion in the Making*, Whitehead says: "This

[43] PR 489 [524], 494 [530]; cf. 491–2 [527].
[44] PR 488 [524].
[45] PR 489 [524].
[46] PR 497 [532].

transmutation of evil into good enters into the actual world by reason of the inclusion of the nature of God, which includes the ideal vision of each actual evil so met with a novel consequent as to issue in the restoration of goodness."[47] We must insist that for Whitehead this "restoration of goodness" is not without its tragic aspect. God is "the fellow-sufferer who understands".[48] He does not deny the reality of evil, but only its finality as resisting all transformation into good.

The question to be raised here is whether Whitehead's account of the divine causality leaves God without concrete power in the world. Put in another way, is whatever power God has exercised only through the creature's experience of the divine wisdom and compassion which are in themselves passive to the world's effort? If this view be held strictly, Whitehead has solved the difficult problem of keeping from assigning some specific effect in nature to the direct causality of God by asserting that God acts only as a lure for feeling, as object of experience, not as one efficient cause among others. But if this be the doctrine, the result is that God acts only by persuasive disclosure of a vision of the transformation in himself of the happenings in the world. He sets certain limits to the creatures and absorbs the world's activities in a certain way. But does he act with power to transform the world beyond presenting it with an ideal aim?

We may ask if Whitehead has replaced the Arbitrary Monarch with a Constitutional Monarch, who to be sure is unlimited in his power to establish the general constitutional conditions for the world's action; but who after having made the initial address to the cosmic parliament, only waits to receive reports as to what his subjects do, and who then is able to see all the concrete acts of the subjects as having an ultimate unity in his divine perspective. My question concerns the divine initiative in history and the way in which it is exercised. Does God only listen or does he speak?

As one thinks of the alternatives in Christian theology, Whitehead's doctrine here seems to me most at home in spirit if not in detail in certain strands of modern Russian theology and in Berdyaev's thought, in which the action of God is seen in the divine humility on the Cross. This is taken as the standard and criterion of all divine action. Persuasion is finally identified as the key to the meaning of love, and the solitary route to redemption. I

[47] RM [155]. [48] PR 497 [532].

mention this as an indication that similar theological outlooks can be developed from rather different metaphysical premises. This is not an argument against the use of metaphysical analysis, but a caution that in any metaphysical system there may be at work a fundamental religious orientation which can achieve articulation in more than one way.

IV

Any simple judgment either on Whitehead's method or his conclusions ought to be immediately suspect. It is a philosophy woven of many strands. He is highly self-conscious as to its sources and criteria, and is disarmingly candid as to the openness of its conclusions. His critique of the Christian doctrine of God is so forthright and so radical that it cannot be ignored by any contemporary theology or religious philosophy which seeks the relevance of religious faith to contemporary culture. I have shown that Whitehead raises very sharply the issue for every theism of how God's action in and upon the world is intelligible.

Two points deserve further comment in conclusion. The first concerns the extent to which Whitehead's critique of the tradition rests upon metaphysics, and the second involves two aspects of the doctrine of God which he proposes as an advance beyond the tradition.

First, Whitehead's method affords opportunity for an important case study in the possibility and the limits of speculative metaphysics as a means of criticism of religious doctrine. It is clear that there is no presuppositionless search for the categories of being, nor is there any purely rational standard to which particular religious doctrines must be brought for judgment. Whitehead seems to acknowledge this in his descriptions of metaphysical method, but he sometimes puts it in such a rationalistic way that the real status of metaphysical reflection is obscured. Is it really clear for example that both the advance of reason and the development of religion show a persistent upward trend? And is not the judgment as to what is *advance* the central problem?

Further, it is possible in judging any metaphysical system to analyse its special presuppositions. Whitehead always calls for this. But we may ask if he has fully applied it to this ethical preference for persuasion which he sees not only as a high value but as the definition of the true nature of all existential striving toward a higher good? It may be that his preference for persuasion as an ethical value led him to an analysis of the nature of God and of his relationship to the world which projects this value as metaphysically ultimate. What does the evidence say about this so far as we can see?

The coercive aspects of being seem as necessary to a real universe as the persuasive aspects if we are to speak accurately about the mode of existence, the relationships, the functioning and the fulfilment of actual occasions. To say this is not to argue for brute force and coercion as ethical norms, but to recognize a fact of experience. Granted all the 'tendernesses' in life (Whitehead's term), no organism would survive five seconds on the exercise of tenderness alone. Whitehead's doctrine, moreover, leads him to ignore the wide ranges of types of force, of coercion, and of mutual interaction. These would seem to have their place in the necessities of being, and therefore require us to find their place in God's being.

The conclusion is warranted then that every metaphysical system is a function of the perspective in which the data are seen as well as of the data themselves. This is not to deny the necessity or relevance of metaphysical doctrines. I would defend the view that there is no reflective interpretation of man's life which does not involve metaphysical structure. But the point is that a metaphysical system has the status of a partially tested hypothesis. In the judgment of its adequacy there come into play elements in the human apprehension of the world which are not derived from metaphysical reflection or a wide survey of experience, but from specific faiths, decisions, and orientations which have within them elements both of historical fate and of personal evaluation.

When we turn to the question of how God acts upon the world we see that Whitehead has thrown important light upon some aspects of this perplexing problem. He has shown how abstract structure can be causally efficacious, and with his doctrine of the mutual immanence of God and the creatures he has developed a conception of how God's way of having his world may in turn enter into the way in which the creatures experience both the world and God.

But it still may be that Whitehead has underestimated the disclosure of the divine initiative in religious experience. I believe it can be shown that he has not carried through with his metaphysical method fully in his interpretation of the being of God. It is precisely in that aspect of God which makes him a fully actual, effective subject where Whitehead seems not to make clearly the affirmations which he needs to complete his doctrine. I suggest that it is because Whitehead has reacted so justifiably against the divine Monarch that he has given a partially inadequate account of the relation between God and the world.

This means that a doctrine of God on Whitehead's own standard will have to analyse the problem of the means of action, and the forms of causal efficacy. A way must be found to deal with the uniqueness and the analogical character of the divine causality. Most modern theology seems to have agreed that Calvin's assignment of efficient causality to God in every detail of existence is impossible.[49] But we still have to interpret that aspect of the total religious problem which Calvin saw clearly, the priority, the initiative, and the efficacy of the divine power. It is not surprising that the difficulties of this problem drive many to the assertion that God's action is not in any way subject to metaphysical analysis. But how then can we call it 'act'?

Finally, there is an aspect of Whitehead's critique which does appear convincing against the divine Monarch, when he affirms the suffering of God. Here is Whitehead's primary objection to the traditional God who has no way of reacting to the world for reaction would mean change. Whitehead's God is not in this difficulty, for every phase of his experience invokes a specific response to the concrete activities of the creatures.

There remains a question as to whether Whitehead's God may fail to find anything less than complete satisfaction in every moment of the world's course. Stephen Ely interprets him as saying that God sees every evil as completely contributory to ultimate good and declares that "it is not likely to give anyone much comfort to know that, no matter what happens in this world, God can see it in an ideal setting that makes it an enjoyable sight".[50]

This criticism must be taken seriously by any Whiteheadian. William Christian holds that for Whitehead no actual occasion can alter the intensity of God's satisfaction.[51] Does this mean that for God the world is a fully realized value at every moment? Satisfac-

[49] John Calvin, *Institutes of the Christian Religion*, Philadelphia, 1936, Book II, Ch. 4; Book III, Ch. 21, 5.

[50] S. L. Ely, *The Religious Availability of Whitehead's God*, Madison: University of Wisconsin Press, 1942, p. 41.

[51] Christian, *op. cit.*, p. 360.

tion, we must note, is a technical term in Whitehead's philosophy. It means the definite outcome of a particular concrescence. Does the measure of intensity of satisfaction then mean that every happening in the world simply confirms an absolute quantum of desire in the divine reality? If this were the real meaning of Whitehead's doctrine, one might charge that he has turned the divine Despot into the divine Aesthete who lacks an adequate principle of discrimination and distils a complete satisfaction out of every spectacle no matter how terrible. William Christian is suggesting an alternative explanation, I think, when he says that the *qualitative pattern* of God's satisfaction varies with the advance of nature while the intensity of his satisfaction is invariant.[52]

The consideration which really corrects Ely's interpretation seems to be this, that while intensity of satisfaction is in the aim of God as in that of every creature, God's aim includes in an absolute love the good of the creatures. His aim for each creature is "depth of satisfaction as an intermediate step toward the fulfilment of his own being".[53] Now it is clear enough that the creatures' satisfactions vary in depth. Any creature may fail to realize a creative harmony within itself, with the other creatures, and with God. It may, tragically, end in self-destruction of various kinds. In some sense, all creatures thus fail. This must mean a genuine loss for God. That which the divine wills absolutely has not come to pass, whatever further good he may bring out of the wreckage. This is to say that Whitehead keeps the tragic element in the divine nature: "Peace is the understanding of tragedy, and at the same time its preservation."[54]

At a critical point therefore Whitehead has transformed the unfeeling and unmoved Monarch into "the fellow-sufferer who understands". That this can be done in a coherent, intelligible metaphysical structure is a great gain for Christian theology which has been burdened for centuries with the Platonic doctrine of the divine impassibility. Whitehead's philosophy is highly relevant to the quest for a theology in which biblical faith will have intelligible expression.

Whitehead once remarked that Christianity is a religion in search of a metaphysic.[55] One may judge from his work that the search must continue, but it is not fruitless.

52 Christian, *op. cit.*, p. 359. (Italics mine.)
53 PR 147 [161].
54 AI 368.
55 RM [50].

6

Religious Issues in Twentieth-Century Culture

Daniel D. Williams

An attempt to identify the major issues in religion which will be faced in the 1960's is complicated not only by the limitations of the writer, but by the many currents of thought and feeling in today's world. We are in a cultural revolution in which traditional forms of religion are being discarded, and yet one of the strong trends in our century is the renewal of loyalty to inherited forms of religious faith and community. Some try to reduce all meanings to scientific terms and dispense with ancient religious symbols, while others assert that the way to understanding man's existence is through exploring the depths of religious symbols. There is a world-wide impulse toward the discovery of a religious unity in which the many faiths can find mutual reinforcement over against the secular spirit, and at the same time our century presents some of the most uncompromising stands on the uniqueness and absoluteness of particular faiths, as in Islam, and in some Christian theologies.

Religion cuts many channels as it flows through man's political and cultural life. Asian political leaders try to relate Buddhism and Marxist ideology to see how they can live together. Western sophisticates discover the spiritual disciplines of Zen Buddhism. A pagan National Socialism exploited the power of religious feeling to create a demonic nationalism, but called forth the resistance of the confessional church and some of the authentic martyrdoms of the twentieth century. In South Africa Christianity is used as a bulwark of the policy of *apartheid,* and at the same time there arises a prophetic Christian protest from within the ranks of the controlling group. Religion can be constructive or demonic, revolutionary or conservative, culturally stimulating or stifling. Therefore, simply to list a number of issues which concern religious people would not be very illuminating. It is more important to ask what has produced the present religious situation, and to see how the issues arise in our common life.

We should be clear about what we are to call "religion." We can say that religion has two aspects. There are the *religions* of mankind. These are communities of faith and practice organized around some response to a divine reality which gives meaning to life and to which men seek to relate themselves. There is also the religious *spirit,* man's response to whatever he holds to be of final consequence for the meaning and destiny of his life. The religious spirit may or may not be expressed within a particular community of faith. At times it may appear as a protest against all traditional forms of religious belief and practice; but we shall say that the religious spirit is present wherever man searches for or responds to something which he takes to have ultimate significance for his life. In the history of religious communities we know that the religious spirit in both its creative and its destructive aspects may appear either within or outside of the traditional forms of religion. It may be expressed as a belief in God or some divine reality, or it may become an iconoclasm or atheism in which all concepts of God are attacked. But it is religious when, in Dr. Tillich's phrase, man's "ultimate concern" is involved. In the twentieth century a tension between the religious spirit and traditional forms of religion is one of the characteristic phenomena.

Dr. Toynbee has said that challenge and response is the key to the history of civilizations. It is also an important key to the history of religions. We can understand the formulation of the major religious issues today by seeing that those who hold some kind of religious faith have responded in one of two ways to the protest against traditional forms of religion. Some have sought to make a creative response from within a religious tradition, the others have sought to find a new religious standpoint beyond the inherited forms of faith.

It is not possible to say that any one element in the life of modern man has been the determining factor in shaping the forms of religious life and thought; but one pervasive factor has been that of modern science and its effect upon man's way of understanding his world. We can well begin by examining the radical new situation created by modern science for religion.

While the nineteenth century and the beginning of the twentieth century are known as periods of optimism in western culture, an undercurrent of disturbance and pessimism grew stronger as the turn of the century approached. Consider these words of Thomas Hardy written about 1900:

> What we gain by science is after all, sadness . . . The more we know of the laws and nature of the universe, the more ghastly a business one perceives it to be.[1]

Hardy was haunted by the disclosure in Darwinism of the ruthless struggle of life with life. He may also have been thinking, as many were, of the second law of thermodynamics with its prediction of the inevitable dissipation of all useful energy. Hardy thought that modern critical thinking left no place for a belief in God which allowed any anthropomorphic elements whatever. Therefore the world is founded on something impersonal.

What in Hardy was still a somewhat wistful longing for religious assurance became as the twentieth century dawned a blunt protest against all religious faith. In Freud's psychology, religious beliefs are illusions, the projection of frustrated infantile wishes. In the revolutionary protest of Marx, religion is declared to be an ideology which covers up the cleft in the human consciousness produced by a divided and unjust society. This theory developed by Marx in the nineteenth century became a main theme of the world revolutionary movement of communism in the twentieth century. A socialist chess set recently designed by a German wood carver in the East zone has the King's place in the set taken by a worker holding the economic plan in his hands. The castles are figures in the uniform of factory defence squads, and the bishops are athletes.[2] It is a fair symbol of one of the major challenges to religion in the twentieth century.

Intellectual skepticism which seeks to dissolve the religious symbols by rational analysis lives in our century in logical positivism. New techniques in philosophical analysis do not necessarily support the positivist attack on all religious language; but they raise serious questions about the possibility of giving rational justification to traditional beliefs about God or indeed about any metaphysical realities.

Finally there is what may be termed the "humanistic protest" often voiced in modern existentialist philosophies. It asserts man's radical freedom in the universe, but his aloneness. Jean-Paul Sartre says that whereas in the Christian tradition God creates the world out of nothing, the existentialist truth is that man creates his world out of nothing, the "nothingness" of his freedom. He must bear the burden of his own guilt. He must live with courage knowing that his life runs toward death. He must refuse to be reconciled to a world in which innocent children suffer. Friedrich Nietzsche was the prophet of this protest when he proclaimed in his *Thus Spake Zarathustra,* "God is Dead."[3]

When we examine the ways in which contemporary religion has responded to these challenges, we recognize that there are inward springs of religious life which do not depend upon external challenges to give their sustenance to the human spirit: but to understand religious life today we must see how these protests have been met.

There are two main ways open for those who resist the disintegration of all religious forms of belief. One is to stand within the traditional religious community, and to reinterpret inherited faith in the face of new needs and new issues. The other way is to step out from the historical religious community and to seek a new standpoint relieved of the encumbrance of tradition. Which issues one will take most seriously is determined by which of these two ways is chosen. I have put their opposition sharply, and would not deny that some mediating positions are found; but an ultimate choice between one or the other would still seem to be required.

1

One of the most striking features of the situation in mid-twentieth century is the reassertion of the vitality of the great religious traditions. It is a world-wide movement in all the major faiths: Buddhism, Islam, Hinduism, Confucianism, Judaism, and Christianity. It may be called a "renaissance" within the traditions, for it involves a turning to the origins and roots of an historic faith in order to rediscover the enduring truth, and it may lead to a reshaping and reinterpretation of the faith. The key to this movement is the preservation of a heritage through examining, criticizing and reinterpreting its central themes. It involves adjusting traditional beliefs in the face of new knowledge, and new cultural demands. Sometimes this reshaping takes the form of a modernism in which old symbols are given new content. Sometimes it takes the form of an explicit reassertion of orthodoxy; but it is often a "neo-orthodoxy," a re-establishment of traditional forms of belief with adjustments to the new knowledge derived from science and from other cultural sources. The depth and extent of this response from within the traditional religions would probably astonish Nietzsche, Freud, and Hardy, if they could witness it. Some interpret it as a natural consequence of modern man's search for spiritual security in an age of anxiety, and surely this is one factor within the movement, but we need to look more closely at how it is that traditional forms of religion have found such a vigorous contemporary response.

First, this reaffirmation of religious tradition has come as a counter protest against the excessive optimism of modern philosophies of progress. It is unconvincing to say that the traditional faiths have persisted only because they offer a refuge from anxiety. Modern man had an alternative refuge, the hope of endless improvement of his life enshrined in the doctrines of progress. It is this optimistic view of history that the traditional religions attack. They have tended to agree with the more severe critics of modern man's self-confidence, that the establishment of a genuine security depends upon a much more radical appraisal of man's plight as a creature subject to the risks of freedom and self-destructiveness. The traditional religions oppose a simple humanistic self-confidence with their sense of dependence upon a divine reality, their drastic demands for repentance and for self-discipline, and their affirmation of a saving reality from beyond history as necessary to the solution of history's dilemmas.

In the Christian Church it is the polemic against an easy self-confidence which has characterized the creative theologies. The two outstanding figures are Karl Barth, the Swiss theologian who led the opposition of the confessional church against the Hitler regime, and Reinhold Niebuhr, the American theologian whose *Moral Man and Immoral Society* published in 1932 near the beginning of the great depression turned liberal Christian theology back to a radical doctrine of man's sin and guilt. Niebuhr combined evangelical theology with a realistic political ethic in which the tragic conflicts of power, and the limits of human virtue and wisdom in history were interpreted in the context of biblical doctrines of the fall and grace. He argued that the Biblical tradition understands man more profoundly than have the dominant philosophies of modern culture. The theological climate in the 1930's became more sympathetic to the critical voices of cultural protest. As one symbol of this convergence of the cultural mood of criticism from the two sides of the religious tradition and the disillusioned philosophies there is the figure of the lonely Danish genius, Sören Kierkegaard, whose existentialist Christianity was a formative influence not only upon theologians like Barth and Niebuhr, but upon modern Jewish thought, and some Buddhist thought, and was a source of both the agnostic and frankly atheistic philosophies of twentieth century existentialism. Through this movement from Kierkegaard to Sartre in both its theological and non-theological forms, there runs the theme of man's anxiety in the presence of an ultimate risk, the mystery of death, and the burden of guilt.

A second reinforcement of traditional religion has come from the protest against the dehumanizing elements of technological culture. Here again the religious traditions tend to join forces with the secular rebels against the assumption that the extension of man's scientific power will solve his problem. Martin Buber's religious philosophy is one of the most important instances of the religious defence of the person against dehumanization.

Buber writes from within biblical and Hasidic Judaism, as he develops this thesis that the I-Thou relationship between persons is radically different from the I-it relation between a person and an object which is something merely to be contemplated and used. For Buber the I-Thou relationship is the heart of human reality, and it is not possible for men to enter into it except on the basis of a recognition of God and a personal relationship to Him who is the supreme and ultimate subject. Buber's doctrine has influenced not only Jewish and Christian thought, but other contemporary philosophies.[4]

The protest against dehumanization has an especial significance in Asia where there is a recognition of the overwhelming power of scientific technology to reshape the world's life, but at the same time a deep fear of being engulfed by a civilization of technological power without spiritual sensitivity. In Islam, Buddhism, Confucianism, and Hinduism the question is being asked, is it not possible to have the scientific method and the knowledge and techniques it produces, but to join these with the spiritual sensitivities of the religious traditions? Those who see most deeply into this question recognize that this is more than a matter of simply joining two sets of concepts and values to one another. Creative reinterpretation of the ancient faith and of scientific values is required if the two are to be brought into one whole.

Finally, among the factors reinforcing the loyalty to traditional religion there is the fact that man has his religious existence generally within communities of religious faith. Religion creates societies and binds peoples together. It symbolizes collective memories and hopes. Hence it has always been close to the historical forms of collective life, and in our day it is deeply involved in the dynamism of modern cultural nationalism which is certainly one of the most powerful forces in contemporary history. The search of peoples for self identity, and for political power and autonomy inevitably involves the religious traditions which have informed the common life. On the whole the trend of modern nations has been to disestablish religious institutions; but at mid-century there is a strong opposing tendency. Pakistan is an Islamic State; Burma and Ceylon are moving toward some form of Buddhist state. The political tensions in India are in part related to struggles between religious traditions as in the case of the demand of the Sikhs for a separate state. It is significant that communism in spite of its ideological critique of all religion still tends to be cautious in dealing with traditional religion in places where as yet it has no preponderance of power. Even in central Europe, in Poland, and in Russia itself there seems to be a policy of at least minimal toleration of the religious communities.

The motives of political cohesion and national self identity are not the only ones which tend to strengthen the hold of religious communities. There are the motives of personal need for the symbols of religious experience, and for the inspiration of religious faith.

Some English interpreters of the present cultural scene recognize a "Braithwaiteian" religious motivation following the philosopher Braithwaite, who after having taken the position that no satisfactory rational grounds for accepting traditional Christian belief can be given, enters the established church because the religious spirit and the symbols of faith give practical reinforcement to integrity in human living. There are universally significant elements in Boris Pasternak's picture of Lara in *Doctor Zhivago:*

> Lara was not religious. She did not believe in ritual. But sometimes, to be able to bear life, she needed the accompani-

ment of an inner music. She could not always compose such a music for herself. That music was God's word of life, and it was to weep over it that she went to church.[5]

For all such people, within the religious community, or standing near to it, and drawn to it, those who have grown up within and have never left, and those who have been outside and have been converted, certain issues appear which must be faced if the tradition is to be possessed and interpreted for contemporary living. The first of these issues concerns the credibility of religious faith in its inherited forms. How can religious beliefs be made intelligible in the thought-world of the twentieth century?

Skepticism about religious beliefs is a perennial aspect of culture; but it is true that the rise of modern science has produced the most severe crisis for belief. Auguste Comte divided the history of human thought into three stages, the theological, the metaphysical, and finally the positivist in which man's reason will be free from the illusion of belief in God. But Comte did not anticipate the development in modern religion of a post-positivist stage. After the work of empirical criticism has exposed the errors of a simple literalism, we may be free to explore the deeper strata of meaning in the traditional symbols as fundamental expressions of the human situation which are not dissolved by the scientific picture of the world. The mystery of creation and man's sense of relationship to a divine creative power remain when the details of creation stories are recognized as myths. The story of the fall of man from an original innocence and perfection expresses man's experience of estrangement from his essential being and a fulfillment for which he longs, and yet which he cannot grasp. The discovery of a mercy and renewal which come from beyond man himself comes as a genuine experience of the divine power, although traditional expressions of its working, whether in the Buddhist doctrine of the Bodhisattvas, or the Christian doctrines of atonement, may be understood as symbolic expressions of truths about the ultimate realities of personal existence and history.

Even if we conclude that these symbols offer a legitimate way of preserving religious truth, we should not underestimate the intellectual struggle which is required to achieve an authentic expression of religious faith consonant with twentieth century science and the new cosmologies. In the Christian tradition the controversy over Rudolph Bultmann's interpretation of the Christian scripture in terms of existentialist philosophy offers an example of the critical issues. Bultmann wants to reinterpret the biblical symbols of the fall, guilt, and redemption by showing how the ancient forms gave expression to man's existential questions and his self-interpretation. Bultmann's analysis of the existential questions is drawn largely from Heidegger's philosophy. He interprets the Christian Gospel as an answer, known only through personal faith, to the question about the meaning of existence. Bultmann is attacked on every side. There are the conservatives who do not want to disturb the ancient modes of expression. There are those who recognize the mythological elements in religion but are dubious of attempts to translate these into philosophical terms. And there are those who stand outside the Christian faith and who ask, "Why is not man's existential self-understanding enough, why should he return to an ancient faith at all?" The outcome in this struggle is not decided by intellectual analysis alone. The depths of spiritual life are involved. It is an issue concerning ultimate commitments and loyalties. It is the issue of how man is to find the meaning of his life.

What is happening in the discussion with Bultmann is happening in all the great religious traditions. In Formosa Neo-Confucians are seeking to show how the Confucian tradition can both absorb and deepen the scientific mentality through reaffirmation of the Confucian moral perspective. Japanese Buddhists are re-examining the Buddhist doctrine of desire in an effort to preserve the vital discipline of the self in relation to a life in a technological age. The Hindu philosopher Radhakrishnan proposes a synthesis of the Hindu tradition with modern idealistic philosophy as qualified and informed by Western themes and motifs.[6] As an example of the intellectual ferment we are describing we can note a report concerning the program of the Ahmadiyya movement of Islam at work in Africa, where Islam is making a strong bid for the allegiance of the emerging nations. A reporter says:

> The Ahmadiyya movement claims to do three things—to reform and purge Islam itself: to express Islam in ways pertinent to the modern world; and to answer the challenge of Christianity by borrowing from Christian faith and practise. It is now proposing to set up a medical mission in Sierra Leone, and its schools are increasing in number.[7]

Is this reinterpretation and adjustment of the religious tradition a genuine advance in man's spiritual adventure or a futile last ditch stand before the onslaught of a radical new human outlook? It depends on where one stands how he answers this question. In Western culture there are some hopeful signs that the inherited forms of faith can receive authentic contemporary expression. Some of those signs are found in the realm of religious art. Matisse's Chapelle du Rosaire in Vence, Le Corbusier's at Ronchamp, and other achievements in church architecture are such signs. Contemporary painting has given only a few examples of convincing religious expression, though many find such in Rouault. But in music the case is clearer. The great *Te Deum* and other choral works of Ralph Vaughan Williams, Benjamin Britten's *Noah,* the Masses by Stravinsky and Poulenc communicate religious meaning in a contemporary idiom. The systematic theologies of Paul Tillich and Karl Barth are reinterpretations of the traditional theological materials in ways which seek to be relevant to the present without dissipating the substance of the traditional faith, though Tillich conceives the method of reinterpretation quite differently from Barth. And it should not be forgotten that those who stand outside the historic faiths often draw directly or indirectly upon their substance. Albert Camus took the title for his book *The Fall* (*La Chute*) from the Christian tradition. This book and many others by him are filled with biblical themes although he rejects in part their traditional interpretation. Religious symbols do retain their power in a scientifically minded age.

2

There are many religions, and the second major issue to be considered is the attitude the religions take toward one another. There is a fundamental distinction here between such religions as Hinduism and Buddhism which in principle claim not to displace other faiths, and Judaism, Islam, and Christianity which have historically claimed a revelation of the divine which in the end must overcome all diversity of faith.

In Christianity today there is a deep self-examination on this issue, for it goes to the heart of the Christian conception of God. How does He deal with His creatures? Is Christianity the climax of a history of redemption which has its anticipations in all human experience? Or does Christianity assert, as some contemporary theologies hold, that the one revelation which created the

Judaeo-Christian peoples leads to the judgment that all man's religiousness outside this revelation is only a misunderstanding of God's nature and a reflection of man's self worship? Professor Toynbee sharply raises the question of what lies back of such an exclusive claim when he asks:

> Does not any creature stand convicted of megalomania if he allows himself to imagine that God can have committed Himself in an annunciation to one or more of His creatures, or, still more preposterous, in a covenant with one or more of them, at a particular point in Space-Time, to making this particular encounter of theirs with Him into the supreme moment in the history of His creation?[8]

Now the charge of megalomania is a hard one to answer. Hinduism with its proclamation of synthesis in which all religions can find shelter, and be reconciled in the Absolute One which dissolves all diversity, is attractive religiously because it offers a way of unity, and ethically because it expresses a spirit of tolerance and understanding.

But there is a danger of obscuring the real issue when the argument is put at the level of megalomania. The question is whether in our relation to the Holy we are led to some decisions as to the character of the Holy and as to the nature of the response which is required of us. One cannot believe all at once in the divine reality in all the forms which the great religions have conceived it, a point Toynbee himself makes. The Buddhist Hinayana goal of the extinction of the self's desire in order that it attain Nirvana cannot be simply reconciled with the Mahayana Buddhist view that the enlightened one may make himself responsible for the salvation of others. God cannot be the absolute spirit of Hindu advaita (non-dualist) doctrine utterly beyond all time and limitation, and at the same time be the creating, caring, responding God of history of the Christian scripture. Whoever the true God is, human culture is full of false Gods and false conceptions of God. Toynbee says that the absolutizing of our particular religious faith comes from the desire to escape the risk of making decisions, which in the end causes us to acknowledge issues between different ways of conceiving the divine.

Once we have seen, however, that the issue cannot be resolved simply by charging with intolerance those who claim a truth others do not have, we can acknowledge that there is one position which can be taken within the exclusive faiths. That is, *no existing conception of the Holy is exhaustive*. What Dr. Hocking has called *reconception* of one's own faith in the light of the meeting with new concepts and experience is always a possibility. That is why the encounter of one religious tradition with another may result in creativity for both. The meeting of the major traditions on a basis of mutual respect is surely one of the significant possibilities in our century. In many places such meeting comes in the course of life as people of differing traditions find themselves with common concerns. One thinks of Moslem business men on Y.M.C.A. boards in the Near East, of Hindus engaged in the discussion of modern philosophy with Western Christians, of humanists and Neo-Confucianists teaching in Christian colleges, and of the wide general interest in the study of history of religions. We may indeed invite disillusionment if we expect from such meeting and discussion any achievement of consensus. Is that even a desirable goal? We may treasure the richness of perspective which comes from the many religions, even if we are among those who hold that one requires a final judgment upon the others. But it requires a commitment to open search and discussion to rise above parochial prejudice. We have to acknowledge that our self interest and defensiveness are inevitably aroused in the meeting of alternative religious outlooks, so Professor Toynbee's warning is relevant.

In this new world-wide encounter the religions are on trial before one another, and before human judgment, for there ought to be that in the religious spirit which makes it possible for men to respect one another's humanity, to listen to one another's view of life, and to exhibit a spirit of charity and humility in human relationships. Can the sorry story of religious hatred be overcome? Can men preserve, treasure and renew their religious loyalties in a spirit of human brotherliness? It is always discouraging to see religious people quarreling over who it is that understands love most fully. The threat of "syncretism" should not be allowed to prevent us from recognizing that a real mutual encounter and influence is inevitable and salutary in the world today. Religion should not be a source of the deepening of the chasms between men. They are deep enough as it is.

Such an encounter of religions presupposes freedom for the encounter, and this means we must here take notice of the issue of the place of the religious community in the state, though in the scope of this paper, we can only mention the complex problems. Persecution both against religion and in the name of religion exists in the twentieth century as it has in every previous one. The religious community which seeks to worship a reality which stands above the state or nation may find itself suspect, and under repression, if not outright persecution. Freedom of worship is still one of the threatened goods of a mature civilization.

Religious communities generally are concerned with more than freedom for their thought and worship. They are concerned with the life of the community and with their contribution to both the support and the criticism of the common life. Most of the religion in the world's history has existed in some kind of social or political establishment. There are many types of establishment today, and many movements toward a more explicit place for the religious community in the natural life. Thailand is a Buddhist state, Islam is the state religion of Pakistan and Malaya. There is the Roman Catholic establishment in Spain, and the Anglican establishment in England. There are strong movements in Burma and Ceylon toward a more explicit established status of Buddhism. These examples can be contrasted with that of the United States where the religious institutions have no establishment. The issues in this case have to do with the areas of remaining privilege, the relationship of state support to religious schools, and with moral issues where the influence of the religious community makes itself felt on questions of state policy.

The forms of the relationship of religious communities to the societies in which they live are varied and complex. No general and clear trend in our time is discernible. Issues concerning religious institutions will continue to be raised in every political community, and many factors of tradition, national ideals, and conceptions of freedom will affect national policies. Every concordat between a religious institution and the state is certain to be an uneasy one in a world where the forces of political life are so explosive. There are many cross-currents of feeling and judgment on this issue within the religious communities themselves. In Malaya there is a law which requires every Moslem to attend the mosque on Fridays, and the religious courts can assess a twenty-five dollar fine for failure to comply. During the summer of 1960 a Malayan official, a Moslem, made a public plea that the courts not enforce this law because of the appearance it would give Malaya in the eyes of other freedom loving countries. Thus nationalistic, democratic and religious motives are intertwined in public policy. Religious groups vary as to the kind of political status they seek. Some are concerned only to secure freedom for worship and beyond that point have no direct interest in the forms of political life. Others hold that the religious community must find ways to bring its inspiration and influence into the common life while retaining the ultimate perspective, and critical judgment without which human affairs tend to lose their true direction.

3

So far we have been asking about those issues which arise within the religious traditions today. There is an alternative position. Many religious people believe that the integrity and vitality of the religious spirit require in our time that it be set free from just those involvements with tradition, those efforts to adjust ancient concepts to present realities which engage the energies of the traditionalists. They hold that a change in religious concepts as radical as that brought about by the modern scientific conception of nature is required, and they believe that the religious spirit can be relevant in our century only as it goes all the way toward adoption of a scientific and rational method of approaching religious truth.

These are the ones who "cannot go home again" to any of the traditions. They see the religious traditions as having been formed in the primitive and adolescent phases of human evolution, and they seek a new and "mature" religious faith. The psychologist Henry A. Murray writes of the need for a "mythology for grown ups" which will preserve the riches of religious tradition, but will bring new insight from new levels of human understanding. Professor Goodenough has entitled his book on religion, *Toward a Mature Faith*.[9]

I shall call those who take this position the New Deists because they have a close kinship with the eighteenth century deists in basic outlook, though this is a *new* deism, based on a new era of scientific thought. The early deists wanted a rational religion free from the encumbrance of outworn belief. They wanted a religious outlook agreeable with and indeed based upon the scientific view of the world which had achieved its greatest triumph in Newton's physics. They believed that Newtonian science supported rational arguments for God, freedom, and immortality. Earlier deism had an ethical concern, and tended to become primarily an ethical faith. Believing that reason unites where tradition divides, the deists sought universal rational moral principles which they believed were legislated and enforced by the Supreme Being as laws of his universe. They upheld religions as the inspiration of virtuous conduct and the encouragement of belief in a heavenly reward.

Most of these themes reappear in the New Deism of the twentieth century. To mention representative figures, there are Julian Huxley, Lewis Mumford, Edmund Sinnott, Erwin Goodenough, Norman Cousins, and Pierre de Chardin, the last a Roman Catholic who explored many themes in the relation of an evolutionary world-view to religious faith. Some aspects of the New Deism are derived from the advances in science since the eighteenth century. Physics has undergone a revolution in basic concepts, and leaves far more open questions than did Newton's science. With Darwin the evolutionary perspective has entered, and the new deism is especially concerned with a dynamic view of the universe. In psychology the new deism is more complex and sophisticated than was the simple associationist psychology of the eighteenth century. Freudianism and the depth psychology movement have stressed the irrational elements in human nature. And no contemporary view of man can help but be sobered and perplexed by the outburst of demonic passion and cruelty in the concentration camps and other exhibitions of twentieth century man's ruthlessness to man.

With these qualifications however, it can still be said that what is characteristic of the New Deism as of the old is its temper of scientific rigor, its belief in moral sanity through rational control, its optimism about man's possibilities and its sense of man's at-homeness in the universe, its preservation of belief in God while it remains highly critical of traditional concepts of God. It is a positive, aggressive, morally sensitive and committed outlook, seeking a faith integrated with contemporary modes of thought. Norman Cousins has put into his *Litany for Modern Man* an articulation of this basic faith. I shall not quote all of it, but hope that these lines convey the sense of the whole:

> I am a single cell in a body of two billion cells. The body is mankind.
>
> I glory in the individuality of self, but my individuality does not separate me from my universal self—the oneness of man.
>
> * * *
>
> I do not believe that human kind is an excrescence or a machine, or that the myriads of solar systems and galaxies in the universe lack order or sanction.
>
> I may not embrace or command this universal order, but I can be at one with it for I am of it.
>
> * * *
>
> I see no separation between the universal order and the moral order.
>
> * * *
>
> The sense of human unity makes possible a *reverence for life.*
>
> * * *
>
> I will work for human unity under a purposeful peace. I will work for the growth of a moral order that is in keeping with the universal order.
>
> In this way do I affirm faith in life and life in faith.
>
> I am a single cell in a body of two billion cells. The body is mankind.[10]

Here rationalism is joined with mystical religious feeling in a way which is not always present in deism, but the central theme of confidence in the unity of man with his world and of man with man through rational insight is the key to the position.

When Norman Cousins here speaks of "reverence for life," he brings us deliberately to the figure of Albert Schweitzer, one of the few persons in the world who cannot be omitted in any study of the religious situation in our time. He cannot be classified among the "new deists" for he does not belong with them philosophically or theologically. His roots are in the Christian faith, and in the spirit of the enlightenment, and he combines these in a way which is peculiar to him, so that he stands apart. In his principle of "reverence for life" he accepts the positive Christian evaluation of life with its doctrine of the goodness of the creation, yet he seems to develop this as a principle which transcends any particular tradition. And in his example of devotion, of moral dedication and the will to reconciliation his spiritual stature makes him the symbol and inspiration of the sacrificial spirit which has commanded the response of sensitive souls throughout the world. It is characteristic of those I have called the New Deists that often they find in Albert Schweitzer a major source of inspiration and insight.

But Schweitzer's complex ethical and religious outlook is at many points at variance with the view that a rationally unified whole can be made out of science and human experience. Schweitzer sees as Thomas Hardy did, an ultimate opposition between the demands of a humane ethic and the ways of nature. Schweitzer says:

> . . . ethics can expect nothing from a true knowledge of the world . . . The world offers us the disconcerting spectacle of the will to life in conflict with itself. One existence maintains itself at the expense of another.[11]

This thesis directly challenges the deistic confidence that the natural order and the moral order exhibit mutual support. Late in 1960 a group of Schweitzer's American followers made a pilgrimage to Lambarene with the specific purpose of asking him about this radical opposition between ethics and nature.[12]

There are two major issues which the new deism faces. The first concerns the extent to which religious faith can find its principles and its rational ground in the objective inspection of the conditions of human life in nature. Deists reject the authority of special revelations or special intuitions of the divine. They want to find a position which in principle is accessible to all rational men, precisely in order to set religion free from the bias, the defensiveness, and the confusion which result from appeal to authorities beyond the reach of criticism. The question arises then as to how religious knowledge is to be derived from experience.

Dr. W. F. G. Swann, director for thirty-two years of the Bartol Research Foundation in Philadelphia, and one of the elder statesmen of modern physical science, writes in a religious vein of the mystery and miraculous character of all nature and life. He raises, in fashion reminiscent of that earlier deist William Paley, the question of whether the universe exhibits a "planned design, whether or not we are willing to admit the notion of a planner, or say what we mean by that postulate?" Then he comments on how we are to deal with such questions:

> In discussing such matters I think it is essential to avoid all theological doctrine as a starting point. I would rather see a theological doctrine emerge spontaneously as part of the over-all scheme of nature, than I would see the workings of nature forced into a frame provided by a preconceived theological doctrine as a starting point.[13]

The thesis of both old and new deism could not be put more succinctly. We are to see the truth of the divine reality by freeing ourselves from the bias of inherited theology, and discovering the truth which rises "spontaneously" from the general scheme of nature.

But what truth rises spontaneously from the face of nature? For Thomas Hardy it was the truth of a relentless machine grinding its way forward. For Bertrand Russell it is the trampling march of unconscious power. For Albert Schweitzer it is the contradiction between the struggle for life and the demands of conscience. Are the issues here resolved by further appeal to the observable facts, or do they lead us into the area of evaluation rooted in the perspectives of different faiths, with their different responses to the facts?

If we read the facts differently, and interpret their implications differently, this must be partly because we seek the meaning of life as different selves, shaped by historical traditions, with different perspectives and different ultimate commitments. How can these differences be adjudicated and by what higher judgments can they be resolved?

At this point even physics raises some questions for rationalists, since the relativity of the perspective in which we see the facts is now a factor in physical theory. And when we make judgments in history we recognize the clash of ultimate values. The issue here concerns the ultimate ground of faith. Is there something which lies deeper than rational thought, because it grasps a reality which can only be known through the total response of the person? Or is it the case that a higher synthesis of religious experience and scientific insight, a reconciliation of intuition and reason, is possible in a more ordered and inclusive view of our life in its cosmic setting? The new deism, I suggest, lives more by the hope of such a synthesis than by its possession, but it may point toward the synthesis which must ever lure those who believe in the unity of truth.

The second issue for the new deism is related to the first. It concerns the view which is to be taken of man's potentialities for good and for evil. Two philosophies of man are in contention in our day. One is that which sees in man an essential goodness, and a creative capacity. He can find the resources within himself to meet the experiences of life and the fate of death with courage and be at peace with them. The other sees a contradiction in man's spirit which he cannot resolve by his own efforts. His existence involves a final anxiety about his being, about the world, and life. He is therefore prone to take desperate measures to assure himself of his security, either in pride or in despairing resignation. The religions have expressed both these attitudes and have ministered to both of them.

The issues here, it may be fairly clear, cannot be resolved solely by an appeal to common knowledge. Every religious outlook will have to come to terms with both human hopefulness and with human desperation. The twentieth century has shown the highest technical achievements in human history. It is also the century of Auschwitz and countless other examples of man's cruelty to man. No theology or religion which does not recognize both sides of man's nature can claim the thoughtful allegiance of twentieth century minds. Here we have raised an issue which helps us see the relevance of the religious traditions with their symbols of man's estrangement from God, and their declaration of the necessity of repentance and regeneration. A superficial rational optimism can be just as completely out of touch with the realities of human experiences as is sentimentalized religious faith. It remains to be seen how far a rational humanism can clarify, purge, and fulfill man's highest capacities without the religious awareness of the divine holiness, judgment, and mercy.

I am trying only to state an issue not to resolve it; but we may have gone far enough in the analysis to see that traditionalists and modernists, mystics and rationalists, and surely those who have high hopes for man and those who see tragic elements in his destiny may speak in the twentieth century with insight, power, and relevance. None has a monopoly on the truth.

The ultimate issue in religion in our century and in every century concerns the meaning of man's life and the question about God as the source and fulfillment of the meaning of all existence. As Alfred North Whitehead has said, "To-day there is but one religious dogma in debate: What do you mean by 'God'?"[14] Is man the creature of a divine reality which gives meaning and fulfillment to his struggles, or is man, alone in the cosmos, required to set his own spirit free, bear his own burdens and become a saint without God as Albert Camus describes man's situation in his novel *The Plague*. We ask this question, not because we have inherited something called religious belief, but because we are men who live and love and die. *In Science and the Modern World* Whitehead states the meaning of religion in these words:

> Religion is the vision of something which stands beyond, behind, and within, the passing flux of immediate things; something which is real, and yet waiting to be realised; something which is a remote possibility, and yet the greatest of present facts; something that gives meaning to all that passes, and yet eludes apprehension; something whose possession is the final good, and yet is beyond all reach; something which is the ultimate ideal, and the hopeless quest. . . .
>
> Apart from it, human life is a flash of occasional enjoyments lighting up a mass of pain and misery, a bagatelle of transient experience.[15]

It may obscure the real issue even to use the word God for that which Whitehead speaks about here, since we have no right to say that only one kind of language is appropriate for that which stands beyond all language. Dr. Tillich has used the phrase "the God beyond God" to remind us that we are speaking about One who cannot be confined to our human perspectives. If God be God, the One who can save life from ultimate chaos, He is not a projection of a father image, or a symbol for our best human ideals. He is the reality which judges all our ideals. As Henry Nelson Wieman has said, "God is more than we can think."[16] He is the truth of all truths, the source of being, the spirit which makes us persons, able to approach Him in thought and worship.

Is such a God real? That is the religious issue in every century, as Thomas Hardy saw. He could not let go of the question. In the closing passage of *The Dynasts* he has the Spirit of the Pities ask if after all the Great Impersonal Source may not be conscious life since it has produced conscious human life, and Hardy allows the Spirits to echo the *Magnificat,* "thou hast put down the mighty [the Dynasts] from their seats."

Can man in this technological age with its high possibilities of creativity and its terrifying possibilities of destruction live with a faith and a hope which will release his full humanity, his capacity to love and to serve in the midst of human problems? That is the religious question to which men of the twentieth century must give such answers as they have.

Notes

1. Quoted in W. R. Rutland, *Thomas Hardy, A Study of His Writings and their Background,* Oxford, Blackwell (1938), p. 64.
2. Reported in the London *Observer,* October 16, 1960.
3. Friedrich Nietzsche, *Thus Spake Zarathustra,* LXVI.

4. Martin Buber, *I and Thou,* Eng. trans. by Ronald Gregor Smith, Edinburgh, 1937.
5. Boris Pasternak, *Doctor Zhivago,* Pantheon Books edition, N.Y., 1958, p. 49.
6. S. Radhakrishnan, *East and West, Some Reflections,* London, Allen & Unwin, 1955.
7. Cecil Northcott in *The Scotsman,* Edinburgh, December 5, 1960.
8. Arnold Toynbee, *An Historian's Approach to Religion,* London, Oxford University Press, 1956, p. 135.
9. Henry A. Murray, "A Mythology for Grownups," *The Saturday Review,* January 23, 1960, pp. 8–12.
Erwin Goodenough, *Toward a Mature Faith,* New York, Prentice Hall, 1955.
10. Norman Cousins, "Litany for Modern Man," *The Saturday Review,* Aug. 8, 1953, p. 22. (Italics the present writer's.)
11. Albert Schweitzer, "The Problem of Ethics for Twentieth Century Man," *The Saturday Review,* June 13, 1953, p. 48.
12. Reported in the *London Times,* December 29, 1960.
13. W.F.G. Swann, "The Living and the Dead," *The Saturday Review,* June 4, 1960, p. 44.
14. A. N. Whitehead, *Religion in the Making,* New York, Macmillan, 1926, p. 67.
15. A. N. Whitehead, *Science and the Modern World,* New York, Macmillan, 1931, p. 275.
16. Henry N. Wieman, "God is More Than We Can Think," *Christendom,* Vol. I (1935–6) pp. 428, 442.

7

HOW DOES GOD ACT?: AN ESSAY IN WHITEHEAD'S METAPHYSICS

THAT THE Christian God acts is one of the main themes of contemporary theology. The Biblical conception of God as Creator and Redeemer involves his purposive working in history. He liberates a people and establishes a covenant with them. He withdraws his favor from them when they are disloyal, he announces his judgment and purpose through the prophets. He gives his son to live and die for the world. He creates a new heaven and a new earth. It is often remarked that such assertions about God mark the primary difference between Greek conceptions of time as cyclical, Asiatic conceptions of the appearances of God in history as theophanies manifesting an ultimate reality which lies behind the illusions of time and space, and the Christian view of a history of redemption with a Beginning, Center, and End.

There are innumerable assertions in the Biblical record of specific acts of God. The regularities of the times and the seasons as well as miraculous suspensions of the expected occurrences in nature come from God's sovereign will. He "sends his rain on the just and the unjust," and he raises his Son from the dead. He clothes the lilies of the field, and he ordains the powers which govern men, using them as his instruments. As Holy Spirit God inspires and blesses, and he holds before every moment as well as before the whole drama the promise of ultimate judgment. In this intensely personal and realistic way the Bible speaks of the acts of God. It has been the task of Christian thinkers to relate this Biblical outlook to rational interpretations of the structure of nature and the occurrences of history. And this has meant that the question of *how* the divine action is to be conceived, both in its "regular" and in its extraordinary manifestations, has perennially exercised Christian thought and given it special problems.

It may be granted that the acts of creation and of eschatological judgment and deliverance are in a special category so far as rational interpretation is concerned. They are generally held to be "events" which cannot be interpreted as observable natural events. They deal with beginnings and endings and, as Immanual Kant claimed, we here move beyond the sphere of a possible basis of knowledge in experience. But most of the biblical assertions about God's action have to do with present experienced happenings in history, the destinies of men and nations, the powers, wonders, diseases, threats, and symbolic significance of nature. Therefore the problem of giving a theological interpretation to the meaning of the divine action in relation to the powers and structures, causes and effects, which we can observe and which the sciences study is inescapable. Newton in the first edition of the *Principia* said nothing about God. He added the famous scholium to the second edition affirming God as *pantocrator*. But as to specific functions Newton could find nothing for God to do once the world was set in motion other than to keep the stars from collapsing in outer space, and occasionally to reorder the world when its motions led to too great a disorder. The problem of first and final causes, of the meaning of force, of the regularities of nature in relation to divine miraculous action, of creativity and evolution, of chance and purpose have thus become the standard problems of relating Christian theology to nature as scientifically understood. In this paper I shall express my conviction that these are genuine problems for religious belief, and that Christian theology cannot assert that God acts without going on to a general interpretation of action in the world and of the meaning of God's activity within or upon the world.

It is a further presupposition of the approach in this paper that the problem of action has three dimensions, theological, scientific, and metaphysical, and that these are so related that the metaphysical analysis must take into account the scientific analysis, and the theological analysis must take into its range of vision both the scientific and the metaphysical analyses. It is less obvious that the metaphysical depends upon the theological and that the scientific depends also upon the metaphysical, although in the end I believe they are so related.

The problem of God's action involves the meaning of action, of cause and effect, of power and structure, of law and chance. Whether we start with scientific concepts or theological assertions we are led to a common ground where the meanings of these general concepts must be given some clarification. The problems are difficult. I shall confine my paper to an exposition which I hope has some measure of accuracy to Alfred North Whitehead's doctrine of action and causality, and then make some comments upon his doctrine and its implications for theology. Concerning its implications in relation to particular scientific concepts I am not able to speak above the level of a lay acquaintance with science, so many points are raised which will have to be pursued in discussion with scientific theorists.

I. *Whitehead as Metaphysician; his Concept of Speculative Philosophy.*

One of Whitehead's most interesting definitions of metaphysics occurs in *Process and Reality* in the opening chapter:

"Metaphysics is nothing but the description of the generalities which apply to all the details of practice."[1]

There are three points to note about this definition:

First, metaphysics is a description of what is experienced, or what is encountered in experience, such as structures, qualities, judgments, errors, minds, and bodies. Whitehead says the final tests of speculative concepts are in their applicability and adequacy to experience and their coherence with one another. That is, *practice* here means concrete observable, experienceable activity in the world.

Second, metaphysics seeks generality. Whitehead believes the chief task of philosophy is to elaborate categoreal schemes within which the world may be coherently spoken about. For Whitehead a category is a structure found in all experience. Hence the method of philosophy is to take some significant area of experience, for Whitehead this is primarily to take the human experience of knowing as a bodily-mental event, and then to elaborate a systematic scheme of concepts which will be adequate to make speech about this reality intelligible. Of course, if we begin with this human experience of bodily-mental knowing we must go on to examine everything within the range of human experience including all the specific data and theories disclosed in science and in the history of human institutions. The goal of the search is for a rational understanding, so far as reason can go, of the *being* of things, and of the ways things are related to one another. Thus Whitehead's fundamental doctrine that real things are actual entities, moments of experience which represent the outcomes of processes which aim at satisfaction, is his answer to the classical question about being. He seeks to give an account of all the conceptions which are

[1]Alfred North Whitehead, *Process and Reality* (New York: The Macmillan Co., 1936), p. 19. (Hereafter, *PR*)

necessary to understanding a world of actual entities related to one another and coming to be and passing away. It is this generality of intent in philosophy, its attempt to grasp the multiplicity of the world's phenomena, its dimensions of finitude and infinity, its goods and evils, its truth and illusion, its appearance and reality which distinguishes philosophy from science. And Whitehead explicitly says that philosophy is not a science.[2] But the concepts which philosophy seeks must be adequate to interpret the data and the meanings supplied by science. Of course we are here stating a goal of speculative philosophy which lies beyond any human attainment. Philosophy is an exercise in the construction and the criticism of metaphysical schemes.

Third, Whitehead's statement about metaphysics leads directly to the topic of this discussion, for the reference to the details of practice means that Whitehead accepts activity, function, and interaction as the context of all theory. In this statement he is very close to John Dewey's outlook. Philosophy itself is activity set in the context of a world of interactive processes. This pragmatic aspect of Whitehead's standpoint is important throughout his understanding of action.

II. *Some Basic Concepts in Whitehead's Metaphysics*

It is a fundamental doctrine of Whitehead's that if God is intelligible at all to us, he must exemplify the metaphysical categories and not be invoked just to "prevent their collapse."[3] Hence in seeking the categories we must arrive at generic concepts which in some way characterize all action including the divine activity. Therefore we must explore some of Whitehead's general concepts first and then see how they are used to interpret the action of God.

(a) Whitehead calls his standpoint the philosophy of organism. What he proposes is a social doctrine of being.[4] He envisions the world as an ongoing complex of real things which act upon one another within the patterns set by a primordial order which includes all the possibilities which may characterize the outcomes of particular activities in the world:

[2]"Mathematics and the Good" in Paul A. Schilpp (ed.), *The Philosophy of Alfred North Whitehead* (Evanston: Northwestern University Press, 1941), p. 681.

[3]*PR*, p. 521.

[4]Charles Hartshorne's illuminating characterization.

> The notion of 'organism' is combined with that of 'process' in a two-fold manner. The community of actual things is an organism; but it is not a static organism. It is an incompletion in process of production. Thus the expansion of the universe in respect to actual things is the first meaning of 'process'; and the universe in any stage of its expansion is the first meaning of 'organism' . . . each actual entity is itself only describable as an organic process. It repeats in microcosm what the universe is in macrocosm. It is a process proceeding from phase to phase, each phase being the real basis from which its successor proceeds toward the completion of the thing in question.[5]

In this quotation Whitehead rejects one approach to the interpretation of causation and interaction which has so often been stated in traditional philosophy. Given individual substances which have no relations to one another and which are not directly experienced by anything how do they act upon one another and how do they become known? The specific doctrine which Whitehead believes the seventeenth century finally worked out in following the implications of this question is that of "simple location." This means that each actual entity can be located in a specific time and place which has no necessary relation to any other time and place, or to any other entities which are in the past or present or future of the given thing. Whitehead believes this was the outcome of the application of the conceptual scheme of seventeenth century physics to the description of the material world, and he believes that Hume exposed the logical consequences of this view. Induction has no rational ground, for the present data have no inherent reference to any other state of affairs. It is impossible to account for living organisms, and valid inference from sense impressions to their origins or causes is impossible.

Whitehead declares that nothing in our experience gives any basis whatever for this doctrine of simple location.[6] He proposes to return to immediate experience and suggests the possibility of beginning with another set of concepts for describing the being of actual things. Further, Whitehead believes the logical and mathematical analysis of spatio-temporal structure requires the doctrine that every region involves a reference to, or "mirrors" every other region.

Through the appeal to immediate experience coupled with a logical analysis of spatio-temporal structure Whitehead gives a char-

[5] *PR*, p. 327.

[6] A. N. Whitehead, *Science and the Modern World* (New York: The Macmillan Co., 1931), p. 85. (Hereafter *SAMW*)

acterization of the metaphysical task which is quite close to Aristotle's. He accepts as a point of departure a world of real things which function in relation to one another and to other realities in processes of becoming. There are causes and effects, and these causes are complex. Final causes are included among the interpretative principles of any action. The problem of philosophy is to describe the interweaving of the many strands of activity and structure in the one world. Where Whitehead differs from Aristotle is in the conviction that the Aristotelian subject-object logic defeats itself by treating the qualifications of substance as accidents which happen to characterize an underlying reality which "possesses" and exhibits these qualities. Whitehead sees no need for asserting an underlying reality beneath or behind the process of the becoming of and passing away of "qualitied" things. There is indeed one actual entity which does not pass away. God's metaphysical status here differs in important respects from that of all other things. His primordial nature, which is the structure of possibility, is eternal, and his concrete nature in interaction with the world is everlasting.

(b) We can always begin with assumptions and it does not take us far to say that we assume interactive processes in a world where there are patterns of organic relatedness. The problem is to give an account of this relatedness. It is here that Whitehead's distinctive doctrines appear. They are illuminating, and they create their own special problems.

Whitehead's term for the relation in which one thing is acted upon by another thing is "prehension" and his distinctive doctrine is that prehensions are "feelings." Actual entities are subjects. They are centers of feeling which weld together the many strands of relatedness to other things in one determinate outcome which is a specific satisfaction.

> A feeling is the appropriation of some elements in the universe to be components in the real internal constitution of its subject. The elements are the initial data; they are what the feeling feels. But they are felt under an abstraction. The process of the feeling involves negative prehensions which effect elimination. Thus the initial data are felt under a 'perspective' which is the objective datum of the feeling.[7]

Two kinds of things are "felt." One is the structure of possibility

[7] *PR*, p. 353.

which includes the logical orders and the qualities which can characterize particular things. These qualities Whitehead calls eternal objects. They are potentials for feeling until they are actually felt in some concrete process. The eternal objects are felt "conceptually." The other things that are felt are actual entities in the world and these are felt "physically." Thus Whitehead generalizes the body-mind duality in knowing. Further, he holds that every real subject-electron, cell, or human person grasps the structure of possibilities beyond itself and in the way in which it relates itself to the possibilities every actual entity makes a "decision," that is it has its world in its own way, contributing an element of its own novel self determination to the final outcome. There is always a way in which *that* subject unifies and possesses *that* set of prehensions. This involves final causation for it is possible for novel decisions to occur only as real things lay hold on a possibility of attainment which lies beyond the present activity.

It must be clear also that Whitehead regards the category of value as constitutive of every actual thing. Everything aims at being something, at realizing some unification of itself with other things and with its world. He writes "To be an actual entity is to have a self-interest. This self-interest is a feeling of self-valuation; it is an emotional tone."[8]

Whitehead has obviously derived his categories from human experience and has generalized them for all levels of nature. He appears to attribute feeling, valuation, subjectivity, decision, and even purpose to every actual thing, including the non-living orders. This may be criticized as naive imagination or speculative irrelevance. I suggest it is neither. Whitehead is quite explicit that he is not asserting consciousness below the human, or, perhaps in rudimentary form, the animal level. He is not a pan-psychist if that means the attributing of conscious decision and awareness to plants and atoms. He says explicitly the physical world consists of "blind" feeling.

> This word 'feeling' is a mere technical term; but it has been chosen to suggest that functioning through which the concrescent actuality appropriates the datum so as to make it its own.[9]

It is in this sense that we can understand Whitehead's startling language about emotion when he says that the key notion with which

[8]*Religion in the Making* (New York: The Macmillan Co., 1927), p. 100.
[9]*PR*, p. 249.

cosmology should start is that "the energetic activity considered in physics is the emotional intensity entertained in life."[10]

What is fundamental here is the social analogy: the real things are the electronic and protonic occasions which form the societies, and their interactions are characterized by laws which "come into being by reason of the analogous characters of the members of the society."[11] . . . "Thus our cosmic epoch is to be conceived primarily as a society of electromagnetic occasions, including electronic and protonic occasions . . ." "The atom is only explicable as a society with activities involving rhythms with their definite period." And he also remarks that since the structural flow of energy has to do with the transmission of simple physical feelings, some sort of quantum theory in physics relevant to the existing type of cosmic order "is to be expected."[11]

One element of this description of actual entities deserves emphasis at this point. There is a novel element in the 'decision' of each individual occasion, which is its own contribution to the uniqueness of its perspective upon the universe. The weakest and most trivial occasion of an electron contributes a unique moment of being to the totality of the universe. Therefore the transcendence of God is not something absolutely peculiar to him. "Every actual entity, in virtue of its novelty, transcends its universe, God included."[12]

(c) We come now to the interpretation of cause.

It follows from the preceding analysis that every actual occasion is in one sense *causi sui*. We have to find the reason for things within the constitution of actual events, and their decisions. Every event prehends the universe in its own way, with some increment of novelty. Its outcome involves the way in which that actual occasion lays hold upon the structure of possibility which stands before it as the foundation of its subjective aim. Whitehead uses the term "final cause" to characterize this aspect of actuality. The feelings involved in any concrete process are to be understood as elements in the aim which is given concreteness by the "feeler" itself. Every process aims at its own satisfaction, that is, at being a certain kind of center of meaning, a

[10]*Modes of Thought* (New York: The Macmillan Co., 1938), p. 232. (Hereafter, *MT*)

[11]*PR*, pp. 121, 139, 141, 389.

[12]*PR*, p. 143.

unity of the universe at its place and from its perspective. "This final cause is an inherent element in the feeling, constituting the unity of that feeling."[12]

There is also efficient causality between one actual entity and another, for to prehend something is to have that something enter into the prehender as cause. The basic discussion here occurs in *Process and Reality*, pp. 361-365. I shall risk this brief summary:

"A simple physical feeling is an act of causation."[13] Actual entities are prehended, that is, felt, by other actual entities. What is experienced is not only the abstract form or quality which characterizes the other entity but in some measure we directly experience, Whitehead holds, the way the other entity entertains its own data. In experiencing the greenness of the forest we are experiencing the way in which trees and leaves entertain the eternal object, greenness. And the greenness of the forest enters as cause into the determination of the person who experiences it at this time and place. It is a constituent in the satisfaction which constitutes this phase of his being. Whitehead therefore terms the mode of perception in which the human body is organically conditioned by its prehension of another actual entity 'causal efficacy'. "Thus the cause is objectively in the constitution of the effect."[14] It should be emphasized that this organic experience of the greenness of the forest is a direct qualification of our organism and its structures by the actual occasions which they prehend. This organic experience is transmuted in the higher organisms into particular and discriminated sense data, which are then projected back upon their source. This later perception is the mode of "presentational immediacy." It is the way the world appears to us after the highly complex tranformation which organic experience undergoes in the body-mind organism. It is necessary to stress this because Whitehead is not declaring that what we consciously discriminate as the "greenness of the trees" is precisely what the trees entertain as greenness. Distortions, error, transformation, are all elements in the final outcome of our experiencing other things.

The primary mode of our experience of causal efficacy is our intuition of our own selves a fraction of a second before the present moment. The self at Time I has now become a datum for the self at

[13]*PR*, p. 361.
[14]*PR*, p. 363.

Time II, is prehended by the self at Time II, and enters as cause into the constitution of the self at Time II.

III. *God's Action Upon the World*

It will be necessary to give some general characterizations of Whitehead's doctrine of God's action before turning to its special aspects.

First, it is required in Whitehead's metaphysics that the notion of God as sole cause of all happenings is rejected. God exercises causality, and in a supreme way (also, I think it must be shown in some special ways) but he acts always in relation to beings who have their own measure of causal self determination in their interaction with other finite things and with God.

Second, the way in which God can act upon other things is categorically determined by the metaphysical order constituted by his primordial nature, and which he does not violate. It would be meaningless to speak of his violating his own essence. This means that God acts upon other things by objectifying his being for them so that he can be prehended by them. God acts by being felt by his creatures, and in this process he enters into the constitution of their successive moments of experience.

Third, the creatures enter into the constitution of God's experience as he prehends *them*. They become causes in his successive phases of experience. He receives from the world as well as gives to the world.

Fourth, causality is complex. This is of fundamental importance in any theological doctrine related to Whitehead's ontological outlook. Causality has complex aspects at the level of bare physical existence, for there are elements of final causation, through prehension of structure, and elements of self-causation, and of efficient causation. In the high grade organisms through their powers of abstraction, consciousness, with its transmutation of the modes in which experience is possible, introduces the complexity of emotion. Consider for example the feelings of mystery, of perplexity in the face of the variety of good and evils, the contemplation of ideals, the feelings of remorse. All these have causal aspects, and enter into the constitution of the occasions of personal experience. When we speak then of causality in God we are stretching our understanding of these structures of our experience far beyond any direct comprehension. But what Whitehead does insist is that if we are to speak intelligibly of God's action, and of God as cause, there must be some real analogy of structure between his being and that of the creatures.

Fifth, it must be shown that on Whitehead's terms there are identifiable ways in which the divine action differs from that of the creatures, differences rooted in the fact that God's metaphysical status is not identical with that of the creatures.

We now turn directly to Whitehead's doctrine of God. He distinguishes between the primordial and the consequent natures of God. I have always thought that his language here was improveable. It suggests two separate beings, or at least "natures" somehow joined together. But it is clear that the intent of Whitehead's view is quite different. The being of God is dipolar.[15] The primordial aspect of his being is his envisagement of the realm of possibility in its abstraction from all particular matters of fact. It is the order which characterizes the world so that it can be one determinate world, and at the same time be a process in which possibilities are realized and expulsion of incompatibles takes place. The primordial nature is actual, that is, there is a definite structure of possibility which characterizes every existing reality; but it is deficiently actual in itself for it has no concrete determination of matters of fact within it. It is the realm of possibility. It is also an order of value, for it includes the structure of relevance, the qualities, and the potential meanings which characterize the world, and it is an ordered realm in which gradations of value are structured.

How does God in his primordial nature act? The most obvious point is that he acts by presenting to the creatures the unity, the richness, and the limits of possibility as ordered by his vision. That is to say God acts in his primordial gift of structure to the world by "not acting." He acts by being. He is the order upon which everything existing must draw if it is to be at all. The primordial nature simply is what it is, and nothing can be anything in particular without prehending that order. Whitehead speaks of the primordial "appetition" which is the basis of all order.

> The universe is thus understood as including a source of ideals. The effective aspect of this source is Deity as immanent in the present experience. The

[15]Again to use one of Charles Hartshorne's accurate phrases.

sense of historic importance is the intuition of the universe as everlasting process, unfading in its deistic unity of ideals.[16]

The view is then that God presents the individual occasions in the world with the possibility of participating in the society of being in certain definite ways, which involve elements of decision and novelty, but also strict conditions of limitation. Nothing is, for Whitehead, except by participation. Thus Whitehead, as in so many ways, repeats a Platonic theme, but on a realistic basis, rather than an idealistic one.

I will make two observations about this doctrine as it bears on the question of how God acts.

First, there is the question of the validity of stretching the category of feeling to cover non-conscious life. Does Whitehead throw any light on the question of how every physical event exhibits the structure expressed in the formula $E = mc^2$?

It is difficult in one sense to say that "feeling" which must be understood from the standpoint of our experience, belongs to non-conscious life. But the critical point is not whether "feeling" as we know it is attributed to electrons; but the point is that the description of an electron requires a doctrine of '"physical memory" and of causal relationship in which there is a structural analogy to our remembrance of things past, and our knowledge of the inheritance of elements of our present actuality from that past. And it also requires some apprehension of a structure which is a form of possibility, applicable to an infinite number of occasions, but which characterizes this actual occasion in its immediacy. Further, Whitehead refuses to leave the problem of the evolution of organisms within the physical world simply with the name "emergence" to cover the mystery. Some kind of appetition toward further possibilities, some way in which even the physical world lays hold upon an order which lies beyond the present must belong to that world, else evolution is completely unintelligible. God, we may say, is that function of primordial order with its potentialities which makes evolution possible.

We note that the theme of the divine persuasion enters here. The primordial nature stands before the decision of each actual occasion; but in itself it does not determine the final outcome in its concreteness.

[16]*MT*, p. 132.

Thus the order of nature, by itself does not make anything happen. Physical law is not a cause, except as it becomes an order prehended by an actual entity. In the view of evolution here proposed then, one might observe physical structures which point toward the emergence of living organisms; but prediction at any given time that the new structure would emerge would be impossible, at least it would have only a probability status.

It can be emphasized that the primordial nature of God is the being of God on the side of absolute structure. No reason can be given for its existence. It is akin to Aristotle's Unmoved Mover. It moves the world by luring the multiplicity of efforts in the world toward as yet unrealized possibilities.

A second observation on the primordial nature of God concerns the problem of "miracle." I would interpret the position to be that every happening in the world has an element of novelty, of freedom. The notion of absolute laws governing existence is discarded in so far as it is taken to mean the exhaustability of meaning of any event through knowledge of law alone. Further, new kinds of beings do appear in history. There are new defining characteristics of new societies.

At the same time there is the primordial order with its ultimate logical structure ordering all potentialities and excluding what is really incompatible. All actions in the world and in God observe this order for without it the world would be no world.

This means that every act of God occurs within the ultimate structure of possibility which makes the world a unity. But any act might "violate", in the sense of transcend, some particular structure of a society of beings by introducing a new level of possibility. The one restriction is that it could not violate the essential unity of being. It could not in other words be a complete discontinuity, nor could it destroy the final possibility of rational understanding, though indeed that understanding might be far beyond the power of any creature.

Such a position does not directly bear upon the "religious" meaning of miracle as a sign pointing to the power and salvation of God. It is a metaphysical understanding which sets certain bounds to what miracle might be in relation to an intelligible world view. Nothing can happen which violates the community of being itself. But, as Schleiermacher saw, to take only extraordinary events as miraculous in a 'religious' sense is surely to limit greatly the religious understanding of the world. Every event which points to God, order as well as creativity, predictability as well as novelty may make manifest God's being. From this standpoint the experiences of order, and of possible rational understanding are also potential miracles pointing to God in his primordial nature and function.

IV. *The Principle of Concretion*

In his first essay on the nature of God in *Science and the Modern World,* Whitehead introduces the concept of God as the principle of concretion. He has discussed the structures of possibility which characterize every existing thing. Then he points to the fact, which is strictly in accord with Aristotle's view, that no amount of analysis of the structures of subjects can exhaust the full meaning of the subject. The "thisness" of this table can never be reached by multiplication of abstract structures of determination. Hence Whitehead argues that for a real world a metaphysical "principle of concretion" is required. There must be a metaphysical function by which a definite outcome is secured from the ambiguous and indeterminate possibilities which hover over every concrete matter of fact. And this function, he asserts, belongs to God.

In what sense, we may ask, is God's being as the principle of concretion a definite action upon the world? Can a principle act, in Whitehead's terms? And if it can, does it follow that God as this principle determines the outcome of every particular event? Whitehead has sometimes been interpreted in this way, and I must agree that some of his language is either unclear, or it leads to this conclusion. Certainly if the principle of concretion itself determines the outcome in every event, there is no freedom whatever except in God. But Whitehead's philosophy is so strongly assertive of radical freedom for the creatures that surely this cannot be his intent; however, his language may lend itself to this view.

In *Process and Reality* he identifies the principle of concretion with God's function as providing for every occasion that "initial aim" from which it takes its rise. That is, there must be an order of participation in an actual world with a definite presentation of this order before there can be a new occasion. Whitehead says, "Apart from the intervention of God, there could be nothing new in the world, and no order in the world."[17] And it is in relation to this doctrine that Whitehead makes his remark concerning the importance of the *secularization* of the concept of God's functions in the world.[18]

My conclusion is that we can keep the principle of concretion only in this sense of the offering by God of an *initial* aim to each creature, thus making its concretion in a new actual occasion possible.

V. *The Consequent Nature of God*

The consequent nature of God refers to God's concreteness as he is related to the world and as the world's events are objectified in him. God receives from the world the effects of the world's action but he receives them in his own way as subject, and in the decision of his freedom. There is a divine passivity as well as divine activity. The content of the divine experience changes with the happenings in the world. It is active, and passive, temporal as well as eternal, patient, judging and redeeming. The life of God is an infinite social order of concrete "havings" of the world in the divine way and in the pattern of the divine primordial nature which defines the order of value for all things.

We must pass over many questions which can be raised here in order to move to our central concern, how does God in his concrete, consequent nature act upon the world? Here he is not only structure, but conscious active and passive being.

On this important point Whitehead is not very explicit. There are a few tantalizing suggestions. He speaks of the "love of God flooding back into the world."[19] But does this mean that we are to add God as efficient cause to the other efficient causes in the world?

In some sense the answer must be yes, for God in his concreteness is in the total datum to which we respond and out of which our moments of experience are constituted. But how can this be construed?

The principle by which an answer can be sought is clearly established in Whitehead's philosophy. The consequent nature acts by being prehended, *felt* by the creatures. This means that not only the primordial structure but the concrete being of God in his relation to

[17]*PR*, p. 377.
[18]*PR*, p. 315.
[19]*PR*, p. 532 (cf. *RM*, p. 156).

the world is communicated to the creatures. God is, in a literal sense for Whitehead, "the love which moves the sun and the other stars," and "communicative immanence" is one mode of divine action (This last phrase is Robert L. Calhoun's in *God and the Common Life*).

We are asking how feeling is communicated and therefore we may legitimately turn to the "natural history of feeling" in human experience. In what ways does the community of feeling with another become an efficient cause of our own action?

If we look for suggestions on this point from depth psychology we are moving into an area which Whitehead does not explicitly deal with but for the interpretation of which I suggest he has made some fundamentally important contributions. In therapeutic psychology we have a great deal of knowledge about the significance of the exchange of feelings, and about its results, whether or not we have much insight into how it comes about. The mechanisms are only partially understood, but the results are observable. It may be that we have here some useful analogies for thinking of the divine action.

The central point is that the discovery of another person who will receive my feelings into his own feelings and neither reject them nor me, is a basic aspect of psychological therapy. The analysis of "acceptance" and of the resulting "clarification" confirms this. There is a transformative power in the knowledge, the *felt* knowledge, not bare conceptualization, that our feelings have entered into the "consequent" nature of another person. Of course we are talking about causal effectiveness, not about the possible evil as well as good in its exercise.

In interpreting this fact of experience we may distinguish three aspects:

(a) This process involves an objectification of the self, so that a position is established from which self-judgment can be made. This objectification seems to make it possible for the judgment to be known partly without the anxiety which normally attends it. The communication of feeling to the other in the accepting situation constitutes a new standpoint in which the self may reorder and reinterpret its experience.

(b) A second aspect involves this element of judgment in another way. To recognize the feelings of another which result from the communication of our own is to be brought up against a judgment which is independent of ourselves and is reflected back then into our being.

Accounts of the therapeutic situation do not always stress this, but it surely is one aspect of what happens. We are made aware of the significance of our acts by the way in which they are received in the feelings of others. We harden ourselves against this, or run from it but this only confirms the causal efficaciousness of the recognition that our feelings have a meaning in the feelings of others.

(c) Finally, there is a transmutation of feeling which qualifies both the aspects already mentioned. To have one's feelings taken in by another and reflected back is to experience a transformation of the meaning of the feeling. This is the central miracle of "feeling" that awareness of the other can result in strengthening or weakening, purgation or enhancement of my feeling. The way the other received my feeling is then a constitutive part of its outcome. When the feelings are received in "love" there is a transmutation which takes on the quality of the love which is given. This process has its conscious aspects; but it operates far below the conscious level. The child feels the mother's feelings long before the child is in any sense a discriminating person.

The use of the category of feeling to describe the relatedness of the world to God does not of course offer a full explanation; but it does sharpen the point that the experience we have of causality at the human level involves a transfer and transformation of energy in personal relationships. In Whitehead's view we do have some basis here for speaking about the way in which God acts. He says, "The power of God is the worship He inspires."[20] The feelings which enter into the constitution of our being are transformed through awareness of their reception in the consequent nature of God. We must speak of persuasion here also, for we can still reject, thwart, revise our reception of the new situation created by communion with God. But I think Dr. Hartshorne is right in stressing also the coercive aspects of our religious experience. To worship God in dependence on his holiness does transform the self, far beyond its conscious intent and understanding. When we oppose God we discover the boundaries of our action, which are starkly there, and the consequences which are visited upon us whether we will or no. There are large coercive aspects in the divine governance of the world. We might summarize by saying

[20]*SAMW*, p. 276.

that God is that metaphysical function in the world by virtue of which sanity becomes possible for the creatures.

VI. *Some Concluding Comments*

The greatest difficulty in relating a theological doctrine of God's action to scientific understanding lies in the problem of assigning specific, observable consequences in the world to divine causality. This always seems to imply an intervention of theological explanation in scientific inquiry. Science must surely restrict itself to the observations and categories of explanation which are appropriate to each special science. It seems meaningless or hopelessly confusing to a scientific physical theory to say that an electron behaves according to the pattern of the quantum theory because God induces it to do so. The statement can be made; but it seems to lie on a different level from that of scientific understanding. One thinks of G. K. Chesterton's remark that "the sun rises every morning because God says to it, 'get up'." This statement is religiously meaningful, but not intelligible scientifically.

But the problem remains because if we assign God's action upon the world to a level of metaphysical causality which lies in a different place from the particular actions and reactions in an observable world, we pay too great a price from the standpoint of religious faith. We are then saying that God's acts make no difference in the observable world. To say that God "judges the nations" or "raises his Son from the dead" would be saying that this all happens without altering in any way the understanding we have empirically of the course of events.

Whitehead seems to me to hold a position between these two extremes. There are specific metaphysical functions which God alone performs. These can be in some measure described. But they involve the assertion that God makes a specific and observable difference in the behavior of things. At the same time Whitehead describes God's actions in such a way that at least some of the traditional difficulties in relating this view to scientific understanding are overcome.

So far as the primordial nature is concerned, it acts only by being presented to the creatures as the integrity of the order of possibility by virtue of which there can be a world. No specific action is completely determined by the primordial order, it only sets limits to what any action may be. There is here no clash with scientific understanding.

The consequent nature acts by being concretely apprehended in feeling in such a way that God's specific response to the world becomes a constitutive function in the world. Here there is specific divine causality. It should be remarked that this assertion in no way denies the operation of all the other actual entities in the world as causes. God's causality is exercised in, through and with all other causes operating. There is no demand here to factor out what God is adding to the stream of events apart from those events. But there is the assignment of specific functions to God's causality. These include the presentation to the creatures of a supremely adequate center of feeling through which the meaning of every occasion is received into and transformed by the divine experience, and this is concretely known by the creatures in such a way as to qualify their experience. Verification here can hardly take the form of precise description of individual experiences. The problem is far too complex and the data are too obscure for that. Verification must take the form of observable results in cosmic history, in human history, and in personal experience. While we are looking for specific causes at the level of observable and controllable data, we also have the question of the interpretation of the meaning of the whole of experience. That interpretation has aspects of faith and commitment which go beyond any precise knowledge. But I have tried to show that the assertion that God acts is neither wholly outside the possibility of verification in the breadth and depth of experience, nor does it conflict with scientific description of any concrete event.

One final point. The standpoint here outlined is, I suggest, compatible with the biblical and Christian assertion about the acts of God. Indeed, such a metaphysical outlook owes its historical development in part to elements in the Christan perspective, as Whitehead and many others have acknowledged.[21] At the same time the development of scientific and metaphysical analysis in the Western tradition has led, and should continue to lead, to a profound caution concerning assertions about the divine action.

The caution has two aspects. One is that every "act of God" is presented to us in, through and with the complex of nature and life

[21] *Ibid.*, chap. I.

in which we are. When we say God elected Israel, or that he sends his rain on the just and the unjust, we must not ignore the complex analysis of assignable causes and factors in Israel's history or in the cosmic record of rainfall. We have no way of extricating the acts of God from their involvement in the activities of the world.

The second caution is that to assign any particular historical event to God's specific action in the world is to risk ultimate judgment on our assertions. Faith leads us to take that risk. We say God sent his Holy Spirit at Pentecost. He spoke to Jeremiah, he heals diseases, he will send the Lord again. But all such assertions in so far as they conceivably refer to historical events require us to acknowledge the limits of our sight and our knowledge. In specific assertions about what God is doing now, or precisely how he has acted, and how he will act, we surely can be mistaken.

Daniel Day Williams

Union Theological Seminary
New York City

8 A Theological View of Identity

Daniel Day Williams

Methodological questions are immediately raised in a theological analysis of identity, for "identity" as usually interpreted is not a theological category. It is derived from the psychology and sociology of personality. A philosophy of identity is not necessarily opposed to a theological perspective, but it may have a different context. Erikson defines identity thus: "Within historical actuality it is the sum of all images, ideas, and forces which —roughly speaking—make a person (and a people) feel more 'like themselves' and act more 'like themselves,'—which means in historical terms: like what they have come to consider their historical selves. By the same token, identity confusion defines what will make individuals and peoples feel that they are betraying their core and losing their grip on 'their' times." [1] Thus understood, identity belongs to the structure of every human life. It is empirically identifiable, within limits, and its meaning can be pursued in psychological and social structures. Erikson shows, however, that identity points toward ultimate questions when he speaks of "the core of the self" and "the times." The real self involves the meaning of history.

Theologically we can ask about identity in the biblical experience, but the biblical account of identity cannot be restricted to cultural and existential categories. The biblical context presupposes that the culture and the times are transcended, though not negated, by the relation of God and man in the history of salvation. The Bible knows no answer to the question "Who am

I?" apart from the history of the God-man dialogue. Our problem, therefore, is to relate two perspectives on human existence, one theological the other psychological. Our attention in this essay is focused primarily on the theological perspective. Whatever significance theology may have for psychology can become clear only if theology clarifies its own perspective and criteria, and the same is true of psychology.

There is a further methodological point to be made. Theology always interprets the biblical faith in relation to a world view, which means a conception of being and a criterion of truth, which are not derived solely from the biblical revelation but from the critical inquiry after truth in all reason and experience. There are theological methods which deny this, but here I can only record my dissent from them and say that the interpretation here given of the biblical categories involves a judgment about the history of Christian thought which can be summarily stated: the Christian doctrine of man as we have inherited it is derived both from the Bible and from the metaphysical interpretation given to it within the Hellenistic world view. The doctrines of the soul, of freedom, of the relation of mind and body, of immortality, of sin and grace, of the individual and society, were woven together partly out of the ancient supernatural world view, partly out of the biblical understanding of God's self-revelation, and partly out of Greek metaphysics. I believe that today this traditional synthesis has to be revised and our doctrine of God and man reconstructed. In giving, then, a Christian interpretation of the doctrine of man, I shall seek to get at its core, that is, what makes Christianity Christian, but I shall do this with conscious acceptance of the new metaphysics of process, of becoming, in which God is related to his world in social interaction so that time and history are real for God as well as for man. What follows, then, is not *the* biblical interpretation of selfhood. It is a theological interpretation from a point of view. In this point of view human nature is in process and exhibits both perennial structures and creative novelty.

First, then, we encounter the theme of God and man in history. I shall try to show how the biblical interpretation of man leads to the christological question. Human life is set within a history which begins with God's creation of the world and man and ends with God's final acts of judgment and redemption. For every man then the question "Who am I?" is bound up with the question "What is God doing in his creation and in our history?" In this perspective personal identity can never be discovered solely within the individual and his immediate personal relations, however important these are, because every man is in a history which embraces the whole creation, and what his life means is bound up with that history. It is true that Augustine says he wants to know only two things—the soul and God—but it is also clear that, in *The City of God,* Augustine had to reflect upon the entire history of salvation in order to say what the relation of God and the soul really is. Consider three aspects of this history.

First, the search for identity always takes place within the history of a people. In the biblical view God engages in a history with the whole creation, and within this history he elects a people to live in a special relationship to him. The witness of Israel is concerned with the life of a particular people under God. In our age of social relativism we are perhaps more prepared to consider seriously the significance of this doctrine. No one belongs only to humanity in general. We live in communities with concrete traditions, values, and faiths. The search for identity involves the search for the people to whom one belongs or can belong. Martin Buber insists that there is here an insight in Judaism which Christianity has never reached. He says: "Reverence for the absolute without the use of an intermediate agency is the principle of Israel's everlasting life. . . . To this day, however, we have not yet learned to revere the absolute by our very existence. What has kept us alive until now is the task itself—not its fulfilment, the task which burns in our blood like a fire, and will not die down. . . . A people has only one means to point to God, and that is through life lived in accordance with his will." [2] He thinks that Christianity has never quite understood the significance of the people as over against the individual.

The issue here has an important bearing on the new nationalism. Innumerable people in our culture find their personal identity in the spirit of nationalism, including American nationalism. The constructive and destructive aspects of nationalism are obvious features of our present situation. Christian interpretation of nationhood still has some critical issues to face. Idolatries, like that of national socialism, fall into a special category perhaps, though let us remember that even that was swallowed by some Christians at certain stages of its development. The passionate new nationalisms, such as some in Africa, which assert the freedom, equality, and dignity of all people require a different analysis. The question of racial identity is often involved. In any case, the biblical view has a kinship with all doctrines of the self which recognize the significance for personal identity of the history of a people.

Consider secondly, sin and grace. To be in human history is to manifest an estrangement from God and our intended being. The estrangement from God is both individual and collective, diverse in forms, but identifiable as unbelief or refusal to trust, hubris, and concupiscence.[3] In the Christian view, I know myself when I know myself as estranged, and in this knowledge I am in some sense one with every man. I participate in a history which is given its character not only by my finitude but also by my sin. In this history the meaning of every individual life and of the collective life involves the history of God's actions of judgment and redemption and of man's response. Therefore in the Christian interpretation the wrestle of the prophets with the meaning of God's redemptive action drives toward the question of his future action, the hope for his kingdom. In the Old Testament there are the first glimpses of a christological answer, especially in Daniel and in the suffering servant figure, though what is to be identified in the Hebrew Bible as Messianic in the strict sense is still a matter of considerable discussion. Thus the history of sin and grace as understood in the biblical perspective drives toward the question of Christology. As Paul Tillich formulates it, it is the question of the appearance in history of a human life in which the break between essential human nature and existential estrangement is overcome within the conditions of existence.[4] This is the third aspect of the bearing of history on identity.

In the Christian perspective my identity is discovered and bestowed (both words must be used) through the action of God in the historical Person, who is not myself but who is every man's elder brother and who stands in a different relation to every man from that of father, mother, siblings, friends. "He who loves father or mother more than me is not worthy of me." (Matt. 10:37.) It is this christological structure we have now to explore.

At this point our theological method opens the way for conversation with those who approach identity psychologically. We may look for analogies to the christological structure in the psychological understanding of identity. There is much theological significance in the remarkable address of Eric Erikson to the American Psychoanalytic Association in 1961 under the title "Psychological Reality and Historical Actuality." Erikson says, "Historians *and* psychoanalysts must learn to grasp fully the fact that while each individual life has its longitudinal logic, all lives lived interdependently within a given historical period share a kind of historical logic—and a-logic. Much of this is contained in the way and in the images by means of which men identify with each other, . . . identify themselves with their leaders and their leaders with themselves, and how, as they thus identify, they repudiate . . . their adversaries and enemies." Erikson develops this theme in relation to the psychoanalytic method and says, "We cannot escape, then, the major task of our time—a task which we have helped to shape—namely, that of participating in historical actuality more consciously and thus responsibly than have the generations before us." He discusses the guilt of passing over the meaning of destructiveness in history, and concludes, "In this time of a tragic confrontation of 'selfless' and 'objective science' with its murderous results, however, it may well be up to psycoanalysis to initiate a self-scrutiny of the scientific mind." [5]

Where is the healing or reconciling reality in the actuality of history as Erikson sees it? It appears in his hope that individuals will "transcend the remnants of the past, and mobilize and cultivate more rational outlooks for the sake of a wider and more inclusive identification among men—such identification as provides the leverage for decisive deeds." Erikson looks for leaders who possess superior gifts and who "create a joint future out of a combination of their own pasts and the typical pasts of the led, and thus acquire and provide a conception of truth in action."[6] We cannot say that this is a christological statement made from a psychological point of view. The frame of reference does not permit that. But it is Erikson's answer within his framework concerning the center of meaning and truth in history. Erikson recognizes that the identity problem requires a historical answer, and he is, so far, close to the biblical perspective.

We can now state more formally a Christian view of the source and structure of identity. The Christian perspective locates the center of identity neither in the individual nor society but in a relationship between persons and the one Person who represents human nature in history and who is the bearer of reconciliation in the midst of alienation. This is the christological structure of biblical anthropology. I know who I am through another who is not myself but who in some way is the key to every self. The main features of this christological structure can be stated under four headings.

I. The Person in History

The God of Christian faith acts in history. He is known through his acts. The context of every assertion of the Christian faith is the history of salvation within the concrete historical life of the world. In this history the center is found in the life of the man Jesus of Nazareth who lived and died in Palestine about A.D. 1-30. There are important issues in this claim.

First, there is the nature of the Gospels, the historical record. They give a report of events, but as seen through the eyes of faith and as interpreted. The debate about the kind of history we have in the Gospels is crucial for the Christian faith. If Jesus is not really there in history, then the Christian understanding of God and man is not true. Yet the record gives us little biographical information about Jesus by himself. It is a record arising from the witness of men to the new reality they found in Jesus and using the symbols of their culture to express that reality. The personal relationship to Jesus Christ is always constituted in part by the symbols by which the meaning of his life is grasped.

A second aspect of the personal relationship has to do with the way in which Jesus is remembered. He is known as the risen Christ, the ever present Head of the Church. He lives "not after the flesh," as Paul says, but in a new kind of memory. All the christological symbols, images, and doctrines enter into the personal relationship in which he is known. Their diversity and mystery constitute both a richness and a problem for the discovery of the true meaning of the Christ. John Knox has put the actual situation of the believer who finds his identity through Jesus Christ in this way: Jesus is known as he is remembered, interpreted, and experienced in the ongoing community which shares in and lives by the faith given by his life and its meaning.[7] Thus Jesus confers personal identity on individuals always within the community which bears the meaning of his life through history.

This raises sharply of course the question of uniqueness and finality in the Christian revelation. Is there no other way by which we may come to personal identity? Is the personal identity known in Christian experience completely different from all other identity? Arnold Toynbee says it is megalomania to say that the meaning of existence must be confronted only in one place in the universe and one point in history.[8] The issue of whether Christianity separates man from every other center of meaning or whether in Jesus there is the center of a historical meaning which embraces all others is a crucial one. I take the view that to assert the finality of Christ is not to reject meaning in other faiths. The Christian finds a solidarity with all others, including unbelievers, through his relation to Christ. The meaning known in Jesus Christ must be reflected in all history if it is valid in any history.

II. Love as *Agape* and as *Eros*

The content of the Incarnation is the love which the New Testament knows as *agape.* It is love given in the midst of alienation. It is forgiveness. It is the basis of the real universal community. It is grace. The question of the relation of love as *agape* to the human loves becomes critical for identity, for if a man is constituted by his loves, as I take it most psychologies would assert, then if there is a love other than human love, it becomes of fundamental importance for the Christian's identity. The question "Who am I?" as a created, loving, sexual being—loving persons, loving the world, art, work, and play—is bound up with the question "Is there another love beyond these?" Now the argument of Nygren in *Agape and Eros* that these are two utterly different loves, that *agape* is different in origin and structure from the human loves, states a radical problem for Christianity. Nygren, to be sure, does not say *agape* rejects the human loves, but *agape* is something utterly different. It moves from God to man exclusively and is the one possible ground of reconciliation for man and, therefore, of human integrity. What shall we say to Nygren's position?

Agape is not the same as *eros.* It does not depend on any particular structure of human relations as does *eros.* It does not have the distinctive emotional components of *eros.* It comes at the edge of human love as a new possibility, and it comes as grace, as undeserved, leading to a reconciliation with others and within the self. It is of critical importance, therefore, to show how *agape* can incorporate the freedom and vitalities of *eros* and not reject them. I am agreeing with Paul Tillich against Nygren here.[9] An absolute separation of *agape* and *eros* is fatal to the possibility of uniting Christian faith and human existence. The direction of the solution is that love as *eros* is never completely self-contained. All *eros* pushes toward the point where the meaning of *agape* looms up as its judgment and its completion. *Eros* does not turn into *agape* automatically, but it can reach toward *agape*. On this point the possibility of the unity of *agape* and the loves of the self depends.

Agape is known within the Christian faith as the love which God has shown in Jesus Christ. It has a center in history, and its definition and power are derived from this historical Incarnation. In Jesus' teaching there is no rejection of the human loves. They are often seen as parables and analogies of *agape* as in the story of the prodigal son.

A further point concerning love involves the historical community which Buber insists is the key to biblical faith. The Christian perspective agrees with this but asks, "Where is that community within which man can find his authentic being?" In the New Testament the community has to be understood in a new way. It is the church, the body of Christ. This new people has a concrete life. Its members are members one of another as participants in the new life which has come through Christ. Since, however, this community is in its meaning and intent the community of the whole creation under God, it is a community of the spirit and cannot be limited to any historical form as defining its boundaries. Here identity becomes an ecumenical issue. It is also an issue concerning recognition of the holy catholic church and its authentic existence wherever the work of love is getting done. Not only is Christ in the least of these who are ministered to, but he is present incognito wherever the way of *agape* is being broken open in the midst of all the human loves. We cannot say that the problem of identity for the Christian can always be resolved within the form of the church as we know it. The real depth of the empirical church is discovered where within it we see the possibility of the spiritual community which transcends the forms in which it lives.

III. Eschatology

Our third topic is the significance of eschatology for a theology of identity. It may be that theology here makes a special contribution to identity theory. Jürgen Moltmann's *Theology of Hope* has become significant for contemporary theology because he has stressed the eschatological dimension in the New Testament.[10] Christ points toward the end of history and time, the completion of meaning. He gives not immediate realization but the promise of a fulfillment yet to come. The very meaning of the cross and resurrection points toward a consummation which is known only in hope. Christ must reign until he has put all enemies under his feet, and the last enemy which shall be destroyed is death (I Cor. 15:25-26).

This eschatological dimension reflects itself in each individual's existence. The life of faith is a progress toward the new life as well as a realization of it. If personal identity is self-discovery through the image of God, the New Testament transfers this identity to the image of Christ and declares we are being transformed into his image. Our becoming has a new structure which is not consummated. We are perplexed but not in despair; cast down but not destroyed; we know in part, and it is only at the end that we will know as we are known, as Paul says (II Cor. 4:8-9; I Cor. 13:12). Identity in the theological sense, therefore, can never be identified with the cultural images and values which enclose us in a particular time and place. From the Christian point of view this given cultural identity is something less than the authentic reality of our being. It is not too strong to say that the Christian gospel introduces a new kind of alienation into history and into the life of the individual. If "alienation" suggests something pathological, then discard the word, but the life of faith involves a break with the enclosure of the present culture and its symbols. It introduces a new element of criticism into all self-definition.

The history of sin does not end with the revelation of grace. It takes on a new character, but it is still present. What ought to be an increase in self-knowledge and in the power of *agape*—love to fulfill the human loves—is at the same time within the mystery of evil and freedom a new temptation. Therefore, the Christian distrusts the identification of his identity with the present structure of his being. In faith he becomes an alien to every cultural satisfaction that seeks to enclose the meaning of his life. He expects his identity to be disclosed, and its essence is "life in love," but its shape and definition are not solely in his hands nor in the hands of any culture, and this includes Christian culture itself, insofar as that is an object which can be identified with particular concepts, institutions, and symbols. There are modern humanisms and other perspectives which have analogous insights into radical freedom.

IV. Vocation and Identity

The christological approach to identity issues in a concept of life as vocation. What is called "vocation" in a secular sense enters powerfully into the identity quest in every human life. We may come to self-knowledge in relation to significant work. In the Christian view there is a vocation within every vocation, that is, an ultimate calling within the specific tasks of life. I shall call this ultimate and unifying vocation the Calling and discuss it as form, as spirit, as suffering, and as decision.

The source of the Calling is given within the christological structure. The Word of God comes to man in Jesus Christ as an offer of grace that summons man to response. Jesus himself is called to his vocation. He is the "elect Man," the elect of God for his task in history. He calls others to follow him, to bear their burdens, to take up their crosses. This is the familiar structure of Christian discipleship. Let us ask about its relevance to the dynamics of the search for identity today.

The Calling involves a definite form of existence. Paul speaks of the Calling as the *locus* in which one hears the gospel. This seems to be the original sense of the statement in I Cor. 7:20, "Let every man abide in the same calling wherein he was called" (KJV). What I am to become in the response to the summons of Christ involves my specific existence in the world with its form, its limitations, and its history. I cannot jump out of this or ignore it and achieve the new being in some unhistorical way. The history of the interpretation of Paul's dictum is of course a long one, bound up on the one hand with the Roman Catholic tradition that only the religious have a special Calling and on the other with the Protestant Reformers' secularizing of the conception to regard every legitimate profession as a Calling. The Reformers, unfortunately, tended to combine this doctrine with the idea that God has decreed the circumstances of every life, and I believe we must reject that doctrine. Process theology can help here, for it asserts that there is a real history and becoming not only for man but also for God, so that no present form of existence should be absolutized as a block against the creative possibilities pregnant in every situation. We are called in a world which has both freedom and form, and we lose our identity if we do not come to terms with this fact. None of this is meant to exclude the truth in the Reformer's emphasis on the providential character of the Calling. There are possibilities of good which God wills amid all the givens in life. We are masculine and feminine, of this race, in this culture, in this time, with this body-mind and this emotional inheritance. Personal identity involves coming to terms with this givenness and yet finding within it that which is not merely given but which can be shaped by courageous response, discipline, and faith.

This reshaping may take the form of rebellion. The Christian view of the Calling cannot be identified with either the conservative or the radical stance. Gauguin leaving his banker's world for Tahiti, Eugene O'Neill leaving family and school to knock around the world on sailing ships—these are authentic contexts of the discovery of identity and vocation. There is no Christian norm which judges as appropriate or inappropriate any human decision apart from its human context and motivation and its relation to love and lovelessness. The Christian faith leads to an acceptance of the givens in any personal destiny, but it sees God himself interacting with the world and with men in the concreteness of circumstances to change them. This is one reason why the identity crisis at age forty can be just as traumatic as the one at adolescence.

The Calling comes from spirit to spirit. Paul speaks of one

Spirit and one Calling just as there is one baptism (Eph. 4:4-5). He treats the question of individuality in vocation through the doctrine of the one spirit with a diversity of gifts. I Cor. 12 is a fundamental New Testament text on identity. The diversity of gifts involves psychological factors, for Paul does not rule out natural and tempermental differences, but these are explained theologically. God has called some to be prophets, some apostles, some teachers. The metaphor of the organism with its various members is here, as everywhere, fundamental for him. The consequence is that the Calling is not to a new life in general but to a new existence in Christ and therefore in the church. That is, the meaning of every calling is disclosed within the history of redemption. Here we encounter the question of finding a new vocation. The break with the old life means the discovery of a new structure of vocation. To be called out of darkness into the marvelous light is also to be given a new path to walk.

Just here the Reformers' doctrine of the Calling is pertinent. They did not reject the secular callings. The work of the world has to be done, and that work includes all the services men may reasonably and effectively render one another. Yet the identification of each vocation as a Calling from God now has a new interpretation. The call to the building up of the body of Christ cannot be separated from the forms of the world's work. We must acknowledge that the actual estrangement in life as men seek meaning in their work is very deep. The present concern with the secular may help eradicate vestiges of irrelevant pietism and simple moralism in talking about Christian Calling. The categories of the Calling in the church, with its witness, discipleship, stewardship, will have to be rediscovered and brought into some kind of unity with living in the world.

The Calling involves suffering. No one has to be called to suffer, but one may be called to suffer in a certain way and for a cause. Paul describes his life as bearing about in the body the dying of Jesus, that the life of Jesus also may be made manifest. The call to the new life has come to the world through the self-giving of

Jesus. Hence life in the church is the sharing of suffering. When one member suffers, all suffer.

Suffering may lead to self-discovery. The suffering which attends the working out of the Calling is one element in the disclosure of the meaning of the Calling. No one really understands a way of life who does not know what it costs. Hence we need to see the significance of suffering not simply at the dramatic level of major crises and tragedies but in the recognition of the omnipresence of suffering in all human response to Calling. Every decision for a vocation is an acceptance of limitation, narrowing of attention, the sacrifice of other goods to this good, and the opening of one's spirit to be reshaped by the experience. When suffering clarifies who we are, what we are serious about, and what we can celebrate, then it may become a healing power.

The second aspect of suffering in vocation is related to conflict with enemies, both without and within. Erikson remarks that a large element in the discovery of identity is the demarcation of what one is against. This belongs to the characteristics of a severe identity crisis. The Christian faith has always provided for this power of opposition in the Calling. Christ's vocation is realized in conflict with principalities and powers which he in essence defeats but which still work in life. Paul's statement that neither life nor death separates us from the love of God is rightly recognized as assurance. It is not so often noted that it is a call to combat.

Finally, the Calling requires decision; this element has been implicit throughout. This must not be obscured by the traditional doctrines of election and predestination. Election is God's affirmation of human destiny as communion with him, and it is meaningless without the free response of man. There is decision at every point, in the acceptance of what must be accepted, in the rejection of what must be rejected, and above all in the risk to face the undefined and open possibilities of the future.

Existentialism has had its powerful impact in facing the actuality of the human situation with the call to assume it with courage and in insisting that man must realize his own becoming without guidelines or guarantees. Sartre says "man is only what he wills himself to be."[11] A contemporary theology, while it will by no means accept the extremism of Sartre's view (which he himself qualifies in all sorts of ways), must assert human freedom and personal creativity in bringing the new into being. Personal identity is not something which God gives simply as it is, but it is discovered and created in a free, hopefully faithful, response to God and the world. To be free, conscious spirits having an identity is to be able to say "yes" or "no" to the forms of our existence as they are and in dependence on grace, to will into being the person we are not yet. That is the ultimate risk of love: to let the other become what he will become—and God has taken that risk with us.

Notes

1. Erik H. Erikson, *Insight and Responsibility* (New York: W. W. Norton, 1964), pp. 203-4.
2. Martin Buber, *Israel and the World* (New York: Schocken Books, 1948), pp. 198, 200.
3. Cf. Paul Tillich, *Systematic Theology*, II (Chicago: University of Chicago Press, 1957), 44-58.
4. *Ibid.*, Part II.
5. Erikson, *Insight and Responsibility*, pp. 207, 211, 212.
6. *Ibid.*, p. 205.
7. John Knox, *Jesus: Lord and Christ* (New York: Harper, 1958).
8. Arnold Toynbee, *An Historian's Approach to Religion* (New York: Oxford University Press, 1956), p. 138.
9. Tillich, *Systematic Theology*, Vol. I.
10. Jürgen Moltmann, *The Theology of Hope* (New York: Harper, 1967).
11. Jean-Paul Sartre, *Existentialism* (New York: Philosophical Library, 1947), p. 18.

DANIEL DAY WILLIAMS

9

The prophetic dimension

Man is the being who tells himself who he is. That is why answers to the question of man's uniqueness differ so widely. Man knows himself, but always with presuppositions. Some experiences are common to all of us. There is the human body with its growth, joy, sickness, and death. There are the processes of human thinking and acting, and the universal traits of culture. We share a common fate as problems of hunger, transportation, crowding, nuclear war, and population explosion press upon us all. But what men make out of their situation and what kind of hope they have does not come simply out of the facts, but out of ways of seeing the facts.

A second complication of man's attempt to say who he is concerns his being in process. Man is the being wo knows he is becoming. He can trace something of his place in the evolutionary process. He writes his history. That history continues, and man is in it. Therefore, every answer to the question of who man is involves the reservation expressed in the biblical word, 'it doth not yet appear what we shall be.'

A third factor involved in man's uniqueness is that man has freedom to reshape his own being, at least within limits. The existentialists have tried to say that the meaning of existence is something for man in his freedom to decide. The ancient text would have to be modified, 'it doth not yet appear what we shall make of ourselves.' And in some sense that must be true. It is man's uniqueness that he can either affirm or reject ways of being human.

Thus contemporary views of man range all the way from the evolutionary cosmic optimism of Teilhard de Chardin to the stoic despair of Jean Paul Sartre: 'Man is a useless passion.' This radical disparity in philosophic hope and despair is matched by the ambiguity of hopes and fears which now arise from scientific knowledge. During the past holiday New York City entertained the American Association for the Advancement of Science. A reporter summed up his reaction to what he had heard thus:

> No fundamentalist preacher ever prophesied doom for most people more emphatically than do some of the 10,000 members of the American Association for the Advancement of Science at meetings here this week. Yet they exhibit their holiday cheer in lobby greetings and at dozens of social gatherings. Visitors question: 'Are they stoics, don't they believe one another, or do they fiddle while Rome burns?'

This picture of the sophisticated community of scientists in cheerful concourse as they discuss the doom of environment pollution, population explosion, and atomic destruction gives a nightmarish quality to our search for meaning today. Never before have the possibilities of human control over the things that lay waste to life seemed greater. Yet never before have men had the imminent doom of all their works through their own self-destruction so clearly portrayed.

In the search for some perspective and direction there are some who say, our problems are so new that ancient wisdom has nothing to tell us. Others fall back on the reiteration of past ways of thinking, whether or not they can see their relevance to contemporary life. I propose to explore one ancient perspective on man which may still illuminate the issues which confront us. I call it 'the prophetic dimension' for two reasons. One is that its structure involves man's historical consciousness, with his knowledge of past and future, and the necessity of understanding himself as the being who is becoming. This historical consciousness is in part the contribution of the biblical-prophetic tradition to our culture. The other reason for calling it the prophetic dimension is that it is the specific view of life which came to expression in the prophets of Israel and which underlies both the Hebrew Bible and the Christian New Testament. I have two main theses about it: first, that the prophetic dimension offers one relevant view of man's uniqueness; and second, that the prophetic dimension must be recognized in new contexts in the twentieth century because of the extraordinary new powers which technological man has acquired. We need to take thought of ourselves in the light of our ethical and spiritual tradition; but it is true we cannot simply reaffirm that tradition in all its old forms. Amos did not know about cybernetics, and Hosea did not understand the physical and psychological causes of schizophrenia. When Paul says the state must wield the sword, he is not dealing with the issues raised when the sword becomes an H-bomb. But there is a clarification in hearing the prophetic view of life in its own terms first, and then asking what it can mean to us.

There are five aspects of the prophetic view of man:

First, man is the creature of the Creator of all things. Man's life is bound up in a personal relationship with God, the Lord of life and history, who has created a good world, and has made man in his own image, to inherit, possess, and be fulfilled on the earth. Man's uniqueness reaches its peak, not in the emergence of his intelligence and culture creating power alone, but in his discovery that he is a responsible being, endowed with a freedom which he can use to serve God and his fellows, or which he can misuse. For the prophets, conscience was as fundamental as consciousness for the understanding of the uniqueness of man. Man is unique among all creatures in that he bears the image of God. His spiritual dignity, therefore, is a reflection of his origin, and it brings its weight of responsibility with it. God has made of one blood all nations to dwell on the earth. Hence responsibility of each man for the neighbor is universal.

Second, man's spiritual greatness is the source of his deepest evil, idolatry. Man's God-likeness tempts him to assume his divinity. The prophets see national life as the key to history. It is primarily nations and men as belonging to nations which exhibit the self-serving pride which leads to monstrous evil. The specific sins of men are largely crimes against men: murder, exploitation, the arrogance of wealth, and the violence of power. Men comfort themselves with smooth words; they cry 'peace, peace' when there is no peace. Jeremiah suggests to the rulers of his day:

> You make a covenant with death saying 'it shall not pass near us.' But when righteousness and justice are made the measure, then your covenant with death shall be annulled; and your agreement with Sheol will not stand. When the scourge passes through you will be beaten down with it. (Jeremiah 38:17)

That is, the prophets see man as one who avoids telling himself the truth about his own death, trying to make a covenant with it so that it will not touch him.

A third aspect of the prophetic action and word is that the prophet himself is in the history for which he speaks the Word of God's judgment and promise. The prophet's work was a response to God's call in the history in which he stood, and the prophet bears this crisis and its meaning within his own life. He is but an instrument of the divine purpose; and he recognizes himself and his suffering within its action. He may be rebellious and unwilling. Jeremiah curses the day of his birth; but he lives in a history which is determined not by his individual wish or will, but by the will of God. His prophesying, therefore, is not something routine; nor is it a profession. It is characteristic of authentic prophecy that it is unpredictable and uncontrollable in its appearance. It comes from the meeting of the Spirit of God with the consciences of certain men. The prophets are individuals. They stand in specific times and seek the meaning of God's word for their time and their people. They do not all see history in exactly the same way, nor do they all have precisely the same forms of hope. But they all see man as confronting the final issues of his life when he recognizes the claim of a divine goodness and purpose, which he ignores at the peril of losing all that matters.

The prophets do hope, and that is the fourth aspect of the prophetic dimension. Their people had experienced a redemption, a release from slavery, and the possibility of a new life in their own land. This pattern remains the theme of prophecy; but here the prophetic message reached its summit. Reliance on past achievement, and on past security brings no salvation. It is the sin of nations to trust their own power and their claim to favor before God. Here the prophetic radicalness appears. All security lies in commitment to what God will do, not to what we have already enjoyed. Salvation lies in expectation of what the divine judgment and mercy will yet bring. This structure of future promise as the ground of salvation is more important than any special form of the prophetic hope. Sometimes the prophets spoke in near utopian terms with visions of universal peace and contentment. Sometimes they left the mode of the divine intervention unspoken. But in the later prophetic movement the hope takes on a new form. It becomes messianic. God will raise up in history his own appointed servant to exercise divine power, establish justice, and bring peace. We see why those who understand men in the prophetic dimension can never accept salvation through progress, or evolution, or power over nature. The reason is not that these are not good things; but that they put our confidence in the wrong place. The issue is the relation between man in his freedom and God in his claim upon the love and loyalty of his creatures. That issue can only be resolved when man himself receives a new heart. As the prophets see it, for man to trust in his own moral achievement is to trust in a broken and treacherous power. The saving way is acknowledgement that what we build cannot stand the judgment of a righteous God and he will have to rebuild. This prophetic messianism came to its supreme expression in the picture of the Suffering-Servant in Second Isaiah. Whether the servant is a messianic figure or not remains obscure. In any case, he is the servant of God at the center of a history which is riddled with guilt. He bears its consequences in such a way that a new relationship between God and man is created.

Here briefly I must turn a theological corner, because Christianity has always understood the prophetic message as preparation for the fulfilment of the messianic expectation in Jesus. I concentrate attention here on one point only, that the prophetic dimension is not set aside in the Christian view that the Messiah has come; but is incorporated into the Christian faith and the Christian view of the future. My colleague Seymour Siegal of the Jewish Theological Seminary has put the two angles of vision, Jewish and Christian, perfectly: The problem for the Jew is: 'since the world is in the condition it is in, why does not the Messiah come?' The problem for the Christian is, 'since the Messiah has come, why is the world in the condition it is in?' The issues here lie at the root of all philosophies of history in the biblical tradition. My thesis is that the Christian faith incorporates the prophetic dimension into its very affirmation that the Messiah has come. The extended defense of this view which should be given can only be summarized in the following points:

First, Jesus himself continued the prophetic ethical message, and preached the judgment and the promise of the Kingdom.

Second, the church has always asserted that Jesus fulfils hte prophetic function because the church recognizes his office as Prophet as well as Priest and King. Since the Messiah has come in part as Prophet, prophecy is not set aside but is given a new foundation.

Third, as the Church lived through those first centuries after Christ, and as history went on, with men still living and dying, experiencing sin and grace, a new view of history had to be worked out. In the life, death, and resurrection of Jesus the beginning of the new Age and the redeemed world is known. But it also points forward. We live between an Already and a Not-Yet. Paul saw the present time as the beginning of life in the new age, but not its consummation. 'The whole creation groaneth and travaileth in pain together until now.' (Romans 8) The vision of last things in the New Testament book of *Revelation* involves the divine proclamation again: 'Behold I make all things new.' So the Christian view of history is prophetic and eschatological. Faith has received a new foundation; but it always in its new form looks forward. 'Now is our salvation nearer than when we first believed.'

We must say something about the prophets' view of nature. Too little attention has been paid to it. The Greeks were the naturalists of the ancient world, and much of our science we inherit from them, as Father McMullin so clearly told us. Have the prophets anything to offer but the limitations of an ancient world-view which we no longer hold?

We must be careful not to try to modernize the prophets! They thought within the world-view of their age. They picture God as immediately controlling and miraculously intervening in events. Modern conceptions of natural processes obeying discoverable laws and developing through infinite time are foreign to them. Yet with all reservations, certain elements in the prophetic outlook are strikingly suggestive to us now. Nature, for all its dependability, we now know, is no fixed order with patterns which repeat themselves in endless cycles. Nature comes from the hands of God and serves his purposes as the prophets see it. Therefore it is the scene of action, of passage, and it can be transformed. Everything in the created world is subject to the limitations of finitude, to passage and death; but everything by the same token can be seen as offering some potential value to man as the dynamic life process goes on.

Again, for the prophets, nature bears the mystery of creation. It is not self-explanatory. Men's attempts to read its secret come up against the limits of human understanding. It is not a sheer riddle nor an arbitrary order, but its meaning is related to what God intends for man within the order of life; therefore, there is always more to be known. The prophets' most radical idea is that nature itself is subject to God's redemptive action. It will be remade and reordered to fulfil the divine purpose. The words are almost too familiar, and we forget their power to release us from a fatalistic view of nature. 'God turns a desert into pools of water, and a parched land into springs of water,' says the psalmist (Ps. 107:33–36). The animal world is included in the transformation: 'The wild beasts will honor me, and the jackals and the ostriches, for I give water in the wilderness.' When we read the prophecy that every valley shall be exalted and every mountain and hill be made low, and that there will be a highway in the desert, we may even feel in the light of modern highway systems that we have been overdoing it.

In any case, nature is the God-given environment for man's use. Jesus says, 'Your heavenly father knows you have need of all these things.' This relation of man to the rest of nature is a critical issue today. We would not have modern science without the sense of nature as an order to be understood, and for that we have both the Greeks with their rational genius and the Hebrews with their sense of the faithfulness of God to thank. But the Hebrews contributed something else: the sense of a necessary moral order in man's relationship to nature, an attitude which combines reverence before mystery with the sense of a purposeful life for all things. What nature will become is related to what man can become. And man will fail if he takes a purely exploitative attitude toward nature. Greed and the exploitative attitude combined can lead to wanton destruction of a countryside, of animal species, of the very possibility of a healthful life for man. The failure then to see a moral demand in nature, the failure to love it in all its mystery and beauty and even its terror is part of man's failure to grasp the key to his own fulfilment. Science as an enterprise and attitude is not committed to the exploitative attitude nor does it require it. Many scientists would strongly say the opposite; they would say that reverence and joy in the face of the great mystery is the most fruitful scientific attitude. But man using science, and developing his technology may lose that moral sense for a humane and mutually fruitful relation between himself and nature which the prophetic dimension requires.

I have summarized the prophetic dimension on these five points. On the last one I have already begun to speak about the relevance of the prophetic view to our present situation, and it is to that topic that I turn for the second part of this discussion.* We can now ask the question, how could man in the twentieth century be understood if we tried to see him with the guidance of the prophetic tradition? If the prophetic perspective has relevant light to throw on man, what does it reveal?

At the outset we see that the historical view of man which has its roots in the biblical-prophetic view has become the almost inescapable presupposition of every outlook in the twentieth

---

* My brief summary of the prophetic outlook covers a very large topic. See: Martin Buber, 1949, *The prophetic faith*, New York, Macmillan (also in Harper & Row Torchbooks, ed. 1960); Abraham Heschel, 1955, *The prophets*, The Jewish Publication Society of America; James Muilenberg, 1961, *The way of Israel*, New York, Harper & Row; Gerhard Von Rad, 1968, *Old testament theology*, Vol. 11., New York, Harper & Row.

century. Whatever else we know about man, we know he has, to manage in the history of an evolving world and changing cultures. He must solve some collective problems of living on this planet, else life will be intolerable for most and perhaps for all. Almost no one today proposes that the lonely flight to the inner world or the seeking of the peace of eternity beyond time is sufficient. Man has to face his becoming in a world which has a history, and where the shadow cast by the risks and possibilities of the future requires responsible action. This historical man is also technical man, armed with knowledge and powers which were unthinkable in earlier times. Some say these new powers make all traditional faiths and views of man's moral situation obsolete. But let us see. There are important ways in which the issues of the technological age raise questions to which the prophetic outlook seems directly pointed. Perhaps the real question of our time is how man can understand himself and face his problems by incorporating his technological skill into a perspective which is founded on the deepest elements in the prophetic view of life.

First, technology brings both threat and promise to man, not only for the higher achievements of culture, but for his very survival. The point is too obvious today to dwell upon; but the confirmation of the prophetic view that human powers are ambiguous in their significance could hardly be more convincing. Man himself is the most lethal and destructive creature evolution has produced. Unless he can manage to guide and control his technical processes, there is no reason whatever to think that he will avoid catastrophe with quite possibly the extinction of his life and perhaps of all life on this earth. The ancient words of the Deuteronomist now have a literal and inescapable force. 'See I have set before you this day life and good, death and evil.' (Deuteronomy 30:15) This crisis produced by technical power and knowledge means that the greater man's power of controlling his environment, the more demands are placed upon his capacity for responsible concern. The self-restraining mastery of his passions is more urgent – not less. Some pictures of human development would make it appear that there is a gradual movement of man to higher and higher planes where his moral problems become resolved and he can breathe easier because he has reached such a high state of skill in dealing with all his difficulties. The very opposite seems to be the case. The greater man's powers the greater threat he becomes to himself. The age of computers, missiles and thought control demands a transformation of the human conscience if it is not to end in disaster.

Not only do the technical powers require a prophetic interpretation, but the prophetic outlook must incorporate into its way of dealing with human problems the obligations derived from technical power. Most of the issues which are matter of critical importance for us today might be called 'moral-technical', that is, they require both man's responsible valuations of human existence and persons and knowledge of the precise modes of relationship of man and nature which are disclosed by scientific inquiry. Moral issues tend to develop a technical dimension. For example, feeding the hungry has been a perennial moral demand. But the mode of providing an adequate agriculture is a problem of chemical knowledge, and getting it into use, a challenge to tasks of literacy, education, and political organization. By the same token technical abilities create moral issues. The heart transplant raises the question of who is to have this service? By what principle of justice do we decide? The possibility of almost unlimited production of standardized goods raises the question of the effect on human beings of the surfeit of such goods, and the advertising campaigns necessary to sell them. This is why a prophetic ethic must concern itself with technical issues. Prophets have not always been strong on details; but we must be. It is an extension of the prophetic outlook, not a contradiction of it, to deal with the effects on human life of the new knowledge. Another example: The search for armaments' control and the international policing of atomic weaponry involves man's survival. But the means of such control requires the most precise knowledge of physical processes and reactions, most of which may be understandable to the layman in their effects but their creation and supervision requires the skill of a very few experts.

I must not use the term 'technical knowledge' here too narrowly – for there is a knowledge of the facts of life which in one sense is not scientific, but which brings to the issues of moral judgment a common sense understanding. Take the question of the rebuilding of the modern city to make it a place where people can live, breath, converse, raise families, do work and come to know their own souls. Cities have always been incarnations of human pride in the achievements of culture. That is why the prophetic words of doom for the cities are so frequent. They see the divine judgment on civilization in the laying to waste of the cities. 'The houses of the kings are torn down to make siege mounds.' 'Famine, pestilence, and sword' level these proud achievements of man. The prophets also express their hopes in visions of the rebuilt city, which shall be 'a name of joy and praise and a glory before all the nations of the earth.' (Jeremiah 32:33)

Today our cities are at the center of the human problem; and the issues are critical. Miss Jane Jacobs' title for her book (1961) has a prophetic ring, *The Death and Life of Great American Cities*. She knows that the problems of the city are, again, 'moral-technical'. Space for living is a moral problem; every aspect of the laying out the life of the city has its human repercussions. Planning for the new city is, therefore, not a violation of the prophetic outlook, but a requirement of it. How can we create livable space, buildings, homes, theatres, schools, so that men can live and breathe, and work and play and learn to love one another? The answer to that question requires the technical knowledge of economists, planners, and architects. But it also requires common sense. Miss Jacobs asks, 'What is it that people really like about cities?' and points out how important diversity and the interest of the street, and the chance to roam in interesting surroundings is. The new city requires, as we know so poignantly, the willingness of people to revolutionize a total social structure so that space and light, education and recreation can be available for everyone, and men can be together in a community of mutual respect and help.

It may be, however, that the deepest problem posed by technology is the control of human behavior itself. Man can conceive the reshaping of his very mind and consciousness through instruments. This is a unique capacity, and it contains a unique threat. Here is one of the clearest demonstrations of the relevance of the prophetic dimension. Man can now plan his own dehumanizing, and there are some who would like to carry it out. There is no assurance in human evolution that men will become more human, more free, more self-directive. Man can seek to divest himself of everything that fills human life with the risks and the surprises of existence. We need to face this question in the context of Auschwitz and Dachau, of the murders of civil rights workers, of the inhuman systems of exploitation of grape and tomato pickers. Man lives to control. So, the promise of controlling others, even if it means their destruction, has its demonic attraction. The issue is the place of technical control in a genuinely human economy. Here again, to emphasize the prophetic claim of man's ultimate moral responsibility for preserving freedom and the integrity of creative response is not to down-grade the use of technical knowledge, but to put it in its place. For example, Dr. Carl Rogers, the psychologist, has insisted as strongly as anyone in present day America on the importance of empirical knowledge of human behavior. He has pioneered in finding ways to document an accurate record of what happens when people engage in the exploration of the inner world. He has developed a highly technical set of concepts of the therapeutic encounter. But he has recently commented on tendencies in the behavioral sciences to make certain presuppositions about the control of human behavior which he believes lead to dehumanization. He does not appreciate the prospect of an 'order in which men will be conditioned ants in a giant ant hill.' Psychology, like physics, can be used to enrich or destroy life. Rogers says pointedly: 'Living is a form of not being sure, and of not knowing what next or how. Man guesses and he may be wrong. But then he does not know whom to befriend, or, for that matter, to marry.' Rogers sees man's unending inquiry for truth as the discerning of the hidden elements of order embedded deeply in nature and experience. Dr. Rogers (1967) quotes Bronowski:

> Order does not display itself of itself... There is no way of pointing a finger or a camera at it; order must be discovered and in a deep sense it must be created. What we see as we see it is mere disorder... We remake nature by the act of discovery in the poem or in the theorem.

The decisive requirement for a humane technology is the achievement of a view of man's relation to nature in which there are infinite possibilities of human discovery and creation, but there are also limitations imposed by the mystery of existence, and by man's requirements for freedom, growth, and expression. The search for sheer control is self-defeating. Every teacher knows it. Parents learn it. We have to rediscover that truth in each generation, and especially now.

Man's problems, then, are moral-technical, but they are also political. Man is a political animal. Here the prophets and Aristotle agree. Here, again, the prophetic perspective is being confirmed in the clash of nations and the search for a world order which can provide a tolerable mode of living together for the nations. The ambiguity of nationalism in its shaping of history runs all through the prophetic outlook, and it is being demonstrated anew today. The emotions and hopes of men are bound up with national destinies. In the developing new nations national pride and power are essential for the emergence of personal dignity and a place in the world for multitudes of people. Man does not live by universal humanity alone; but by tradition and language, and the sense of belonging in the group. Without the nourishment of personal life through the intimate group, the family and neighborhood, the larger community and the national community, men cannot have the sensitivity, the sense of belonging and the self-recognition which is required for creative living.

Yet the ancient prophesy still stands against the temptation to make an idol of national power, to claim superior wisdom and righteousness for our group or nation. This people which in some sense gives me my identity, my homeland, my chance of being effective in the world, this people which becomes my 'cause', almost inevitably makes a claim for an absolute devotion which can become uncritical and in which the power of my group against the other is made the goal of history. So political messiahs appear, sometimes in expectation, sometimes in the flesh. They appear as omniscient leaders, as demi-gods, as persons who are the incarnate symbols of national destiny. Their claims become fantastic. Their power feeds upon itself. No view of man which ignores the fanaticism of totalitarianism and the self-righteousness of national power can begin to cope with the facts of man's existence. Nkrumah of Ghana has had his downfall; but his inscription on the center of the capital city stands for one of the demonically persuasive views of human life: 'Seek ye first the Political Kingdom and all these things will be added.'

The prophetic view here makes one of its most important contributions. It accepts the nation as God's people. We can generalize this Old Testament idea for all the nations. History is determined by the relations not of individuals alone but of nations to one another. The Hebrew prophets never rejected the notion of Israel's peculiar election as a nation. At the same time they saw the divine judgment against every nation, including Israel, and they rejected utterly the attempt to make out of national power and success the equivalent of the fulfilment of life under God. If the prophetic view is right, then it should be possible for us to discover both the greatness and the limits of national life. We can learn the meaning of nationhood and of belonging within a national political tradition without making an idol of our group and its power.

It is a sober fact of history that it takes more than our own wisdom to temper national absolutism. The necessities of survival in a world where others are armed with the means of destruction has its own way of teaching us what we need to know. We proceed partly by moral discernment and partly by the stark realities of history. But if by the prophetic dimension of man's uniqueness we understand that view which sees man discovering his membership in the family of many peoples and seeking a viable justice and peaceable order among them, then the prophetic dimension is critically important today. In 1960, Eugene Rabinowitch writing in the *Bulletin of the Atomic Scientists* was willing to push the scientists' clock back to 'a few more minutes before twelve' on the ground that this new collective consciousness is penetrating our world, and wrote in 1962:

> In our time the survival and prosperity of any individual or group is becoming more and more obviously tied up with the well-being and security of mankind... No nation has either the moral right or the objective possibility of existing indefinitely as an island of prosperity in a sea of want.

But on the day on which I wrote this paragraph about turning the clock to a few minutes earlier before twelve, Rabinowitch was quoted in the *New York Times* that we must again move it closer to twelve.

We have taken notice of the prophets involvement in the history to which he announces the divine judgment. His word is not a professional pronouncement. He doesn't choose the role. He is called against his will. He protests his guilt and inability as does Isaiah. He curses the day he was born to such responsibility, as does Jeremiah. And as the prophetic movement develops, the prophet himself in his own loneliness, his suffering and his anguish, becomes along with his people the bearer of the pain of the divine judgment.

The prophetic view of politics requires man's commitment at the risk of power, position, and prestige. There is no way to the responsible meeting of contemporary issues other than sharing the political struggle. This means that the ethical way requires more than adopting a moral attitude, however sensitive and well considered at any time. It means to act in history, to assume its burdens and to bear the consequences. The greatness of man not only in the sensitivity of his conscience, but in the willingness to risk the resentment, the disfiguration which occurs when he acts according to conscience; to make himself a reproach as he shares in the moral burden of history. The atomic scientists became politicians at the outset of their project and in its aftermath.

I take another example of prophetic involvement. Erik Erikson remarks that Luther and Freud each did the 'dirty work' of their generation, and it is to Dr. Erikson the psychoanalyst that I turn for this example of the prophetic dimension in a contemporary perspective. Erikson's address to the Psychoanalytic Association in 1961 on *Psychological Reality and Historical Actuality* is directed to the role played by psychiatry in the modern period. It is a plea for a recognition by the psychologist of his responsibility in history. Psychology, he tells us, has a share in creating the romantic optimism which hopes of an 'id-utopia' to be arrived at through the release of infantile sexuality. He calls on his profession to assume a new responsibility in culture. But Erikson goes deeper as he asks what has contributed to the reluctance of the psychiatrist to see the struggle for power in history as a source of dynamism and of evil. He concludes that one source has been the psychologists' own failure to recognize this aggressive drive in his professional activity (Erikson, 1964).

Here is the prophetic turn to the conscience. 'Woe is me, for I am a man of unclean lips and I dwell amidst a people of unclean lips.' Erikson takes note of Robert Oppenheimer's use of the word *sin* to describe man's fall into the corruptions of injustice and indecency. Here the language of secular prophecy beginning with issues of contemporary professional responsibility has become the language of traditional prophecy. I am not trying to say that Erikson would reinstate the traditional perspective as I have been pleading for it, but only to show that the prophetic pattern recurs as men grapple with contemporary responsibilities.

We see that this prophetic word in its contemporary form is not spoken apart from technical understanding, but it makes use of that understanding. Erikson draws upon his psychological knowledge of repression in order to call his colleagues to a deeper assumption of responsibility in history. This welding of prophetic judgment to scientific understanding is something new in human history. The ultimate issues still lie in man's moral assumption of responsibilities, his acknowledgement of the evil he does, his resolve to seek a wider justice. But those issues require him to know himself with every resource of modern knowledge. Technical knowledge does not create the prophetic outlook, but it may immeasureably contribute to its effectiveness.

I come, then, to the last and the profoundest issue which the prophetic perspective raises for man today. Is man unique in the world as its only spiritual inhabitant, finding his way alone to his natural environment, dependent wholly upon his own resources for wrenching some meaning out of this strange material of life? The prophets do not see man that way. The sources of hope and renewal do not lie in man alone because his uniqueness is a reflection of the image of his creator. His hope lies not only in what he can make out of life, but in the creative power which remakes his life and consciousness, and offers him a hope founded upon the eternal and ever gracious source of his being.

In a full discussion of the prophetic standpoint I should, of course, give fullest attention to the concept of God. The prophets leave us many problems about God, since they speak and think within the ancient world view with its supernatural structure, its tendency to see extraordinary intervention as God's primary mode of working, and the too simple equation of suffering with moral punishment. The prophets did not have the modern view of nature, nor the conception of an eternally creative life which is manifest in the great sweep of evolutionary history. But the prophets do know God as living, present, creative Spirit. They see God entering into an adventure with his creatures in this freedom, as establishing a personal covenant with them, and as bearing with them in their groping, their failures and their hopes. They think of God as setting limits to man's evil and the manifestation of those limits is the divine judgment. They think of the future as holding in store a new act of God in which his Kingdom will come through his own power and will. But they always think of that future act of redemption as conforming in meaning to the previous acts in which God has set men free. Its meaning is bound up with the divine purpose in history and man's response to it. It the last resort the prophets are not concerned with pictures of the new age; these are prophesies but they are not prophetic. They are concerned with the trust and hope which belong to those who believe that with God a new order is possible, and that it will fulfil the ultimate need of men for righteousness and peace. Therefore, in the prophetic perspective the uniqueness of man is understood only when we see that 'it is the God-relationship which makes a man a man', as Kierkegaard says. Man is the God-seeking creature.

Just here, let's notice that the prophets seem rather unconcerned about religion. Indeed if religion means comfortable feelings of being on the divine side, or impressive ritual observance, or the prestige and power of religious institutions, the prophets are unimpressed. Their message is sometimes one of downright rejection: 'I hate, I despise your feasts, and I take no delight in your solemn assemblies... But let justice roll down like waters, and righteousness like an ever flowing stream.' (Amos 5:21, 24) But if religion means that man bears within himself the question as to who he is, where he comes from, and to whom he is beholden, then man cannot fulfil his humanity without discovering who God is. In that sense, man is the religious animal and the question about God will burn within him forever. The recent episode of the 'Death of God' thinkers certainly indicates a widespread dissatisfaction with the repetition of ancient formulas for God's relationship to the world and to human action. But it also seems to show that the announcement that there is no God is but the prelude to a more intensive search for that ultimate reality in which man's life is set, and that is just the question about God.

Believing as I do that an interpretation of the prophetic message in our time requires a re-thinking of the conception of God's relationship to the world, of God's relationship to time, of God's becoming as well as being, of God's relationship to natural law. It would be quite tempting here to plunge into those issues upon which, it seems to me, Alfred North Whitehead among the philosophers has the most light to throw. But there is no time for that and we are talking about man and I shall turn to the practical question about what difference this faith in the God of the prophets makes to man's conception of his uniqueness and his destiny.

Among the many views of man taken today I shall contrast two. They are not the only ones, but they are both contemporary and they are both concerned with man in the scientific and technological age. They are both realistic, combining hopes with a knowledge of the risks of freedom. They are both authentic expressions of human conviction and disciplined belief. I shall call them the way of the Self-Transforming Humanist and the way of the Celebrating Servant.

The Self-Transforming Humanist has learned that humanity is involved in a long evolutionary development and that man has power to understand, reshape and direct some of its processes. Man's task now is to realize his fulfilment through the exercise of his natural and yet unique capabilities. I am thinking here of Lewis Mumford, surely one of the most profound and most informed of the humanists of our time. Mumford does not believe in any automatic progress. In his book *The Transformations of Man* (1966, p. 124) he writes bluntly of the impending degradation of man to a power serving automaton:

> If the goal of human history is a uniform type of man, reproducing at a uniform rate, in a uniform environment, kept at constant temperature, pressure, and humidity... all inner waywardness brought into conformity by hypnotics and sedatives... a creature under constant mechanical pressure from incubator to incinerator, most of the problems of human development would disappear. Only one problem would remain: Why should anyone, even a machine, bother to keep this kind of creature alive?

Mumford believes that what man must achieve is what he has never yet accomplished, the affirmation of his wholeness, to realize the many-sidedness of his nature in its bodily, mental, sexual, artistic, technical and emotional aspects. The man who can live in this new age which is come to birth must 'renounce perfection in any single field for the sake of balance and growth'. Mumford (1966, p. 170) says, 'The self we seek, one that will have a heightened consciousness of its own still unused resources, has still to be created.' In the 'fullness of time', a unified self will bring a world culture into existence, and that world culture will in turn sustain and bring to a higher pitch of development this new self.

Mumford thus calls for human effort, directed by a new philosophy of wholeness. This effort to create the new civilization should claim our energies and our devotion.

Surely here is the uniqueness of man stated with nobility of purpose and openness of mind. Mumford has no blueprint for the future. He recognizes that man is cooperating with many integrating processes, and with the promptings of divinity within him. His view is Faustian in its heroic optimism about man. It is sane, humane and dedicated in its search for the deeper springs of human action. Who could conceive a finer or more sensitive vision of man realizing his unique capabilities?

And yet – something makes us pause. Is it only the echo of an ancient warning that man cannot count on his own perceptiveness and goodness? Or is it the knowledge of what man has done to man with the brutality, the horror, the hatreds which divide men, and the great and as yet unsolved problems of humans living together.

There is an alternative form of faith for contemporary man. The Celebrating Servants find themselves saying 'yes' to life, not because they see the way to wholeness, or because they are drawn by the prospect of such a civilization in the future, good as these things are. They say 'yes' to life because they find its meaning in God's work in the midst of the present tragic and comic circumstances. They do not depend upon the assurance of wholeness for man. They depend on the discovery that the broken fragments of human effort are yet good and whole when they incorporate the love of life and faith in the gracious working of God. This is the prophetic form of hope. It believes that God uses what man discards, that suffering with the agony of mankind is the only way to peace, and that life holds a glory for him who lives by faith. And so the Servants celebrate life, while they work at it. They believe in an unimaginable good in the future, even when they cannot see it coming. They are Servants, not as a term of self-congratulation, but because they see all good as a gift from the source of life which is God, not man.

I am thinking here of another of the great citizens of our time, Dag Hammarskjöld. He was something of a renaissance man himself in his abilities and tastes. He would understand Lewis Mumford's call for the wholeness of life, the uniting of emotion and intellect, the love of mountain climbing, the delight of friendship. He worked at the center of the political effort of the nations to find some way of peaceable and tolerable community with one another. But instead of offering a broad philosophy for the transformation of man, he left us only a set of fragments, 'markings' or scratchings. But in them we catch the accents of a way of being fully human and of saying 'yes' to life which expresses the faith that man is the servant of God and that the meaning of life is in accepting that service with its demands, while we do not know the end. He says in his book *Markings* (1964, p. 125):

> There are actions, justified only by faith – which can lift us into another sphere, where the battle is with 'Principalities, Dominions and Powers', actions upon which – out of mercy – everything is staked. For the holy life is our way, and your adorable patience the road by which we must approach thee.

He joins the note of celebration to the note of strenuousness and of peace in the midst of the unfinished business, as he says (*Markings*, p. 127):

> To love life and men as God loves them – for the sake of their infinite possibilities,
> to wait like Him
> to judge like Him
> without passing judgment,
> to obey the order when it is given
> and never look back –
> then He can use you – then, perhaps He will use you.
> And if He doesn't use you – what matter. In His hand every moment has its meaning, its greatness, its glory, its peace, its coinherence.

In this prophetic perspective man's most important capacity is not his dream of being fully realized in a new civilization, but his capacity to give thanks on the way to it, his courage to do what needs to be done when he is surrounded by darkness, and his possibility never to lose heart. Lewis Mumford uses a prophetic phrase when he says the great new civilization will appear 'in the fullness of time'. But for the prophets the fullness of time is in God's hands, and it is a mystery.

Man, then, is becoming, and it does not yet appear what he shall be. In the prophetic view man's hope is most securely founded when it expresses his celebration of a life to which he says 'yes' in the midst of its good and its evil. Man's uniqueness finds its fulfilment in this, that he can recognize and trust in a goodness which is at work in all things, which works in strange ways, and which holds an even greater promise for every time and every future than man can conceive or plan.

References

Erikson, Erik, 1964. Psychological reality and historical actuality, in *Insight and responsibility*, New York, W. W. Norton. The reference to Luther and Freud is in Erikson's *Young man Luther*, 1958, New York, Norton.

Hammarskjöld, Dag, 1964. *Markings*, transl. by Leif Sjöberg and W. H. Auden, New York, Alfred A. Knopf, pp. 125, 127.

Jacobs, Jane, 1961. *The death and life of great American cities*, New York, Random House.

Mumford, Lewis, 1966. *The transformations of man*, New York, Collier Books, pp. 124, 170.

Rabinowitch, Eugene, 1962. Pushing back the clock of doom, in *The atomic age* (Morton Grodzins and Eugene Rabinowitch, eds.), New York, Basic Books, pp. 606, 607.

Rogers, Carl R., 1967. Some thoughts regarding the current presuppositions of the Behavioral Sciences, in *Pastoral psychology* 18, 177, Oct. 1967, p. 45. The quotation is from J. Bronowski, 1956, *Science and human values*, New York, Harper & Row Torchbooks, pp. 23–24, 32.

Knowing and Hoping in the Christian Faith

1

In his book *Eros and Civilization* Herbert Marcuse indicts religion and contemporary philosophy for their affinity with death which is the symbol of unfreedom and defeat. He says:

Theology and philosophy today compete with each other in celebrating death as an existential category: perverting a biological fact into an ontological essence, they bestow transcendental blessing on the guilt of mankind which they help to perpetuate—they betray the promise of utopia.[1]

My concern in this essay is with the meaning of hope in the Christian faith and the relation of hoping to knowing. Hope has become the central theme of much contemporary theology and has arisen with surprising power throughout our culture. I have begun with this quotation from one of the leading philosophers of the revolutionary spirit for three reasons. First, Marcuse states the familiar Marxist thesis that the forms of religious hope are ideological projections whose real function is to distract attention from the divisions in present society and therefore to block action toward the good society. Second, Marcuse links theology and philosophy together as betrayers of utopia. Presumably he is thinking of the Existentialist doctrine of authentic existence as the recognition that we run toward death, and the Stoic attitude which has no real hope but only courage in the face of the ultimate negation.

But it is what Marcuse goes on to say about death to which I call particular attention. He asserts, "Men can die without anxiety if they know that what they love is protected from misery and oblivion." [2] "If they know. . . ." Here he binds hoping and knowing together. To know something which gives hope for the future is in some way to grasp that future.

What I propose to do is to explore the relation of knowing to hoping, first as it appears in the Christian faith. But I also want to show that there is a remarkable convergence of theology, revolutionary philosophy, and the impact of modern science on our present experience, so that the present concern with hope is appearing in different contexts but with a measure of shared understanding. The possibility of a deeper reconciliation between religious, political, and scientific traditions appears when we tackle the subtle problems involved in the relation of knowing and hoping. The prospect of a greater mutuality between theology, philosophy, politics and science is so great that it may justify the risk of exploring our thesis on a very broad scale.

We begin with knowing and hoping in the Christian faith. Of course this comes directly to the heart of the biblical perspective. Human existence has a beginning and an end. The life of faith is lived in history before and with God who is working out his purpose. Hence the theme of promise and of hope is fundamental in the Bible.

Certainly the expectation of salvation and the Kingdom is essential to the structure of the Christian faith. There are the words of Jesus. "He who endures to the end shall be saved." "Blessed are the meek for they shall inherit the earth." Paul says we are "saved by hope." "Now we see in a mirror dimly but then face to face. Now I know in part, then I shall understand fully even as I have been fully understood." The words of 1 Corinthians 13 about faith, hope and love abiding are so familiar we easily miss the powerful paradox involved in the affirmation that hope *abides*. It is no temporary expectation to be immediately fulfilled, but a dimension of all life before God until the last enemy has been put down, and the last enemy is death.

The relation of hope to knowledge contains a powerful inner tension which lies at the roots of the Christian faith. What we hope for is bound up with our knowledge of who God is and what our existence means. The word of the Fourth Gospel has been a major motif of all Western civilization. "You shall know the truth and the truth will make you free." The promise is for a future fulfillment. The reference in the Fourth Gospel is quite clearly to the sending of the Spirit, the Comforter, who will lead us into all truth. But that promise is meaningless apart from the belief that Christ who is the Truth has already come to us, and we have beheld his glory "full of grace and truth." Thus hope in the Christian perspective is rooted in *the faithfulness of God,* as the Old Testament continually asserts, and in the personal Word of God who is Jesus Christ, the Truth. In the New Testament to know God in his Word is to hope. We live in a dimension of expectation which stretches into the future and beyond death, but we hope on the basis of a knowledge of our real situation before and with God. "Brothers, now are we the sons of God; it does not yet appear what we shall be." There is of course in human life a kind of hope which is sheer unknowing leap into the future; but that is not the hope of the Gospel which is founded on what we can now know.

If we consider the *content* of the hope the New Testament holds we encounter the same inner tension between knowing and the not-yet. For we do not fully know what we hope for; yet our hope is meaningless apart from what we have already seen in Jesus Christ of life on the other side of the estrangement of sin.

The relation of knowing and hoping for Christian faith is brought to its clearest focus when we consider the meaning of Christ for *forgiveness*. It is clear that Paul's theology, whatever its dimension of futurity, unequivocally rests on a present reality: God's acceptance of us now while we are yet sinners. The Gospel message is not, "God *will* forgive," but "God *does* forgive"; not that we will one day be free of condemnation but that we are now free; not that we will at some time enter into a new relationship to God through Christ, but that God has now made us a new creation in him. "Now there is no condemnation to those who are in Christ Jesus."

The content of the new life is freedom to love, to grow in grace, and it is freedom to hope; but it is freedom given to us now. So Paul pleads with the Galatians: "For freedom Christ has set us free, stand fast therefore, and do not submit to a yoke of slavery" (Gal 4:1). This life in the new freedom has one of its dimensions in the future. It is bearing about in the body the dying of Jesus that his life also might be manifest; but both the dying and the manifestation have a present reality, as well as a future expectation—for "we shall be like him."

The foundation in Christian faith of our knowledge of the new life and its hope is the story of Jesus with its climax in the crucifixion and resurrection. Here knowledge and hope are indissolubly together; for while Christ's resurrection has taken place and therefore we are no longer dead in our sins, we are yet waiting for fulfillment. Paul says, "For if we have been united with him in a death like his, we shall certainly be united with him in a resurrection like his" (Rom 6:5). The tenses become strangely mixed here. Paul thinks of the new life in Christ as partaking in the resurrection; yet he also speaks of the resurrection in future terms: "We shall all be changed." As Paul says:

> Therefore since we are justified by faith we have peace with God through our Lord Jesus Christ. Through him we have obtained access to this grace in which we stand, and we rejoice in our hope of sharing the glory of God.

Peace now, glory later. What holds these together is the Spirit. It is the new life in the Spirit which both knows the power of the resurrection, that is what it means to die to sin; and which also hopes for what is not now consummated, that which we cannot now see. But the peace and the glory are mutual implicates. Without the peace of reconciliation there is no meaning to the hope for communion; and without the hope there can be no real peace in the present experience, for it is filled with suffering, with the not-yet.

If this be in barest outline the relation of knowing and hoping, in the New Testament we find three central questions which are insistently asked today, and which have led to an increasing emphasis on the importance of hope in Christian faith.

First, there is an increasing recognition that the forms of our knowledge and the language of its expression have their limitations which come from finitude, and from diverse cultural perspectives. The symbols of our knowledge and our hope point beyond themselves. We are reluctant to claim for the forms of our knowing an absoluteness and finality; there is an aspect of incompleteness, an expectation of correction. The language of the Kingdom is not yet our language except in expectation. But notice this also means that the specific forms of hope are subject to the same limitation. The eschatological concepts are notoriously "symbolic." They reach for that which is beyond our present grasp: resurrection; apocalyptic visions; heavenly expectations which lie beyond anything we can imagine. I shall not dwell on this new sensitivity about the forms of knowing and hoping, but it is important for our present situation in the expression of the Christian faith, and for the relationship between theology, philosophy, and science.

The second question arises from an honest confession of what we are doing when we claim a present knowledge of God's saving power. What kind of knowledge do we really have? When we say we know we have been set free from sin and death our statements invite an immediate disclaimer of authenticity. Do we really experience freedom from the law when we see ourselves contending for our small righteousness? Have we really been set free from the bondage of guilt into the glorious liberty of the sons of God? Ask the psychotherapists what they find in us professed believers. We believe Christ has openly triumphed over the principalities and powers and authorities; but history moves on with the principalities and powers wielding enormous force, and making a strong bid to bring the whole to a catastrophic end.

The problem here is a very old one—Is faith knowledge, or is it essentially hope? John Calvin defined faith as

> . . . a steady and certain knowledge of the Divine benevolence towards us, which, being founded on the truth of the gratuitous promise in Christ, is both revealed to our minds, and confirmed to our hearts, by the Holy Spirit.[3]

This phrase, "the truth of the promise," embraces the mystery of hoping and knowing in the Christian faith. Without the truth we cannot believe the promise, but we can have the truth only with a dimension of promise.

It might be proposed here that we will be on safer ground if we always understand knowing in the Christian faith as believing. We hope that what we believe is true, even if we cannot know it to be true. And we can hope that what we believe we shall know in the end. But hope wins out now, for believing is subject to all the risk of our finitude, our uncertainty, and our sin. Believing always bears an inner counterpoint of disbelief. Luther says:

> For this is the nature of faith, that it dares trust in God's grace. . . . Faith does not require information, knowledge or security, but a free surrender and a joyful daring upon an unfelt, untried, unknown goodness.[4]

Yet the dialectic of knowing and hoping cannot be overcome by believing, for belief without any basis in experience is purely arbitrary and therefore any hope founded upon it is arbitrary. We hope in the Christian faith because we have already seen a reality which makes life whole; the incarnate mercy of God and therefore a new possibility for ourselves. We are touching here upon the meaning of assurance in faith, a perennial theological topic. I am appealing to the authority of Christian experience: not for the absoluteness of the forms of expression of our knowledge, but for that real knowledge which is essential to the very hope which we hold. Unless we experience the leading and creativity of God there is no ground of hope. We can believe the promises of God only if we believe in the Promiser. What we know in Christian experience is a grace, a power, and a life which is beginning to be opened to us, and which leads us toward a future disclosure. This knowledge should prevent us from absolutizing our present state of understanding or practice. "It does not yet appear what we shall be."

The third issue is that between our ultimate hope and proximate hopes for this world and its life, the hopes for justice, for a peaceful and creative world civilization in history. Has theology here betrayed Utopia? The answer so far has to be, in part, yes. We have yet to find an adequate view of the relation of hope in time and history to the ultimate promises of the Gospel. It is surely not the case, as Marcuse and Marx and others charge, that the Church has not wrestled with this issue, or that it has always turned attention away from earthly causes. One can easily refute that from the beginning of Church history, but our concern is with the issue today. We have to solve concrete problems of social control, international war, human justice, and technological adjustment to our environment; otherwise the whole human enterprise faces catastrophe. We can understand those who say it is not ultimate reconciliation but drastic change which is required. We need not ultimate assurance but the release of human energies for survival. We need hope for present human effort.

We turn therefore to the new revolutionary philosophies. But in anticipation of our conclusion, there are two major affirmations about the relation of ultimate to proximate hopes which grow out of our analysis of the relation of knowing and hoping in Christian faith that can be stated here.

The first has to do with the new openness concerning the precise forms of hope. The future is not determined according to a pattern which has been revealed to us. All literalizing of eschatological symbols, all prediction of the future course of events, all enclosing of the Christian view of the future in optimistic or pessimistic modes must yield to a proper sense of the limitations of our sight as we learn what it means to live in hope before God. The Christian faith has always had as its deepest note the call to entrust life to God in all things in life, and in death. Our times and all times are in his hands. Providence means that God goes before us wherever we are to go. There is therefore an existential courage and commitment to serve God in present history as we have light on his purposes, even when the outcome of his working is by no means fully known to us. Against Marcuse and Camus, I am arguing that one of the contributions of Christian faith to civilization has been its ability to sustain hope in an undefined future, and to nourish a trusting expectancy for new good in history. There is a link between present action for justice and humanity and the final purposes of God.

The second observation has to do with the specific content of Christian hope. The central theme is the Kingdom of God, and that means God's reign over all things. The Kingdom is therefore a social reality. It involves the fulfillment of the kinds of relationships between man and man and man and God which show forth the divine image in human affairs. There have been, to be sure, forms of Christianity which have so individualized the meaning of the Gospel that it has been drained of its social relevance; but these are aberrations, and there is almost universal recognition in our century that the social gospel with its drive toward a new social order has its warrant in the deepest understanding of the biblical message.

The humanity for which we hope is defined by the humanity we know in Jesus Christ. It is the humanity of the servant, the man free to serve other man, and to give life for the meeting of other men in love. We have no blueprint for a Christian civilization. We have to find our way in the imitation of Christ in our time and with our problems. Christ is the Type; but the type leaves us open to the creativity of freedom itself when that freedom is exercised in love.[5]

It is this concrete human and social content of the hope for the Kingdom that gives us the basis for translating our ultimate hopes into concrete decision in history. There are principles and requirements of human justice which are the historical and present forms of what God's righteousness requires. The new theologies of hope have been asserting this but sometimes they give the impression that we have to derive all our guidance for present action from the eschatological Kingdom alone.[6] But the hope we have now is grounded in what we know about God's action, although even as we say this we recognize that our ways are not his ways and that therefore while we seek the justice we believe God requires we cannot simply identify our plans and programs with his will. Secular justice is ultimately worthful even if it does not have the absolute worth of perfection.

We turn now to the contemporary alternatives to Christian faith in the hopeful new revolutionary philosophies.

In *Man's Nature and His Communities* Reinhold Niebuhr speaks of that "wonderful combination of hope and despair which has been the motive power of all rebellions against injustice." [7] All revolution lives from some kind of hope. There must be a conviction that a new order is possible, and there must be some idea of what that new order could be in contrast to the present. It is in this sense that Marcuse uses the term *utopian.* It does not mean dreaming a glorious picture of the future with all the evils rubbed out; it means the hope for a new order which is based on a new principle, achieves a new justice, and promises human fulfillment.

Every revolutionary philosophy therefore relates knowing and hoping. What I shall try to show is that now there is a shift in this relationship in revolutionary philosophy which is akin to what we have seen in theology.

First let us look at the revolutionary philosophical stance in its own terms. I am focusing on the movement from Marx to Marcuse. The revolutionary is in the following situation with respect to knowledge and hope: As a revolutionary he must break with the present structure of knowledge which characterizes the mind-set of the established order. This mind-set is illusory, ideological, and untrustworthy. The content of the revolutionary hope is the new order, but it is just that which we do not have in our experience. How can we move from our present distorted vision to what we can hope for tomorrow?

There is a way of making this move. If not wholly discovered it was at least systematized by Hegel, and that is why most revolutionary philosophy since Hegel has directly or indirectly drawn upon him. It is the dialectical way. We can go from present knowledge to future hope when we discover that history moves according to a pattern in which the new order arises as an opposition to the old, and the new content will be that which both negates and fulfills the present order. The dialectical key to hope is that history exhibits its own structure which guarantees the shattering of the present order to make way for the new.

As we know, Hegel's version of the dialectic reaches its consummation in the Prussian State, and Hegel is the philosopher who understands the whole process. As he says magisterially in the preface to his lectures on the philosophy of history: "In the World nothing else is revealed but the True, the Eternal, the absolutely powerful essence of reason—a result which happens to be known to me, because I have traversed the entire field." [8]

Emil Fackenheim in his recent book on Hegel reminds us that in his last lectures on philosophy of religion, after Hegel has demonstrated the power of philosophy to express the absolute truth, which is for him the truth of the Christian revelation, he looks about him and finds very few people who understand the absolute Idea. Philosophers remain an isolated order of priests who cannot mix with the world.[9]

Not so with Marx. For him the point is to change the world. His view of the relation of knowing and hoping has its clue in Hegel but it has the structure of a dialectical, economically determined process. That structure can be known, because it is objectively embedded in reality, and the observer who is not confused by ideology can know it. Here is Lenin's claim for objective knowledge:

Materialism in general recognizes objectively real being (matter) as independent of the mind, sensation, experience, etc. of humanity. . . . From this Marxian philosophy, which is cast from a single piece of steel, you cannot eliminate one basic premise, one essential part, without departing from objective truth, without falling a prey to a bourgeois-reactionary falsehood.[10]

Once the nature of alienation is understood man's true essence becomes intelligible. All the oppositions in man which frustrate his full humanity are to be overcome. So the content of revolutionary hope is derived from this dialectical affirmation of the overcoming of what is at present disrupted. Marx says in his economic and philosophical manuscripts:

Communism is the positive abolition of private property, of human self-alienation, and thus the real appropriation of human nature through and for man. It is, therefore, the return of man himself as a social, i.e. really human being. . . . Communism . . . is the *definitive* resolution of the antagonism between man and nature, and between man and man. It is the true solution of the conflict between existence and essence, between objectification and self-affirmation, between freedom and necessity, between individual and species. It is the solution of the riddle of history and knows itself to be this solution.[11]

We need not dwell on the often repeated observation that Marx is giving us a secularized version of prophetic eschatology. If we substitute a completely this-worldly vision of the future society for a transcendent kingdom of God, and see the primary agency not as God but as the dialectical structure of history, the agreement with the biblical hope for the overcoming of alienation is patent. Objective scientific knowing has replaced the traditional revelation. Hope is grounded in knowledge, and the content of the hope is man's fulfillment of his essence objectified in a new order of life.

It is the fate of this Marxist confidence to be giving way in the twentieth century to a reassessment of the relation of knowing and hoping not unlike what we have seen in theology. If we can penetrate this phenomenon we may get some light on the movement toward a new stage in the form of man's hope.

The confidence which Marx had in grasping absolutely the structure of history and predicting the complete overcoming of alienation has given way to a more open, less deterministic conception of hope. Much contemporary revolutionary philosophy (not the doctrinaire kind of party propaganda) shows a kinship with the theological interpretation of hope in which there is a present insight into the reality of redemption and yet an acknowledgment that the mystery of the future remains. In place of a claim for absolute knowledge of the future, there is more readiness to wrestle with the present, and move into the future as an exploration of possibility rather than the realization of a pre-arranged plan. Put in another way: utopia seems to be taking on a new function. It is not the complete determination of hope and the pattern of the future; but it is the assertion of judgment on the present in order to win freedom from the present, and to draw upon the power of hope to create a new reality. One of the chief complaints of the critics of the new youth revolution is that it is vague in its objective. "Precisely what do you want?" the moderate elders ask. I am pointing out that it is just the unwillingness to answer that question which characterizes some of the new revolutionary stance. While this may produce a considerable confusion so far as a sense of direction is concerned, it also shows an openness which may be more flexible and revisable than the dogmatic secular eschatologies of the past. Here is a characteristic statement from a student of the new left:

The present day stranger hung-up on every cross in town may be that so-called hippie, who is unself-consciously developing a revolutionary style in technological America through his *ad hoc* participation in all of life, creating a "bottom-up" revolution with a new style (a highly individualized style learned largely from the black movement, where oppression has preserved black men from white contamination, wherein they created their manhood out of suffering, as Fanon has said), a new style that makes leaders unthinkable and exploitation impossible for each man now becomes his own leader. The new style is directed toward a shared community of quality in which each man's genius is recognized, an infinitely humorous situation in which the Kingdom of God is seen as present. Jesus the revolutionary is Jesus the hippie, disguised in four parts as the Beatles. "Heaven sneaks in in unsuspecting ways" as John of the Cross might say.[12]

The utopian note here is unmistakable as it finds theological expression, yet there is no plan for the future, and no prescription for its attainment.

Two main issues have led to this new openness in revolutionary philosophy, and therefore to a new assessment of the relation of knowing and hoping.

The first point concerns the determinism in the traditional Marxist solution. The criticism of this comes out clearly in the Polish Marxist philosopher, Kolakowski. I must here rely on Professor George Kline for my knowledge of Kolakowski's thought, and I have implicit confidence in Professor Kline. The Polish Marxist finds that absolute determinism takes all the sense out of moral obligation. He draws upon Kant and the Existentialists to recover the element of subjectivity which is essential to authentic humanity. He sees both Marx and Hegel as caught in historiosophy in which there are no more individuals:

. . . they appear only as instances of general ideas, bearing the mark of their species upon their foreheads. In that world, we do not eat bread and butter; we restore our labor power, which is consciously organized for purposes of socialist construction. We do not sleep, we regenerate cerebral tissue for creative work in realizing the *Weltgeist.* We talk not to men but to carriers of ideas, which are themselves only representatives of certain conflicting social forces in the gigantic march of history.[13]

Within this dehumanization there is a failure of ethical judgment; for in a completely determined history we will judge right and wrong by the success of particular movements. Moral sensitivity is dulled by the "opiate of the Weltgeist." Hence, "between obedience to history and obedience to the moral imperative yawns an abyss on whose brink the great historical tragedies have been played." [14]

Here the relation of knowledge and hope is being redefined through the grasp of a moral imperative which transcends historical success or failure. What we know leads to a judgment on immediate history and its forms of hope. The hope which guides action will be redefined in the light of this moral dimension, for now all values have to be re-examined in the light of a moral absolute which transcends any predictable realization. Kolakowski has opened up what may be a new form of revolutionary doctrine based on a new anthropology; for if there are depths in man's self-knowledge which disclose his relation to something beyond historical actualization, then the relation of knowledge to hope must be restated.

In Ernst Bloch this new openness in the structure of revolutionary hope becomes the dominant theme. For Bloch, Marx is the prophet of liberation; but Bloch sees in both man and nature a creative becoming, which is the context of man's self-understanding. Man has to live into his future in order to know who he is, and Bloch's thought here is indebted to the biblical structure of knowledge and hope.[15]

Bloch retains much of the classic Greek view of nature. With Aristotle he sees nature as the scene of processes with potencies to be realized, primordial matter to be shaped, natural powers achieving ends. Transposed into modern evolutionary thought this means that man is the creature of an unfinished nature. His hope then is bound up with his expectation of a future which is not wholly predictable. Nature has her own mysteries.

But the greatest mystery to be explored is in man himself. For Bloch, man lives by hope, because he has unexplored depths within himself. He is the self-discoverer through his grasp of the future, a grasp secured not only by rational thought but by imagination, dreams, fantasies, constructions of what is not yet actuality. Asked to sum up his philosophy in one sentence,

Bloch is reported to have said: "S is not yet P." [16] Predicates of man the subject have not yet been actualized. To live by hope is to know existence as bearing a depth and possibility which we cannot fathom through present knowledge.

This theme of man as *homo absconditus* living toward his future reality, not possessing it, is reinforced by Bloch, in spite of his atheism, with an affirmation that we must preserve the affirmation of the *deus absconditus*, the ultimate mystery of being, else the human mystery will be robbed of its full depth. Here again the philosopher is drawing upon a theological theme for the sake of a revolutionary anthropology. It is some evidence of the move toward internal communion between radically different modes of thought.

As we assess the relation of knowledge and hope today we have to introduce a third approach, that of Science. Whitehead points out that modes of thought which have characterized modern science are now spread throughout the civilized world.[17] These include empiricism, the search for the stubborn and irreducible facts; the relation of facts to general theories which give intelligibility to the facts; and the spirit of tentativeness concerning all conclusions. There are always more data. Science must be revisionist in its attitude toward theory, for the method is the practice of critical reflection moving toward new exploration. It is science above all which has caused the revision of our world-views, and it has had much to do with modifying the relation of knowing and hoping in both theology and philosophy. From Bergson to Whitehead and Teilhard de Chardin the story of metaphysics is the struggle to get time into being. Now the relation of knowledge and hope has a new metaphysical context.

It is instructive to ask about the specific relation of knowing and hoping in science, for here it appears to have a somewhat different structure and in some measure a distinctive outcome. After all, in science we really *do know*.

All science implies a relation between present inquiry and the possibility of future truthful resolution of inquiry. The structure of past, present, and future is inescapable. Present knowledge leads to new hypotheses, and we learn by predicting future consequences and testing them. Notice the hope in science is *not* that a particular hypothesis will be confirmed, but that out of experiment and confirmation or disconfirmation more fruitful hypotheses will emerge.

What becomes then of the truth which makes us free when the absolute truth can only be spoken about as a limit? Charles Peirce defined truth in the following way:

> The opinion which is fated to be ultimately agreed to by all who investigate, is what we mean by the truth, and the object represented in this opinion is the real. That is the way I would define reality.[18]

Thus the hope of future agreement becomes the very meaning of the scientific process. William James continually declares the significance of truth as the end of inquiry. It does not negate the past, but it must weld the past to new experience:

> New truth is always a go-between, a smoother over of transitions.[19]

> The absolute truth, meaning what no further experience will ever alter, is that ideal vanishing point towards which we imagine that all our temporary truths will some day converge. . . . Meanwhile we have to live today by what truth we can get today, and be ready tomorrow to call it falsehood.[20]

James' word falsehood might be too strong, for a fragmentary truth corrected is not necessarily a falsehood. But he says the absolute truth will have to be *made,* made as a relation incidental to the growth of a mass of verification-experience, to which the half-true ideas are all along contributing their quota.[21]

Now this conception of truth as being made in history, startling as it appears, converges with the theological and philosophical standpoints we have been examining. Truth in history rests upon the present reality of a community of shared experience and of inquiry, but that community can grasp truth only as having a dimension of hope.

We seem to have come upon a guiding conception of the relation of knowledge and hope as inhering in communities which bind time with hope. Our communal theory of truth would hold together present knowledge born out of communal experience and mutual criticism, with an expectation of correction and fulfillment in the future. As Josiah Royce said, to live within a community in history is to experience a sharing of memory and hope.[22] Here James' and Peirce's pragmatism and Royce's idealism tend to converge. They all claim to be giving an interpretation of truth which conforms to the scientific mode of knowing.

There has been a considerable reinforcement of this view of science as the function of communities of inquiry in Thomas Kuhn's book *The Structure of Scientific Revolutions*. Kuhn comes close to denying for example that there is such a thing as linear progression toward truth in science. Rather, there is a series of revolutions in which new statements of problems appear, and new questions are asked. No scientific theory ever fits the facts completely, and the choice between competing paradigms "proves to be a choice between incompatible modes of community life." [23]

Kuhn may not give sufficient weight to the cumulative achievement of science, especially in the more precise realms such as physics; but he shows that science lives in communities which move into the future armed with theories which have attained verification yet which are subject to radical revision in the light of new problems, new data, and new shifts of interest. This is not to deny the reliability of science in the ordinary sense of that term but it is to deny the finality of any particular stage of scientific theory. Kuhn feels constrained to ask whether we may not have to surrender the view that "there is some one full, objective true account of nature and that the proper measure of scientific achievement is the extent to which it brings us closer to that ultimate goal."[24] The real mystery, Kuhn says, lies in the question of what kind of world we must be living in so that science is possible at all, and that question remains unanswered.[25] There begins to appear in science a structure of hope for a future truth which cannot be clearly defined in the present, a hope whose fulfillment is eschatological.

Scientific knowing then has its own internal dialectic between knowing and hoping. It appeals to a radically open future into which the scientific community moves, along with the rest of the human community, as an essential dimension of science itself.

Beginning with the question of knowledge of God and salvation and its relation to hope in the Christian faith we have been led to a reconsideration of the general theme of the relation of knowledge and hope. As we draw the threads of this discussion together certain conclusions emerge. We see a convergence of perspective on knowledge and its relation to hope in theology, in philosophy, and in science. Our age is certainly not conspicuous for its tendency to achieve agreement on major articles of faith, yet it may be that there is a deeper current of common searching and outlook in our time than the outward appearance shows. If so our exploration of knowing and hoping might lead to a reinforcement of hope for mutual understanding and relevant criticism among these different perspectives. I do not believe we are grasping at straws when we detect in the analysis we have made a basis for these conclusions:

1. Man's existence has a thrust into the future so that the dimension of hope is an essential constituent of humanity. The meaning of the present is not derived from the past or present alone; it is derived from its linkage with a future toward which we move.

2. The future is the unfathomed realm of possibility. Our relation to it, while grounded in present knowing, is a relationship to an as yet unencompassed, and unobjectified reality. Man bears a depth within his own being which is not only the

abyss of negation and death–*pace* Heidegger–but the depth of openness to possibility beyond what he now is, and in that sense beyond death itself.

3. Hoping is meaningless apart from knowing. The grounds of hope and the content of our hopes are always rooted in what the past and present of experience give us by way of values, goals, frustrations, and expectations. We clash about what we hope for indeed; but the remarkable fact today is a tempering of the forms of the hope by a sense of our limitation, a recognition that hope lies deeper than its particular forms.

4. The truth which makes us free is a truth which is both present and future. It must be grasped as we live into it. It is that which is the ground of our humanity, yet its promise looks toward what we may become.

This discovery that what we know includes a dimension of hope beyond what we can fully know could open the way to a mutual interchange between Christian theology and revolutionary hope, between humanists, scientists, and theologians. The Christian affirmation of the Kingdom of God at the "end" of history is not a restriction on hopes for this world, but rather a release of hopefulness without dogmatic prediction. Whatever man does in history he lives in the light of the Kingdom which fulfills life in freedom. The biblical eschatology so understood ought to release human energies for the most strenuous action toward the reconstruction of existence.

I have argued that theology has been helped to understand more profoundly the relation of knowing and hoping by what revolutionary thought and science have given it in criticism. But does the Christian faith with its view of the relation of knowing and hoping have any distinctive truth to speak to our culture?

I return to Professor Marcuse's statement: "Men can die without anxiety if they know that what they love is protected from misery and oblivion."

The theological question could not be put more sharply; and woe to theology if it offers a glib answer. The Christian faith does claim a knowledge that what we love as God loves it is protected from misery and oblivion. This would be faith's testimony to a time wracked with agony, death, and frustration; not the avoidance of effort but the release of it, knowing creative action is worthwhile.

But here theology does speak a strange language, of death and resurrection; of the earthly passage as a pilgrimage to eternity, of knowledge of God who ventures into the future preserving what "in the world is mere wreckage," as Whitehead says.[26] That knowledge has never been a simple objective knowledge which can be spread out for everyone to see. It is the knowledge shared in a community of living and dying people whose faith has been transformed by the experience of Israel and the life of Jesus seen in the light of his death and resurrection.

Do we leave this world of real things and "betray utopia" when we talk of knowing the power of the resurrection and the hope it brings? I do not believe so. The resurrection is the sign of the hope which gives life in the midst of death. We do not know fully what it means, but in its light we have begun to know that there is a God who does not leave us in despair or death.

Marcuse closes his book *One Dimensional Man* with the statement that his critical theory of society cannot bridge the gap between present and future. It remains negative, and yet must not refuse to stand by those who are without hope yet refuse to submit to present inhumanity. He quotes Walter Benjamin at the beginning of the Nazi era:

It is only for the sake of those who are without hope that hope is given.

But surely all men at some time are without hope, or tempted to be without hope. That is why the theological question about the sources of hope, and its witness to the reality of God who gives hope, remains relevant to every age and every time, including our own.

NOTES

1. Herbert Marcuse, *Eros and Civilization*, Boston, 1955, p. 236.
2. *Ibid.*
3. John Calvin, *Institutes of the Christian Religion*, Bk. III, chap. 2, 7.
4. Martin Luther, wks. Weiman ed., 10, III: 3, 329. Quoted in Wilhelm Pauck, *The Heritage of the Reformation*, Boston, 1950, p. 20.
5. Cf. James Gustafson, *Christ and the Moral Life*, New York, 1968.
6. It seems to me that the connection between eschatological hope and present social action is insufficiently made in Jürgen Moltmann's *The Theology of Hope*, New York, 1967.
7. Reinhold Niebuhr, *Man's Nature and His Communities*, New York, 1965, p. 102.
8. G. W. F. Hegel, Preface to the *Philosophy of History*, trans. by J. Sibree, *Modern Student's Library*, New York, 1929, p. 350.
9. Emil Fackenheim, *The Religious Dimension of Hegel's Thought*, Bloomington, Indiana, 1967, p. 235. Cf. G. W. F. Hegel, *Lectures on the Philosophy of Religion*, Eng. tr., 3 vols., London, 1895, Vol. 3, pp. 149-51.
10. V. I. Lenin, *Materialism and Empirio-criticism* (Selected Works, Vol. XI), New York, p. 377.
11. Karl Marx, *Economic and Political Manuscripts* in Erich Fromm, *Marx's Concept of Man*, New York, 1961, p. 127. Italics omitted.
12. Robert Hundley, an unpublished manuscript "Revolutionary Youth Movements." Quoted by permission.
13. Quoted in George L. Kline, "Leszek Kolakowski and the Revision of Marxism," in Kline ed., *European Philosophy Today*, Chicago, 1965, p. 146.
14. *Ibid.*, p. 149.
15. Ernst Bloch, *Das Prinzip Hoffnung*, Frankfurt, 1959.
16. Harvey Cox, "Ernst Bloch and the Pull of the Future," in *New Theology* No. 5, edited by Marty and Peerman, New York, 1968, pp. 193-94.
17. Alfred North Whitehead, *Science and the Modern World*, New York, 1931, p. 3.
18. Charles Peirce, *How To Make Our Ideas Clear*. This and the following quotations from William James will be conveniently found in Konvitz and Kennedy, eds., *The American Pragmatists*, New York, 1960. Peirce quotation, p. 38.
19. William James, *What Pragmatism Means*, p. 36.
20. William James, *Pragmatism's Conception of Truth*, p. 55.
21. *Ibid.*, pp. 55-56.
22. Josiah Royce, *The Problem of Christianity*, New York, 1914. One volume ed., Univ. of Chicago Press, 1968.
23. Thomas S. Kuhn, *The Structure of Scientific Revolutions*, Chicago, 1962, p. 93.

24. *Ibid.*, p. 170.
25. *Ibid.*, p. 172.
26. Alfred North Whitehead, *Process and Reality*, New York, 1936, p. 525.
27. Herbert Marcuse, *One Dimensional Man*, Boston, 1964, PB 1966, p. 257.

1[illegible]

PHILOSOPHY AND FAITH: A STUDY IN HEGEL AND WHITEHEAD

Daniel D. Williams

The question of what philosphy can do in giving credibility and intelligibility to Christian faith is one with which Albert Outler has concerned himself throughout his lifework of interpreting the history of Christian thought. His own work has shown that the relation of faith and reason must be re-examined in every era, for the modes of reasoning change in the light of science and new experience. The self-understanding of the Christian faith confronts new issues within the believing community and in relating faith to the changing and often explosive cultural scene.

This paper proposes to examine one strand of the classic and contemporary discussion of faith and philosophic reason by analyzing the way in which Hegel and Whitehead give philosophical accounts of Christianity. Alongside Hegel's claim to show the truth of Christianity as the absolute religion in the form of absolute knowledge achieved by philosophy, we shall set Whitehead's more modest but similarly rationalistic faith that the essential truth of Christianity can be exhibited in its universality through a philosophic critique of the theological tradition and the elaboration of a theistic cosmology. In so doing, we may be able to identify certain critical issues concerning the limits of reason in interpreting Christian faith, and we shall try to see what it is that Christian theology must consider in the work of philosophers who give their own account of the intelligibility of faith. Finally, we shall identify one important issue that emerges between the Hegelian and Whiteheadian accounts of reconciliation as the overcoming of tragic history. In dealing with the meaning and overcoming of evil Hegel and Whitehead stand very close together, yet there is a critical difference between them.

Since they think within the same philosophic tradition, the issues between Hegel and Whitehead offer an especially illuminating study of the limits and possibilities of reason. Whitehead disavowed ever having read much of Hegel, partly, he says, because he once found Hegel talking some "complete nonsense" about mathematics. But Whitehead acknowledges that his philosophy is of the Hegelian type, and the historic route of Hegel's idealism runs through Bradley and McTaggart to Whitehead.[1] When Whitehead says he is transposing some of the main doctrines of idealism onto a realistic base, his statement is supported and clarified by comparison of his doctrine with Hegel's.[2]

Hegel claims that religion, which is the knowledge Spirit has of itself as Spirit, finds fulfillment in the Christian religion; but the truth is expressed in Christianity in pictures and images that need to be given scientific rational form before Spirit can achieve its goal of absolute Truth.

Out of the richness and complexity of Hegel's philosophy of religion, from his early theological writings to the last lectures on the philosophy of religion, I shall concentrate on just two aspects of Hegel's view of religion and Christianity:

first, his view that reason can objectify the truth of religion as universal knowledge; and second, his view of what it is in the nature of reason that lends it this supreme power.

Hegel sees the work of Spirit (*Geist*) in history as the search for the coming to full consciousness of absolute truth. "The truth is the whole," he says in the preface to the *Phenomenology of Mind*[3] Therefore, religion is the human search for the reality that constitutes the absolute and all-inclusive truth. That reality for Hegel must be found in the coming of self-knowledge of Spirit itself. Thus religion seeks what philosophy gives:

> The aim of philosophy is to know the truth, to know God, for He is the absolute truth, inasmuch as nothing else is worth troubling about save God and the unfolding of God's nature. . . . Philosophy has been reproached with setting itself above religion; this however is false . . . it sets itself merely above the form of faith, the content is the same in both cases.[4]

The universal reality of Spirit which religion seeks and philosophy knows is not the abstract universality of concepts or ideals. It is the one concrete and absolute truth embracing the whole of the cosmos, history, and eternity. It is God knowing himself in the history of the world.

Hegel sees in Christianity the religion that has fully grasped the relation of God to the world. It is the Christological affirmation: God has become man. The Christian faith declares that "Spirit is accordingly the living process by which the implicit unity of the divine and human natures becomes actual and comes to have definite existence."[5]

The unity expressed in the incarnation is not, however, given as a bare idea or principle. It has to be won through the process of Spirit's self-alienation, which gives rise to the story of finitude and history. The full power and profundity of Hegel's view of reason is exhibited in his account of world history as the life of Spirit returning to itself, that is becoming conscious of itself as Spirit. It is the process of alienation and return that constitutes the truth of the whole, and within this perspective Hegel works out the meaning of the biblical drama of Creation, Fall, Incarnation, Atonement, Crucifixion, and Resurrection, the rise of the new community of Spirit and its participation in eternal life.

The Crucifixion can be spoken about as the death of God, for it is the point at which Spirit achieves its self-disclosure as the absolute limit of the experience of finitude. "This is the deepest depth." Here Spirit comes to self-recognition, grasping and overcoming the meaning of its own alienation:

> This death is thus at once finitude in its most extreme form, and at the same time the abolition and absorption of natural finitude, of immediate existence and estrangement, the cancelling of limits.[6]

The theme of the universality of Spirit is repeatedly affirmed in Hegel's account:

> When the fullness of time was come, God sent his Son, *i.e.*, when Spirit had entered so deeply into itself as to know its infinitude, and to comprehend the Substantial in the subjectivity of immediate self-consciousness, in a subjectivity however which is at the same time infinite negativity, and is just, in consequence of this, absolutely universal.[7]

The real internal history of Christianity therefore is the history of the Spiritual Community brought into being through the Crucifixion and the Resurrection. It is the community that bears the authentic universal within its faith, since the history of Christ by which the community lives is absolutely adequate to the Idea.[8] God is eternal love, and this absolute truth that God is not an abstraction but absolutely concrete is unfolded by philosophy; and it is only modern philosophy that has reached the profound thought thus contained in the Notion (*der Begriff*).

For Hegel, then, it becomes possible to speak of Christian faith as a justification of the ways of God to man. The story of Spirit is packed with tragedy, illusion, suffering, and death. To live as finite person struggling for understanding means to experience infinite sorrow, for we live in contradiction. The "I," the natural will, seeks particular fulfillment, It loses the concern for universality. But Spirit coming to itself in Christianity knows that this evil of self-isolation is overcome:

> Spirit can make what has happened as if it had not happened; the action certainly remains in the memory but Spirit puts it away. . . . For the true consciousness of Spirit the finitude of man is slain in the death of Christ. . . . The death of the natural gets in this way a universal signification, the finite, evil, in fact, is destroyed. The world is thus reconciled, and through this death the world is implicitly freed from its evil.[9]

Hegel thus assigns to reason the highest possible function. It is nothing other than the divine and human spirit together attaining a self-conscious grasp of the saving truth. Reason understands and fulfills what every creature and every life really needs. Reason's service to religion is to give permanent form to the message of reconciliation. Christianity therefore is rational belief. Faith attains understanding. God is known, for He is Spirit itself, the absolute source and principle of intelligibility.

These magisterial claims for reason are the hallmark of the Hegelian philsophy. They sound somewhat strange a century and a half later, even perhaps vulgar or naïve. We cannot assess his claim until we understand what he meant by reason and his view of how its work gets done. For Hegel, reasoning is not abstract reflection, nor is it the application of an analytic method seeking to achieve clarity of logical form. Reason is the progress of the total self-reflection of Spirit moving through the whole of time and history, and probing for the pattern of being as this unfolds in the total history of nature, life, and culture.

Hegel did indeed believe that there is a logical structure in existence, and his logic is a brave and obscure attempt to set forth that structure in itself. But it is no simple formula of dialectical progression, nor does it yield a simple logical pattern that can be applied forthwith to the description of every experience. The logic is the interweaving of all basic concepts with one another so that the incompleteness of every abstract concept taken by itself is exhibited, and its meaning as involved in the interlocking web of meanings is articulated. Hippolyte has called Hegel's logic a "poetic of being," and the phrase is apt.[10] Reasoning, for Hegel, is the process of bringing every partial concept and structure into relation to its history, its context, and its participation in the final truth that is the whole. Until the fundamental pattern of Spirit seeking its own self-consciousness is grasped, we do not really understand anything in particular. Hegel's ultimate assumption is that to be human is to want to know who we are, why we are what we are, and what it is that makes us what we are. It is truth that "makes us free." Every Hegelian philosopher can quote the Fourth Gospel assertion as the New Testament charter of the vocation of truth-seeking. And again, the Apostle Paul puts knowledge at the center of the Christian hope, even if he does not make it the sole content of that hope: "Now I know in part; then I shall understand fully, even as I have been fully understood" (1 Cor. 13:12).

Knowledge comes through the concrete experience that conscious beings have of the world process, and philosophy is the final expression of that knowledge. History must be lived through for Spirit to know itself, for it has no knowledge apart from that history. Here is the key thesis in the Hegelian perspective. "It is the very nature of understanding to be a process, and being a process it is Rationality." Note particularly, then, this conclusion: "This alone is what is rational, the rhythm of the organic whole. It is as much knowledge of content as that content is notion and essential nature."[11] We see that Hegel's claims for reason, whatever their exaggerations, are meaningless apart from his conviction that truth is given in the life process itself. Truth is at work shaping all things, and at work in the life of subjects who are coming to reflect on their own being. It is here that Hegel stands in the Aristotelian tradition as one of those who sees both scientific and philosophic inquiry as the search for the forms embedded in things; but for Hegel the final principle of intelligibility is not an Unmoved Mover, but the total history of Spirit's self-movement, its self-emptying, and return.

The life of reason, then, is the pilgrimage of the human spirit toward the light. Hegel's description of the pilgrimage in the *Phenomenology of Mind* reflects the ladder of mystical ascent, beginning with sense experience and its subjection to critical reflection, opening the way to the dialectical penetration of all forms of being, and moving toward the ultimate structure that they all exemplify.

> Consciousness first finds in self-consciousness—the notion of mind—its turning point, where it leaves the parti-coloured show of the sensuous immediate, passes from the dark void of the transcendent and remote supersensuous and steps into the spiritual daylight of the present.[12]

The century elapsing between Hegel's last lectures on the philosophy of religion and the period of Whitehead's metaphysical reflection is filled with revolutions of monumental significance in human thought. There is the collapse of the idealist philosophies of nature and the conquering progress of scientific empiricism in Darwin, the revolution in modern physics, the transposition of the Hegelian dialectic of Spirit into the revolutionary dialectical materialism of Marxism, the inauguration of a new era for logic and mathematics exemplified by Whitehead and Russell's *Principia Mathematica*, and the new "age of analysis," as Morton White has called it.

Christian theology has participated in this revolution and the new modes of thought, and has found in Karl Barth what appears to be the most decisive rejection of philosophic reason as having any place in the articulation of Christian faith. Yet the question of the relation of faith to reason does not go away, and we shall see in Whitehead the continuation of that mode of philosophical interpretation of Christianity which continues to pose the issue of the place of reason.

In spite of the radical new perspectives in the twentieth century, Whitehead's doctrine bears very strong resemblances to Hegel's rational vision of the meaning of Christianity. It must be said at the outset that Whitehead rejects the imperious and absolute claims that Hegel makes for speculative reason. For Whitehead philosophic reason, including its speculative search for metaphysics, is indispensable to civilization; but philosophy must live in a critical give-and-take with all other inquiries, including science and theology. "There is no short cut to truth." It follows that Whitehead rejects every claim for finality for any philosophy, including his own:

> Systems, scientific and philosophic, come and go. Each method of limited understanding is at length exhausted. In its prime each system is a triumphant success: in its decay it is an obstructive nuisance.[13]

Yet Whitehead has a high place for reason that seeks the "essence" or the essential structure of reality, and his metaphysical vision is very close to that of Hegel, as is his view of the necessity of metaphysics for religion.

To begin with, Whitehead, like Hegel, is concerned with

the two major questions of permanence in the face of flux and the relation of universality to individuality. With this emphasis on the necessity of overcoming the evil in death and passage, Hegel and Whitehead may be said to stand closer to the Eastern Orthodox tradition of Christianity than to the Western, with its central emphasis on guilt. For Whitehead it is temporality that constitutes the deepest threat to the meaning of life. He says: "Religion is the art and the theory of the internal life of man, so far as it depends on the man himself and on what is permanent in the nature of things."[14] Again, he asks theology

> to express that element in perishing lives which is undying by reason of its expression of perfections proper to our finite natures. In this way we shall understand how life includes a mode of satisfaction deeper than joy or sorrow.[15]

Process and Reality closes with the declaration that the vision of God there expounded aims to show how zest for existence can be refreshed "by the ever-present unfading importance of our immediate actions, which perish and yet live forever more."[16]

Whitehead associates the religious spirit closely with the search for "universality"—that is, the reach for a universal truth, and participation in reality which fulfills the meaning of life by binding all things to one another. It is instructive to read Whitehead's *Religion in the Making* and *Adventures of Ideas* together as a twentieth-century *Phenomenology of Mind*. As in Hegel's great work the philosopher here traces the history of culture as the search for participation in the universal and enduring values. The statements that "religion is world loyalty" and that "generality is the salt of religion" put succinctly the significance of universality, which Whitehead elaborates in many ways.[17] The decisive formal statement of the relation of the religious quest to universality of meaning is found in the following passage from *Process and Reality:*

> Religion should connect the rational generality of philosophy with the emotions and purposes springing out of existence in a particular society, in a particular epoch, and conditioned by particular antecedents. Religion is the translation of general ideas into particular thoughts, particular emotions, and particular purposes; it is directed to the end of stretching individual interest beyond its self-defeating particularity. . . . Religion is the ultimate craving to infuse into the insistent particularity of emotion that non-temporal generality which primarily belongs to conceptual thought alone.[18]

It scarcely needs remarking how closely this doctrine stands to Hegel's view of religion as Spirit seeking its own self-conscious grasp of the truth. But again, as with Hegel, we must recognize that for Whitehead the work of reason discerning the universal structure is never in abstraction from experience. Surely as clearly as does Hegel, Whitehead remains an empiricist so far as the test of truth is concerned. Reason attempts to find the general concepts that pertain to all the details of practice. Whitehead allows, of course, for logical coherence as an important aspect of the test of truth; but the final test is "wide-spread recurrent experience."[19]

It is clear why religion and theology need philosophy and science. The truth is found only in the interaction of experience with all the modes of rational, aesthetic, and symbolic expression. The same internal drive in religion and morality toward universality of outlook is present in philosophy. "All general truths condition each other."[20] "Reason is the safeguard of the objectivity of religion: it secures for it the general coherence denied to hysteria."[21]

The question of what does secure objectivity for human thinking and how far reason can be relied upon for this is a topic of much importance. It is our purpose here not to defend Whitehead's confidence in reason but to recognize that when philosophers make the claim that universality of meaning can be attained only through the exercise of philosophic reason, theologians must take account of this claim. If it be true, it says something decisive about the task of understanding religion and faith. In our time, when there is such fragmentation of experience and such despair about communication between different perspectives, both secular and religious, it is certainly worth asking whether there is a function of reason that can aid common understanding.

We turn now to Whitehead's interpretation of the place of Christianity in the history of religion. He never uses the term "absolute" for Christianity. He was clearly interested in the possibility that aspects of his own cosmological outlook might be close to some elements of Buddhism, which he describes as a metaphysic generating a religion in contrast to Christianity as a religion seeking a metaphysic.[22] But Whitehead does find in Christianity the decisive insight that became his basis for judging all traditional doctrines. Whitehead's two theses about the significance of Christianity are, first, that Christianity as expressed in the initial testimony of the Gospels understands that the salvation of the world lies in the triumph of persuasion over force; and second, that this insight was lost when Christian dogma degraded its vision of the divine persuasion by combining the concepts derived from Semitic religion of God as omnipotent will with the Unmoved Mover of Aristotle and the Neo-Platonic conception of God as the eminently real, thus producing a conception of God as world ruler which contradicts the ethical sensitivity affirmed by the Gospel itself.[23]

Here Whitehead the philosopher appeals in the name of reason and ethical sensitivity against the theological tradition to what he finds deepest in the Christian experience. He appeals to our direct intuition of the meaning of the Gospel story:

> The essence of Christianity is the appeal to the life of Christ as a revelation of the nature of God and of his agency in the world . . . there can be doubt as to what elements in the record have evoked a response from all that is best in human nature. The Mother, the Child, and the bare manager: the lowly man, homeless and self-forgetful, with his message of peace, love and sympathy: the suffering, the agony, the tender words as life ebbed, the final despair: and the whole with the authority of supreme victory. . . . Can there be any doubt that the power of Christianity lies in its revelation in act of that which Plato divined in theory?[24]

A certain contrast with Hegel appears here. Hegel sees the end of Spirit's work as freedom; but he draws no absolute opposition between freedom and coercion. Hegel sees the whole process of Spirit as having its self-regulating necessity, and his picture of the world spirit tramping, and sometimes trampling, through history does involve an acceptance of God's agency as manifest in many apparently ruthless forms, and not stopping for the niceties of moral sensitivities.[25] Whitehead on the other hand represents what was in the early part of the twentieth century called "ethical theism." He believed that the concept of God's mode of dealing with the world must be brought into harmony with an ethical view of what freedom entails. Hence God for Whitehead does not drive the world; he lures it through the power of the vision he inspires. It is a Christological perspective compatible with the Gospel word: "I, if I be lifted up from the earth, will draw all men unto me" (John 12:32).

The critical issue for Whitehead, then, is the meaning and possibility of the "supreme victory." For Hegel it is guaranteed; but is it so for Whitehead? What is the status of evil? These are pressing questions, and Whitehead was fully aware of them. In trying to trace out his answer we find where he remains very close to Hegel; yet there is a difference about good and evil and their destiny, and it may make all the difference in two different religious understandings.

The question is, what kind of hope does Christianity hold. Both Whitehead and Hegel see history as tragic viewed from one side. Yet both come out with a positive affirmation of hope, so that Hegel can state that Christianity really belongs to Comedy rather than Tragedy, and Whitehead affirms the reality of Peace in the religious Spirit. Here some careful analysis is needed.

Whitehead clearly believes that evil is real. The Hegelian side of Whitehead is found in the way in which he sees present evil woven into ultimate good:

> The Kingdom of heaven is not the isolation of good from evil. It is the overcoming of evil by good. This transmutation of evil into good enters into the actual world by reason of the inclusion of the nature of God, which includes the ideal vision of each actual evil so met with a novel consequent as to issue in the restoration of goodness.[26]

It would require a study of a great many passages in Whitehead to get a full textual basis on which to judge what he really believed about the destiny of evil. It is clear that the "greatest evil," temporality, is overcome through participation in the everlasting life of God.[27] But do the real evils of actual events lose their quality of evil in God's assessment of them? That is the critical issue, and it is because Whitehead says some things about it which seem to suggest a complete transfiguration of all evil, that Stephen Ely could interpret Whitehead's God as the divine aesthete enjoying the world spectacle with undiminished intensity no matter what takes place in history.[28]

There is an alternative interpretation of Whitehead's view of evil which makes a much sharper difference with Hegel's doctrine that evil is always taken up into the absolute good of Spirit. I am not sure that all the Whiteheadian texts are in agreement with one another here. What saves Whitehead from the view that all evil becomes transformed into good in God is his doctrine that God and the world are together in process toward as yet unresolved issues and unachieved goods. God guides the world with an ideal vision. He imparts to the creatures the harmony and lure of the new good, including the transformation of the world that comes through God's perfect understanding and care. But for Whitehead there is no completion of this process in the sense of a static resolution. There are continuous resolutions of particular issues which enter permanently into God's experience of the world. But that experience includes the world's becoming, its limitations, and the losses attending every decision. Whitehead insists that wherever there is a choice between possibilities, something is lost as well as gained; and this is as true for God as for the creatures. Hence the world story is not the achievement of all possible good. It has its tragic side.

> There remain the final opposites, joy and sorrow, good and evil, disjunction and conjunction—that is to say, the many in one—flux and permanence, greatness and triviality, freedom and necessity, God and the World.[29]

Another way of putting the decisive point is that in the divine wisdom evil is judged. Whitehead affirms the importance of each individual occasion. It is one of his clearest differences with a purely organic idealism in which nothing is really real except the whole. For Whitehead there is an absolute importance for every individual occasion of experience, but this importance is not understood apart from the achievement and the failure of each act in experience to realize at least some of the possibility lying before it. "Every act," Whitehead says, "leaves the world with a deeper or a fainter impress of God."[30] If one takes this text as the real key to his view, then it is clear that there is loss and tragedy in all existence, but that God brings all such loss within the orbit of his understanding, his wisdom and his unflagging vision of the good. He is "the fellow sufferer who understands."[31]

> The consequent nature of God is his judgment on the world. He saves the world as it passes into the immediacy of his own life. It is the judgment of a tenderness which loses nothing that can be saved. It is also the judgment of a wisdom which uses what in the world is mere wreckage.[32]

"Nothing lost that can be saved." This is the vision of God as absorbing the world's effort into his ongoing experience. It holds with Hegel that no event is defined in its value solely by its immediacy of achievement or failure. God brings new good out of evil, and there is worth in every experience, no matter what the loss. It is the intuition of this final importance and worth of individual action which gives the sense of Peace. "Peace is the understanding of tragedy, and at the same time its preservation."[33]

In this way Whitehead's search for a rational vision does embody in its estimate of evil an alternative religious position to that of Hegel. They both hold that reason can penetrate to a supreme victory affirmed in Christian faith, but Whitehead believes that reason must acknowledge an element of incompleteness and divine suffering in the ultimate outcome.

Our point of departure was the question concerning the significance of philosophic reason for Christian faith. Both Whitehead and Hegel claim that reason can penetrate the metaphysical order on which all good and salvation depend, and give an account of alienation, estrangement, despair, and renewal of hope. Whitehead, as did Hegel, assigns to philosophy a special role in the advancement of civilization.

> . . . in unthinking Nature "natural selection" is a synonym for waste! Philosophy should now perform its final service. It should seek the insight, dim though it be, to escape the wide wreckage of a

> race of beings sensitive to values beyond those of mere animal enjoyment.[34]

This assigns a high vocation to philosophy. Like Hegel, Whitehead believes that in carrying out this task philosophy can draw upon insight derived form Christianity. They both see in the Incarnation the key to Christianity's distinctive place in world religions. For Hegel it is the unity of God and man. For Whitehead it is the victory of persuasion over force.

My aim has not been to judge between these two systems; but to show that Christian theology cannot ignore these philosophical interpretations of faith. The case can be stated in two points. First, the philosophers claim to set forth the universal meaning of human experience and therefore of the religious quest. The claim to universality cannot be bypassed by theology, for theology makes it also.

All great religious faiths claim to have hold on the universal meaning of life. The God of Christian faith loves the world, not just a portion of it. The Christ is the Way, the Truth, and the Life. Karl Barth has disavowed the help of philosophy in stating Christian theology, but when he says that "the truth of Jesus Christ . . . is *the* truth, the universal truth that creates all truth" we are driven to ask how this universal truth is to be given such form that its universality can be an intelligible hypothesis.[35]

Of course, it can be said that both Hegel and Whitehead work within Christian culture and consciously set out to reason about Christianity, so that we are dealing here with a "Christianized reason," not a universal reason. There is indeed no absolutely universal standpoint for reason. And there is no way of knowing what modern philosophy would have been without the history of cultures—Eastern, Western, and Judeo-Christian—in which it has participated. But the claim still remains that the human power of reasoning has a place in the critical interpretation of all traditional religious doctrines.

The second argument for the involvement of theology with the philosophic task is closely related to the first. Is Christian faith to be understood within the history of religions, or, as some modern theologians have held, is it a perspective that transcends religion?

It is the tendency of philosophers of religion to see all religions and faith in some kind of interrelationship. This may be dangerous to the individuality of particular faiths, but it is hard to see how Christianity can understand itself internally unless it takes up the biblical theme of the witness the one God has given of himself in every land. The notion that the search for communication and understanding among religions is an exercise in human good will and the desire to live in some kind of community of understanding is true but inadequate. The question is whether any religion can understand itself apart from the structure of human existence and the search for meaning in the face of alienation and despair. The search for the universal element in religion may or may not succeed, but it is essential to the religious spirit itself to find within the experience of the holy that which illumines every experience.

There is finally to be noted a difference between the way in which Hegel and Whitehead view the work of reason. While Whitehead has great confidence in reason, he does not share Hegel's belief that the whole can be brought into a completely self-conscious structure of knowledge. For Hegel the world exists to be known; for Whitehead it exists to be felt. Thus, in the response of the human spirit to God, Whitehead leaves the final word to Vision and Insight, which run beyond adequate rational articulation. Reason is an instrument of the divine Eros in achieving the higher purposes, but it is not the only instrument, since concrete reality is feeling, adventure becoming. Whitehead says that the doctrine of God in *Process and Reality* is only an attempt to add another speaker to Hume's *Dialogues Concerning Natural Religion*. The dialogue continues.

Theologians may see here the philosopher acknowledging the reality of faith as necessary to the life of reason itself, if faith is the living personal response to that reality which draws us, with our reason, out of self-preoccupation into self-transcendence.

NOTES

Note: I have given references to the paperback edition of Hegel's *Phenomenology of Mind* (trans. J. B. Baillie), and all of Whitehead's books. Most Whitehead works are out of print in the original editions.

1. Alfred North Whitehead, *Process and Reality* (New York: The Free Press, 1969), p. 194 (hereafter *PR*). The reference to Hegel on mathematics is quoted in a memoir by William Ernest Hocking in George L. Kline, ed., *Alfred North Whitehead: Essays on His Philosophy* (Englewood Cliffs, N.J.: Prentice-Hall, 1963), p. 11. On Hegel's influence on Whitehead see Gregory Vlastos, "Organic Categories in Whitehead" in the Kline volume, and Victor Lowe, *Understanding Whitehead* (Baltimore, The Johns Hopkins Press, 1962), pp. 254-56.

2. *PR*, Preface, p. 7.

3. G. W. F. Hegel, *The Phenomenology of Mind*, trans. J. B. Baillie (New York: Harper Torchbooks, 1967), p. 81 (hereafter *Phenomenology*).

4. G. W. F. Hegel, *Lectures on the Philosophy of Religion*, trans. from 2d German edition by E. B. Speirs and J. B. Sanderson. 3 vols. (London: Kegan Paul, Trench, Trubner & Co., 1895, 1968), 3:148 (hereafter *Lec. Ph. Rel*).

5. Hegel, *Lec. Ph. Rel.*, 2:349.
6. Ibid., 3:60, 93.
7. Ibid., 3:112.
8. Ibid., 3:111–13.
9. Ibid., 3:96; cf. 3:130.
10. Jean Hippolyte, *Studies in Marx and Hegel* (New York: Basic Books, 1969), p. 169.
11. Hegel, *Phenomenology*, p. 115.
12. Ibid., p. 227.
13. Alfred North Whitehead, *Adventures of Ideas* (New York: The Free Press, 1967), p. 159 (hereafter *AI*).
14. Alfred North Whitehead, *Religion in the Making* (New York: World Publishing Co., Meridian Books, 1960), p. 16 (hereafter *RM*).
15. *AI*, p. 172.
16. *PR*, p. 413.
17. *RM*, pp. 59, 42.
18. *PR*, pp19.
19. *PR*, p. 21.
20. *PR*, p. 13.
21. *RM*, p. 63.
22. *RM*, p. 50.
23. *PR*, pp. 403-4.
24. *AI*, p. 167.
25. See Preface to Hegel's *Philosophy of History*.
26. *RM*, pp. 148–49.
27. *PR*, p. 410.
28. Stephen Lee Ely, *The Religious Availability of Whitehead's God* (Madison: University of Wisconsin Press, 1942).
29. *PR*, p. 402.
30. *RM*, p. 152.
31. *PR*, p. 413.
32. *PR*, p. 408.
33. *AI*, p. 286.
34. *AI*, p. 159.
35. Karl Barth, *Dogmatics in Outline*, trans. G. T. Thompson (New York: Philosophical Library, 1949), p. 26.

BRUNNER AND BARTH ON PHILOSOPHY

12

DANIEL D. WILLIAMS*

The publication of Emil Brunner's *Revelation and Reason* marks a decisive point in the maturing of his own distinguished contribution to Protestant theology and in the total search of Protestantism today for theological reformation. Brunner has had his disagreement with Karl Barth and has gone his own way. That disagreement involved the problem which is dealt with in the new book, the relation of Christian faith to human reason. Here we have Brunner's statement of where his chosen path has led him. The book covers a host of theological issues, and these must all be dealt with in a critical review. My purpose in this article is not to review the book but to use it as the basis for an evaluation of Brunner's treatment of the relation of philosophy and faith. With this definitive statement in *Revelation and Reason* before us, we should be able to come to some conclusions concerning the fundamental direction of Brunner's thought. While we shall depend mainly on this work, some references to earlier books will also be made. The basic issues can be sharpened by reference to Barth's alternative way of dealing with faith and reason and to his difference with Brunner.[1]

Brunner and Barth are evangelical Protestant theologians who have striven to set the Christian gospel free from what they regard as the illusions, errors, and false ways of thinking which have become associated with it in the modern period. These false ways of thinking are, on the one hand, the naïve, prescientific supernaturalism of orthodoxy and, on the other, the mysticism, rationalism, and idealism of modernist Christianity. Within Protestantism these have been the subversive elements. Outside, there stands Roman Catholic Christianity, with its absolute claims and its subtle capacity for adjusting all religious and cultural values within its own being; and, finally, there is neopaganism, with its ultimate nihilism, as exemplified in national socialism, the incarnation of human evil erupting into full rebellion against God.

To set the gospel free in the face of all these forces and to do it both with loyalty to the Christian revelation and yet as men who know modern science, modern philosophy, and the values of modern culture is the central problem of these two theologians. They see the problem from very nearly the same standpoint. They have come to disagree as to its solution. We shall turn, first, to Brunner's discussion of the relation of faith and reason and then see why Barth rejects Brunner's solution.

* Dr. Daniel Williams, associate professor of Christian theology in the Federated Theological Faculty of the University of Chicago, took the M.A. degree from the University of Chicago and the Ph.D. degree from Columbia University. He is the author of *The Andover Liberals* (1941) and of articles published in various scholarly journals. Dr. Williams was the Rauschenbusch lecturer for 1947 at Colgate-Rochester Divinity School. The present article was presented at a recent meeting of the Theological Colloquium of the Federated Theological Faculty.

[1] Emil Brunner, *Offenbarung und Vernunft: Die Lehre von der christlichen Glaubenserkenntnis* (Zurich: Zwingli Verlag, 1941). References are to the English translation by Olive Wyon: *Revelation and Reason* (Philadelphia: Westminster Press, 1946). A review of this book will appear in a forthcoming issue of the *Journal of Religion.*

I. BRUNNER'S ANALYSIS OF REASON AND PHILOSOPHY

Brunner's writing has a deceptive smoothness and simplicity on the surface. Underneath there is a dialectical restlessness and a continuous subtle movement. I hope also to show that there is a strong undercurrent which runs in a quite different direction from the main tendency. If we are to understand Brunner, it is important to try to enter into the dialectical movement of his thought, which gives life to his formal conclusions.

We need, first, to see how Brunner uses the terms "reason," "philosophy," and "faith." But, before we come to these specific concepts, there is a general consideration of Brunner's way of thinking which must be stated.

Brunner deals with all basic concepts in theology and with all the major movements of religion and culture by the use of a "typological" method. This means that he abstracts from the historical concreteness of human experience certain fundamental structures and certain basic types. Theological analysis for him consists in setting forth these "types" and contrasting them with one another. For example, he states clearly his way of dealing with the history of philosophy:

> All the systems of rational metaphysics that have so far emerged can be classified under a few main types—those of antiquity as well as of the modern period. In the course of time the arguments may have altered, but even here the main types seem to persist. Scientific progress possibly affects some of them in detail, but it is evidently unable essentially to alter the situation, so far as these traditional main types are concerned.[3]

One cannot say explicitly just how Brunner arrives at his typological schematisms, for he does not state his method in this respect. He simply states his principal concepts and works with them, illustrating these "ideal" formulations by reference to their exemplification in particular thinkers or movements. I do not mean to suggest that he deals woodenly with these formal concepts. He often gives a penetrating analysis of important differences within the same general type, as, for example, his discussion of the difference between the idealism of Hegel and that of Schelling; but the main argument is always based upon acceptance of certain ultimate distinctions which underlie his analysis. This method sounds, at first, like that of Hegel, and it is characteristic of the whole tradition of German thought. But there is one important difference in Brunner's use of it from that of Hegel. For Brunner these ideal types tend to be absolute. They do not flow into one another, either logically or historically. For him idealism is a finished type of philosophy, and there is no possibility of any important modification of its traditional formulations. If a system tends toward pantheism, it is hopelessly caught in the identification of God and the world, and it must be rejected completely. The truth of faith is what it is in its own unique character, and it is different in kind from other truth.

To say that Brunner works with these typologies is not to question the usefulness of his method or the adequacy of his treatment of it (questions will be raised later in the paper). But it is important to keep in mind this fundamental pattern of Brunner's way of thinking, since it has significant consequences for the way in which he states the problem of faith in its relation to philosophy.

This statement about method furnishes a necessary introduction to the problem of the meaning of terms like "reason" and "philosophy" in Brunner's

[3] *Revelation and Reason*, p. 343.

usage, for its explains why he never defines these terms. To be sure, he gives many quasi-definitions; but he never says: "Here is exactly the sense in which I mean to use these words." What he does do is to give examples of the work of reason and of the achievements of philosophical thinking and then leave the reader to see the "pure type" standing forth. He gives us illustrations, examples, contrasts, until we are to understand "reason" by seeing what he has to show us about its essential character.

We have, therefore, to make our own definitions when we try to be specific about the meaning of words like "reason" in Brunner's work. And we have a right to our suspicions concerning whether his "pure type" really fits the stubborn facts of the living movement of human experience.

He uses the term "reason" in three general senses. First of all, reason means our human capacity for thought, for speech, for communication. This is the *humanum*, the endowment of intelligence which God gives to man. Brunner quite readily speaks of this reason as a reflection of the divine in man. Without it man could not be responsible, nor could faith have any meaning for him.

Second, "reason" means the activities and the principles of "reasoning" as these are exemplified in logic, science, ethics, and metaphysics. Common sense also belongs here, as human intelligence dealing with the practical problems of living. All this reasoning, as it goes on in human life, grows out of the *humanum*. It is necessary to life, and its use is never to be opposed by Christian faith. Notice, however, that man naturally reasons about ethics, about ontology, about the meaning of life. Here man becomes involved in questions and decisions about ultimate truth and value. Human reason begins to accept and to reject answers in these areas. It can be offended when its basic norms are contradicted. We are led, then, to a third meaning of "reason."

"Reason" in this third sense consists in the attempt of the human mind to discover and express the truth about existence. This reason is philosophy, as Brunner interprets it. It is the effort of man to achieve knowledge of God, or of whatever is ultimate, through the use of his own powers. Brunner does not always use the term "philosophy" when he is thinking of reason in this third sense, sometimes he uses the term "reason" itself; but it is important in reading him to realize that when he is criticizing "reason" adversely it is this third sense of the term which he means for us to have in mind.

Now, from one point of view, Brunner's whole work consists in a polemic against philosophy, this third kind of "reason." Yet, if philosophy, as reason seeking understanding about the meaning of life, is rejected as misguided and inadequate, must he not also reject the whole inquiry after valid principles of reasoning in logic, in ethics, and in metaphysics? Here lies, on the formal philosophical side, Brunner's central problem. His basic thesis is this: There is given to us in the Christian revelation apprehended by faith the one real, saving, unique, and final truth about the meaning of our existence. We come to know this meaning, that is, we come to know God through his revelation given to us, and this is the revelation in Jesus Christ. Unless we receive and believe this revelation, we cannot know God. Hence all philosophy outside that revelation must be shown to be inadequate, else the truth of Christian faith will be compromised by being made subservient to a "philosophical" truth which is really a misunderstanding of God. The theme of the whole attack of Brunner and Barth on philosophy is perfectly summed up, I believe in a saying of Augustine's: "Si comprehendis, non est Deus," the sense of which may be stated thus: "Whatever can be grasped as an object of your comprehension cannot be the true God."[3] It will not do, then, for the Christian thinker simply to ignore philosophy; for the philosophic claim reaches into the sphere concerning which Christian faith has its own word to say. And, by the same token, Christian speech about God is still human speech, making use of the language, the forms, and the principles of intelligent discourse—the same mental equipment with which the philosopher works. There is no way out of the effort of the Christian mind to reach a settlement with the claims of philosophy.

Brunner's evaluation of the claims and limitations of philosophy can be interpreted at two levels. The actual movement of his thought can best be exhibited if we begin at the more superficial of these levels and see how it leads to the more fundamental analysis, in which certain distinctively Christian insights are brought into play. At the first level Brunner simply contrasts the philosophical way of seeking the meaning of existence with the way of faith, and, by setting forth the essential character of the philosophical type of thought, he aims to show its inherent weakness. When we ask, then, for the cause of this weakness of philosophy, we are led to the second and deeper level of his criticism.

At the first level Brunner characterizes philosophy as the search for objective truth. The antithesis between subject and object and the necessity of getting from one to the other is presupposed. Philosophy analyzes experience to abstract from it the basic principles which can be used to exhibit the pattern of relations between our subjective experience and what is actually out there to be known. These principles and structures can then be analyzed and criticized from the standpoint of logical coherence and adequacy to the data. Hence philosophy always has as its object the impersonal, timeless, abstract orders, the analysis of which makes the world intelligible. Brunner uses the terms "abstract" and "impersonal" in connection with his characterizations of philosophy literally hundreds of times in his writing. They resemble the Wagnerian leitmotiv which is heard every time a particular character appears or is even remotely referred to in the drama. "All rational knowledge is impersonal."[4] Philosophical truth has no concern with time.[5] All rational thought is deterministic. "This is the curse of theoretical thought that it kills the future by regarding it as already fixed."[6] In ethics, reason remains outside the sphere of personality, for its concern is with universal, timeless principles, applicable to all men in all times. "Reason is the abstract way of thinking which is concerned with argument, this is its character in so far as it refers to idea, law, value, and norm."[7]

One additional point concerning philosophy as a human activity must be made here. The products of philosophy are the products of human effort, working with the resources of human faculties and moving always within the sphere of human experience. That is, philosophy

[3] Quoted in P. Erich Przywara, *Polarity* (English trans.; London: Oxford University Press, 1935), p. 76.

[4] *Revelation and Reason*, p. 364.

[5] *Ibid.*, p. 369.

[6] *The Divine Imperative* (English trans.; London: Lutterworth Press, 1937), p. 200.

[7] *Man in Revolt* (English trans.; New York. Charles Scribner's Sons, 1939), p. 244.

must always be seen within the circle of immanence prescribed by its own limitations, it cannot transcend itself. "The truth of reason is that which we as rational beings can tell ourselves; the truth of revelation is that which, by its very nature, we could not tell ourselves, which by its very nature is truth that has been communicated, and indeed is transcendent, communicated truth."[8]

A consequence of this analysis of philosophy is that there is always a fundamental isolation of the knower from that which he is trying to know. The most important instance is our isolation from one another as persons:

> It is true of course, that between me and my fellow man as I perceive and experience him, exchanges of various kinds take place. We work together and we speak with one another. He allows me to share in his knowledge; he "has something to say to me," and even very much to say. In the last resort, however, what he has to say to me is something that comes to me from him accidentally. He does not break through the circle of that which I could have told myself. . . . . Nowhere in the sphere of rational knowledge does there emerge truth of such a kind that essentially, of necessity, it could reach me only by way of the "other"—truth which I, in the very nature of the case, could not have found out for myself. . . . . Thus in principle even rational knowledge leaves me isolated.[9]

It becomes clear, then, in a first sense why that which we can comprehend cannot be God. Reason cannot tell us about anything but ourselves, and what it can tell us is abstract, impersonal truth. It can tell us nothing of events, of this concrete historical uniqueness of personal being. It offers us no real bridge between ourselves and other persons, let alone ourselves and God. Brunner here is pushing his typological method to the limit. "Reason," by which we understand here primarily "philosophy," is set forth in its essential character as a way of thinking which inherently possesses radical limitations.[10]

Now set over against this analysis the conception of truth as grasped in the Christian revelation. Here the general becomes the concrete, the universal is supplanted by the unique and particular content of the truth as given in the revelation in Jesus Christ. Nontemporal truth is supplanted by truth in event. The deterministic cycle of history is broken, and history is understood as the realm of freedom. Our isolation is broken through. Our thinking loses its independence, but it gains a new freedom in dependence upon God. Here, then, Brunner has outlined two conceptions of truth, two different ways of apprehending the world. What is limited and fundamentally inadequate in philosophy becomes fulfilled in the truth which the Christian has by faith.

If we ask what it is that we know through revelation which philosophy cannot attain, we come to the second level of Brunner's analysis of reason, for we begin to discover an explanation of this failure of philosophy. In Jesus Christ I come to know for the first time (for reason cannot know it otherwise) what it really means to live in responsible community with God and my neighbor; and my coming into this knowledge is, at the same time, the discovery of what my

[8] *Revelation and Reason*, p. 207.

[9] *Ibid.*, pp. 365–66.

[10] In *The Divine-Human Encounter* (English trans.; Philadelphia: Westminster Press, 1943) Brunner has used this analysis to interpret the significance of the influence of Greek philosophy on Christian thought. He argues that the recasting of the conception of revelation under the sway of the "objective" mode of thought has resulted in the evils of rationalistic orthodoxy, in which doctrine rather than personality is made the content of revelation, and has also led to the identification of Christian faith with non-Christian elements in philosophy, as in liberalism and modernism.

actual estrangement from God and my neighbor has been. I now know myself as a sinner, one who is in rebellion against God with my whole being; and that rebellion has its effect on my reason.

This new discovery, which is yet not my discovery but truth given to me by God in Christ, now leads me to a more profound understanding of what has gone wrong with my reasoning about the meaning of life. This reasoning was, however sincere, a manifestation of self-will, of pride, and of the desire to dominate my world. I want life to be fitted to my formula. I want an objective truth which I can manage. I want to attain God for my own purposes. "Knowing, thinking, possessing something, is thus, first of all, something over which I have disposal; secondly, something that does not essentially change me; and thirdly, something that leaves me solitary."[11] And I deceive myself into believing that I have truly achieved knowledge of God. I identify my system with God's truth. This abstract impersonal idea becomes my idol. Here Brunner sets the whole philosophic enterprise in a new perspective. The philosophic quest is really an exhibition of the spirit of proud, sinful, self-deceived man: "The spirit which thinks creatively leads man astray into self-deification, into a confusion between the spirit of God and the spirit of man."[12]

We are bound to recall, in the face of this strong criticism, that philosophy as an enterprise grows out of and makes use of that natural human reason which Brunner has accepted as a part of the divine endowment of man. Human thought must be rigorous, logical, communicable. Does Brunner mean that all the standards of intelligent human discourse are to be rejected for the sake of the truth of revelation? Has man so lost the image of God that there is left to him nothing whatsoever in his reason which can serve his knowledge of the Creator? Brunner does not accept such a radical outcome. He explicitly reminds us that the theologian reflecting on revelation must speak in grammatical sentences and participate in the appreciations and concepts which are part of the total culture. Were this not so, all distinctions between truth and error, good and bad, in the culture, would be irrelevant to Christianity, and this is a conclusion Brunner believes Christianity cannot accept.[13] No, the image of God does remain in fallen man and in his reason, but how?

Here Brunner gives the key to his understanding of the whole problem. The secret of the abstraction, the impersonality, the inadequacy, of our fallen reason is that sinful man thinks legalistically. When the sinful man tries to understand God and His good, he is, to be sure, reaching toward the true God. We are not wholly without knowledge of our true source. But what we do with this knowledge is to conceive it as a norm, a standard, a law which stands over against our conscience as requirement and as condemnation. If we would understand in its full depth Augustine's "Si comprehendis, non est Deus," we must put the emphasis on the pronoun. That which *thou* canst comprehend, thou sinner, can only be God as law, God as abstract principle, standing over against you. He becomes the God of wrath who drives us to despair, or else we engage in the ultimate self-deception of supposing that we are one with God. This is why we can say with Brunner that as philosophers we do know that we ought to love God and our neighbor; but we cannot know why we should love or what this

[11] *Ibid.*, pp. 87–88.

[12] *Man in Revolt*, pp. 248–49.

[13] *Ibid.*, p. 95.

love truly means.[14] What Brunner has done is to show that the problem of the relation of the law and the gospel is basic to the understanding of the problem of philosophical interpretation of our existence. The very great importance of his analysis on this point cannot be doubted.

II. BRUNNER ON THE PHILOSOPHICAL SYSTEMS

At this point we can briefly summarize Brunner's conclusions concerning what has actually been achieved in the major philosophical systems. He has four main theses concerning the history of philosophy.

First, one of the manifestations of sin in human history, and of the break in the community of human life brought about by sin, is the splitting of thought into contending "schools," which carry on a continuous and unresolved warfare between their claims to truth.[15]

Second, from the Christian standpoint it must be said that certain elements in philosophical idealism bring it nearer to the truth than are materialism, naturalism, and positivism because idealism is able to show that reason points to a transcendent object, though as reason it cannot understand this "object." Philosophy, of course, is full of reasonings about God, "proofs" of his existence, interpretations of his good. Must theology cast all this aside? Brunner will not go so far. There is no true knowledge of God outside the Christian revelation; but there can be a human pointing to God, and this is what the transcendental reference of philosophic ideas can accomplish. Brunner himself uses the term "transcendental" here; but he calls it an "immanent transcendentalism," for that which points the human mind beyond itself is still the human mind. The light of reason "does indeed point back to its origin in God, but in so doing it does not open a way to the knowledge of God."[16]

Third, Brunner sees the tendency toward self-deification in human reason manifested in the systems of pantheistic idealism and deism. Brunner freely uses the term "pantheism" to refer to all systems of the Hegelian type, and he regards the deism of the Enlightenment as caught in the same fundamental error, though the formulation is different. For the famous statement "the intellect is a born atheist" Brunner could substitute another, "the intellect is a born theist," and this is worse, for "theism" as a system always results in the identification of the highest in man with the goodness of God. Since pantheistic idealism is an ever present danger, Brunner accords to positivism a valuable function. "This view has some perception of the truth that man cannot know God by his own efforts, that all rational knowledge of God is to the highest degree hypothetical and uncertain. . . . He [the positivist] has a feeling for the arrogance of all rational metaphysical systems."[17] Theology thus can make a certain use of this warfare of the philosophers. Idealism refutes materialism and points to God. Positivism shows that idealism does not know the God to whom it points and refutes the systems in which God is claimed to be understood.

Fourth, Brunner has a theory of the inevitable decline of philosophic insight

[14] The limitations of moral knowledge outside revelation lie for Brunner in four points: "in the incapacity to determine whence this law comes, in the incapacity to know evil in its depths, in the abstract nature of the demand, and in its impotence to overcome resistance" (*Revelation and Reason*, p. 326).

[15] Brunner's essay in the Oxford Conference volume, *The Christian Understanding of Man* (Chicago: Willett Clark Co., 1938), p. 166.

[16] *Revelation and Reason*, p. 355.

[17] *Ibid.*, p. 357.

when it is cut off from the Christian revelation. I do not know that he has anywhere stated this in detail; but he suggests that there is a progressive loss of all religious belief whenever reason strikes out on its own, apart from revelation. The stages of the decline are first idealism, then humanism, and then nihilism, in which all truth and values disappear.

III. PHILOSOPHY WITHIN THE SPHERE OF FAITH

We have seen what philosophy is or becomes when it is without faith. But suppose the philosopher is a Christian believer. Suppose he has become the new creature through his apprehension in faith of the truth of the personal, loving, forgiving God disclosed to us in Jesus Christ. How is this new life reflected in the reason of the Christian thinker? Can he become a Christian philosopher?

We have already noted that the basic tools of reason, language, logic, and cultural patterns of understanding are reflections of the divine image in us. Further, we have, according to Brunner, discovered a slight positive achievement of the unregenerate mind, the knowledge that man is related to God, and we have some apprehension of the divine law. May it not be possible, then, for the Christian to create a true philosophy because his mind is now open to the real character of our human existence? Perhaps reason can now be used to correct and fulfil what before was misguided and insufficient.

The most important discussions in Brunner of the problem of Christian philosophy are Appendix IV in *Man in Revolt* and chapter xxv of *Revelation and Reason.* The outcome, particularly in this latter chapter, is somewhat surprising. Not only is there Christian philosophy, but there must be such. Consider the areas of ethics, of politics, the theories of scientific concepts, the problems of the categories. Here the Christian thinker stands in the same sphere as that of the secular philosopher. Here theology and Christian philosophy will speak about the same things, "though in different ways." The relation between them should be "fluid." The dialectical restlessness of Brunner's thought now begins to manifest itself: "Every systematic theologian . . . . is philosopher and theologian in the one person."[18] There is a sphere in which the Christian mind must reflect in such a way that it makes use of philosophical methods and concepts. The Christian philosopher has the advantage over all other philosophers, for only the Christian can be the truly critical philosopher who understands the fallen state of human nature.[19]

How can theology and philosophy exist side by side in the same mind? Brunner's answer, in sum, is this: When I think about the revelation of God in Christ testified to in the Bible, I am thinking theologically. When I think as a believer in this revelation about a general human problem, such as that of justice, I become a Christian philosopher. But does this Christian philosophy have norms and principles which contradict those of secular human thought? Here Brunner is extremely careful. He denies that there is a Christian mathematics or a Christian logic. There is, however, a general law of Christian thinking. The further I move toward the periphery of personal experience, into the realms of science, of logic, of the principles of natural knowledge, the less distinctiveness I find in any Christian approach to understanding in these areas. But the closer I move toward the central

[18] *Ibid.*, p. 390. [19] *Ibid.*, p. 393.

problems of the meaning of personal existence, the problems of good and evil and the meaning of life, the more distinctively do the Christian insights take control, until, when I come to the idea of God, secular thinking vanishes altogether, and it is a case of the "complete substitution" of a new idea of God for any secular notion about him.[20] This general principle does not, however, bring the dialectical movement between revelation and general human experience to rest, for we must ask: How is Christian theology different from Christian philosophy? because theology is not revelation. It is thought about revelation. It takes revelation as its object, and as theology it is caught in the same problems of the relation of subject and object, of the application of general principles, as is all philosophy and, indeed, all human thought.

The answer that Brunner gives is clear when we remember that for him one thesis holds: *no reason*, not even Christian reason, can understand God. There is a final break with all human thinking, even the most disciplined Christian thinking, when we try to understand God's forgiveness of the sinner, his gift of himself in Jesus Christ. The true sphere of theology is this innermost circle of our experience, the point where faith is born of the encounter with God. There is no "understanding" this encounter. Brunner says that the decisive break is not between theology and philosophy, it is between both of these, on the one side, and faith, on the other. Theology is not sacred truth. Brunner makes a brilliant application here of the doctrine of the "priesthood of all believers." The theologian has no preferred position as thinker alongside of any other honest seeker after truth. The devil can pass a superior examination in systematic theology.

What theology does is to point to that truth which faith alone can "know," to say in human words whatever can be said about it; but its words are not the Word itself. Faith has its own way of knowing. This position makes it clear why at decisive points where the Christian assertions appear to contradict reason Brunner freely admits the break. The gospel is an offense to any human reason which insists on trying to understand the real nature of human existence. "Si comprehendis, non est Deus" is spoken even to the theologian.

Theology does, of course, use reason in expounding the nature of revelation. Brunner does not analyze this aspect of the relation of faith and reason very fully. He does say that the "tyranny of logic" must be resisted, and he suggests that any theological idea thought through to the limit on a strictly logical basis must lead to "horrible results," and thus he leaves room for a continued dialectic within theology itself.[21] Yet at the same time Brunner insists that the Christian believer is set free to use his reason fully, and he even says: "Faith itself is truly rational thought about God and about life as a whole."[22]

The basis of the dialectical movement of Brunner's thought lies in his conception of the inherent instability of human reason when it is seeking to understand ultimate matters. The believing Christian has received a truth which differs from all other truth. His mind has been transformed and given its ultimate norm by an event which is beyond the grasp of reason. Once this event of revelation has taken place for the believer, he may then reason about all things; but he must always in faith keep in view that reality

[20] *Ibid.*, p. 383.

[21] *Ibid.*, p. 351.

[22] *Ibid.*, p. 429.

which transcends all human understanding, namely, the redemption of the sinner through God's love given in Jesus Christ.

IV. CRITICAL REMARKS ON BRUNNER'S POSITION

A first question to be put to Brunner's polemic against philosophy is: What philosophy does he have in mind in his characterization of it? It is obvious that Brunner thinks primarily of philosophical thought about religion as represented in German philosophy, with the names of Hegel, Kant, and Feuerbach most prominent. Indeed, outside of Feuerbach's naturalism, one gets the impression that all real philosophical development stopped with Kant. *Revelation and Reason* is addressed to the contemporary mind, but Brunner does not find it necessary to deal with any of the philosophical movements of the later nineteenth century. There is nothing of British philosophy outside a reference to A. E. Taylor. There is brief mention of William James. And, most remarkable of all, the whole personalistic movement, the theme of which is so close to Brunner's own argument, is ignored.

Surely, it is important to ask whether, in the achievements of classic Greek philosophy and in the modern developments which have taken account of the knowledge provided by modern science, there are not corrective tendencies through which philosophy itself has overcome some of the errors which Brunner rightly criticizes. In particular, it certainly is true that both the Greeks and modern philosophers have tried to view the world in terms of living processes, to take account of time, and to understand the nature of personal existence. In view of all that Brunner charges philosophy with leaving out, one statement of his seems to offer its own criticism of his position. He says in chapter xxv of *Revelation and Reason* (already noted):

> The thinker must reckon seriously with the fact that the material of thought does not come first from the reason. Even the most strictly philosophical thought is obliged to depend upon experience. This experience includes not only the variety of sense impressions; it also includes the inward variety and multiplicity of the human mind, the moral, artistic, religious experience. Philosophy has not to produce experience or to replace it by its own concepts; but it is its business to set it in order and to present it in its right context.[23]

But this drives us to ask: Would a philosophy which has this relation to human experience be the impersonal, abstract discipline which Brunner says it is? Consider in this connection a very revealing remark which Brunner makes on the relation of values, ideas, and laws in his discussion of ethics. He says that, in their pure meaning, value and idea must be identified with law and not confused with the "aesthetic," that is, the personal element of desire. Then he remarks: "Neither Plato nor Aristotle has made this distinction quite clearly; the confusion exists in the fundamental Greek conception of *kalokagathia*."[24] Now why were the Greeks confused in this notion which fused together the concepts of desire, logical structure, and moral command? That is, why is it confusing to introduce actual living process into the notion of what determines the moral obligation? The answer is clear: the Greeks must be confused because, if they are not, then Brunner's conception of what philosophy is breaks down. My point is not to argue that Greek philosophy did not need to be corrected by the new understanding of personality which Christianity brought. But it is to say that, when philosophy does its humble and

[23] *Ibid.*, p. 392.

[24] *Ibid.*, p. 324 n.

rightful task of seeing human existence as clearly as possible, it does take account of the character of man's experience as a person in history. The correction of the abstractions of the Kantian analysis of experience is not to get rid of philosophy but to develop a better philosophy, one illuminated by Christian insight.

A second comment is that Brunner has a philosophy of his own which furnishes an important part of the structure of his thought. This is the undercurrent which actually moves against the main line of his argument. Brunner introduces a philosophical idea into his theology at the very point where he says it does not belong, namely, in the description of the encounter between God and man.

Formally, of course, he states that this conception of the event of revelation is derived from the Bible. But this biblical account must be set forth and given intelligible expression. The Bible never states a "concept" of revelation. There are, indeed, many notions about revelation in the Bible and many descriptions of events of revelation; but no *definition* of it. Where, then, does Brunner's description of the event of revelation as the encounter of person with person come from? It comes from a general conception of the nature of personal relations which has been given classic expression in Martin Buber's *I and Thou*. Philosophically speaking, Buber's world view is based on a distinction between two kinds of relations, those between persons, defined by "I-Thou," and those between persons and things, defined by "I-it." Buber has analyzed the structure of personal relations and has stated what he sees as its distinguishing features. The most important of these are the freedom of each person, the replacement of all objectivity by interpersonal subjectivity, the absence of the will to control the other, the appreciation of the other's worth as a personal subject.[25]

What Brunner has done is to take this pattern of personal encounter and to use it to interpret the meaning of revelation. The event which is supposed to transcend all philosophical understanding is described by the use of a philosophical structure, drawn from human experience and subject to criticism by the methods of philosophical analysis. It is true that Brunner is aware of the possibility of this criticism. He struggles mightily to avoid identifying this philosophical idea with the actual nature of the event of revelation. He says that relations between human persons are but feeble analogies of the relation between man and God. But the choice which the theologian must make is plain enough. Either we interpret revelation in some relationship to human experience, or else the whole attempt to speak about it intelligibly must be given up. If Brunner's thought were not so great as it is in his effort to do justice to the facts, he might have avoided this outcome, which has a certain irony. But the conclusion must be stated that the theologian who has spent his life in an effort to free Christian theology from entanglement with mysticism and with philosophy has in his own theology developed a perspective which embodies a philosophical mysticism whose classic exponent is a philosopher who does not depend upon the New Testament.

A brief comment must be made about the charge that philosophy is an expression of sinful pride. Admitting the truth of this criticism, one may still ask whether it throws any light on the problem of the relation of philosophy and theology, for even the regenerate Christian is sub-

[25] Martin Buber, *I and Thou* (English trans.; Edinburgh, 1937).

ject to sin, as Brunner continually insists. There is other pride besides pride of reason, and it is necessary to point out that the honest philosophical search for principles and accurate definition can be an expression of humility. I suggest that Brunner's too sharp distinction between legalism and the freedom of the spirit of the gospel has obscured the truth here. As William Ernest Hocking has made abundantly clear, the search of men for principles and laws by which they may understand one another and form stable human communities can be an *expression* of personal worth and not a denial of it. Legalism is an evil; but there can be a nonlegalistic search for the kind of law which will support and release the personal life.[26] Philosophy has its rightful place in that search.

V. BARTH'S CRITICISM OF BRUNNER

The danger which Barth sees in Brunner's concessions to philosophy may be illustrated by a story which Kierkegaard uses to similar purpose in his *Journal*.

> Imagine a fortress, absolutely impregnable, provisioned for an eternity.
>
> Then there comes a new commandant. He conceives that it might be a good idea to build bridges over the moats—so as to be able to attack the besiegers.
>
> *Charmant*. He transforms the fortress into a country estate—and naturally the enemy takes it.
>
> So it is with Christianity. They changed the method—and naturally the world conquered.[27]

Barth believes that, by allowing any claim that the divine image remains in fallen man, Brunner is building the same bridge which has allowed Catholicism and modernism to be, as Barth holds, overwhelmed by secular thought.

One is sometimes tempted to think that Barth's radical denial that there is anything in our human nature which reflects the being of God is an exaggeration, a curiosity. Surely, he cannot mean it. But he certainly does mean it, and the whole development of his theological position depends upon it. Allow human nature to shine ever so slightly with the reflected light of God, and you have prepared the way either for secular culture or for Roman Catholicism to engulf the Christian gospel. Barth believes that Kierkegaard and Brunner, who depends heavily upon Kierkegaard, have done exactly this. He has said that if he accepts Kierkegaard and his Christian existentialism he might as well go over to Rome.[28] In this he is supported, of course, by Roman Catholics, who believe that Kierkegaard was on the road to Rome and that, given the map he was using, he would have arrived there in the end.

We understand, then, why there is little frontal attack on philosophy in the later writings of Barth. He sees that to argue with philosophy as an alternative to Christian faith is in some way to become a philosopher. To some degree one has to stand outside the faith in order to contrast it with other ways of thinking. And this outside standpoint can only be something common to human experience. Brunner has found it in the experience of responsibility; but for Barth this human experience is no clue to our responsibility before God.

What Barth does attack directly is "natural theology," for this kind of philosophic thought has appeared and has

[26] W. E. Hocking, *Man and the State* (New Haven: Yale University Press, 1926), chap. xxii.

[27] Quoted in W. Lowrie, *Kierkegaard* (London: Oxford University Press, 1938), p. 536.

[28] W. Lowrie's Introd. to *Kierkegaard's Attack on Christendom* (Princeton, N.J.: Princeton University Press, 1944), p. xvi. Cf. Lowrie's comment in his translation of Kierkegaard's *Repetition* (Princeton, N.J.: Princeton University Press, 1941), p. 209.

made its claim within the sphere of faith itself. It has had its place in both Catholic and Protestant thought, in both orthodoxy and modernism. And it is here that the issue is explicitly joined with Brunner. Barth's problem is set by the fact that the Scripture certainly speaks of revelation in the creation, in the heavens, in historical events, and in the human conscience. Barth's position is that, while therefore we can say as Christians that God is revealed in the creation, so far as our knowledge of God is concerned there is only one revelation—Jesus Christ. He rejects the whole structure of the *analogia entis* in Catholic theology, that is, the claim to find analogy between the being of God and that of his creatures. Barth calls this principle "the invention of Anti-Christ." Even when the truth of faith is given, Barth does not believe we can "look again" at the world and find God's revelation in it. We believe that he is revealed there, but we cannot experience him there.

Because of the famous discussion between Barth and Brunner over this issue, the pages in *Revelation and Reason* in which Brunner comments on his understanding of Barth and the difference between their theologies are of especial interest.[29]

Brunner agrees with Barth that we cannot know that God is revealed in the creation apart from our knowledge of God through Jesus Christ; but Brunner holds that, given the revelation, we can apprehend God in the creation. Hence he takes a positive attitude toward the *analogia entis*, once the standpoint of faith is presupposed. But the difficulty in which this position involves Brunner is quite clear. He distinguishes between saying that God's being is reflected in the world and that it is reflected in our knowing. But our minds are a part of the being of the world. If there is some positive analogy between God and his creatures, that analogy will be reflected in the human mind itself and in its philosophical quest. Brunner himself says: "What is decisive even for the Christian thinker, is that in the human mind we come upon something that points beyond man to the dimension of God."[30] But can the mind "point" to God without having some real knowledge of him? It is difficult to see that such a distinction can be maintained. Brunner's problem is the same as that which appeared in his distinction between the *imago dei* as form and as content. If the mind points to God, then it has some knowledge of him. And the philosophical task of interpreting this knowledge has its validation. Brunner is closer to the methods of modernism and liberalism than at first appears possible.

If Brunner's thought is pulled irresistibly toward some kind of philosophical theology, Barth's thought is pulled strongly toward a theology which remains in splendid isolation from all efforts at human understanding. The basis of theology is the Bible, and the Bible is God's language, but it is also human language. Hence Barth's heroic solution—the Bible is God's mystery hidden under the form of human language.[31] The possibility of grasping the truth of Christian faith does not lie in us or in anything we possess as men. It lies in God alone. Barth makes the startling assertion that the Holy Spirit is not only the objective possibility of revelation, but it is also the subjective possibility of revelation.[32]

[29] *Revelation and Reason*, pp. 77–80.

[30] *Ibid.*, p. 344.

[31] Karl Barth, *The Doctrine of the Word of God*, I, Part I (English trans.; Edinburgh: T. & T. Clark, 1936), 188.

[32] Barth, *Die Lehre vom Wort Gottes*, Zweiter Halbband (Zollikon: Evangelischen Buchhandlung [illegible]

Thus our knowledge of God is really God knowing himself in us. It is a daring solution. Must we choose between Barth and Brunner?

VI. THE NECESSITY FOR PHILOSOPHICAL THEOLOGY

Apparently, there are three ways in which the Christian mind can relate itself to the cultural forces which surround it—accommodation, defiance, or critical analysis and adjustment. Barth's way is defiance, and one must admit that he gains a certain initial advantage over all his opponents by the sheer violence of his solution. He does not in any way seek to mitigate or explain away the mystery of the gospel. He flies it from the masthead of his ship. He seems to say: "I have nothing to do with philosophy. I do not argue with it, or about it. I tell you what it means to believe as a Christian!"

Can Barth really escape the dialectical process of conversation between theology and philosophy? Surely, he cannot. The theologian is a human being, speaking human language. His thought is full of "scraps" of philosophy (the term is Barth's own). If he thinks about the high mystery of the Trinity, he begins with the familiar notions of one, two, and three. At the end of his marvelous essay on the Trinity in the first part of the *Dogmatics*, Barth pauses to ask himself whether, after all, he has not been speaking in a human way about the mystery of God.[33] There is no escape from the implications of the inevitable answer. Barth's whole system (and all theology with it) is something different from what he says it is. It is an appropriation by human experience of a revelation which enters into direct contact with the structure of our creaturely existence.

[33] *The Doctrine of the Word of God*, p. 397.

Emil Brunner would appear to be right in accepting the necessity for some real point of contact between human nature and God's revelation. But, if our interpretation of the movement of his own thought is valid, this should lead to the admission that there is more of a unity between the tasks of theology and those of philosophy than he has recognized.

If we say that what Christian life and preaching needs today is a theology which brings faith and reason into a mutually complementary and harmonious relation, we do not commit ourselves to saying that any of the historic attempts to unite the two have been altogether adequate or are beyond criticism. The warning which thinkers like Barth and Brunner have given against allowing the distinctive message of the mercy of God to be obscured by secular philosophy is always to be heeded. They have seen with their own eyes what a terrible and destructive idolatry can seize upon the spirit of modern man when he no longer believes in the God of justice and mercy. But the task which must still be done if our culture is to receive the guidance and empowerment which Christian faith can give is to show how all our human experience is illuminated when we see life under the aspect of God's search for man. It must be shown that the honest quest of the human mind for adequate understanding of the problems of life receives its answer and its fulfilment in Jesus Christ. This means that we must continue to seek a theology which will be both Christian and philosophical at the same time. There is warrant for believing that this is possible. God is one, and he is truth. Augustine's "Si comprehendis, non est Deus," must give way to the New Testament's "The *logos* became flesh and dwelt among us."

NIEBUHR AND LIBERALISM

13

EVERY theologian interprets the Christian faith from a standpoint in which his own cultural heritage plays a formative rôle. Reinhold Niebuhr's theology has arisen within American Christianity in its liberal period. But he is our foremost critic of "liberal Christianity." No theme recurs more frequently in his writing than the polemic against "liberal culture" and against the liberal Christianity which he regards as having capitulated to that culture. It is due more to Niebuhr's influence than to that of any other single thinker that liberalism in America has come to a period of radical self-examination. In consequence, for many there now must be a re-establishment of faith on other than liberal foundations.

Niebuhr's evaluation of liberalism is not exclusively negative. He sees modern liberalism as the heir of the discovery of creative possibilities in human nature in the Renaissance, and he has stated the central problem of his theology as an attempt to combine the insights of the Renaissance and the Reformation.[1]

The fundamental problems which Niebuhr sets out to solve are the characteristic problems of liberalism: the discovery of the meaning of the Bible beyond a literalistic orthodoxy, the establishment of the practice of tolerance, the relating of the Gospel to cultural movements and the search for its intelligibility in relation to human experience, the discovery of the theological basis of democracy. Certainly these are the problems which liberal theology has raised and left for the "post-liberal" work of theologians such as Niebuhr. When we examine now Niebuhr's relation to liberalism, we do not hold up "liberal theology" or "the liberal spirit" as the norm by which his thought is to be tested. Christian faith transcends every culture in which it may be expressed. No theology of great stature

[1] *The Nature and Destiny of Man*, II, 207.

like that of Niebuhr's can be forced into the position of dependence upon a single cultural outlook. Still, it remains true that his thought bears a special relationship to liberalism, for his early thought was formed by liberalism, and he has developed his own theology largely by working out his criticism of liberal presuppositions. Therefore, by examining his relationship to liberalism we have one way of getting at the meaning of his theology. Further, an inquiry into Niebuhr's critique of liberalism raises some of the questions which to me, at least, remain unanswered in his own theology.

I propose, then, to ask what Niebuhr means by liberalism and liberal Christianity, to summarize briefly his evaluation of them, and then to ask what light this view of liberalism throws upon the method and content of his theology.

I. NIEBUHR'S METHOD OF INTERPRETING LIBERALISM

When we ask what Niebuhr means by the "liberalism" and "liberal Christianity" he criticizes, we have to take account of his method of characterizing broad cultural movements and theological positions. He views the history of human thought as exhibiting a series of "types" of outlook. He arranges these according to certain key concepts and problems in which he is interested. For example, he distinguishes between "classical" and "modern" cultures according to their views of time, and contrasts both of these with the "Biblical" view of time. Again, he classifies modern philosophies as "vitalistic" or "idealistic" as they find their principle of meaning in nature or in spirit. Thus Niebuhr is not so much concerned to trace nuances of meaning in different philosophies, or to work out the complex lines of historical development. He is rather an apologist and critic who tries to get directly at the basic principles by which various faiths grasp the meaning of life.

This "typological" method seems to me one of the major reasons that Niebuhr's cultural criticism has been so effective. His great genius in using the method permits him to go swiftly to the heart of a vast and complex cultural movement, to lift out the central idea which gives it its drive, and which also betrays in many cases its weakness. Though the method produces a considerable oversimplification, it permits the discovery and concise statement of fundamental issues. Its disadvantage is that it permits Niebuhr to deal with the point of view he is criticizing by using its most exaggerated, and sometimes even its most fatuous, expressions to represent the entire position. It is so important to understand this method as Niebuhr uses it in dealing with liberalism that I illustrate the point by quoting one paragraph in which Niebuhr sums up the kind of liberal Protestant faith which he rejects:

> The mystery of creation is resolved in the evolutionary concept. "Some call it evolution and others call it God." The Bible becomes a library, recording in many books the evolutionary ascent of man to God. Sin becomes the provisional inertia of impulses inherited from Neanderthal man against the wider purposes of mind. Christ is the symbol of history itself, as in Hegel. The relation of the Kingdom of God to the moral perplexities and ambiguities of history is resolved in utopia. The strict distinction between justice and love in Catholic thought is marvelously precise and shrewd compared with the general identification of the *agape* of the New Testament with the "community-building capacities of human sympathy." (Rauschenbusch) This reduction of the ethical meaning of the scandal of the Cross, namely, sacrificial love to the dimensions of simple mutuality imparts an air of sentimentality to all liberal Protestant social and political theories.[2]

Now this paragraph tells us what Niebuhr sees in liberalism, especially its limitations. But what liberalism is he looking at? Hegel cannot be reduced to these dimensions. Neither can Rauschenbusch. Niebuhr himself once refers to Albrecht Ritschl as "the most authoritative exponent of liberal Christianity."[3] But there is not a single statement in the above paragraph which can possibly be said to represent Ritschl's view. He could hardly be thinking of Ritschl here, nor could he be thinking of his own teacher, D. C. Macintosh, whose *Social Religion* he has also characterized as a representative statement of liberal Christianity. His statements would have to be radically qualified if he tried to document them from the thought of his late colleague Eugene W. Lyman or that of Robert Calhoun. He rarely discusses in any detail the thought of Josiah Royce or William Ernest Hocking, both exponents of versions of liberal Christian faith. In short, the "liberal Protestantism" which Niebuhr is getting at is not to be found in this "pure form" in the more adequate expressions of liberal theology. I do not mean that it does not exist. It certainly does exist in naïve simplicity in much popular

[2] "Coherence, Incoherence, and Christian Faith," *Journal of Religion*, Vol. XXXI, No. 3 (July, 1951), p. 162.

[3] *The Nature and Destiny of Man*, I, 178.

Christianity, and in the extreme views of a few theologians. The point is that Niebuhr here gives exaggerated statement to what he regards as the essential tendency and outcome of all liberal faith. He exposes the heart of the issue about moral progress in history which is the central difficulty of liberalism. The danger in the exaggeration is that some of the truth for which liberalism contended may be overlooked. I believe this to be the case in Niebuhr's critique of liberalism. But first we must see what his main theses about it are.

II. WHAT NIEBUHR MEANS BY "LIBERALISM"

Our main concern is with "liberal Christianity," but Niebuhr sees liberal Christianity as having very close connections with liberal culture, so we must examine his characterization of both.

Liberal culture is essentially the spirit and outlook of the middle classes in the modern period. It is a phenomenon of the ascendancy of the bourgeois. The most characteristic idea of the liberal is his faith in historical progress. The values which are usually placed foremost as criteria of progress are individual freedom and the practice of tolerance.[4] John Locke, John Stuart Mill, and John Dewey are among the typical interpreters of the liberal faith in its widest context.

Niebuhr sees liberal Christianity as a phase of this cultural liberalism. He says, "Christian liberalism is spiritually dependent upon bourgeois liberalism and is completely lost when its neat evolutionary process toward an ethical historical goal is suddenly engulphed in social catastrophe."[5] The liberal faith is the child of the age of reason, and Thomas Jefferson is one of its most characteristic prophets.[6]

Behind this characterization of liberalism as a function of class structure is Niebuhr's indebtedness to the Marxist analysis of society. Especially in his *Reflections on the End of an Era* he tends to look at liberal politics and social philosophy with the presuppositions of a modified Marxism. He never accepted the Marxist oversimplification of its picture of society; but he found a large element of truth in it, and he accepted its catastrophic view of history. In the light of this doctrine of historical conflict, he criticized liberal programs which hoped to avoid class conflict through amelioration. At the same time Niebuhr has always regarded dogmatic Marxism

[4] *Reflections on the End of an Era,* p. 88. [5] *Ibid.,* p. 135.
[6] *An Interpretation of Christian Ethics,* p. 170.

as falling into the characteristic errors of liberal culture when it absolutizes the rôle of one class as the bearer of perfect justice and looks forward to a utopia in which all historical injustices and contradictions will be overcome.

Christian liberalism then for Niebuhr is that phase of modern Christianity which has taken over from the Enlightenment a conception of man's goodness and his potentiality for moral improvement, and which has reinterpreted the Gospel according to rational methods, and with a system of values which includes individualism, tolerance, and progressive achievement of a free and just order of society. Wherever we encounter the belief that "all social relations are being brought progressively under the law of Christ," and wherever we see the Christian Gospel expressed as a moral pronouncement which can be made intelligible as a purely rational ethical ideal, there we have encountered the liberal Christian spirit as Niebuhr sees it.[7]

III. THE CRITICISM OF LIBERALISM

"The real basis for all the errors of liberalism is its erroneous estimate of human nature."[8] This is the key point of Niebuhr's attack. Faith in man's reason, in his goodness, and in his power to overcome the limitations of existence has led liberalism to a view of the progressive fulfillment of good in history which simply does not conform to the facts of experience. "There is not a single bit of evidence to prove that good triumphs over evil in this constant development of history," declares Niebuhr.[9]

When we seek the explanation of the naïve optimism of liberalism, we are led by Niebuhr to several important historical insights and judgments. In the first place there is the expansive period of modern economic and political life in which new freedoms were won by the rising classes. Men in the more favored groups at least

[7] *Moral Man and Immoral Society*, p. xxi.

One of Niebuhr's characteristically pungent descriptions of Christian liberalism is the following:

"This 'pure Gospel' which we claim to have rescued from the obscurantists and dogmatists, including St. Paul, is little more than eighteenth-century rationalism and optimism, compounded with a little perfectionism, derived from the sanctificationist illusions of sectarian Christianity" ("Christian Moralism in America," *Radical Religion*, Vol. 5, No. 1, 1940, p. 19).

[8] *Reflections on the End of an Era*, p. 48.

[9] "Ten Years That Shook My World," *Christian Century* (April 26, 1939), p. 544.

were easily persuaded that the possibilities of overcoming threats to man's happiness or success were unlimited. The liberal mind usually went on to trace the evil in human life to specific causes which time or effort could eliminate, such as outworn and unjust institutions, or the remnants of animal nature yet to be sloughed off; or, in the case of the Marxist, all evils were derived from the character of the economic order. Niebuhr sees all this as a naïve judgment on the historical realities, for there is nothing to prevent new sources of evil from emerging.

Even more important than the optimistic social climate is the error in the understanding of the nature of man. The problem of evil in human nature lies precisely in the character of man as a being who in reason and imagination can transcend particular historical circumstance. This higher capacity of man offers no guarantee of victory over evil. It is the source of the profoundest evils in human life. It is in the corruptions of the life of the spirit that sin lies. Man who sees beyond himself becomes anxious about his ultimate being and security. He falls into the sin of identifying some particular interest or vitality with God, or he seeks redemption by trying to establish himself and his partial values more securely than in fact they can be established.

Here Niebuhr's critique of liberalism reaches its prophetic height. He sees the liberal spirit in both its secular and its Christian forms as essentially a sentimental obscuring of the truth. But behind that sentimentality there lies that which the Christian Gospel enables us to expose: man's sin of thinking of himself as possessing disinterested good will and as able to solve his problems, perhaps with the help of God, but with progressive expansion of human powers. Thus man denies his dependence on the mercy of God who transcends all historical processes, and whose work of redemption must be fulfilled at the end of history or "beyond history." Liberal optimism has the sin of pride in it.[10]

In refuting specific liberal claims Niebuhr points out how ambiguous are the instruments and powers in which men have put their faith. Scientific knowledge does not give man control over himself. It can become the means of inhuman exploitation and the imposition of tyrannical power. The development of high civilization does not remove the threat of fanatical tribal idolatry. Consider the emergence of the Nazis in Germany. The development of demo-

[10] *Faith and History*, p. 85.

cratic processes of persuasion is extremely valuable; but it may lead men to feel that they are free from the temptations and brutalities of conflict when actually they have only covered them up. One reason modern men have felt more "humane" is that they have transferred their vices to larger and larger groups.[11] Beneath the façade of peaceable economic relations there lies a struggle for power which may erupt into overt conflict.

Neither secular nor Christian liberalism has really understood man because of their failure to see the full dimension of his being. Niebuhr sees man as rooted in nature, subject to the power and vicissitudes of finite existence. Man's mind enables him to transcend time to a limited degree, and it permits him to organize his experience into wider and wider circles of coherence. Yet mind is not the full height of man. Man transcends *himself;* this is spirit. He is aware of a mystery beyond all rationally determinable coherence. He can imagine possibilities beyond the given order of things. The self then is a three-dimensional reality. Niebuhr turns this analysis against liberal faith in reason. It is just because man lives both in the depths of nature and on the heights of spirit that his deepest anxieties arise. The corruption of the self affects the whole man. He falls into the sins of pride or sensuality precisely to escape the threats which his peculiar situation involves. Liberals generally have assumed that mind can lift man beyond the frustrations of nature, and seize control of history. But they forget that mind itself is limited in its reach, and is subject to the corruptions of fear and pride.

Niebuhr's interpretation of the liberal confidence in reason is so fundamental for understanding both his criticism of liberalism and his own theological method that we need to examine an additional aspect of it here. One of the themes which runs through his work is that liberal culture has not understood the organic unities of life because reason does not offer an adequate grasp of organic processes. He makes this point in connection with his analysis of individualism in liberal culture. "The organic character of the individual's relation to society can be comprehended and illumined by an adequate mythology, but hardly by rationalism, for reason mechanizes human relations."[12] The rationalistic approach leaves the in-

[11] I heard Dr. Niebuhr make this point in a lecture. I do not know whether he has written it.

[12] *Reflections on the End of an Era,* p. 93.

dividual rootless. He is bound to his neighbor only by mechanically defined contracts which envisage no deeper participation in concrete community. Reason in ethics reduces all moral issues to a matter of calculated prudence. This is what Niebuhr means by the failure of "mutuality" as an ethical ideal. In "mutuality" the ethical goal leads to the satisfaction of the other's interests only so long as mine are taken care of. Liberalism therefore misses the meaning of sacrificial love in the Gospel. It reduces the Cross to a "success story." It cannot understand the radical giving of the self beyond any visible or historical reward.[13]

Niebuhr's judgment on rationalism in ethics has therefore an intimate connection with his insistence that our interpretation of the Christian faith must keep a tension between faith and reason in which the ultimate mysteries of faith are expressed in mythical symbols, for only in myths of creation and redemption has Christian faith been able to express its truth and yet preserve the realm of mystery and the appreciation of organic realities within and beyond the coherences and processes of nature.[14]

Liberal theory has led to one very nearly fatal consequence in Western civilization, as Niebuhr sees it. Those who rely on rational persuasion have weakened themselves before the attacks of the forces which would destroy the free society. He charges liberals with failing to realize the significance of Hitler's movement, because there was nothing in the liberal view of history which comprehended the possibility of a Hitler.

This point about liberal reliance on persuasion is of course directly related to Niebuhr's rejection of his early commitment to pacifism. He has come to analyze the problem of power in history in terms which lead to a complete rejection of the pacifist ethic as a sufficient strategy for dealing with social problems. In *Moral Man and Immoral Society* he argued that the refusal of exploited classes to use coercive means betrayed society into the hands of oligarchs. Bourgeois liberalism contributed to the betrayal by putting too great reliance on the power of rational ideals to cure social injustice. The error of Christian liberalism here was doubly serious, for it "appropriates the prestige of the religiously inspired absolute ethic of Jesus for the ideals of prudence which have developed in a com-

[13] *Moral Man and Immoral Society*, p. 263.

[14] "The Truth in Myths" in *The Nature of Religious Experience* (New York: Harper and Brothers, 1937).

mercial civilization." Niebuhr is here thinking of the way in which the claim of absolute disinterestedness may cloak private interest and satisfy the privileged by reducing Christian ethics to a "prudent and utilitarian altruism."[15]

Much of Niebuhr's polemic against the social policy of Christian liberalism is directed at Christian pacifism. He recognizes, of course, that not all Christian liberalism has taken the pacifist position; hence I shall not dwell here on his arguments against pacifism. It is probably true that some of the extreme things Niebuhr says against liberalism in ethics are colored by the fact that he is thinking primarily of liberal pacifism. He does believe that no Christian liberalism has really resolved its dilemma between reliance on the persuasive power of ideals and the necessities of coercion in securing justice. Christian liberalism has not known how to relate its view of the ethic of Jesus as a program for direct social action to the necessities of social existence. Hence it makes pragmatic concessions to the use of violence, or tries futilely to justify strategies of non-violence on practical grounds. Niebuhr believes that the liberal position actually came to bankruptcy in dealing with the ethical problem.[16] It has simply not understood the full dimensions of the Christian's ethical situation as he stands between the absolute ethic of Jesus and the requirements of social strategy in a sinful world.

In sum, Niebuhr sees all liberalism as lacking in depth of understanding of who man is and what his problems are. "The liberal soul," he says, "is pedestrian and uninspired. Its moral philosophy is always utilitarian and practical. It avoids the fanaticism and passion of the servants of the absolute and goes about its business to tame life and bring larger and larger areas of human society into its circles of humane good will and prudent reciprocity."[17]

IV. THE WORTH OF LIBERALISM

Niebuhr argues against liberalism from a broad base of rational and ethical criticism, as well as from strictly Christian premises. He does not affirm a simple Christian orthodoxy or an exclusively Biblical norm against liberalism. He argues from within a framework which is largely dominated by the liberal problems, including the relation of reason to revelation and the relation of the Gospel to

[15] *Reflections on the End of an Era*, pp. 268–269.
[16] *An Interpretation of Christian Ethics*, p. 179.
[17] *Reflections on the End of an Era*, p. 261.

social ethics. He sees positive values in the liberal outlook, and his own method is dependent on the liberal achievements.

There are values in the liberal spirit of tolerance. Reason has its rights and its constructive function. Niebuhr says, "The extension of rational justice and the encouragement of a tolerant attitude toward life is the very essence of liberalism."[18] Coupled with tolerance is liberalism's outstanding achievement of the "discovery and affirmation of the rights of the individual."[19] Reason has played a part in the discovery of the worth of the individual and is necessary to the achievement of tolerable justice in human relations. The very reliance on reason does tend to achieve something of a balance of power.[20] The liberal spirit in morals is of most value in working out pragmatic adjustments within a fairly stable situation. It does not know so well how to cope with major upheavals and conflicts.

Christian liberalism rightfully used scientific reason to destroy crude supernaturalism in the understanding of nature. Science discloses a realm of law in the processes of nature, and theology must respect this aspect of the truth in its doctrine of God's action. Liberalism applied the scientific historical method to the records of Christian origins. This was necessary as a criticism of pre-scientific supernaturalism, and it had important ethical results. It saved the Christian mind from the error of making an inflexible and infallible law out of the historically conditioned precepts in the Biblical record. Thus liberalism recognized the law of love as the final norm for Christian ethics; and it made possible in principle the criticism of every historical dogma and ethical system.[21] Niebuhr's own critical method in theology which allows him to reject the absolutizing of any single theological doctrine is certainly in the liberal spirit, even though his ultimate presuppositions about Christian knowledge look for truth beyond the realm of rational intelligibility.

Most important of all in Niebuhr's positive appreciation of liberalism is his assertion that liberalism was right in declaring the relevance of Christian love to social issues even though it understood this relationship far too simply. He acknowledges a "prophetic element in the passion for justice in eighteenth and nineteenth century moralism."[22] Niebuhr is never more blunt than he becomes

[18] *Ibid.*, p. 252.
[19] *Ibid.*, p. 88.
[20] *Moral Man and Immoral Society*, p. 237.
[21] "Ten Years That Shook My World," *loc. cit.*
[22] Title essay in *Christian Faith and the Common Life* (Chicago: Willett Clark & Colby, 1938), p. 91.

when he criticizes theological ethics which try to keep the realm of law and social order sharply separated from the imperatives of the Gospel. He once wrote against a view which upheld such a separation: "Any judge who seeks the aid of psychiatric specialists to understand the causes of the criminal's wrong doing and thus to mete out punishment with an eye to his reformation is closer to the Kingdom of God than this theological pessimism."[23]

This positive appreciation of the worth of relative moral gains in social action enters directly into Niebuhr's conception of the authority of the Biblical revelation. The issue is whether Christian ethics is to be allowed to derive some supplemental insight from cultural standards. Niebuhr believes that Christianity must recognize such insight and allow it to supplement the ultimate standards derived from the Biblical faith. One of the essays which reveals most vividly Niebuhr's appreciation of cultural values comes in his discussion with Karl Barth about the authority of the Bible. Niebuhr argues that the exclusively Biblical approach to every moral issue which he finds in Barth prohibits any attempt even to discuss Christian ethics with non-Christians. It leads to a "torturing" of Biblical texts to prove that certain newly discovered values, democratic ideals for example, were there in the Bible all the time. Niebuhr declares that it was modern secular culture which first granted women full recognition as persons. "There are certain insights about the political order which come to us in the same way from modern secularism, despite its libertarian or equalitarian tendencies."[24] He concludes that the Christian's appropriation of the mind of Christ requires a continual analysis of values discovered in human experience. In the end all cultural insights and ethical systems raise problems which cannot be solved apart from the standpoint of faith in God's sovereignty over history which is revealed finally in the Cross. Once this truth of faith is apprehended, we may be brought to a fuller coherence in our understanding of life, though it is the kind of coherence which acknowledges ultimate mystery beyond any definable structure of intelligibility.[25] Niebuhr is further agreeing with one point for which Christian liberals have contended when he acknowledges that a "hidden Christ operates in history," so that some men come to the truth He reveals outside Christian culture.[26]

[23] *Ibid.*, p. 89.

[24] Reinhold Niebuhr, "An Answer to Karl Barth," *Christian Century*, Vol. 56, No. 8 (Feb. 23, 1949), p. 236.

[25] *Faith and History*, p. 165.

[26] *The Nature and Destiny of Man*, II, 109n.

Yet in spite of its elements of permanent validity, liberal culture, both in its secular and Christian expressions, remains in Niebuhr's eyes inadequate to preserve the very values it cherishes. The preservation and renewal of what is good in civilization depend upon its establishment on the foundation of the Christian faith which apprehends the true depth of man's problems and the source of his ultimate redemption.

V. THE CENTRAL THEOLOGICAL ISSUE

It is necessary to confine my critical questions to the problem of the liberal theology itself rather than to try to deal with the whole of Niebuhr's critique of liberal culture. It must surely be allowed that Niebuhr has raised the crucial difficulty in the liberal theology, that is, the question of whether the course of history exhibits any such progressive movement toward redemption as the liberal theologians held. He has shown that the "long run of history" is a false asylum for refuge from the realities of historical evil. He believes that the meaning of redemption in Christian faith must be expressed in symbols which point beyond history to a fulfillment which is disclosed and promised by the revelation in Christ but which lies in a realm that transcends the ambiguities of temporal human existence.

Since Niebuhr holds that an interpretation of redemption as progressive fulfillment of the Kingdom of God in history cannot be sustained, has he put in its place a more adequate expression of the Christian faith that redemption is accomplished through the goodness and power of God revealed in Jesus Christ? It is in relation to this question that I wish to make my critical remarks. Liberal theologians were trying to formulate and protect the truth that God does achieve his redemptive purpose in the concrete transactions of his dealing with his creatures. Niebuhr has shown that this faith was formulated too simply and superficially in the liberal period. But it is worth asking whether in his tendency to look mainly at the more exaggerated expressions of liberal optimism he may not have overlooked the significance of the preservation of this central Christian theme, that God does transform human life. It is Niebuhr's own doctrine of the actuality of redemption which remains less clear and convincing than it might be.

I restrict my comments to three points: (*a*) Niebuhr's conception of the meaning of history; (*b*) his view of God's action in history, and especially of the significance of God's suffering; and (*c*) his conception of the ethical decisions which Christians must make in this kind of history.

VI. THE RELATION OF MEANING TO HISTORY

No term appears more frequently in Niebuhr's writing than "meaning." What Niebuhr seeks in the Biblical revelation is its "meaning," that is, the truth which cannot be literally defined in a text, but which constitutes the revelation which comes through Christ. In that revelation, he says, the "meaning of man's historic existence is fulfilled."[27] Again, he views history since Christ as "an interim between the disclosure and the fulfillment of its meaning."[28] Obviously this is a key term; but I know of no place where Niebuhr isolates it for analysis. What is the "meaning of meaning" for Niebuhr?

The term seems to be used in two ways. Often it refers to any realm of coherence or order. It can designate ethical principles as relevant to moral behavior, or it may refer to scientific theories. Any system of principles or any orderly relationship has "meaning."

But there is another and more fundamental usage. Meaning signifies the victory of good over evil. Further, meaning usually refers to the completion of this victory. This completion involves both God's judgment upon history and his mercy overcoming its evil; but both of these constitute the complete victory over evil.

There is no single text which clinches this interpretation, but a careful reading of the Gifford Lectures and *Faith and History* seems to support it. History has a "true meaning" which is contradicted in part by actual history, but which nevertheless is the reality which "bears history."[29] The Christian revelation in all its aspects "points to the impossibility of man fulfilling the true meaning of his life."[30]

Niebuhr has a Calvinistic doctrine of meaning. God's sovereignty asserted in complete victory over evil is the very meaning of meaning itself. My comment here is that this gives a clue as to where Niebuhr's real divergence with liberal theologies of history comes.

[27] *Faith and History*, p. 139.

[28] *The Nature and Destiny of Man*, II, 13. Cf. his statement in the same book that if the idea of progress were to be rejected, "the whole liberal structure of meaning would collapse" (p. 240).

[29] *The Nature and Destiny of Man*, II, 51, 61. On p. 61 Niebuhr seems to equate "eternal meaning" with eternal purpose and power.

[30] *Ibid.*, p. 98. Cf. p. 67: "History is meaningful but its meaning is threatened by meaninglessness."

He finds meaning ultimately only in complete victory over evil. Therefore history depends upon something "beyond history" for its meaning; because there is no complete victory in history. Profound liberalism always regards the struggle with evil as meaningful in itself. Some liberalism, it is true, found meaning in history only by believing in a complete victory over evil in time, the building of the Kingdom of God on earth. But the more realistic element in the liberal spirit was not so concerned about complete triumph. Can we not believe in an actual redemptive working of God in history without falling into the utopianism which Niebuhr rightly exposes and rejects?[31]

VII. HOW DOES GOD REDEEM MAN?

The central theological issue is the account to be given of God's redemption wrought in Jesus Christ. Niebuhr's position I take to be this: God has disclosed both his wisdom and power in Jesus Christ; but this very disclosure required Jesus' disavowal of historical power in order that he could express the disinterestedness of the divine love. What his life and death shows is that God suffers and takes up into himself the sin of man. In the light of this revelation men can be brought to repentance. By discovering that God suffers for them they have discovered the reality of his forgiveness. But they have also been freed from the false notion that the meaning of history can be fulfilled in history. They come to hope for and expect a completion of life "beyond history." This hope enables them to live in history a life of serenity and creativity.

Now what I should like clarified is the relation of God's action in Christ to this beginning of redemption in history. It is the question of Niebuhr's view of the relation of time to eternity. Put in another way, it is the question of whether *God has a history,* so that He fulfills the meaning of life in a real history of redemption. Or is the ultimate "meaning" of life something beyond concrete action and events?

Sometimes Dr. Niebuhr seems to argue in a way which separates God's mode of being sharply from the actualities of existence. He seems to think in a Kantian framework in which God is a reality behind the phenomena. Here it makes sense to talk of something "beyond history," for this means beyond time and space and beyond

[31] Royce, Whitehead, Dewey, Ritschl, Wieman are examples of liberals who could not be said to hold the simple utopianism which Niebuhr criticizes.

the whole phenomenal order. Redemption in history therefore means that in Christ we know a symbol or pointer which permits us to anticipate a fulfillment beyond all events. History continues on its own tragic and ambiguous way forever; but its meaning lies in another realm of being.

But there is much in Niebuhr's writing which does not seem to be in harmony with this Kantian metaphysic. Take these sentences from *Faith and History:*

> The climax of the crucifixion and resurrection thus becomes not merely the culmination of the whole series of revelations but the pattern of all subsequent confrontations between God and man. They must contain the crucifixion of self-abandonment and the resurrection of self-recovery. Men must die to sin with Christ and arise with him to newness of life.[32]

This surely is the language of concrete events. It speaks of the new life of the Christian as something begun here and now through God's present working. And it seems to say that this confrontation of God with the sinner is a real event for God also.

Another passage is relevant here. Niebuhr speaks in *Faith and History* of the "transfiguration" of nature and history. What is this transfiguration? Is it an event? Is it something that God actually accomplishes in history? In Christ, Niebuhr seems to say, this transfiguration has begun. But if that is so, then the Christian lives not merely in an interim before the fulfillment of history's meaning, but he already participates in a new history which has begun with the transfiguration of the old.

In his discussion of the resurrection Niebuhr again comes close to this view when he places the resurrection "in a different order of history than the story of the crucifixion."[33] But surely this "different order" is still a history, and not "beyond history." And again we cannot overlook such a striking affirmation as this: "The goodness of Christ must be embodied in the stuff of history."[34]

We cannot claim, and Dr. Niebuhr has made us see this clearly, that this transfiguration which God accomplishes removes all evil from life. History is full of unresolved issues of injustices and broken projects. But if this second interpretation be correct, then redemption is something in history and not beyond it. The problem is to understand the relation between two aspects of our actual history: the ongoing of human events with all their mixture of good and evil,

[32] P. 149. [33] *Faith and History*, p. 147. [34] *Ibid.*, p. 213.

and the history of God's redemptive activity culminating in Christ and continuing in His Church. It seems to me this is the way the Bible views the matter. The Bible sees these two histories as finally one; for there is one God and one creation, and real history is simply the story of God's dealing with his creation.

A closely related theme in Niebuhr's theology of redemption concerns the meaning of the suffering of God. He says that the Christian answer to the problem of life is that "a suffering divine love is the final coherence of life."[35]

Surely, however, a suffering love is not "beyond history." Love suffers precisely because it is engaged in this kind of world. When Niebuhr says that redemption consists in the agony of existence being "taken up into the divine life," then he is hardly saying something different from what liberal theology declared when it found the meaning of life in the history of the actual dealings of God with men. The doctrine that God deals with sin and evil in part by suffering their consequences in love does not lead to a simple utopianism. Indeed, it excludes utopianism. The meaning of life lies in participation in the whole drama of God's working and in dependence on the sustaining reality of his forgiveness. It is true that this leaves many questions unanswered about future events, about the meaning of life in God beyond death, and about the last things. But whatever good we hope for in this realm beyond our sight, it is not something outside the history of God's redemptive working but an actual fulfillment within that history.

My question to Dr. Niebuhr, then, is, How does he conceive the relation between what he refers to as "beyond history" and God's suffering and redemptive working in history? If he asserts God's actual transforming power in history, then it seems to me that his view comes close to what a realistic liberal theology of history would be. But if Niebuhr holds that we must think of a "three-storied" system of meaning, in which the realms of nature, history, and beyond history are somehow ultimately separate, then I have to say I do not believe that this is the way the Bible regards God's relationship to time and His creation, or that an adequate Christian interpretation of God's saving work in Christ can be put in this way. It seems to me to be an imposition of a Kantian epistemology and a Greek metaphysics on the Bible's dynamic conception of time as the form of the concrete encounter between God and man.

[35] "Coherence, Incoherence, and Christian Faith," *loc. cit.*, p. 159.

VIII. MUTUAL AND SACRIFICIAL LOVE

The question about Niebuhr's critique of liberal ethics with its definition of love as mutuality can be put more briefly, because it is closely bound up with the distinction we have been examining between what is in history and what is beyond history.

It is not valid, Niebuhr holds, to regard the love which is revealed in Christ as a simple possibility for human action. It requires a heedlessness of self-interest which sinful man in his anxiety and sin is not able to achieve. But more than this: it is not possible on the grounds of purely historical observation and experience to justify complete self-giving, for history does not prove that such sacrificial love ever receives an adequate response, or that it leads directly to the fulfillment of good. Niebuhr therefore holds that we must distinguish mutual love which seeks a community in which each is fulfilled through what he gives and receives, from sacrificial love which transcends all requirements of reciprocity. It gives itself up for the other. Since mutual love can be shown by rational historical analysis to be the highest ethical possibility which can be explicitly justified on the basis of reason and experience, and since sacrificial love transcends all such rational justification, we can see that Niebuhr's distinction between history and what is beyond history has its ethical relevance. Although sacrificial love cannot maintain itself in history, it is yet essential to bring the ultimate judgment of the spirit upon all human ethics. Once sacrificial love is understood by faith, it has power to qualify, purify, and renew man's ethical life, which always tends to bog down in calculated systems of mutual harmony.

I have the same difficulties with this distinction between two kinds of love that I do with the distinction between history and what is beyond history. It seems to me to leave the Christian with two kinds of obligations, one to honor the good in the world, even his own good, the other to obey the spirit of sacrificial love which cannot take account of his own good. This leaves the Christian caught between two worlds which have two differing ultimate norms, and therefore distraught and divided in all ethical decision.

The issue here is what it is that love rightly intends and seeks. Is it a good which lies beyond history and therefore beyond any envisaged fulfillment of the person who loves? Or is it a real community of good in which all life, including my own, is intended to share? There is a Christian ethical tradition from St. Augustine to present-day liberal theories of mutuality which says that love is one because its object is one. What love seeks is the full community of each with all. It may be remarked here that profound liberal ethical theories never defined mutuality as a simple calculation of mutual reward. Such systems as Wieman's have held that the new community of life which love seeks requires the transformation and the continual sacrifice of the present good to which the self clings.

Now Dr. Niebuhr always affirms that Christianity does not require the annihilation of the self or its interests. "It is . . . not the highest perfection for man to achieve a unity of his being from which all natural and historical vitalities have been subtracted. The highest unity is a harmony-love in which the self relates itself in its freedom to other selves in their freedom under the will of God."[36] But he believes that while the ultimate goal of the spirit of love is fulfillment for the self, this cannot be the *intended* goal; because as soon as we intend our own good we have lost the freedom from self-interest which can enable us to enter into the fulfilled community. Thus he wishes to leave the paradox of losing one's life and saving it a real paradox which defies strict rationality, but which describes the reality of the human situation.

My difficulties come at the point where we try to pass from this paradox as Niebuhr interprets it to our making concrete decisions in history. Shall one honor the demand of sacrificial love and become an ethical absolutist, recognizing that the proximate problems of society cannot be directly solved in this way? Or shall one be guided by the demands of mutual love and justice, which may include justice even for oneself? How can this be decided? How is *agape* as the ultimate norm related to a sense of responsibility for the proximate problems of human life and history?

Surely if relative justice and systems of mutuality are good, and if the self is not to seek its own annihilation, then *for the sake of love* we must undertake to construct communities of good in history in which we can share. Cannot the labor leader who fights for justice for his own union have a Christian vocation to do so? Surely it is not only the ethical absolutists who have a vocation to express the love we know in Christ. But if this be the case, then there cannot be an absolute distinction between sacrificial love and mutual love. Christian love must involve the seeking of community of life, and in the end must be one love which embraces all possible good.

[36] *The Nature and Destiny of Man,* II, 94–95.

Certainly there are levels of community, and no historical community adequately expresses love. Perhaps it is almost impossible for any human life fully to express the full meaning of love. But the love revealed in Christ does lead us to seek a fulfillment of all life in the relationship which God intends. There is no way to that fulfillment apart from a continual self-giving. But it is giving for the sake of the Kingdom of God which includes all good.

In any case, if my question is a legitimate one, perhaps Dr. Niebuhr would restate his conception of the way in which we move from the distinction between mutual and sacrificial love to concrete and responsible Christian decisions in history.

IX. CONCLUSION

There are, I have argued, two insights in the liberal tradition which must be brought within an adequate Christian theology. One is that God's dealing with man is a matter of concrete events, of processes of personal confrontation and renewal. The other is that Christian love has its unity in the truth that God intends a community of all life, and that this love is the basis for the vocation of the Christian in the midst of the ethical struggles and dilemmas of history. I am not quite sure whether to interpret Dr. Niebuhr more in the light of the Kantian and Platonic strains of his thought in which he distinguishes between history and a realm beyond it, or whether to emphasize those tendencies which seem to be closely akin to the most realistic liberalism when it has asserted God's present redemptive action in history.

I close with a personal confession. Whenever the case is argued for a more positive view of redemption in history, Dr. Niebuhr's theology comes to trouble and disturb. For he has shown how every theology which has tried to affirm unambiguously a conception of God's redemptive action in history has ended by sanctifying some partial cultural or religious perspective. He has uncovered the pervasiveness of sin and the persistence of self-centeredness in the Christian life. He makes us wonder whether the paradoxes and radical distinctions which he holds between what is possible in history and what is possible only beyond it may not be necessary warnings against this inevitable tendency to allow the hope of redemption to hide the depth of human corruptibility.

In any case we can be grateful that one of the most discerning of all interpreters of the Christian faith has brought a whole generation to see more clearly the full dimensions of sin and reconciliation. We can be grateful also that liberal Christianity helped to provide the freedom and the critical methods by which its own most trenchant critic has sought to establish the values achieved by liberalism upon firmer Christian ground.

DANIEL D. WILLIAMS

FEDERATED THEOLOGICAL FACULTY
UNIVERSITY OF CHICAGO
CHICAGO, ILLINOIS

Tillich's Doctrine of God* 14

I

It is the purpose of this paper to raise certain questions about the meaning of Dr. Tillich's doctrine of God. Such questions should be preceded by a full exposition of that doctrine as the questioner understands it, an exposition which would draw together all the available texts. For limitations of time in this paper I am foregoing such an exposition and proceeding directly to certain issues. Such a method may lead to the overlooking of aspects of his doctrine which are treated at many points in the system. On the other hand, this may have the value of leading directly to some pertinent issues. In any case, the raising of the questions may uncover some discrepancies between what this writer has understood Dr. Tillich's meaning to be and his actual intention.

Since my major questions have to do with the relation of the ontological aspect of the doctrine of God to the Christian faith, I should state at the outset that these questions are raised from a standpoint in which Dr. Tillich's method of correlating philosophical-ontological questions and theological answers is fully accepted. Since I do not believe that there can be any Christian faith without implicit or explicit ontological elements, I have no interest in trying to show that the tensions in Dr. Tillich's thought could be avoided if he would renounce the ontological quest. Further, since I do not believe that the Christian revelation would be meaningful unless man has in his created structure a prior knowledge of God to which specific historical revelation can be addressed, I have no interest in trying to show that Dr. Tillich has confused the task of Christian theology by appealing to a knowledge of God which is prepared for outside the Christian revelation.

My questions have to do with the specific ontology which Dr. Tillich proposes, with the grounds upon which he appears to rest his case for this ontology, and with the relation of that ontological doctrine to the meaning of the Christian revelation with its center in the New Testament picture of Jesus as the Christ.

The general thesis I shall defend is the following: Dr. Tillich has sought to interpret the Christian faith in relation to

---

* This paper was presented originally at a meeting of the American Theological Society.

one ontological tradition which is essentially that of the neo-Platonic vision of the mystical quest for unity with God. This rich and powerful tradition has had its logic, its epistemology, and its ontological structure prepared and interpreted through a long line from Parmenides, through Plotinus, down to Boehme and Schelling. Being appears as the abyss of all finitude. It is the One in which all differentiation and all categories disappear. All the polarities are transcended, but in such a way that their union cannot be understood from the side of existence. There is a process in the divine life; but it is the process, in earlier thought, of the continual emanation of particular existence from being. Later it becomes the creative process in which non-being gives rise to God's freedom to create, and finitude thus mixed with non-being becomes the estranged and threatened existence we experience in our human life. One can trace from Eckhardt through Boehme and Schelling to Tillich a continuing and increasing assertion of the dynamic element of non-being in the divine life and the radical freedom both for God and man it provides. At the same time, it is significant that Tillich finally classifies Schelling among the dualists because of the latter's solution of this problem.[1] For Tillich there is a process in the divine life, the process in which being overcomes non-being; but it is not possible in any sense to speak of this as a temporal process, for time as a category of existence disappears in the divine life.

My first attempt, therefore, is to identify the ontological tradition in which Tillich stands. My second assertion is that Tillich interprets the meaning of revelation and specifically the final revelation in Jesus Christ in terms which are consonant with this ontology. Revelation becomes the manifestation of being. The final revelation is the manifestation of being itself in a human life, under the conditions of finite existence, yet in such a way as not to destroy his finitude and its conditions.

I raise three questions about this program:

First, there are difficulties which appear within the ontological structure itself, difficulties which do not seem to yield a clear answer in Tillich's terms.

Second, this position of religious experience remains somewhat ambiguous in Tillich's doctrine of our knowledge of God, since there appears to be a religious experience which is appealed to to confirm the ontological analysis even though experi-

---

[1] Paul Tillich, *Systematic Theology*, Volume I (Chicago: The University of Chicago Press, 1951), p. 232.

ence itself is not supposed to yield knowledge of God, but to be only the medium of revelation. It is the relation of this ultimate experience to the structures of its interpretation, both ontological and theological, which I wish to discuss.

Finally, there is the question of the meaning of the Christological assertions in the Christian faith, and their bearing upon the doctrine of God. I wish to ask whether another ontological structure may not be more adequate to interpret the meaning of being as disclosed in the New Testament picture of the Christ.

II

God as being itself is not bare identity or lifeless structure, Tillich says:

> If we call God "the living God" we deny that he is a pure identity of being as being; and we also deny that there is a definite separation of being from being in him. We assert that he is the eternal process in which separation is posited and is overcome by reunion.[2]

In one passage Tillich seems even to allow for some meaning of time in the divine life itself, "for time is the form of finitude in the creative ground of the divine life as well as in creaturely existence."[3]

But we must take this to mean that being itself includes time as a structure of the total process of creation. It does not mean that time can be asserted of the divine life itself. Tillich's statements on this point are unequivocal:

> There is no difference in the divine life between potentiality and actuality. . . . The creative process of the divine life precedes the differentiation between essences and existents. In the creative vision of God the individual is present as a whole in his essential being and inner *telos*, and, at the same time, in the infinity of the special moments of his life-process. Of course this is said symbolically, since we are unable to have a perception or even an imagination of that which belongs to the divine life.[4]

---

[2] *Ibid.*, p. 242.

[3] *Ibid.*, p. 257.

[4] *Ibid.*, pp. 254-255. Cf. pp. 280, 281.

While we must not forget the "symbolic" character of ontological assertions about God, it is made plain here, it seems to me, that Tillich stands with St. Augustine's *Totum Simul* as his doctrine of the eternal being of God. He must do so since any qualification would lead to some doctrine of potentiality in God.

Further evidence of Tillich's strict adherence to the consequences of this conception of the divine life occurs in his rejection of patri-passionism. This is stated as follows:

> God himself is said to participate in the negativities of creaturely existence. This idea is supported by mystical as well as by christological thought. Nevertheless, the idea must be stated with reservations. Genuine patripassionism (the doctrine that God the Father has suffered in Christ) rightly was rejected by the early church. God as being itself transcends non-being absolutely. On the other hand, God as creative life includes the finite and with it, non-being, although non-being is eternally conquered and the finite is eternally reunited within the infinity of the divine life.[5]

There may be some tendency to qualify this in the second volume when Tillich speaks of "the suffering of God, universally and in the Christ,"[6] but again this suffering does not contradict God's eternal blessedness and "aseity" in which he is beyond both freedom and destiny.[7]

All such ontological analysis of the nature of God rests for Tillich upon something more than rational reflection on being. His method makes this clear throughout that without revelation, i.e., without special correlations between existential concern and the manifestation of being, man has no knowledge of God, only the question. Thus Tillich rejects the ontological argument, and of course all the other classic arguments for God. They point to the question, or express it; but do not in themselves make God known or make his reality a matter of rational conclusion.

III

We have to pass then to the question of the nature of our knowledge of God. On what grounds does this ontology rest?

All knowledge of God rests upon God's self-manifestation. The name for this is revelation. It is marked by ecstasy and

---

5 *Ibid.*, p. 270.

6 Paul Tillich, *Systematic Theology*, Volume II (Chicago: The University of Chicago Press, 1957), p. 176.

7 *Ibid.*, p. 175.

miracle. All preparatory revelation is judged by the final revelation. Final revelation carries its own criterion of finality with it. It is the offering up of everything finite in an unbroken relationship to God. Nothing final can be claimed for the man Jesus, his personality, his ethical insight, his religious teaching. All these are the media of revelation, but they are not the revelation itself:

> Knowledge of revelation does not increase our knowledge about the structures of nature, history, and man. . . . Knowledge of revelation is knowledge about the revelation of the mystery of being to us, not information about the nature of beings and their relation to one another.[8]

This statement is intelligible within the structure of Tillich's doctrine. Revelation cannot increase our knowledge of particular structures, for they are symbols pointing to being; not being itself. They all disappear in God. And it cannot increase our knowledge of the revelation of beings to one another because God is not a being among others, having relationships in a community in the sense in which finite things have such relationships.

In view of Tillich's doctrine that experience is a medium of revelation, but not a source of it, I am driven to ask further about the nature of the revelatory situation. Precisely what is it here that gives knowledge. I press this question because there is much in Tillich's writing which suggests that there is an *experience* of God, of a depth and penetration which does yield knowledge of God's being. My question concerns Tillich's final settlement with the mystical experience. Is it present at the foundation of this theology, or is it not?

I bring together here some texts which suggest this question. Speaking of ontology as inquiry, Tillich says: "Ontology presupposes a conversion, an opening of the eyes, a revelatory experience."[9]

Again, in a discussion of mysticism and the possibility of absolute faith which transcends the mystical union, he still does not seem to leave the ground of experience: "The courage to be which is rooted in the experience of the God above the God of

---

[8] *Systematic Theology*, I, p. 129.

[9] Paul Tillich, *Biblical Religion and the Search for Ultimate Reality* (Chicago: The University of Chicago Press, 1955), p. 65.

theism unites and transcends the courage to be as a part and the courage to be as oneself."[10]

In a critique of process theology Dr. Tillich objects to the doctrine of God as "becoming" and says that the error of these doctrines is their "metaphysical constructive character. They apply the ontological elements to God in a non-symbolic manner and are driven to religiously offensive and theologically untenable statements."[11]

There are two points of special interest in this passage. The first is Tillich's objection to "metaphysical construction" which suggests that he tries to hold a distinction between ontology which points to being itself, and metaphysics which tries to discern the structure of that being. (Such a distinction between ontology and metaphysics is more explicitly affirmed in *Love, Power and Justice.*) The question is, then, what is ontological knowledge if it does not include knowledge of the structure of being?

The second point is the reference to "religiously offensive statements." The nature of this offense is not here made explicit. I presume such statements as "God waits upon man's action," or "God has new experience as time goes on" would be examples of such statements. But what is it they offend? Is it a religious experience or insight? How is the relation between a religious or theological statement and the origin of religious insight to be judged?

Confirmation of the view that Tillich really appeals to a special experience of the divine is yielded also in his reply to Dr. Hartshorne. In rejecting the doctrine of God's finiteness in relation to the world Tillich says, "My resistance against this doctrine (not against the positing of the finite in God) is rooted in the overwhelming impression of the divine majesty as witnessed by classical religion."[12] Here again the reference to the "overwhelming impression" can be interpreted as reference to a religious experience, or insight, or impression, which yields some kind of ontological knowledge, and which implies a specific resistance to one kind of ontological doctrine and affirmation of another type of ontology.

A specific discussion of the methodological problem occurs in Dr. Tillich's paper published in the *Journal of Religion* in

---

10 Paul Tillich, *The Courage To Be* (New Haven: Yale University Press, 1952), p. 187.

11 *Systematic Theology,* I, p. 247.

12 Charles W. Kegley and Robert W. Bretall (ed.), *The Theology of Paul Tillich* (New York: Macmillan, 1952), p. 341.

1947 in which again he explicitly separates "revelation" from "religious experience." The following quotation must be given in full:

> There is, however, one point (which is only a point, without length or breadth) in which medium and content are identical, because in this point subject and object are identical: It is the awareness of the ultimate itself, the *esse ipsum,* which transcends the difference between subject and object and lies, as the presupposition of all doubts, beyond doubt; it is the *veritas ipsa,* as Augustine has called it. It is wrong to call this point "God" (as the ontological argument does), but it is necessary to call it "that in us which makes it impossible for us to escape God." It is the presence of the element of "ultimacy" in the structure of our existence, the basis of religious experience. It has been called "religious *a priori*"; but if we use this phrase (in the sense of *anima naturaliter religiosa*), we must remove every content from it and reduce it to the pure potentiality of having experiences with the character of "ultimate concern." Every content of such an experience is dependent on revelation, namely, on the special way, form, and situation in which this potentiality is actualized by a concern which is concrete and ultimate at the same time. While the certainty of the pure ultimacy is ultimate, conditioned by nothing, its concrete embodiment in symbols and acts is a matter of destiny and venturing faith. Whenever we speak of religious experience, it is important to distinguish these (inseparable) elements: (1) the "point" of immediate awareness of the unconditional which *is* empty but unconditionally certain; and (2) the "breadth" of a concrete concern which is full of content but has the conditional certainty of venturing faith. Theology deals with the second element, while presupposing the first and measuring every theological statement by the standard of the ultimacy of the ultimate concern.[13]

This statement bristles with difficulties. Unconditional certainty is surely certainty of something. An awareness, or experience, or certainty which is only a point, without content, is, it

[13] Quoted in Will Herberg (ed.), *Four Existentialist Theologians* (Garden City, New York: Doubleday Anchor Books, 1958), p. 249.

seems to me, unintelligible. It cannot be used as a basis for affirming or refuting any particular ontological, or metaphysical doctrine. For the "point" does not apparently guarantee its own content. If it does, then it is more than a point. If it does not, then the criterion for the adequacy of various interpretations of the content must be derived elsewhere.

My query is, upon what does the specific ontology which Dr. Tillich affirms rest? Does it not require some affirmation of an immediate encounter with the divine which has content, the kind of encounter which the mystical tradition has affirmed, and for which various modes of interpretation have been proposed?

IV

What means do we have of sustaining, or correcting an interpretation of man's experience of the ultimate reality? An element of interpretation certainly enters into everything we say about that experience. What correctives are to be found in experience or elsewhere for analyzing the interpretations? It is here that we come directly to the theological dimension of our problem. For Christian faith it is the revelation in Jesus Christ which gives the final criterion for judging every interpretation of the divine reality. This must mean that theology can examine any ontological statement for its adequacy as a dimension of the interpretation of the revelation in Christ. "The name 'Jesus the Christ' implies an ontology."[14] What ontology? This question cannot be avoided, though Dr. Tillich does take the position in the work just quoted that "there is no special ontology which we have to accept in the name of the Biblical message."[15]

Still, Tillich seems to hold that the doctrine of God as being itself, with its implications, must in some sense be required in order to do justice to the biblical revelation. Therefore, we are back with the problem of what ontological structure can give meaning to the Christian assertions about the Christ. There must be some kind of integrity between the ontological vision and the assertions of faith else the theological structure breaks down. The method of correlation requires that the assertions about the Christ come as answers to the ontological question.

As we turn, then, to the question concerning the adequacy of the ontology of "being-itself" to interpret the Christian faith, we may first notice that there is an integrity between Tillich's christological formulation and his doctrine of God. Jesus is

[14] *Biblical Religion and the Search for Ultimate Reality*, p. 76.
[15] *Ibid.*, p. 85.

the medium of the final revelation by giving up everything that is finite in himself to God.[16] The revelation in Christ is the negation and the affirmation of Jesus.[17]

In these formulations the acceptance of the risks of finitude and their overcoming through such acceptance which points beyond all finitude to the absolute overcoming of non-being in God is affirmed. Thus the work of Christ and the ontological structure seems to yield a mutually supportive interpretation.

I ask whether in this formulation, however, the dimension of finitude in the revelation in Jesus is sufficiently accounted for. If we attend to the New Testament picture of Jesus as the Christ, is it satisfactory to identify its inner meaning with the eternal overcoming of non-being by being in which time disappears, in which God does not suffer? That Jesus gives himself up to his vocation is clear. Everything in his life and being is devoted to the realization of that vocation. But this "giving up" is a human action, worked out in history, through the meeting of concrete issues, temptations, and problems, and resulting in the life of a community which has to press forward through history, making decisions, suffering the consequences of freedom, and expecting a future action of God. There are the Pharisees, there are the money changers, the sick, the dying. There is the man going about, wrestling with his vocation, speaking, healing, facing a final decision, sweating it out, dying, and in his death tasting the full mystery of man's estrangement as he seeks to obey the divine will. He appears surely as the central figure in an historical drama. God is at work in and through him; but far beyond his specific conscious awareness. "If it be possible, let this cup pass from me."

There are two implications in this picture which appear inescapable; real freedom in the man, and real suffering in God.

As to the freedom in the man, this means that what is taking place here is a genuine adventure with risk of the divine creativity. That the freedom of Jesus is related to a destiny which is determined from God's side is not to be doubted. But it still can be real freedom. This is not a question of making salvation dependent on a contingency. It is a question of the reality of the human side of the revelation. One of Dr. Tillich's statements seems to me exactly to agree with this:

> Both infinite divinity and finite human freedom make the world transcendent to God and God transcendent

16 See *Systematic Theology*, I, pp. 132-135.
17 *Biblical Religion and the Search for Ultimate Reality*, p. 85.

> to the world. . . . Transcendence demanded by religious experience [N.B.] is the freedom to freedom relationship which is actual in every personal encounter.[18]

But if this position is taken, it surely follows that God cannot be "being itself" without any distinction of actuality and potentiality, for this would destroy the freedom in the creature.

And second, it must follow that God does suffer, and that the divine life is in some way actually affected by the relationship to the creation which God sustains. The suffering of the Christ is, of course, the clearest aspect of the New Testament story. This suffering is not only in the agony of rejection, and the crucifixion, it is in the "suffering of our human lot," the bearing with the slow of heart, the reluctance of man to face the truth, the mystery of man's sin, the waiting for God. Christ bears with a creation which groaneth and travaileth and does not yield up its full truth to any. He counsels the disciples to expect their own suffering and the necessity of waiting for the Kingdom which has no sign save the sign of Jonah.

Now this can be expressed as "participation in the overcoming of non-being by being" but is that a sufficient interpretation of the historical dimension? History in the light of the Gospel, seems rather like a participation in and response to the divine creativity. God is working something out, shaping a world, sending his spirit to raise up a people and a church, preparing the way for man's response but not coercing it, waiting until the "end." There is mystery in all of it; and most of all, in the infinite future with its "not yet." But is it not the mystery of a love at work, and therefore of a suffering love?

I do not mean to overlook the important discussion of the temptations of the Christ in the second volume of the *Systematic Theology*. But here again Dr. Tillich seems to hold to the real freedom of Jesus and yet preserve the element of destiny by the assertion that in God these are united.[19] But how they are united there, without one qualifying the other, is something we cannot say.[20]

My argument is that whatever is to be said about religious experience as pointing to being itself beyond the categories and ontological elements, there is a polar opposition in religious

---

18 *Systematic Theology*, I, p. 263.

19 *Systematic Theology*, II, p. 130.

20 See the reply to Hartshorne in *The Theology of Paul Tillich*, p. 340.

experience and one which is underlined in the Christian revelation. It is the experience of the mystery of being which has an unfinished work, which involves real risk, in which destiny is not wholly determined from the side of the divine. This seems to me as inescapable an aspect of the religious apprehension of ultimacy as any other element.

Perhaps this is what Dr. Tillich means by the assertion that faith can be interpreted as the "courage to be"; but such courage is surely bound up with time, with the sense of the not-yet, with the genuine risk of life moving into a future which is real future, even for God.

I am suggesting that the problems which seem to be unresolved in Dr. Tillich's doctrine might be resolved in an ontology which really accepted both time and eternity as real for God. I do not see the necessity of clinging so tenaciously to the classical ontology of the mystical neoplatonic tradition. And I see some good reasons for rejecting it.

In all this I confess I am not sure that I am really disagreeing with Dr. Tillich. In my desire to understand his doctrine, and in my conviction that he has given us a genuinely contemporary and profound Christian theology, I find these questions arising. His gracious willingness to answer questions and to discuss them further makes it worthwhile to write a paper in this exploratory vein.

DANIEL D. WILLIAMS
Union Theological Seminary

15

Daniel Day Williams

WIEMAN AS A CHRISTIAN THEOLOGIAN

Judgments of Henry Nelson Wieman's relationship to the Christian faith and tradition vary all the way from seeing in his empirical theology the only possible way of saving the truth of Christianity for the modern world, to viewing him as one who has cut away all the distinctive elements of Christian faith and who proposes a radical alternative to anything resembling Christian doctrine. A discussion of his work as theologian must try to explain how such divergent views are possible.

The thesis I shall state and argue is the following: Wieman's thought arises within the Christian community as an expression of the essential truth of the Christian faith. His development of an empirical philosophical interpretation of Christian belief has always been regarded by him as an aspect of the theological task. Through personal conversations over the years, and in the reading of his works, I conclude that he has never disavowed either the significance of the theological task or his own involvement in it. What has to be understood in order to see the meaning of his work as theologian, is that Wieman is one of the radical modernizers who believes that, for the sake of the truth of the Christian faith, its interpreters in our day have a primary responsibility to turn to philosophical methods for the analysis and exposition of that truth.

I must also state two subsidiary theses which follow upon this first. One is that Wieman has developed an explicit theory of the relation of his method of inquiry in religion to the Christian community and its faith, and has always shown how his conclusions may be interpreted in the light of understanding the meaning of traditional Christian doctrines. He has a definite theory of the function of theology as a discipline different from philosophical inquiry. His standpoint, therefore, does not bypass the theological problem, but puts it into one of the possible frameworks in which it can be interpreted.

Second, I shall argue that, in working out his problems Wieman did adopt some positions in relation to the tradition and task of theology which disclose what seem to me rather arbitrary and unexamined aspects of his own position; and that the viewpoint he finally came to take regarding theology, while intelligible from the standpoint of his presuppositions, contains some inadequate conclusions. I believe that contemporary theology must face seriously the questions he raises, but that valid answers to the problem of truth in theology and philosophy require a more complex analysis than he has given.

I. Wieman's View of the Present Situation of Christian Thought

Western man, Wieman believes, stands in a crisis which reaches to the roots of his being. Not only is his culture faced with choices which mean life or death, but the religious tradition by which he has lived (this means for Western man the Judaeo-Christian tradition) has largely lost its power as it stands, to guide and shape life in a technological age. Even where the tradition is held and proclaimed with great intellectual subtlety and profound devotion, it actually has become more and more detached from the concrete choices which our living demands.

Man cannot live without the guidance, the emotional sensitivity, and the depth of association which the religious tradition and community provide. Wieman has stressed this point continually. In the past, he holds, greatness of devotion has been sustained and enhanced by the wealth of insight, symbol, and truth which were embodied in the church, with its theology, liturgy, and all the intellectual structures by which the faith was interpreted. But no matter how imposing and rich a tradition, it can break down in its capacity to guide the minds and hearts of men to an adequate faith. This theory of a breakdown of the tradition in the face of new conditions and a new understanding of the world is the key to the modernist position. Tradition must be reinterpreted. Revered doctrines and symbols must be re-evaluated; modern knowledge has made this necessary.

This modernist attitude has seemed to some the only alternative to obscurantism. Certainly, in the 1920's and 1930's in America it had a powerful hold upon honest minds. Those who recognize the validity, now at mid-century, of Bultmann's thesis of the necessity for an existential interpretation of the Christian message which will set it free from the mythological world view in the Bible, can appreciate the way in which the intellectual problem of religious belief appeared to the liberal modernists in the early twentieth century. The theme is the same: Reinterpretation is necessary if the truth of faith is to be available to twentieth-century men.

What needs to be clearly understood is that this was a Christian modernism, arising within the church, and faced with the question of the relevance of the church's message to the world. Wieman has always stressed the point that his own thought is shaped by the Judaeo-Christian heritage in which he stands. It is an illusion to think that one can stand outside of his heritage, and Wieman explicitly accepts the responsibilities implied in a conscious identification with this tradition. As he says in his essay on *The Promise of Protestantism—Whence and Whither:*

> If other forms of religion are equally endowed with Protestantism for doing the religious task of our time, so be it. But being a Protestant myself, my responsibility is to see what my form of faith can do when it corrects its faults and exercises its capacities to the full.[1]

There is a further aspect of this explicit Christian responsibility affirmed by Wieman. His concern with the truth of religious belief has always been directed toward the practical issues of commitment and the growth of the community of faith. For all his emphasis upon the need for intellectual inquiry into the meaning of religious belief, and for all his insistence upon empirical method and scientific rigor, Wieman has never had a

[1] "The Promise of Protestantism—Whence and Whither," PC, edited by Vergilius Ferm, p. 163.

speculative aim as his chief concern. In writing and teaching, he has insisted that science and intellectual analysis are to serve religious devotion and not the other way around. Thus, his program of religious-philosophical analysis has arisen within the concern of the church and is directed toward clarifying and making more adequate the grasp of that truth by which alone the church can adequately serve God and man.

II. God or Man; the Critique of Humanism

The consideration of Wieman as theologian raises the question of what makes a religious thinker a theologian. Is there a fundamental difference between theological thinking and philosophy of religion? Tillich has thrown much light on this problem by pointing out that thinking which expresses an ultimate concern by which one is grasped and which compels his commitment is different from that which seeks the objective structure of being in itself unmixed with personal and subjective devotion. As Tillich points out, every philosophy has implicitly or explicitly involved this existential element and has therefore been "theological." Yet there is a difference in position between the thinking which affirms an ultimate concern and that which does not. It is important to see Wieman's thought from the standpoint of this analysis, for here his position as "theologian" is unequivocal. The purpose of his whole work is to point to the reality of God and to call upon men for that change in the direction of commitment which alone can redeem life from triviality and destructiveness and open the way to salvation.

The key to Wieman's theological position is to see that his entire work has been a meditation on God, a struggle with the problem of truth in God, and a dedicated, persistent, often grim battle with the humanism which looks only to man for achieving whatever meaning and fulfillment he can. A stoical humanism, seeking the courage to be through the affirmation of human life and freedom against a barren and unresponsive universe, appears today as the supreme rival of Christianity, whether it expresses itself in Marxist form, or in the profound ethical humanism of an Albert Camus, or in atheistic existentialism. Wieman has held from the beginning that there is a fatal weakness in humanism—one which must be opposed, not for the sake of a traditional or abstract belief in God, but for the sake of the truth and fulfillment of man's life. And he has sought to expose that weakness through concentrated argument which appeals to the experience open for examination by humanists as well as theists.

When Wieman came to the University of Chicago in the late 1920's, he stood in an environment suffused with the optimism and humanistic enthusiasm of the liberal period at its height. The religious claim of this humanism was heard everywhere, and it had the confidence of a conquering power. Away with superstition in the theological tradition! Let us bow respectfully to the religions of the past as they have enshrined human ideals; but let us affirm man's intelligent search for the fulfillment of his ideals, and the conquest of all the things which stand in his way. This viewpoint was upheld by the brilliant historian of religions, A. Eustace Haydon at Chicago; by Max Otto at Wisconsin; and in a form which took a somewhat more positive attitude toward theism, by Edward Scribner Ames.

To this humanistic faith, Wieman threw down the gauntlet of battle. He made the issue sharp, unavoidable, and compelling for us who studied with him in those days. We began to see what many of us who had combined a traditional Christian piety with a kind of liberal optimism had not seen: that the issue was not to be solved by showing that Christianity could do more for man than any other view. The issue is whether it is man or God who is to be served. A profound abyss separates the way of idolatrous humanism from the way of God.

All of Wieman's writings declare this theme. *The Issue of Life* is not one of his major works, but the chapter in that volume in which he points out the difference between humanistic devotion to ideals and the theistic way of devotion to that reality which is working in and through human life—but beyond human intent—to generate and sustain the actual good which is never fully envisioned in the human definition of the good, is one of the clearest and most decisive statements he has ever made.[2]

It may be readily acknowledged that in his earlier writings Wieman uses much of the language of humanism and sometimes seems close to its perspective. His early emphasis upon the defi-

[2] IL, VI.

nition of God as that which supports the best in human life or yields the greatest good for man may seem to make God a function of the quest for human fulfillment. But this came, in part, from the apologetic search for a common meeting point with the one who does not believe in God. As Wieman's thought moved forward along the line he had blocked out, the sharp distinction between the good which God creates and all human ideals of the good is increasingly emphasized. Wieman himself tells of the way in which the full significance of this distinction grew upon him. In 1939 he wrote:

> Sin is not the impossibility of attaining our highest ideals. The assumption that our own ideals, no matter how far beyond our attainment, can be identified with the infinite riches of God, is itself a sinful and arrogant presumption. . . . God, I have come to see with increasing clarity, is not merely man lifted to the *nth* degree of perfection. . . . God is different from man. God works concretely. Man cannot possibly do that. . . . Recognition of the otherness of God, I hold, is the next step which man must take in his climb up from the idolatry which makes a god in man's image.[3]

When Wieman's theological intention is put in relation to traditional modes of Christian thought, it is clear where he belongs. His is the spirit of high Calvinism. God's sovereign creativity works amidst the wrecks of time, taking its own absolute direction, plowing up human purposes and institutions, breaking down and rebuilding. Man's one course which will lead out of despair is to open his life completely to this transforming power and to serve God above every created good.

Critics of Wieman's naturalistic philosophy have often missed the depth of his doctrine of God. They have seen him as apothcosizing some natural force or part of the world, and calling it God. But if my understanding of Wieman's view is correct, nothing we can humanly grasp or define can be identified with the full being of God. We know him indeed as the operative power in our midst which brings forth the good. But, in the mystery of his working, God is the power of correction and judgment on all our human attempts to grasp his being. No human philosophy or theology or political order or religion

[3] "Some Blind Spots Removed," *The Christian Century*, 56:117–118.

should be allowed to take the place which belongs solely to God. To put anything else first in understanding or in value is the very core of sin.

It was this theme of the centrality of God which so powerfully grasped those who sat under Wieman as teacher. His own genius in making clear what religious devotion means beyond all sentimentality and self-righteousness came to us as the renewed assertion of the meaning of Christian faith, before which humanism was a noble but inadequate gesture.

III. The Work of Philosophy in Interpreting the Christian Faith

Once we see that traditional interpretations of Christian faith have come into conflict with the knowledge and world view of modern man, the question is, what can be done, not just for the sake of preserving a tradition but for the sake of the truth which has heretofore been grasped in ways appropriate to other times. Wieman sees the problem in these terms, which are those of the modernists. Let us now examine the method by which he seeks the solution through philosophical analysis of the fundamental concepts in religious living.

Wieman asserts a thoroughgoing empiricism as the only adequate method for getting valid concepts, supported by evidence, and useful in the further clarification of the realities with which we are confronted. Others in this volume are discussing Wieman's empiricism in detail, and I do not propose to examine it here. Clearly, Wieman stands in the broad stream of radical empiricism as developed by James, Dewey, and Whitehead—an empiricism which seeks to bring within the net of rational analysis the broad reaches, variety, and depth of man's concrete being, including his religious experience. Reason serves as guide to the clarification and testing of concepts. The canons of rational consistency are important, not because all experience can be presented in a rational scheme, but as man's protection against illusion, nonsense, and the imposition of untestable doctrines upon his religious search for truth.

Empiricism is a philosophical doctrine, a theory of knowledge. Why is Wieman confident that religion can be protected from superstition and error by philosophical means? To turn from other theological methods to a complete acceptance of rational empiricism would seem to involve a decision based on faith. And on what basis is that decision made? Does it come from within the Christian standpoint?

Here we are dealing with a position which reflects Wieman's historical situation, in which modern science seems to many to have provided the sole corrective to historical errors and illusions. It cannot be denied that it was modern science and historical scholarship which brought about the transformation of the church's conception of its origins and its scriptures. Wieman believes, and he certainly is not alone in this, that a drastic shift is required in man's understanding of how truth arises and is tested in the central matters of faith. For him, "evidence" is a word which reaches to the very heart of our human problem. We know when we can find concrete confirmation of our theories and doctrines, and not otherwise.

However one assesses the ultimate roots of Wieman's decision for the empiricist philosophical position, one aspect of his analysis of the problem of knowledge is of special relevance to the view he takes of the Christian tradition. This is the distinction he has lately stressed between "cognitive" and "non-cognitive" modes of apprehension, and consequently between literal and symbolic statements.

What Wieman sees in the religious traditions is the accumulation of a wealth of mythical (which for him means non-cognitive) symbols by which men have grasped, served, and tried to express their relationship to God. Wieman has always held that such modes of religious thinking and practice are absolutely necessary. Man cannot live without myth. The great symbolic expressions of the past have guided whole generations and cultures in the religious and moral life; and as long as the myths function in this way, men will not only find life in some measure fulfilled but they will probably be unaware that there is any discrepancy between what the myths say when taken literally and the ultimate truth.

But myths and symbols which function practically are not literal statements of truth. This I understand to be Wieman's position. Nor are they to be regarded in any sense as cognitive. To hold them or to believe them is not to know; it is only to have a practical means of functioning in relation to some reality. This sharp distinction between the literal and the non-literal, the cognitive and the non-cognitive, is the key to much of Wieman's method in dealing with the meaning of the Christian faith. If we accept his distinction here, it is clear what view we must take of much Christian theology. We cannot take it as literal statement for which empirical evidence can be adduced. Therefore, we must take it as a structure of non-cognitive symbols. It follows that the only way to save the truth of Christian theology is to turn to philosophical analysis of the truth of its statements when these are put into the form of literally meaningful and therefore testable hypotheses.

Wieman's view here is consistent with his treatment of the Christian theological tradition, and it anticipates many of the problems which have recently appeared in connection with the proposal for the demythologizing of the New Testament message made by Rudolph Bultmann. What Wieman proposes is a thorough and radical demythologizing of all tradition. This is to be done by means of a transposition of the problem of religious knowledge into the area where empirical rational method can be used on assertions about the most important human realities.

Wieman's position here recalls most nearly that of Hegel in the historical development of Christian thought. As for Hegel, so for Wieman: it is philosophy which examines Christian belief in its historical, mythical, or symbolic form. Philosophy then gives the higher, pure form of rational statement to the real inner meaning of the truth which myths and symbols have only practically grasped. Whereas for Hegel the final method is rational logical analysis as it grasps the pattern of history, for Wieman it is rational empirical inquiry grasping the structures exemplified in the flow of experience. And Wieman does not make the absolute claims for his or any other philosophical doctrine that Hegel sometimes made for his.

Has Wieman therefore left the standpoint of Christian theology and identified himself as a philosopher of religion who bears a relation to the Christian tradition, but is not involved in the specifically theological task?

Before we answer that question, there is a third aspect of the problem of the nature of theology which we must examine in Wieman's analysis. He specifically discusses the task of theology in his papers "On Using Christian Words" and "The Need of Philosophy of Religion."[4]

Wieman states the central task of religious inquiry as the clarification of our understanding of the supremely worthful reality. This inquiry is related in complex ways to the traditional language of the religious community. The problem of theology is bound up with the attitude we take toward the traditional language in which the Christian faith has been expressed. Here, Wieman's radical modernism comes clearly to the fore. He holds that meaning shifts from age to age, so that we cannot say that we mean the same thing by words like "redemption" or "Son of God" as other ages meant.

Since the total complex of ideas in the minds of men today is radically different from that of two hundred years ago, and this in turn vastly different from the mind of the first century, it is plain that the traditional Christian words cannot carry the same meaning in all these different periods.[5]

This is a sweeping statement, and it is not substantially qualified by anything else Wieman says. But he does say that the traditional language dealt with the supreme source of good and truth as men understood that source in past ages—hence, we can say that the divine reality by which we are grasped is that same reality, even though our understanding changes. God is still God, whatever concepts or symbols we use to designate him.

Why should we cling to the language of the past at all? The answer is that religious words must do more than simply designate realities. They must "incite to action, generate attitudes, and awaken sensitivity. Symbols acquire the power to function in this way through social interchange, and this means through the communication in human groups of the responsive awareness associated with the familiar symbols.

Here we come to the difference between theology and philosophy of religion. Theology undertakes to do all its thinking and intellectual seeking in terms that are traditional. Philosophy of religion is free to use any terminology which the best thought of the day may provide

[4] "The Need of Philosophy of Religion," *The Journal of Religion*, XIV, 4 (October, 1934). "On Using Christian Words," *The Journal of Religion*, XX, 3 (July, 1940). [5] "On Using Christian Words," *loc. cit.*, p. 258.

or which experts in the field of philosophy of religion may devise for that time or for special problems. Both these disciplines have their own peculiar dangers and weaknesses. The weakness of theology is that its traditional terms are not always the best fitted for the intellectual problems which it undertakes. The weakness of philosophy of religion is that its terms will not always be fully translatable into the words by which people actually conduct their religious living. Therefore we need both kinds of inquiry in the field of religion, and whenever theologian or philosopher disparages the importance of the other's work, he is obstructing the good of Christian living.[6]

Wieman here sees the difficulty of theological terms, in that they may not be fitted for the intellectual task. But the difficulty of philosophical terms is purely practical, as they may not be responded to by people in practical living. It is clear that Wieman accepts the intellectual task of theology as distinct from philosophy, but it is hard to avoid the feeling that this is only a concession to practical needs. This view is strengthened by his analogy which relates the philosopher of religion and the theologian as the dietitian and the cook. The scientific knowledge of nourishment belongs to the dietitian. The cook (theologian) can make food palatable and therefore available for the religious life.[7]

Does Wieman then separate his inquiry from theology? The answer is No. He says that we should use the Christian words: "There is no entry into the Christian community, no participation in the stream of Christian history, no power that can transform ordinary human living into the noblest Christian living, no effective leadership, and no purifying and redirecting of Christian life except through the use of Christian words."[8] Wieman bends every effort to discovering an adequate philosophical language, but he uses the philosophically developed instruments of analysis to interpret the basic Christian themes. Indeed, one of the characteristics of Wieman's writing is that, while his general mode of analysis and expression are philosophical, he shifts without warning both in point of view and in style, and begins to speak in terms heavily laden with emotion, using the language of religious feeling to evoke a response which goes far beyond intellectual clarification. As one instance, notice the paragraphs in

[6] *Ibid.*, p. 265. [7] *"The Need of Philosophy of Religion,"* p. 380.
[8] "On Using Christian Words," p. 267.

The Source of Human Good in which Wieman is discussing his four-fold doctrine of God, and has come to the analysis of the third subevent, "the expansion of the appreciable world." He points out how the occurrence of this event can make a man more lonely and unhappy than before because he is sensitive to new deeps and riches of experience. Here Wieman suddenly turns to a meditation on the meaning of such loneliness, and the exposition becomes a powerfully written and evocative paragraph which is a vision of the work of Christ. It closes with the words: "perhaps such loneliness, born of such craving for love between men, would drive a man to the desperate madness in which he dreamed that by dying on a cross he could somehow bring this kingdom of love into existence."[9]

Now if we apply to such a passage the analysis Wieman has made of traditional language, we can only conclude that he mixes the philosophical and theological modes in his exposition, and that far from eschewing theology, he might more properly be charged with shifting to theological language without warning.

IV. The Interpretation of the Christian Faith

So far, it should be clear that Wieman's approach to the interpretation of Christian faith is undertaken as an act arising within the Christian community and its concerns, and that he does not reject the theological problem if that is understood as the clarification, analysis, and interpretation of the meanings of Christian language about God.

We have now to see his specific approach to the meaning of Christianity. Here it must be recognized that Wieman identifies his position with a type of contemporary philosophy which he and others call "the new naturalism." This appears in the early pages of *The Source of Human Good* as both an epistemological and a metaphysical doctrine in which all transcendental reality is rejected as irrelevant and inefficacious. Processes in existence are the only realities we can know. It is important to note also that Wieman believes this philosophical position to be based "on thorough analysis of the method by which any knowledge whatsoever can be obtained."[10]

In stating this philosophical position, he asserts that a choice

[9] SHG, p. 63. [10] *Ibid.*, p. 7.

is involved between the Jewish-Christian and the Greek-Christian traditions, and he stands with the former, since it sees God as creative power and not as form. One is driven by the brevity of the discussion to ask whether Wieman sees the choice between these two traditions as purely arbitrary, or whether it is dictated by the naturalistic doctrine itself. (For example, there is the option of George Santayana's naturalism which is Greek rather than Hebraic.)

Wieman turns, then, to a contemporary naturalistic philosophy as offering the only adequate instrument for analyzing the meaning of God so as to provide a basis for interpreting the central realities of the Christian faith. He looks at all Christian assertions about God's revelation and working in history in the light of this philosophical clarification of what we can meaningfully say God is, and how his working is manifest to us. Such a program, fully carried out, would either be a philosophy of the Christian revelation or else a theological restatement, carried out by philosophical methods, of the content of Christian faith.

The fundamental method in Wieman's treatment of the Christian *Kerygma* is his use of a scheme of value analysis to provide the structure in which the meaning of the faith may be stated for our time. His fundamental distinction between creative good (which is God) and created goods, and his insistence that only through the breaking of man's bondage to created goods and through commitment to the creative good can life be saved from what blocks its real hope, are made the key to the content of Christian faith. "This reversal in the direction of human devotion is not new. It is, we believe, the very substance of the original Christian faith."[11] What Wieman does, therefore, is to treat the original Christian expressions of this transformation through God's working "myth." As Wieman uses this term, it refers to beliefs concerning the "metaphysically transcendental," and all characterization of God as "personal" must be understood as myth.[12]

What Wieman now carries out is a rigorous program of demythologizing the Christian tradition; but, in contrast to Professor Bultmann, the philosophical doctrine which is used to give a contemporary interpretation of the myth is naturalistic process

[11] *Ibid.*, p. 39. [12] *Ibid.*, pp. 264–268.

metaphysics rather than existentialist anthropology. There are, of course, important consequences of this difference in philosophical standpoint, but the interpretative program has much in common with that of Bultmann.

We turn first to the interpretation of Jesus and the meaning of the Christological affirmations. Wieman says that we should be able to discover what happened in the rise of Christianity "by simply looking objectively at the events which originated the Christian faith."[13] There could not be a clearer statement of Wieman's positivistic confidence in observation and description to yield the truth sought by religion.

What he sees in the story of the New Testament is Jesus engaging in communication with the little group of disciples with such depth and potency that the organization of their several personalities was broken down and they were remade. "They became new men, and the thought and feeling of each got across to the others. . . . Something about this man Jesus broke the atomic exclusiveness of those individuals, so that they were deeply and freely receptive and responsive each to the other." Wieman describes this new responsiveness in the terms of his analysis of the four-fold process. The creative event was occurring in the fellowship around Jesus. An especially important point for the understanding of Wieman's Christology is that the creative event always involves an interaction of personalities. It is not confined within any one personality. Rather, Jesus was within the event. "It required many other things beside his own solitary self. It required the Hebrew heritage, the disciples with their peculiar capacity for this kind of responsiveness, and doubtless much else of which we have little knowledge."[14]

What happened at the resurrection was the shattering of previous bondage to established expectations and commitments, and the reversal of human devotion. The creative event rose to dominance in the lives of the disciples. They discovered the transforming creativity at work in their midst as "the Living God that works in time."[15] They began to live the crucified life in which every human wish and value is brought under judgment of the God who judges and transforms all human righteousness.

Since faith is interpreted as the act of commitment to creative

[13] *Ibid.*, p. 39. [14] *Ibid.*, pp. 39–41. [15] *Ibid.*, p. 44.

good, the analysis of sin in this view begins with the insight that sin is whatever obstructs such commitment, no matter how noble, righteous, or high minded the devotion with which we cling to our ideals and virtues. Wieman's insight into the transmoral dimension of the category of sin is profound. He sees the greatest destructive power of sin at the very peak of human goodness when that goodness is allowed to obstruct the commitment of life to the transforming power of God. Wieman's identifying the Beatific Vision as the devil when that vision is allowed to stand in the way of creative transformation is surely an insight plumbing the profoundest depths of the mystery of human good turned evil.[16]

Salvation is being transformed in the direction of devotion, which God accomplishes in human life; and it involves the forgiveness of sin. Forgiveness is interpreted in process terms. It is an act of God. Perhaps we could say it is one aspect or consequence of God's penetration to the core of whatever obstructs the creative working. Thus, forgiveness is an active expression of the power of God's working in life, overcoming the estrangement brought about by sin. If Wieman's discussion of forgiveness does not appear to involve personalistic terms, it does make of forgiveness and therefore of the work of atonement an actual process in which God accomplishes what men cannot accomplish with their evil involvements. Should Wieman's implicit doctrine of atonement be developed, it would be analogous to what Gustaf Aulén has designated as the "classic motif" of the victory of God over evil through the death of Christ.[17]

Wieman's process theology offers a basis for a high view of the significance of the church. It is the community raised up by the creative working of God, continually judged and renewed through that working. This view stands in sharp contrast to existentialism with its disparaging of historical relatedness. Historic community constitutes the very substance of the process in which personality is created and men discover the meaning of supreme devotion to the source of all good. The church's prime concern is to be the community in which the crucified life is lived, all lesser devotions are challenged, and men are together in such a fellowship that they are directed to a deepening knowledge of the presence and

[16] *Ibid.*, pp. 128–129. [17] G. Aulén, *Christus Victor* (London: S.P.C.K.), 1931.

demands of God. Thus one of the chief concerns of the church is worship and the nourishing of the life of prayer. Wieman has written much on prayer, and his book, *Methods of Private Religious Living,* is a most refreshingly unconventional treatment of the life of prayer.

When he turns to the eschatological questions—death, eternal life, and fulfillment in history—Wieman seeks to stay within the bounds prescribed by the method of rational inquiry.

Wieman asserts that high religion will not prescribe what the outcome of history must be. It will not erect a series of beliefs which go beyond the evidence. Wieman holds that we do not know what lies beyond death. What we must do is to commit ourselves completely into the keeping and power of God. He points out that the way in which death is met can yield present good. "This we know by the death of Jesus, if in no other way." Wieman's treatment of the meaning of death offers religious devotion as a synthesis of courage and trust. Whatever may lie in the power of the creative event can be released fully only as such devotion becomes the ruling spirit of life.[18]

We still have the question of what the actual course of history means from the standpoint of faith. Is it progress? Is there fulfillment? Or is Wieman's a tragic vision in which the achievements of creativity and the obstructive powers are forever locked in struggle? Here I believe that Wieman means to assert the priority of religious devotion and the trusting acceptance of God's working, in spite of what outcome life and history may provide. At the same time, his doctrine of the immanent working of God leads him to look for signs of concrete achievement in history, and I find what he says on the question of fulfillment in history to be something of a blend of utopianism and the tragic vision.

It should be remembered that in spite of Wieman's metaphysical tendency, the background of his thought is the doctrine of creative evolution as developed in Bergson, Whitehead, and others. He often points to the creative working in time and history as displaying a series of crises and creative thrusts toward higher levels. He speaks of three great victories of creative activity: the creation of the living cell, the creation of man, and the creation of the living Christ in history.[19] He writes as if another

[18] SHG, p. 280. [19] *Ibid.*, p. 274.

transformation of man were possible which would lift life to a new level of existence. There is a great divide separating us from "the end of history" and that great good which will be produced when man is able to receive it and do his part.[20] He sometimes speaks as if the new age were trembling to be born in this present. "We are passing over one of the great divides of history; possibly it is the last high pass over the top mountain range before we enter the valley of abundance. . . . Perhaps beyond the high pass, flinty and cold and narrow, is a region where men may live richly under the rule of a redirected devotion for a thousand years and more."[21]

This passage, which breathes the spirit of chiliastic hope, appeals to what might be rather than to evidence for what is. And it is not quite clear just what expectations Dr. Wieman finds it legitimate to hold for the fulfillment of the creative work of God. "The struggle was, and the struggle still is, to save man from self-destruction and from internal disruptive conflict within the individual and within society, and finally to establish the Kingdom of God. The Kingdom of God is a world so transformed that every part responds with rich delivery of meaning to every other part and supremely to the spirit of man." He adds that the victory is already won in the sense of "winning the strategic battle which determines the outcome."[22] But what is the evidence here? What of the fact that time "takes all our goods away," to paraphrase the familiar hymn? "The great struggle of man is to overcome the perishing of time and conserve the qualities of past events by which alone the present can have depth and richness of meaning."[23] But to what extent does experience justify the hope for overcoming the perishing of time?

I may summarize this discussion of Wieman's eschatology by saying that, on the whole, this doctrine seems to assert an immanent eschaton in which the triumph of creative good may be realized in actual history; but that he thinks this fulfillment can be frustrated (temporarily, at least) by men, and perhaps by other forces working against God. I would like to ask just how far Dr. Wieman believes that an empirical theology can anticipate such an historical fulfillment. The point seems to me of special importance, as it bears on the kind of expectation we may have concerning specific historical movements and programs.

[20] *Ibid.*, p. 289. [21] *Ibid.*, p. 52. [22] *Ibid.*, p. 272. [23] *Ibid.*, p. 22.

V. Our Knowledge of God: Some Critical Questions

Theological critics of Wieman's doctrine frequently assume that they need go no further than to point out his naturalistic conception of God; therefore, he cannot be regarded as a theologian, but rather as one who proposes an alternative to Christian faith.

I have pointed out the reasons why I think such a judgment is superficial. Wieman stands in a positive relationship to the Christian faith and the Christian tradition. His work is not theology in the sense of a formal system in which the traditional dogmatic material is all reorganized and interpreted. But he is a philosophical theologian who has treated the major Christian themes in the light of a metaphysical and epistemological doctrine. True, he has not covered all the aspects of traditional Christian thought, and indeed it is characteristic of his work that not even the most important themes such as the nature of God are elaborated in relation to the traditional problems such as creation and final judgment, time and space, God's freedom in relation to the creatures' freedom, and many other important problems and relationships. Rather, Wieman has stuck to his fundamental theme concerning the nature of our knowledge of God, with the basic distinctions which make it possible to have *tested* knowledge of the source of human good. But this is the root problem of all theology, and concerning his teaching on that central theme I must raise my central queries. Has Wieman correctly formulated and assessed the problem of our knowledge of God? That seems to me the critical question, whether we raise it from a Christian theological point of view or any other. For if Wieman is right that the empirical method can solve the problem of how God is known, then this is true for Christian faith as well as for any other faith. No tradition, however sacred, should stand in the way of our determining the validity of our beliefs. On this point, anyone who accepts the Christian faith that God is truth must agree that Wieman has raised the crucial question for theology.

There are four points at which it appears that Wieman has not adequately stated the problem involved in our knowledge of that upon which we are dependent for all good. I shall state these four points in general terms, and I shall not conceal my belief that part of the difficulty lies in the fact that Wieman has not taken seriously enough the tradition of Christian thought, in either its theological, biblical, or philosophical aspects. But, I repeat, the crucial question is whether Wieman's doctrine is adequate to the total dimension of our human problem in the search for God, not whether he satisfies some traditional criterion of belief.

Briefly put, my criticism is that Wieman has adopted a much too simple positivism in his epistemology, and then has tried to bring all the cognitive aspects of religious knowledge within the narrow framework of that positivism. This method is inadequate in at least four instances in dealing with even the more salient aspects of religious experience.

First, the knowledge of God involves a transformation of the perspective in which we see the world. It simply is not the case that a sufficiently clear definition of God will make his reality plain to any honest observer. Second, there is no meaningful concept of God which does not involve some metaphysical assertions about his being; that is, assertions about God's unity, his relationship to all other beings, and to time and space and eternity. But metaphysical structures require something more than scientific empirical validation; they require a method which can deal with the problem of being at the level of utmost generality. Third, the knowledge of reality in its metaphysical depth—and certainly the knowledge of the objects of religious concern, such as values, other persons, and God—involve us in the attempt to grasp what cannot be fully caught in the net of our literal formulations. Any absolute distinction between cognitive and non-cognitive expressions is therefore misleading. Most of our knowledge, and most of our cognitive language, lie somewhere in between the absolutely literal and the metaphorical, analogical, and symbolic modes. Finally, Wieman's doctrine of the creative good involves as its second step the integration of new meanings with the old. Applied to religious knowledge, this would require attention to the traditional meanings and their formulation, not for the sake of revering the past but for the sake of present truth. But it seems to me that Wieman believes we can make an almost absolute distinction between the purely pragmatic meanings of the past and the literal truth yielded by scientific method. This means relegating traditional modes of expression, such as those of the Bible, to a purely pragmatic status. But when we are trying to know the depths and meanings of human existence, can we dismiss the past formulations as intellectually insignificant just because they involve prescientific or nonscientific modes of expression?[24]

I will develop each of these four points briefly. As to the "obviousness" of God as Wieman defines him, it is clear that he wants to remove the question of the existence of God from debate. In this, he is in agreement with recent philosophy which has held that "proofs" of God are futile. God must become manifest to us, else we cannot know him. But is it true that God should be manifest to anyone provided he is not confused by traditional definitions of God? Present-day discussion makes it plain that the *recognition* of God's presence is far more than a problem of empirical cognition. It involves the stance of the observer. It involves the kind of religious questioning with which we search for the meaning of life. It involves the mystery of the disclosure of the depths of our being and of God's presence. That God is to be known as a structure and process of existence is a supremely important thesis. But how he can be known in this way, as the power which is the source of all good requires more than analytical objectivity in order that we may see it? Of course, Wieman has insisted that something more than observation *is* required to know God. But it seems to me that this acknowledgment should lead to a much more serious wrestle with the problem of faith, of intuition, and the preparation of the mind for recognition of God.

This first point is bound up with the second. Part of Wieman's confidence in a positivistic description of God to make his being manifest is related to his increasing tendency to dismiss metaphysical problems as his thought has developed. To identify God as the source of human good immanent in the processes of human existence is, he believes, the primary task. The question of the creative event at other levels is not set aside, but it is not brought into a positive relationship to his whole doctrine. But the questions of the unity of God and his eternity are so pressing for any religious view (how can we be completely committed to a power which is not involved in all good whatever, past, present, or future?) that Wieman does introduce some discussion of this in the appendix to *The Source of Human Good*. But we have to ask whether the religious search for an object of absolute devo-

[24] *Ibid.*, p. 41.

tion can be satisfied with anything less than some grasp or apprehension of the metaphysical unity of God's being. If we have any metaphysical insight at all into the nature of being (and, of course, this is often questioned both by nonreligious positivists and by religious believers), then the question of the metaphysical search for the structures involved in all experience is fundamental, not peripheral. It makes a profound difference to religion how God is seen in relation to time and eternity, to power and causality, and to the personal symbols and analogies used in religious discourse. It is indeed part of Wieman's greatness as a religious prophet that he refuses to become immersed in such problems. Commitment to the present working of God is what he rightly holds to be of supreme importance. But when all the metaphysical questions are pushed into the background, then there results something flat and, in the end, superficial about the doctrine of God. Many of Wieman's readers may believe as I do that his discussion of the problem of religious knowledge in the early book *Religious Experience and Scientific Method* is the most satisfying analysis he has made, because the role of contemplation is stressed, and the awareness of the "total datum" in all its richness is given as the content of genuine religious knowledge. But, toward the close of that book, there occurs a curious sentence which seems to anticipate the later position. Wieman says, "The exact nature of God is still problematical and may be for many years to come."[25] But if seeking to know the nature of God involves our vision of being, then surely there is something wrong with this positivistic anticipation. One recalls Whitehead's warning: "The metaphysical categories are not dogmatic statements of the obvious. They are tentative formulations of the ultimate generalities."[26]

It is Whitehead also who has stressed the inadequacies of language for the expression of our basic experience. This insight, it seems to me, should play a larger part in Wieman's reflections on religious knowledge. One cannot be too appreciative of the integrity and creative freedom represented by his determination to get tested, valid statements in religion. But as Aristotle pointed out long ago, the degree of exactness expected in any inquiry

[25] RESM, p. 381. [26] A. N. Whitehead, *Process and Reality* (New York: The Macmillan Co., 1926), p. 12.

should be seen in relation to the particular subject matter. There are many questions here concerning the use of analogy, of myth, and of other symbolic statements in expressing the nature of God, which need long discussion. The question of analogy and symbol in religious language is in a highly confused state right now, and a gigantic task confronts those who would bring some order and critical judgment into the confusion. But, on any reckoning, it seems far too simple to say that symbolic terms and myths have a purely pragmatic function, and that all cognition is bound to strictly literal terms. Much depends on what "cognition" means here. But the recent discussion in philosophical analysis seems to indicate that a simple empirical theory of meaning will not do, and that religious assertions, such as those about God, have a status which raises profound questions about their similarity to, and difference from, scientific, empirical statements.[27]

Finally, I have raised the question of meaning in history. If it be true that growth of meaning involves the integration of past with present apprehension of God, then does not the intepretation of the meaning of religious living require a persistent re-examination of those historical meanings and structures, without which present interpretation is likely to be shallow? It is not simply that without this the power to communicate through historically enriched symbols is lost, but that the actual grasp of truth is thinned out.

I am not arguing only to defend the theological standpoint in which the tradition of a particular community is accepted as the context of religious inquiry, but since Wieman himself stands within the Christian tradition, the point here may be sharpened by calling attention to his position regarding our understanding of the significance of Jesus. In approaching his account of Jesus' communication with the disciples, Wieman says that if the reversal of human devotion there accomplished is intrinsic to the tradition, "we should be able to see the truth of it by simply looking objectively at the events which originated the Christian faith."[28] But this is to claim for a purely objective description of events something which they will not bear. How could we understand the significance of the Biblical story of Jesus just by

[27] See, for example, the discussion of the meaningfulness of religious assertions in A. Flew and A. Macintyre, eds., *New Essays in Philosophical Theology*. [28] SHG, p. 39.

looking at the record? It is a strange record, as indeed all genuine records of human history are. The meaning is tied in with a complex of a thousand years of religious experience in Israel, and with the structures of interpretation and symbol which had grown up. The relation between faith, observation, and historical understanding cannot be solved by the simplifications of positivist epistemology.

In arguing that the knowledge of God requires an appreciation of truth in traditional symbols, I shall adduce the matter of commitment as a striking example. Wieman often seems to write as if commitment to God were an absolute possibility in human life; but the truth would seem to be quite otherwise. The life of faith surely involves a becoming, a being transformed, and a continual struggle with the persistent sin in the life of the redeemed. All the subtle issues of self-deception in the life of faith, of the meaning of trust in forgiveness rather than moral accomplishment, as worked out in both the Catholic and Protestant traditions, are of utmost importance in interpreting the religious life. One must see how the life of nations and civilizations is a mixture of high commitment, self-interest, and self-deception. It is never true that a whole nation or culture makes an absolute choice to submit its ideals to the transformation of God. Such a commitment might be a leaven in the historical situation; it cannot in any foreseeable future become the dominant way of life for man. A more realistic facing of the tension between faith and unfaith as depicted in the theological tradition might save Dr. Wieman from a tendency toward simple utopianism. On the other hand, I would like to stress the depth and perceptiveness of his ethical insights as witnessed, for example, in the superb discussion of justice in *The Directive in History*.[29]

The essential rightness of Wieman's insight into the ultimate problem of man's existence under God seems to me to stand out beyond these difficulties in the way he expresses his doctrine. It is impossible to put into words the indebtedness to him which many of us share. His teaching and writing pointed us to the reality of God when theological tradition seemed no longer relevant, and when both liberal idealism and romantic humanism were revealed as incapable of coping with the realities of tragic

[29] DH, III.

history. Wieman set us free to think about God's presence in a dynamic history, and to understand the final issue between that faith which is merely a glorification of man, and faith in the God who alone can sustain an absolute and sovereign claim for man's trust and commitment. However difficult it is to discern the outlines of God's working in experience, unless he works there he cannot be the God who redeems. On the foundation of that theological assertion, Wieman has helped our generation to build. And this is an immeasurable service to theology and to the Christian faith.

DANIEL DAY WILLIAMS

UNION THEOLOGICAL SEMINARY
NEW YORK CITY

The Theology of Bernard E. Meland

Daniel Day Williams

An Introduction

For thirty-five years Bernard Meland has worked within the main stream of American liberal Protestantism and has given thoughtful, constructive interpretation to its expression of the Christian faith. From 1930 to 1964, through the shocks of depression, war, atomic destruction, and the emergence of the twentieth century world he has reflected upon and interpreted the meaning of the Christian faith as it can be held by those who cherish the freedom of Protestantism, the richness of tradition, and the need for constructive new expressions of the Christian perspective.

We can see three main motifs in Meland's theological development. The first is the demand for theological understanding of the American religious experience from within the perspective of the Christian faith. Meland has devoted himself to a persistent, critical reflection on the American experience with its interweaving of secular and religious elements. To read his works is to live through the reflection of a sensitive mind the struggles of American liberalism to come to terms with the realities of contemporary history and to find poise and guidance within the Christian tradition when it is creatively appropriated.

The second motif I find in Meland is a constant protest. His theology contains a running critique of the Christian Church, both conservative and liberal. He protests against the disavowal of responsibility for culture, and he protests against a church whose grasp of its cultural context is thin, trivial and tasteless.

He has protested against a theology which knows nothing of the depths of anguish in life, the reality of tragedy, the mystery of good and evil. Meland as a liberal has continually disproved the trite and stale image of liberalism as superficial, sentimental and unrealistic. At the same time he has protested against any disavowal by theology of responsibility for cultural appraisal and appropriation of the vitalities and sensitivities of the secular order.

He has protested against that side of American culture which leads to the proud, calculating, technologically efficient but emotionally arid spirit. And he has protested against a religiousness and pietism which can find no positive and sound health in a democratic culture and which is indifferent to the task of liberating the best in the secular order. Meland's *Higher Education and the Human Spirit*[1] is one of his most important books in his endeavor to show how theology can be relevant to the problems of a significant area of human life and work for the salvation of human values in a technological age.

But there has been more than protest. Meland has sought to recover and construct a viable theological perspective. The constant theme of his writing has been the necessity of orienting the religious spirit to repossess the depths of insight and power in the Christian heritage. He does not write simply as a critic, appraising the religious situation, but as one who calls upon men both within and outside the church to discover in a new synthesis the faith which informs their deepest valuations with an objective, empirical understanding of the realities of human existence. The words "recover," "reorient," "re-possess," "re-awak-

[1] *Higher Education and the Human Spirit* (Chicago: University of Chicago Press, 1953).

Daniel Day Williams was a colleague of Professor Meland for many years in the Federated Theological Faculty of Chicago, and is now Roosevelt Professor of Systematic Theology in Union Theological Seminary, New York. He has written *God's Grace and Man's Hope* (1949), *What Present Day Theologians Are Thinking* (1952), *The Advancement of Theological Education* (co-author, 1957), and *The Minister and the Care of Souls* (1961).

en" occur as variations on a leitmotif in Meland's writings. Of course they indicate the sense of loss in the present life of Protestantism. The story of modern religion, as Meland tells it, is the tragedy of a supreme insight and guiding heritage dissipated, abandoned, or trivialized. Theology must undertake the task, at the intellectual level, of seeking to "repossess the primal meanings of the Christian ethos."[2]

I
The Meaning of Culture

Since the term culture plays such a large role in the context of Meland's theology it will be well at the outset to get his definition of the word and to see how he uses it. In doing this we will come upon some of the most important themes in Meland's view of man.

The key to Meland's thought here is that he thinks of culture not only as an objective structure, but as a stream of life which bears certain valuations and sensitivities and which becomes therefore a dynamic, formative power in all human living. He defines culture thus:

> It is the human flowering of existing structures and facilities, becoming manifest as an ordered way of life in the imaginative activities and creations of a people, their arts and crafts, their architecture, their furniture and furnishings, their costumes and designs, their literature and their public and private ceremonies, both religious and political.[3]

And he comments:

> Each new generation comes into an organic inheritance greater in depth and range than the perceptions of any living person who is a member of it. Thus people live in a context of feeling and awareness that is always beyond their grasp emotionally or cognitively.[4]

Notice moreover the emphasis on the dynamic in culture:

> The culture is always an exemplification of the structures of consciousness which are available within the region to initiate psychical responses as well as to express and to assimilate meanings.[5]

The meaning of spirit in relation to culture must be clearly understood. Spirit for Meland is the result of the creative process at the human level. He speaks at times of spirit as the realm of meanings, values, responses and sensitivities in which man's creativity participates. The realm of spirit is therefore empirically accessible as the created structure of meanings. Meland rejects tendencies such as those in Berdyaev's theology to oppose spirit to culture. At the same time neither culture nor spirit should be used as an honorific term. Culture can be degraded, narrow and stultifying; and spirit can be demonic. Christian theology works within specific cultures and must seek to discover the issues which concern the spiritual life in every cultural context.

II
The Development of Meland's Thought

Meland stands, I have said, in the liberal stream of American theology. He reacted against the emotionalism and anti-intellectualism of a type of evangelical pietism and he began his theological work as a liberal interpreter of Christianity. But there were three elements in the intellectual foundations upon which Meland built which had for him an especial significance beyond that which is usually characteristic of liberalism. Understanding of these foundations is essential to the grasp of the distinctive character of Meland's theology.

First, there was the assertion of knowledge of God through religious experience, and a formulation of this knowledge through a critical method which can be broadly interpreted as scientific method. This religious empiricism Meland found in the thought of Henry Nelson Wieman, and it has remained a fundamental element in his theological method. Much liberal theology never accepted a radical commitment to empirical method, but Wieman and Meland made this the key to the validation of theological assertions by reason and experience.

Second, there was the metaphysics of emergent evolution as developed by S. Alexander, Henri Bergson, and especially Alfred North Whitehead. Wieman's first metaphysical formulations were put in Whiteheadian terms. Here again there was affinity with the main currents of liberal thought; but with a difference. The theology of divine immanence and the acceptance of the pattern of cosmic evolution as the context for the Christian understanding of God were characteristic of American liberalism; but the Bergsonian-Whiteheadian strand was more radically naturalistic. A metaphysical doctrine of God and the world was proposed as an alternative both to idealism and to materialistic naturalism. I have heard Dr. Meland describe the force of this new metaphysical perspective as an earthquake breaking through the crust of traditional patterns of thought and offering a new conception of the being of God and the nature of the world, along with a functional empirical doctrine of knowledge.

Evolutionary concepts led to the new theism with its doctrine of God as involved in time and

[2] *The Realities of Faith* (New York: Oxford University Press, 1962), p. 56.
[3] *Ibid.*, p. 212.
[4] *Ibid.*, p. 195.
[5] *Faith and Culture* (New York: Oxford University Press, 1953), p. 85.

process. This did not mean the identification of God with process, at least in its Whiteheadian form it did not; but it made a radical break with the classical tradition with its being above time and becoming by asserting a temporal aspect of God. Meland often speaks of God as the sensitive "nature within nature." It is the affirmation of God as involved in becoming, though "God" is not another name for the world.

We must indicate that while Meland adopted these positions of the new empiricism and emergent evolution, he early gave his characteristic emphasis to each of them. In the pattern of emergent evolution Meland saw the real context for a philosophy of culture. He speaks of culture itself as an emergent, it is the product of cosmic and historical processes, and it always reflects something which is deeper than culture that lies at the heart of being. Culture manifests that dynamic becoming which is the key to reality.

When he interpreted God's working within nature and culture Meland early adopted a theme of Whitehead's which sees God's characteristic mode of action in and upon the world as persuasion. It is the gentle, quiet, often hidden, ofttimes slow and tender leading of the world toward finer outcomes which impresses Meland; and I should say that this theme, which is prominent in Whitehead but is not his sole mode of describing the divine activity, has been for Meland the real key to the doctrine of God's power. This has ethical as well as metaphysical implications which we shall need to point out.

Finally, while Meland accepted the thesis of scientific empiricism as the mode of religious knowledge, he tended to focus his own attention from the beginning on the origins of knowledge in the depth of concrete experience, rather than upon the precision of formulated laws and structures. He never rejects the need for rational formulation and criticism; but he constantly calls for renewed awareness and grasp of the fullness of experience which eludes all conceptual formulation.

The ultimate source of theology for Meland is not in the schemes of meaning in culture by itself, but in nature; that is, in the encounter of man with the depths of the reality which brings him forth. The encounter means direct experience of the divine; but to yield knowledge it has to be given an interpretation and a continual critical reflection.

III

The Early Period

From *Modern Man's Worship* in 1934 to *Realities of Faith* in 1962, Meland's theological writing spans about thirty years. My thesis is that these years show a gradual development which has one significant and decisive break within it from an early stance to a later one. The new theological outlook does not repudiate the old, it builds upon it. Yet Meland shows a radical reorientation of his thinking, especially with relation to the distinctively theological task of appropriating the Christian heritage and faith.

One may describe the progress and reorientation of Meland's thought in various ways. He moves from progressive optimism to the tragic view of life. He moves from mystical experience to faith as the key to religious knowledge. He moves from an interpretation of Christianity as merged with the universal history of spirit to the Christian faith as bringing a special and decisive judgment upon man and as requiring a unique commitment. And through it all there is an increasing criticism of the purely rationalistic and scientific formulations of religious knowledge and a deeper concern for probing the roots of experience in which the elemental encounter of man with God takes place.

It is not possible within the compass of this article to document fully the many stages in Meland's theological pilgrimage. Some of the major works can be briefly noted here and we must begin with *Modern Man's Worship*, one of the outstanding books on worship and liturgy written in this century. It is a significant analysis of the tendencies in liturgy, church architecture and the theology of worship as these appeared in the first third of the century. The interpretation of religious knowledge which Meland offers expresses a type of cosmic mysticism. He is openly critical of Rudolph Otto and Karl Barth because of their extreme doctrines of the otherness of God. At that time he thought he could identify a tendency in Barth's theology toward a catholic type of objectivism in worship. Meland pleads for a radical freedom to reinterpret traditional religious concepts which have lost the feel of reality.[6] The new theism is rooted in a sense of "at-homeness in the universe."[7] And again:

> The impetus to set up religious relations with the universe issues, not so much from a conviction concerning the conservation of human values as from the present experience of sustaining cosmic reciprocity in the sheer act of living.[8]

Meland here regards the mystical attitude "as the supremely significant form of religious response . . . the deep fountain of all life, the inmost spring

[6] *Modern Man's Worship* (New York: Harper and Brothers, 1934), p. 124.
[7] *Ibid.*, p. 141.
[8] *Ibid.*, p. 142.

of religion."[9] And it is noteworthy that in this earliest book the theme of the appreciative consciousness is stressed. The pervading buoyancy which results from the appreciative spirit "helps to protect aspiration and thus unifies the personality."[10]

The quest for the recovery of the depth of religious experience in which man finds the meanings and empowerment for the creation of significant cultural structures continues through Meland's writing through *Seeds of Redemption* (1947) and *America's Spiritual Culture* (1948). There is more emphasis on explicit appropriation of the Christian tradition as embodying the elemental religious power in symbolic form increases, and this is the theme of *Seeds of Redemption*. In this work Meland wants to blend the biblical mythical insight with modern metaphysics.[11] He says:

> The ancient tales communicate this relationship in the imaginative vivid language of myth and poetry; modern metaphysics employs its modern myths to articulate on a vaster scale than the descriptive word affords the scope of human destiny.[12]

The stress on mythical expression is emphatic. The literal-minded cannot enter the Kingdom of Heaven.[13]

Meland develops the theme of the gentle working of God and the contrast of that power which the religious discernment finds in the divine with the ruthlessness and brutality of the expression of power of much human culture. We need the higher sensibilities which will enable us to use rightly the vast technical powers now in our hands.

Meland writes with prophetic insight against the crass and ruthless tendencies in culture, and he is no superficial optimist. The working of the gentle might of God involves destruction and suffering. Man the triumphant sufferer is man made in the image of God.[14] And there is this Christological passage:

> I look upon this figure of the Christ as pre-eminently a sensitive and solitary embodiment of those creative capacities that enabled Him to live beyond the mediocrities of His time.[15]

So far it is fair to say, I think, that Meland remains within the framework of the liberal expectation that the discovery and adoption of the right religious attitude will lead to adequate knowledge of God and point a clear way to cultural fulfillment.

[9] *Ibid.*, pp. 292-293.
[10] *Ibid.*, p. 303.
[11] *Seeds of Redemption* (New York: The Macmillan Company, 1947), pp. 40-41.
[12] *Ibid.*, p. 41.
[13] *Ibid.*, p. 43.
[14] *Ibid.*, p. 111.
[15] *Ibid.*, p. 107.

There is a sense in which this position remains through the later period; yet there is a decisive shift of emphasis on the content of the religious affirmation.

IV
The Later Period

There are signs in *Seeds of Redemption* that a new perspective is being born in the midst of the old. I have noted that Meland here brings the theme of suffering into his description of the religious life. Faced with the mystery of the unfulfilled life Meland even asserts skepticism about Whitehead's solution in his doctrine of the consequent nature of God, and Meland takes the position that the only answer to life's evil is the practical one of commitment to creative goodness. He does speak, however, of this commitment as something which can be achieved with ever more sureness.

The decisive shift to the new perspective comes, I suggest, in the brief but trenchant essay *The Reawakening of Christian Faith* in 1949. (It may be observed that the word "faith" appears in the titles of Meland's last three books.)

Take the opening words of this book as indicative of the way the problem of faith is now viewed:

> The conviction has grown upon me in recent years that the human mind struggles against almost undefeatable odds to understand its existence. . . .
>
> Reason and observation give only truncated accounts of existence. . . . The great epics in poetry and in music become as a new source of sight and insight. Their affirmations of faith as well as their tragic laments take on more sobering appeal, and one realizes that all these are the heightened, and sometimes desperate, utterances of men confronting the edge of their being.[16]

The prophetic note sharpens in Meland's appraisal of the crisis of culture. "Our society is hell-bent in this accumulative devotion to mass and brute power."[17] Now the source of hope is much more explicitly identified with that which can be recovered through the appropriation of the Christian Gospel. It is Christianity which has borne within its own deepest intuitions the knowledge of God's tender working. And now Meland lays more stress on faith as the mode of appropriation of the Christian heritage. This outlook on life and this conception of God's gentle yet transforming power "must ultimately be embraced on faith . . . but it is congruous with a conception of life in which tenderness . . . is sovereign over force."[18]

[16] *The Reawakening of Christian Faith* (New York: The Macmillan Company, 1949), pp. vii-viii.
[17] *Ibid.*, p. 103.
[18] *Ibid.*, p. 122.

What this statement means as I interpret Meland is that he now sees the theological task as requiring a more explicit analysis of the nature of faith itself, and of the significance of the primordial institutions and myths of the Christian heritage as the indispensable fountain and source of redemptive insight. Without giving up his earlier concern with religious experience and the significance of cultural experience for religious living, he now sees that the problem concerns the nature of faith itself, the question of what is fundamental in the Christian faith which must be asserted over against other options. He is therefore led to a more explicit concern with the structure of Christian faith itself.

In *Faith and Culture* and *Realities of Faith* Meland has been working at this task. The nature of faith and the relation of Christian faith to culture has been his theme and he has dealt with it with a patience and penetration which have led to some important insights into the nature of faith and to a reinterpretation of the meaning of revelation.

The argument of *Faith and Cuture* begins with what may be called an anthopological analysis of the nature of faith and moves toward an interpretation of the meaning of revelation in the context of Christian faith.

Meland begins by interpreting faith as an ingredient in the human psyche which is encountered by anthropologists, psychologists and philosophers as they try to uncover the deepest strata of human behavior. "Faith emerges before articulate speech formulates its communicable symbols."[19] It persists as a power giving direction and structure to human living in the form of a "structure of experience." This is a crucial term in Meland's outlook. It points to the dynamic power of particular ways of feeling and living as these function in a given culture. It means a structure of social as well as individual experience. Thus faith is to be encountered not only within the person but in the formative elements in the social body. It is a "thrust of the human psyche," it knows no bounds, it involves an act of decision.[20] Faith is later identified as "appreciative awareness," and as "an attitude of trust assuming explicit cognitive concern."[21]

While faith is here interpreted so as to be an object of empirical understanding as it functions within culture, Meland begins to deal with the problem of religious knowledge in a way which appears to transcend the empirical position as he has stated it before. He criticizes religious naturalism for being too concerned with criteria. This means, I take it, being preoccupied with objective rational and empirical confirmations of the beliefs which arise within faith. And he says that a retreat to contemplation and to mysticism offers no solution of the problem of religious knowledge. He is led therefore to a reconsideration of the meaning of revelation. He is dealing now with that given element in faith which cannot be derived from a prior or more general outlook but which is constitutive of a particular religious perspective. Revelation now is seen to mean the "breaking into" the stream of history and into the human consciousness of "a more complex and sensitive" structure of meaning, "impelling . . . to a new level of awareness and sensitivity."[22]

The revelation of God in Christ is the source of the Christian structure of experience. It is the formative, shaping, dynamic reorientation of the human spirit, born along in a living community which accepts the message of judgment and grace as the meaning of its existence.[23] It is clear that Meland succeeds here in keeping his doctrine within the perspective and framework of the emergent evolutionary view. His interpretation of revelation gives it a functional, empirical significance in the life of culture. Regarded objectively, revelation appears as the emergence of a new structure of meaning which becomes the foundation of a way of life for a human community. But Meland points to the revelatory action of God as it is grasped within the Christian faith as a given, which cannot be proved wholly by objective criteria or made to fit into some total structure of metaphysics or theory of value. It is faith which is primordial and formative; reason and experiential exploration of faith's meaning come after.

In *Realities of Faith* Meland has given his fullest and most systematic statement of the theological outlook to which his struggle with the distinctive nature of faith and the significance of the Christian faith has led him. The argument of this book is complex and important. I can here only note a few of the main lines which Meland works out.

What remains to be faced, we may say, is the ontological issue. What is the ultimate context to which faith points? Is man finally limited to the horizon of the world as he experiences it, or is there a dimension of transcendence in man's understanding of his being as related to a source which cannot be wholly bound within the order

[19] *Faith and Culture*, p. 6.
[20] *Ibid.*, p. 16.
[21] *Ibid.*, p. 120.
[22] *Ibid.*, pp. 213-214.
[23] *Ibid.*, p. 215.

of the world as experienced, and as accessible to our direct awareness? Meland now declares for both an immanent and transcendent dimension of faith. The first is the aspect of faith as primordial trust. This is given in the structure of man. It is given in creation.[24] But there is also faith as an ultimate assurance which comes to man as a movement of transcendent grace. This is the redemptive act of God, and is "a dimension of spirit which transcends both experience and culture."[25] Meland sees the insufficiency of humanistic idealism where it fails to find in man any need to recognize the creative ground of his being and to be open to that which comes to him from beyond the horizon of his own insight. Faith appears at the point of man's discovery of his insufficiency, and it perhaps always has the aspect of the venture of trust answering the threat of despair.[26]

Yet Meland does not believe that the transcendent dimension of faith allows the theologian to avoid the ontological problem. Assertions of faith say something about the relation of man to God and God to the world. The explication of that which is implied is the ontological task and Meland makes in this latest book some important progress toward what he describes as an ontology of spirit, or of spiritual encounter. He speaks now of the "transcendent life of spirit" which is interpreted as the life of man when he is aware of and grasped by the reality of grace. This is encounter with the depths of being, for man's life is never something by itself, but arises from a "communal ground," that is from the ultimate reality which gives rise to and holds together the diversity of creatures. Meland says he arrives at this ontological outlook through a doctrine of internal relations. I take this to mean that he holds to the logic of organic relatedness as alone adequate to describe the being of man and his relation to the creative ground. As does Whitehead, Meland wants to keep a place for freedom and diversity in external relatedness among the creatures. It is in the higher ranges of the spirit that we become more clearly aware of the kind of internal relatedness which spirit implies and requires.

This doctrine implies that faith witnesses to a good which transcends all human forms and images, even though it works immanently within all human good. The witness of religion, Meland says, "transcends all cultural goods," though to live with faith as Christianity understands it is to accept responsibility for the culture. We must see that

> It is the best that we do in response to the act of faith which bears at once the transparency of a faithful witness and the marks of our own ambiguities as creatures under God. It is in this sense that religion must always stand in the "crisis" of faith.[27]

What then of the diversity of faiths, and in what ways can there be dialogue across the boundaries of the faiths? Meland deals with this question in what is surely one of the most sensitive, thoughtful, and constructive analyses yet given of this problem. He does not blink at the difficulties. Each faith has its own structure of meaning woven through the cultural ethos in which its witness is carried. Yet "men have access to one another as human beings in ways that transcend all cultural and historical barriers."[28]

V
Conclusion

Looking back over this theological pilgrimage we see that Meland has moved within the liberal stream of theology, but that he represents in his own way a development characteristic of the major theological tendency of our time. He has come to assert that the Christian message of divine grace and forgiveness affords the real foundation of meaningful existence. The good news of the new power which leads to a new order of human existence is the redemptive theme which offers the real hope to our distraught world.

What is most characteristic of Meland's thought, however, is that while he has more and more brought the distinctive aspect of Christian faith to the fore and made it determinative over all rational and experiential search for religious truth, he has never lost his sense of responsibility for understanding, interpreting and relating the Christian faith to the context of man's total cultural life and his search for the understanding of nature.

The Christian faith points to the ultimate ground of all life, not just Christian life. It affirms that God works in his grace and redemptive power everywhere. We are not to sit in simple judgment upon other faiths, but rather to acknowledge a judgment which rests upon all things in human existence, and try to point to that reality out of the perspective of our life in faith. Thus the end of the pilgrimage for Meland is neither nature nor culture, but faith created by and expressed in a transcendent disclosure of meaning to man. It is the task of theology to interpret the meaning of faith, not only in such terms as may have been given in the history of the Christian

---

[24] *Realities of Faith*, p. 217.
[25] *Ibid.*, pp. 217-218.
[26] *Ibid.*, p. 221.
[27] *Ibid.*, pp. 303-304.
[28] *Ibid.*, p. 357.

community, but in relation to all the concerns of human culture and in relation to all the issues which are raised for critical intelligence in trying to understand the truth about things.

It is this sense of responsibility for culture, both in judgment and in appreciation of the residual good which lies in all things human, which has remained with Meland throughout. Every book bears the stamp of a profound, honest, patient and unspectacular, but thorough attempt to see the full problem of faith as men have to appropriate it in the human world, and to bring to bear the resources of the Christian tradition to illuminate the way through to a decent and sensitive mode of human living.

The pilgrimage has always been within the liberal doctrine of freedom, the freedom to inquire, to criticize and to believe. The liberal man, the free man, remains uncompromised in Meland's theology. It is a part of freedom to recognize the determinants and the limitations in one's own perspective. Meland has shown that within liberal theology there can be a decisive movement from a generalized religious philosophy with a perspective which stands outside any particular religious tradition to the affirmation of a witness in the Christian revelation to that which cannot be wholly grasped by any human philosophy.

To hold this decisive witness of the Christian faith and yet to avoid parochialism, irresponsibility and arbitrariness of theological assertion is the great task of the new liberalism in Christianity. The theologian must work and the Christian must live within the faith and within the culture. I believe that when our theological era is appraised in a time when there can be some more objectivity about it, Meland's work will be recognized as having achieved not only an insight into the issues but a balance in the handling of those issues which is sound and prophetic.

Some Queries to Professor Meland on His Paper

How Is Culture a Source of Theology?

Daniel Day Williams

Hebraic mythos; Platonic mythos; modern mythos

This paper has interested me, moved me to an even deeper appreciation of Mr. Meland's capacity to go to the heart of the theological problem, and it has raised some questions in my mind. In spite of the many years I have been associated with Professor Meland and learned from him, I had not quite grasped the direction of his thought as it appears in this paper. Or perhaps what is here represents a further movement in a direction which caught me somewhat unprepared. If I exaggerate to the point of misrepresentation what he says it is for the purpose of grasping some important tendencies in his present thought.

I do not need to dwell on the fact that my understanding of the theological task as it appears to us who stand in the liberal tradition with Dr. Meland is very close to his. Through the years I have been aware of his ever deeper insistence on two things: first, that the theology adequate for our situation cannot be confined to the strictly scientific modes of expression, fundamentally important though those are. And second, his insistence upon the radical character of the Christian revelation of the situation of man, the reality of estrangement, and the central need of the grace of forgiveness which the Christian faith brings.

And I have shared with the overall theme of this present paper that theological method cannot be restricted to an explication of any one source in the tradition, even the Scripture; but that it must somehow relate or correlate the biblical perspective with secular modes of understanding and with the concrete experience of us who live in this century, facing these kinds of problems, having to find our humanity or lose it in our kind of world.

I found especially pertinent to our present situation his remarks toward the end about the difficulty of realizing the heights and depths of the life of faith within the established religious institutions. This fact that in some way our very life in this kind of community relieves us of the necessity of examining first hand some parts of "the tough world" haunts me continually. The great respectabilities and economic securities which lend a certain necessary peace and serenity to our lives tend to remove us one step from the ruthlessness and pathos of life as it is for most people.

I do not know what we can do about this and remain theologians; but I know we had better acknowledge the fact and make it a subject of continual personal reflection, self-discipline and prayer.

I must add that we should resist the tendency to adopt only a negative attitude toward the church's cultural sensitivity and power. I believe Vaughan Williams' music will endure as long as anything being produced in the world of secular art today. And we can be grateful for the honesty, originality, and power of much contemporary church architecture, to mention only these examples.

. . . .

Now to the paper and Dr. Meland's interpretation of his theological method. I come directly to the point which has given me the shock of surprise and a new look at his movement of thought. It is the very strong emphasis on cultural relativism as determining the ultimate context of theological thought. I have never before in reading Meland been moved to think of H. Richard Niebuhr's *The Meaning of Revelation* as close to his position; but in this paper I see this perspective looming up.

> The tendency of every people is to employ the terms of their orbit of meaning universally; i.e., to speak for every man. The effect of this tendency has been to impel each cultural faith to conceive of itself and its perspective as being singularly significant, if not absolute, and thus to resist alien forms of religious witness. A first step as a prolegomenon to theological method is thus to attain self-understanding as a participant in a cultural faith, and to acknowledge as well as to accept the limitations of its historical witness.[1]

There is indeed a second step, "to bear witness to an ultimate reality." But I take it that the terms of the problem for theology in its relation to culture are set by this fact that there are elements in the cultural stream which perforce make us what we are and which determine the limits within which we can grasp ultimate reality.

Granting this element of relativism — and who can deny it — everything for theology depends upon where and how we find within this culturally-given context and meaning the criterion and the avenue of approach to ultimate reality.

Now what impresses me in Professor Meland's paper is that he wants to say that to be born in the Western tradition is to depend upon the *mythos* of the Judaeo-Christian tradition. And here he says his own method moves beyond both orthodoxy and liberalism because the traditional categories of liberal theology cannot handle the task of showing that it is the Christian *mythos* which underlies the structure of meaning in Western culture as it is today lived and experienced. We must therefore turn to the data which comes from the witness which shapes the culture within which both church and individual have achieved their historical forms of experience.

If I understand what is implied by this it means that these data have to do with the underlying *mythos*, the *given* in our culture which we cannot escape. This is born out by Meland's statements:

> My method, I am inclined to believe, rests precariously upon the assumption that our culture cannot extricate itself from the Judaic-Christian *mythos* any more than any existent event can relinquish its past as it lives on in the shaping of its present structure and dynamics.

In an earlier passage he has said:

> The Judaic-Christian *mythos*, I contend, underlies and is formative of the sensibilities and psychic outlook of our Western culture. The Christian expression of this *mythos* bears witness to a specific occurrence in our history in which the saving work of God becomes manifest as a New Creation; that is, the creative work of God assumed a new and decisive degree of concreteness. This, I am inclined to believe, was made possible by the emergence of a sensitivity and qualitative response within the human structure, enabling God to assume a new degree of concreteness in human history.

Now in the passages I have quoted the terms of the problem which raise my question are stated. Here cultural relativism becomes decisive for theology. There is no way to achieve a valid interpretation of the orbit of meaning in our culture apart from a recovery, a grasp, a reassertion of this deepest stratum of the *mythos* by which we live. We must actively appropriate it indeed; but it transcends in its significance and decisiveness any other categories or meaning which we may bring to it. It is what makes us what we are; it is where we recognize the working of God in our midst, and when we begin here we become theologians, not philosophers, or scientists, or poets only — but theologians.

So, baldly stated, one might find oneself bidding goodby to Professor Meland the philosophical theologian, the interpreter of Whitehead and Wieman, the affirmer of radical empiricism. But no, these old friends are not dismissed. They are still present, but Meland will go his own way even if he must move some distance from them. He does not dismiss the metaphysical vision, he "projects" a metaphysical vision (albeit a modest one) of his own.

In other words Meland recognizes that to grasp the underlying *mythos* one still needs a *logos*, and this *logos* is present in philosophical form in radical empiricism.

But now the situation is complicated because from the standpoint of this *logos* one may select among different elements in the tradition, or one may interpret the meaning of the myth differently.

And here Meland's encounter with Whitehead leads me to my first real puzzlement, both concerning what he says and the theological methodology which is implied by what he says. Meland says:

> My response to Whitehead with regard to this crucial empirical datum has been qualified by preferences of my own. For example, Whitehead, in considering where one might begin in one's metaphysical explication of the creative act of God, pondered the primal alternatives which Western history offered, namely the Hebraic and Platonic myths. Whitehead decided that the Hebraic myth of creation was too primitive for modern metaphysical speculation and thus chose to build upon the Platonic myth.

And then Meland remarks:

> I have chosen otherwise . . . but on grounds indicated by hints from cultural anthropology.

[1] All quotations are from Professor Meland's paper, "How Is Culture a Source for Theology?"

Now I must pause to meditate, reflect, and ask some cautious questions. We are seeking a metaphysical explication of the creative act of God. But we are confronted with an alternative between the Hebraic and Platonic myths. Evidently there is more than one myth in our culture, and we are given a choice.

But I am puzzled about the nature of this choice. What are we choosing about? Of course it might be said that the point here is a rather peripheral one in theology; it is only a matter of some special problems concerning the nature of creativity. But I cannot dismiss the problem so easily. Whitehead did not, and I don't believe that Mr. Meland regards the matter as peripheral. It makes a great difference how we think of the creativity of God as it is related to the world, how God acts, and what this means for human action.

I have several comments to make and some of them involve the interpretation of Whitehead on points where I must admit there are rather difficult problems both of what he intends to say and of some aspects of his doctrine of God. But on one point Whitehead is quite clear. It is not simply that he regards the Hebraic deity as "too primitive" for modern metaphysics; but that he regards at least one major strand in the Hebraic conception as presenting us with an imperious tyrant, overriding ethical considerations and in the end repudiating human freedom. The church gave to God the attributes which belong to Caesar, Whitehead says. Further, he argues that the Semitic monarch was united in Christian theology with the sophisticated notion of the Unmoved Mover in Aristotelian metaphysics. What has to be criticized here, according to Whitehead, is not something merely primitive, but something far more effective, contemporary, and dangerous than any strictly primitive notion could be.

I am aware that Mr. Meland makes much the same criticism of certain strands in the tradition which override freedom. Indeed I have always thought of Meland as having drawn out Whitehead's theme of the divine tenderness to its uttermost limit and affirming it with an absolutism which presents some genuine ethical difficulties. Whitehead says that the heart of the Christian revelation is what Plato discerned intellectually, the victory of persuasion over force, and I find this a major motif in Meland's work. I am therefore genuinely puzzled by Meland's statement that the Platonic myth has been only "marginally and intermittently effective" in our culture and then only at the intellectual level. Are we talking about the same thing? If the Platonic myth is that of the divine persuasion then it surely underlies Meland's interpretation even of the Hebraic myth.

I am, I admit, betraying a bias if not a theological prejudice. But I think the attempt to solve the theological problem by repristinating something called the Hebraic myth or world view, or the "biblical way of thinking" over against the philosophical way, has led us into some blind alleys in contemporary theology. It has split the mind of our culture, and it has led to some fantastically wrong-headed, if not just plain wrong interpretations of the first centuries of Christian thought. One only needs to read James Barr's discerning analysis in *The Semantics of Biblical Language* to see how parochial and mistaken the attempt to bypass the complex issues of the cultural background of the biblical view has been.

I am aware that Mr. Wieman has made a similar argument against Whitehead in *The Source of Human Good*. And I understand this in Wieman for he does not like the structure in Whitehead's doctrine and he tends to be skeptical of any metaphysical order or *logos*, and so he chooses what he calls the Hebraic view over against Whitehead. But Meland does not renounce metaphysics, he projects a metaphysical vision, he has a doctrine of God which he claims allows for precisely the kind of freedom for the creatures that Whitehead was concerned about. What then is involved in this choice of the Hebraic over against the Platonic myth? I would like to understand this.

We can pass more quickly over a second point because it has to do with Whitehead more than with Meland, but while I grant that Whitehead is not too clear on how God acts in the world other than through the primordial nature with its Platonic and Aristotelian offer of a lure to the *eros* of existence, surely when we consider the consequent nature of God, the tender care that nothing be lost, the work of the cosmic artist and poet, the love which floods into the world, the notion that God as an actual entity is the supreme exemplification of efficacious creativity, I cannot see that his doctrine is just to be *opposed* to the Hebraic myth of creation. Indeed Whitehead himself is far more Hebraic without surrendering his Platonism than his formal statements make clear.

But I stay further with this passage of Meland's and raise now a methodological question. Meland says a choice must be made between Hebraism and Platonism. And he chooses other than Whitehead, not on philosophical grounds but on grounds indicated by "hints from cultural anthropology."

I find this statement truly fascinating, especially from the standpoint of theological method. A decisive choice in the grasp of our underlying *mythos* is hinted at by, of all things, cultural anthropology.

Surely Meland means more by this statement than I have grasped. Taken as it stands it would seem to indicate that a particular science, cultural anthropology, can show us the way to the most fundamental of theological decisions. But Meland says it only "hints" and I would like to know what these hints are, and how they can lead us in this kind of choice.

What I am really arguing is that the choice is not a real one, that theology stands in the stream of a total culture, having to appropriate truth which comes from a dialectic between *mythos* and *logos*. While this does not allow us to transcend our cultural heritage absolutely, or jump out of our cultural skins, it takes the issue of truth as one which drives us continually out beyond any particular formulation of the ultimate myth to a radical, experimental, dialectical re-examination of its meaning.

In the end I know of course Mr. Meland is arguing for this too. I am only trying to understand why on the way to the method which he finally defends with its three "vortices" he arrives at this kind of transcendent position for the Hebraic myth in isolation. Where then does the structural aspect of our understanding of the world and the creative action of God come from?

Turning now to Mr. Meland's doctrines of God and of Christ — I seek a further insight as to how his post-liberal method leads to doctrines about the ultimate realities; for I am sure this is what his theology is aiming at. And here I come upon what seems to me again a somewhat startling *dénouement* in Meland's paper; for he goes further than I had thought in rejecting the task of developing an ontological doctrine of God. He says,

> For reasons which may become clear, I have recoiled from trying to envisage or to define God in any complete, metaphysical or ontological sense, preferring instead to confine attention to such empirical notions as the creative act of God and the redemptive work of God in history.

The word "complete" may be the key here; but surely Meland does not mean to reject the metaphysical task. His own statements about God are surely ontological. God is "Creative Passage," and God is "ultimate efficacy within relationships." He says this is an empirical statement but I would have difficulty construing it except with reference to some metaphysical generalities. What is *ultimate*, what is *efficacy* and what are *relationships?*

Now this doctrine of God, whether it be ontological or not, is the foundation of Meland's Christology. And here I have always thought of Meland's work as a profound interpretation of the significance of the pattern of emergent evolution for the interpretation of Christian faith.

In Christ there comes into our existence a creative good, a New Creation; Meland says, "the creative work of God assumed a new and decisive degree of concreteness." I hope I am not just seizing upon a phrase, but it was the reference to God's "assuming a new concreteness" which started my thought on the trail of what Meland is saying. He remarks that the New Creation "I am inclined to believe was made possible by the emergence of a sensitivity and qualitative response within the human structure, enabling God to assume a new degree of concreteness in human history." And he goes on, "nothing ontologically new occurred in this New Creation, that is nothing new ontologically occurred in God's character."

The energies of grace and judgment are present in Christ vividly, decisively, and creatively and they become the deepest vein in our structure of experience. We are encountering God's work released in Christ wherever these energies are found at work in our culture. And that may or may not be within the institutionalized cult with its objectified presentation of the Christian myth.

Thus Meland finds his synthesis between the decisive and inescapable biblical revelation and the turning of theology to the culture for the data which illumine our situation and which allow us to repossess what is fundamental in our being.

This union of the doctrine of emergent evolution with the biblical doctrine of the new creation is a fundamental thesis of the process theologies. I am eager to affirm it with Dr. Meland and to express the deepest appreciation for his interpretation of it.

At the same time I find the methodological issues here real; and I am asking for more insight as to just what is involved in his version of this synthesis. I can put my question this way: Is there not something more here than affirming the underlying *mythos* of the Judaeo-Christian tradition? Is there not a further step of interpreting that *mythos* through an ontology which is neither Judaic nor Platonic, but rather modern, the *mythos* of the evolutionary world view? But if this is so then do we not have to be much more specific and thorough about showing how we get to a *doctrine of* God both *ontological* and *theological*, and a viable doctrine of Christ which can really illuminate the meaning of faith in our culture?

I find three aspects of this question pertinent and I will state them, in each case not challenging what I take to be the direction of Meland's methodology, but presenting a query as to whether he is really representing to us the full dimensions of what is involved in carrying it through.

There is first the metaphysical question which I have already been discussing. But now it appears with even greater insistence. For Meland claims not only immediacy but ultimacy for the content of the faith. How is this ultimacy discovered, asserted and explicated?

The statement about "creative passage" here leads to some queries. God assumes "a new degree of concreteness in human history."

Does this mean that the creative passage is less than "concrete" in itself? This seems to suggest an ontological pattern. And what is meant by degrees of concreteness? If the pattern is that of an ultimate abstractness or potentiality which becomes concrete in history by degrees, then the pattern seems not Hebraic but indeed Platonic and Hegelian.

What I see here is that the relation of the Creative Passage to the actualities of history is an ontological problem. It is the question of the power of God, the nature of God's action, the question of the right categories for God, including person, spirit, structure, form, being and non-being. If we are going to use the pattern of emergence in this way we cannot recoil from the ontological task. It must be carried through. We must make it clear how and where this dimension of ultimacy is disclosed and what it means for the creatures. In what sense is there an ultimate in creative passage, *ultimate* in power, in value, in the order of explanation? Or in what?

The phrase "degrees of concreteness" leads to a second question – this one about Christology. We can remark that Meland has shown himself much more adept and profound than a good deal of contemporary theology. He was demythologizing before Bultmann, and yet without that tendency to the reduction of mythological language which seems to leave Bultmann sometimes rather arid.

Meland seems quite untroubled by questions about the historical Jesus, and in rereading his books I have been struck by how little interest he shows in the internal problems of biblical theology and especially of biblical Christology. But I am left uneasy here. It is good to extract the essential matter and say that energies of judgment and grace are released in history through the good which was in Christ. Meland is a profound interpreter of these energies. But I keep wanting to ask, "Just how are they released, what is it in the New Testament story that happens both to judgment and to grace?" What are the aspects of the concrete history (we say we are empiricists) which have this decisive significance in the preaching, the healing, the Cross, and the Resurrection? It is not enough to be impressionistic about this. Our problem is "culture as a source of theology." We need to know what it is that is given to us by way of grace and judgment in this decisive event which gives us a *criterion* with which to move through our culture. And we need to know how this disclosure in Christ is related "by degrees of concreteness" to the histories of grace and judgment before and after Christ.

It is here that the problem of biblical theology seems to me crucial for the theological task, and whatever our resources for dealing with it we cannot finally meet it without trying to penetrate the *mythos* at the focal point of its expression. And this seems to me, the more I meditate about it, a profoundly challenging, difficult, and as yet unresolved task. How much is history, and how much metahistory? What do we do with the extraordinary symbols, the special vocation of the Christ, the healing, the cry of dereliction, the resurrection?

And does our Christology in the end force us to choose between the Synoptics and John, or does it become Pauline, and if it does, then what is our doctrine of atonement, of the church in history, and of *last things?*

I realize I am laying about with large questions which no theology can neatly answer; but I am asking Dr. Meland for two things: for more insight into the methodology of dealing with the Scripture and the tradition, and for a more explicit offering of *doctrine*. Christian theology is the search for the doctrines of God, of Christ, of salvation, of history, of eschatology. And granting the supreme importance of the openness and dialectic and freedom which Meland gives to theology, I ask for a clearer delineation of the structure of the faith.

I come to the third aspect of my queries. It is the question about the place of ethics in theology, and of the implications of Meland's perspective for ethics. This is surely a crucial issue for any relating of theology and culture. It is with this that the church has struggled from the beginning. How is the new energy of grace and judgment related to the answer to the question, "What ought we to do?" We have to move from *ethos* to *ethics*.

Here it has always seemed to me that Meland not only appropriated Whitehead but absolutized one very important strand in Whitehead's thought, namely the opposition of persuasion to brute force as the key to the Gospel. Whitehead seemed to find here an ethical criterion for the direction of human action, if one not always immediately realizable. In fact, in his *Social Essays* Whitehead shows himself an astute commentator on the problems of political and economic power.

But if culture is a source for theology in any sense we have to say that the history of Western culture either has proved that anything but an absolutizing of the gentleness and tenderness of the spirit is a complete failure and therefore Christianity really stands over against the whole history, or it has shown that an ethic of sheer persuasion will not work. Society does not live by persuasion alone; justice is not secured by persuasion alone; man does not advance by gentleness alone. And there is a great problem for the Christian *mythos* here, for the revelation in Christ stands in judgment over all that seems to be an adjustment to or acceptance of the struggles of power in history, and yet we live in those struggles.

Meland surely is right in seeing energies of grace and judgment in the culture outside the Christian community. But are we seeking theological criteria now for identifying such energies, and for relating them to the transcendent criterion in Christ? It is not enough just to say that they are here, or to be moved and persuaded by outstanding demonstrations of humanity and sensitivity. We also have to find a meaning in the obscurities and unclarities and relativities of historical action, and we have to do this within the *mythos* which makes love the meaning of our existence. We have to reckon with the demonic in culture.

I am not arguing against Meland's standpoint but saying that the relating of theology and culture requires a specificity about the ethical dilemmas, and a Christian view of the structures of nations and powers in history which enclose, break, shape, and shatter our human destinies.

There is a temptation to say that Meland really retains much more of the liberal perspective than he acknowledges, that lurking through and underneath his view is the doctrine of progress and the idea that the liberal virtues of sensitivity, tolerance, rationality, and gentle love are really the key to the ethical problem.

But in the end this would not be fair to Meland's view. I am especially impressed by his later articulation of the tragic sense of life, by his refusal to resolve the eschatological problem too simply, and by his emphasis on the spirit of trust and the courage to relinquish the world that we may be prepared for whatever the future holds.

But I am asking about the relation of the tragic sense of life to the ethical task of our time. And surely here Christian theology has a major responsibility to show how the underlying *mythos* of the Scripture is really the key to salvation and to ethical guidance for contemporary man who now keeps the peace in part by preparing such utter and immediate destruction for all that no one will risk setting it off.

. . . . . .

Standing with Meland in his analysis of the theological problem and deeply indebted to him for his probing insight and refusal to seek the easy solution, I am saying that I believe process theology must not only affirm the three "vortices" but that in doing this we must carry through the ontological task of rendering our conception of being. That cannot be solved simply by affirming a particular *mythos* within our culture, but it requires identification of the universal questions which belong to our humanity. And it requires further the pushing through to the doctrines which arise from our encounter with the formative myth in our tradition. And this in turn means that we cannot escape the question of the *final criterion* of theological judgment, and the relationship of that criterion to the biblical record, and to our ontological understanding. Only when we have clarified the final criterion that we see or have given to us can we move with any sureness of appraisal of the claims of secular culture and only then can we fully and truly learn from that culture.

If I have raised many large questions I do it because they are my questions too. I am eager to discuss them so that the weight and depth of Mr. Meland's thought becomes more available to us all.

17

MARTIN BUBER AND CHRISTIAN THOUGHT

DANIEL DAY WILLIAMS

To discuss Martin Buber's influence on Christian thought is a very large task whose dimensions have loomed steadily larger as I have considered it. There is the richness and depth of the work of this great philosopher and interpreter of religion. There is the wide spectrum of Christian theologies from conservatism to neo-orthodoxy and all the way to extreme liberalism. There are many different responses to Buber's thought. But most important of all, we are led by Buber into a discussion of fundamental issues, and the shape of the discussion is just beginning to appear to us not only within Christianity and Judaism but within the whole of modern man's search for reality. This means that we must do much more than simply try to make an historical catalogue of Buber's influence. (That, indeed, would be to make him an "object" and violate the spirit of his philosophy.) We must speak within a dynamic process in contemporary Judaism and Christianity which is leading us all into paths we never walked before. Martin Buber has had a direct part in creating this situation.

What I shall say here, therefore, is in the spirit of adding another speaker to the discussion. I should also say at the outset that, while my interest in Buber's thought has extended over many years, my philosophical roots lie in a different place from the German idealism and existentialism which is his philosophical homeland. My background is in American empiricism, pragmatism, and the metaphysics of Alfred North Whitehead. On the philosophical side, therefore, I may have a less than adequate grasp of his position.

Few of us, however, who think about religion today are without personal and intellectual indebtedness to Buber. I shall never forget the excitement with which I read *Between Man and Man* for the first time, and realized that here was an existentialist interpreter of Kierkegaard who saw beyond Kierkegaard's individualism and who was establishing a fully social-historical doctrine of human existence. I heard Dr. Buber give two public lectures, the one on "Religion and Modern Thinking" at the University of Chicago with its superb critique of Heidegger, and a lecture on apocalyptic and eschatology at Union Theological Seminary in New York. Most important for me was the privilege of sitting in on the two extended Columbia University Seminars in 1957–58 where I could hear Dr. Buber in discussion and enter into some dialogue with him.

I shall give a brief characterization of the main influences of Dr. Buber's thought on Christian theology. Then I shall single out for discussion three major issues which he raises for Christian thought. My thesis is that he has opened the way to a discussion of Christian and Jewish thought which can lead us all to some new insight on perennial problems in man's knowledge of God.

I

There have been roughly three phases in the impact of Buber's thought on Christian discussion. They are to some extent chronological, paralleling developments in his own thought, but they also overlap. These are: first, the period of widespread acceptance and adaptation of the philosophy expressed in *I and Thou* in 1923. Second, there is a period of dialectical exploration and criticism of that philosophy and its implications for religious knowledge. Finally, there is the stage of listening to and response to Buber's characterization and critique of Christianity, especially in his *Two Types of Faith* in 1950.

As to the first phase, the appropriation of *I and Thou* by a wide range of theologians, the sheer list of individual thinkers and their positions could occupy us a long time. Buber's wedge between the primary words of I-Thou and I-it was used as a decisive key to the interpretation of theological method by Emil Brunner, Karl Barth, and Karl Heim, and in ethics by Friedrich Gogarten and Edward Grisebach. In Britain the group includes John Baillie, J. H. Oldham, Ronald Gregor-Smith, and H. H. Farmer, who made it the basis of his book on the nature of preaching, *The Servant of the Word*. In this country there is the powerful influence of Buber on H. Richard Niebuhr, Reinhold Niebuhr, and Paul Tillich, to mention only these leaders of Protestant thought. Until recently explicit influence of Buber on Roman Catholic thought has not been so apparent, partly perhaps because in such thinkers as Gabriel Marcel personalistic existentialism had found its Catholic spokesmen. But there is Father S. J. D'Arcy to be mentioned, and more recently Bernard Häring, whose ethical outlook is so important for the present situation in Catholic thought and who has explicitly acknowledged his indebtedness to Dr. Buber. Hellmut Gollwitzer's recent book, *The Existence of God as Confessed by Faith*, has many positive references to Buber and would seem to indicate that for Continental theology the movement against all "objectifying thinking" and rational metaphysics has grown even more radical.[1]

There are indeed some ironies in the way Buber's thought was used by the theologians. In the neo-reformation theologies of Barth and Brunner, and to a somewhat lesser extent in those of Reinhold and Richard Niebuhr, there was a concern to show that Christian theology

[1] Maurice Friedman's chapter "Buber and Christianity" is excellent in his *Martin Buber, the Life of Dialogue*, University of Chicago Press, 1955, and Harper and Row, 1960. Cf. Hans Urs von Balthasar, *Martin Buber and Christianity*, London, Harvill Press, 1961. (German original, 1958).

has its base in the New Testament revelation and not in any philosophy. Yet Martin Buber, the Jewish Hassidic philosopher, has given the key to the interpretation of revelation and religious knowledge and he does not depend on Christian faith. Karl Barth in his later system develops his doctrine of man and nods slightly in Buber's direction, acknowledging as Christian theologian that what he is saying about man is close to Buber's doctrine, but he goes on to say that Christianity alone knows the spontaneity of the I-Thou relationship. Buber quite charmingly and I think devastatingly reminds Barth that he, Buber, finds all the spontaneity he needs in this relationship without depending on Barth's special source of knowledge.[2]

What so many theologians found in Buber was a way of freeing knowledge of God from the scientific and rationalistic models. And further, Buber had shown that his conception of personal knowledge was born out of the Biblical outlook, yet it could become a general philosophic insight into man and his way of knowing. Hence Buber had shown theology a way of becoming free to develop its Biblical sources of knowledge and its method of expressing the truth of faith.

We see, however, that this freedom included the freedom to adapt the I-Thou doctrine to the purposes each theologian had in mind. It is a predictable fate of Buber's view, therefore, that it would be used to interpret such Christian dogmas as the Trinity and the Incarnation, the New Testament view of Revelation, the extreme individualism of Gogarten's ethics, and the element of mystical awareness as the ground of metaphysical knowledge in Paul Tillich. It may be that, of all the theologians, H. Richard Niebuhr came the closest to the spirit and intent of Buber's thought with his social existentialism, his ethics rooted in the relationships of personal loyalty, and his deep concern to unite faith in revelation with ethical obedience.[3]

There is perhaps further irony in that, while the more orthodox theologies found in Buber a way to defend the exclusive claim to revelation, the left wing of liberalism also turned to him as the liberator of religious thought from the parochialism of tradition. Many liberal moralists, theologians, and religious educators discovered in Buber the way to a vital and experiential humanism asserting the value of the person against a dehumanizing society and a rigid ecclesiastical establishment. They warmed to his teaching that the I-Thou relationship can occur in relation to nature as well as man. Buber opened up a fresh, hopeful valuation of the world as seen through religious eyes.

Paul Tillich appropriated Buber's philosophy in a special way, for Tillich belonged neither to the exclusive biblicism of neo-orthodoxy nor to the immanental humanism of the liberal left. He found in Buber the

[2] Martin Buber, "Afterword: The History of the Dialogical Principle," translated and reprinted in *Between Man and Man*, New York, Macmillan, 1965.

[3] H. Richard Niebuhr, *The Meaning of Revelation*, New York, Macmillan, 1941; and *Christ and Culture*, New York, Harper & Bros., 1951.

union of the prophetic and mystical in Biblical religion. Tillich adopts the doctrine of the I-Thou relation to God, but he does not make it the exhaustive description of that relationship.[4]

The second period I have called one of dialectical consideration of the implications of Buber's doctrine. He himself felt the need for this and made important clarifications in his exploration of aspects of personal being in the essays which make up *The Knowledge of Man*, and in his postscript to the later edition of *I and Thou*. Theologians and philosophers of many persuasions have entered into this discussion and it would be interesting to follow it here, but it is not possible in the scope of this paper. It is important to mention, however, the two major points where the questions have come. One concerns the interaction of the I-Thou and the I-it relationships as these occur in the complexity of human life. This primordial distinction tends to become blurred in actual experience, and many questions about the complex dimensions of human relationships have to be faced. The other primary point of questioning concerned the relation of man and God. If God is "Thou," and not "it," then does this give us a way of speaking about God's being? Is there a new metaphysical standpoint in Buber's vision? What will he say about God and the metaphysical categories of time and space and individuality and freedom? This is a critical question for theology, engaged as it is on all sides today with the question of whether there is any metaphysical knowledge, and if so how we can have a language for speaking about God's being. To all this discussion, Buber answers with a disclaimer of any metaphysical system. We speak of God as absolute Person because this is a way of rendering the meaning of the personal encounter with Him. But this does not allow us to develop objective concepts of God's being, nor are our symbols images of his being. Myths arise out of the human appropriation of God's self-revelation, but there are no images for God. In view of the importance of the question about being for our speech about God in the face of the criticism of contemporary philosophy, it is not surprising to find these issues being raised continually with Buber, and the *Interrogations* and the volume on his philosophy edited by Paul Schilpp and Maurice Friedman contain many important papers.[5]

The third phase of the influence of Buber's thought on Christians came late in his work and its real significance has just begun to dawn. It is the reaction to Buber's interpretation of Christianity, his assessment of the relations between Christianity and Judaism, and especially his view of the meaning of redemption from evil which is at the center of every reli-

[4] Paul Tillich, *Theology of Culture*, New York, Oxford University Press, 1959; *Biblical Religion and the Search for Ultimate Reality*, Chicago, University of Chicago Press, 1955.

[5] *Philosophical Interrogations*, edited by Sydney and Beatrice Rome, New York, Holt, Rinehart and Winston, 1964.

The Philosophy of Martin Buber, edited by Paul Schilpp and Maurice Friedman, The Library of Living Philosophers, Evanston, Illinois, 1963.

gion, and concerning which Christianity and Judaism have their deepest point of meeting and of difference.

Buber gave fifty years of study to the New Testament. He said with candor and blunt realism what he saw in Christianity. He gave his interpretation of the figure of Jesus and his teaching, and his criticism of what Christian faith and theology have done with the messianic hope of Israel. Buber spoke of Christianity with such scholarly mastery, such clarity about his own position in relation to the Biblical history, and, one may say, with such a spirit of judging and yet understanding love that he created a new situation for Christians who seek to understand their faith and to hear what others see in it. The response to Buber's work here has, I suggest, only barely begun to take shape. One thinks of four Christian thinkers in particular who have directly concerned themselves with Buber's critique of Christianity: Eugene Rosenstock-Huessy, Emil Brunner, Reinhold Niebuhr and, in 1957, Hans Urs Von Balthasar, the Roman Catholic theologian in his *Martin Buber and Christianity: A Dialogue between Israel and the Church.*

Rather than review the specific positions and replies of these thinkers, I shall enter the dialogue and raise what I see as three major questions which Buber has posed in his characterization of Christianity.

I need to state here what I believe is involved in this discussion. The important questions are not simply those which involve Jewish and Christian doctrines on specific points. The most important questions are those which go to the roots of all human existence. They are questions which both Judaism and Christianity have tried to answer. To be sure, these questions are raised by Martin Buber in part in a direct discussion with Christians, and they probe to the center of the nature of the two faiths. But it is man, not just Christian or Jewish man, who is seeking God and the meaning of life and who wrestles with evil in himself and his world. What Buber asks us Christians to consider again is, I am saying, what all of us must consider if we are to grasp our faith and seek God's word today. The ultimate questions of theology are every man's business even as we approach them from within the perspectives of particular faiths. In this I believe I am agreeing fully with Martin Buber's view of what is at stake in the discussion between Judaism and Christianity.

First, there is the problem of the I-Thou doctrine itself. I do not believe that the deepest problem of the dialogical philosophy has been fully met, that is, the relation between I-Thou knowledge and objective rational knowledge. This question I realize is a general philosophical question, but it cannot be omitted from our consideration of the issues raised for Christian thought by Buber, because it concerns the nature of man, his knowledge of God, and his knowledge of his world. One of Buber's great strengths is his refusal to separate theology and philosophy. All religious thinking must now come to terms with his fundamental thesis.

Clearly, Buber gave a powerful means of rescuing man's self-understanding from bondage to the analytic, piece-meal, and abstract approaches which have characterized much of modern science and philosophy. He shows that when we know other things as objects we ourselves are sharers in the objective world, and we lose in some way the depth of personal being. This is the ground upon which Buber stands and I, for one, would certainly not want to dislodge him from it.

But the question which remains is, what is the relation between fully personal knowledge and rational understanding of the structures of the world and of personal existence? And this question must be asked in the full seriousness of our realization that, whatever else man is, today he is technological man. He has remade his world by technology. He meets his problems of hunger, disease, mental illness, and social disorder with resources gained by scientific knowledge and rational criticism. But does this not tell us something about man himself, and does it not tell us something about the nature of the world, and indeed about God himself? What is the significance of the fact that man has created his new world by becoming objective in scientific knowledge? Why is it that this knowledge becomes to important to man?

I know that Martin Buber and adherents of his philosophy always say here, and I accept it, that they do not mean to disparage the I-it relationship in its proper place. They mean to say only that it must be rooted in the I-Thou relationship and not detached from it. But this leaves us with the question of how the two dimensions of man's knowledge support and enrich one another, and I do not find in the dialogical philosophy as yet a concern to explore this issue in depth. For it seems to me true that I can only serve another person in love if I am willing to become objective about the structures of his experience and to be willing to have the objective structures of my history and experience disclosed. And by the same token it seems to me that we can only understand what God is communicating to us through his world when we understand that world in its structural aspect as well as its personal aspect. We need a philosophy of existence in which the element of structural order, of objectivity, is not relegated to a subpersonal level, but is brought into the center of personal existence.

Technological man needs above all to find the personal meaning of his techniques. Just here it seems to me that American pragmatism and Whitehead's philosophy have a surer grasp of what is required for a fully personal philosophy than many personalisms. In the background of the dialogical philosophy there is the awesome and brooding figure of Immanuel Kant with his restriction of all objective knowledge to the categories of a deterministic physics, his skepticism about metaphysical knowledge, and his rigid conception of reason as it comes out in his ethics. We need a new philosophy of science and of rationality, not merely a separation of personal knowledge from objective knowledge. The implications for theology are clear, for what is at stake is the nature of our language about God. How can we speak of God's reality, his acting, his loving, his judging, his knowing, unless we have some way of speaking about the nature of being?

Such a plea for the work of reason in arriving at a doctrine of man and of God is not, I should say, typical of much contemporary Christian theology. Especially in Continental theology, there has been a radical appropriation of Buber's anti-metaphysical standpoint and the splitting of religious knowledge from all scientific and philosophical objectivity. But on whatever ground we stand here I am sure we cannot escape the critical nature of the issues. The quest for God and the quest for man is a quest for being, and the way we use reason in that quest remains a point of critical concern for every serious interpreter of religion.

II

We turn then to Buber's view of Christianity. Shall we call it his characterization of Christianity or his criticism? There is an interesting ambiguity which runs through Buber's analysis of the concrete forms of religion. On one side he often speaks as if it were the task of the interpreter of religion to recognize in each civilization its religious principle, and to accept the fact that each will work out its realization of its vision in its own way. For example, in *At the Turning*, Buber begins by saying that each great historical civilization can be understood as a life-system, built up around a supreme principle. All spheres of existence are essentially determined by that principle.[6] He gives a general law that "every civilization strives increasingly to render itself independent of its principle."[7]

From this point of view it could be the philosophers' task to characterize the spirit of each religious outlook, to let it stand by itself, and to take the position that each can only be judged from within. Sometimes Buber seems to take this view in what he says about Christianity, for he does not claim to understand it from within.[8]

But there is another strand in Buber's thought which moves quite against this historical relativism. He really believes each religion must confront others, and that the differences challenge a response. He believes that in one civilization, that of Israel, there was a recognition of God's command for all of life of "unique pregnancy," for "only Israel knew a God who had chosen a human people — just that people — to prepare the created earth as a kingdom for Him by the realization of justice."[9] Thus the more fundamental pattern of Buber's thought is that of a history in which man comes to self-understanding through the special witness of a people who point to God and know him in a way which is the paradigm of truth for all. Here Buber becomes not only an objective

[6] Martin Buber, *At the Turning*, New York, Farrar, Straus and Young, 1952, pp. 11-12.

[7] *Ibid.*, p. 15.

[8] Martin Buber, *Kirche, Staat, Volk, Judentum: in Die Stunde und die Erkenntnis*, p. 152.

[9] *At the Turning*, p. 14.

interpreter of the different outlooks of Christianity and Judaism but also a forthright critic of Christianity, its original formation, its understanding and misunderstanding of Jesus, its redefinition by Paul, its view of the church and the nations in history, its conception of faith, and its interpretation of the meaning of Judaism. Surely one cannot write, as Buber does, that "everything creative in Christianity is derived from Judaism, and that what is not Judaic is compounded of a thousand rites and dogmas, and speaking as Jews and as men we have no intention of trying to adjust our feelings to it" — one cannot write thus, and not expect the discussion to go on.[10] Or again, one cannot assert that the I-Thou relationship is the meaning of human existence, with the I-it relation a derivative and incomplete relation, and then describe the faith, *emunah*, of Judaism in I-Thou terms and the faith, *pistis*, of Christianity in I-it terms, and not be aware that one has raised a critical question which needs to be explored.[11] We can then, all of us, be thankful that Buber forsakes the objective "history of religions" stance and says how Christianity looks from his standpoint, especially its failure to appreciate the truth in which its ultimate sources lie.

Buber's view of Christianity is well known. I trust the following brief summary includes the main themes.

Christianity's departure from the prophetic faith is rooted, not in Jesus' teaching, or his self-understanding, but in Paul. Buber sees Jesus in the line of the prophets. Indeed, Buber speaks of him as the first in a line of messianic figures whom God raises up as his witnesses in history. Jesus understood man before God in the freedom of personal relationship which is at the base of Israel's faith. In the Sermon on the Mount he gave concise and powerful expression to the demand of God as it brings all of life under the divine rule. It was Paul who turned this prophetic outlook into something entirely different. Paul fell into the pattern of the apocalyptic view of history, which to be sure had been prepared in late Judaism and with Iranian and gnostic sources. Paul's world view includes a transcendent realm of demons and evil powers who have to be conquered in a heavenly warfare. He has a deterministic world view in which all follows a divine plan which is worked out, so to speak, over men's heads. It was Paul who took the concept of *Torah*, which for Buber never means "law" but divine command in the concrete historical situation, and understood the Torah not only as an objective set of regulations but regarded it as something which God himself has interposed between himself and man. The Law is the enemy of man, which yet fulfills the divine purpose of condemnation first and reconciliation afterward. God has consigned man to disobedience that he might have mercy. So the concept of faith itself is transformed. It is no longer man's free response

[10] *Die Erneurung des Judentums* in *Reden über das Judentum*, Martin Buber, *Gesamtausgabe*, 1923, p. 54.

[11] Martin Buber, *Two Types of Faith*, English Translation, London, Routledge & Kegan Paul, 1951, *passim*.

to God, but it is belief in an objective truth concerning the acts of God, acceptance of dogma, and God has decreed who shall have faith and who shall not have it.

Christianity thus dominated by Paul becomes an individualistic religion preoccupied with the salvation of the individual soul. This individualism is the real secret of the conception of the Church, for the Church is no longer an historical people, a concrete locatable people of God, but a supranational people without a place, abstracted from the concrete demands of particular histories. Therefore the church develops an ethic of two realms in which the Church lives from the command of God, but the world is alien, it lies in bondage to evil powers, obeying laws which are ultimately God given, but which are concessions to human sin. The directness of the prophetic demand to serve the Kingdom of God in the world is lost amid the mysteries of the Church, which is a figure of the Kingdom but freed from the obligations of historical realization.

Thus constituted, Christianity has regarded itself as the fulfillment of Judaic expectation, and its Lord as the expected Messiah. Yet Judaism remains the people of the Book who in their essential witness announce that God has made himself known; his demand is laid upon men and they can in freedom respond. Man needs nothing less but nothing more than just this witness and his personal response to it. Here is, as Buber sees it, the real source of the dark and tragic reality of anti-Semitism in the Christian attitude toward Judaism.[12] It has distorted its own image of Judaism by seeing the God of the Hebrew Bible as the God of Wrath who only judges man and in whom there is no salvation but only hope for a future mercy. This is the Marcionite theme which Buber believes is always present in Christianity, though he acknowledges that Christian theology has always fought against it. But it has never been eliminated; and when it appears, as it does in even the benign and liberal spirit of an Adolph von Harnack, it leads to the abyss of persecution and that blackest page in the whole history of humanity, the mass murder in Hitler's Reich.

Such a radical, probing characterization of Christianity must lead us in these days to a significant theological exploration of the meaning of the Biblical truth for civilization. We shall live with these issues a long time.

It is not my purpose here to try to answer Buber's position in detail. That would take literally years of work, a work which I hope will go on. What we can do here is to point to a fact in the present situation which is that in the present theological transformation within Christianity, and I think we need that strong a word to describe it, most if not all the trends are in the direction of recognizing aspects of the truth for which Buber is calling, which he rightly finds in the prophetic faith, and which he rightly says have been lost or obscured in the traditional expression of Christian faith. From Karl Barth's interpretation of Paul in the light

[12] Martin Buber, *Israel and the World*, New York, Schocken Books, 1948, pp. 189 ff.

of Kierkegaard's personalistic existentialism to the Second Vatican Council just concluded, the major movement of Christian theology has been toward a deepening of theological emphasis upon the freedom of God and of man in the real life of history. Every major theme — Creation, Revelation, Christology, sin and grace, election and ethical responsibility, redemption and eschatology — has been recast in terms which try to break through the rigidities of traditional dogma. For some of those rigidities the apostle Paul may be responsible; but we also know that they resulted in part from the adaptation of Christian doctrine in the first centuries to the patterns of Greek metaphysics, with its absolute which transcends all time and becoming.

For this new freedom and personalism in theology we have in part to thank the work of modern Biblical scholars, and I can only mention Dr. Buber's contribution to this which has been widely recognized by Christian Biblical interpreters. We are dealing with a movement of thought to which he has given a powerful impetus, and its results are apparent in Christian theology almost wherever one looks today.

If we look at the achievements of the Vatican Council II, for example, we can say that the entire direction in Biblical interpretation, in ethics, in the qualification of traditional views of natural law, and above all in the open spirit toward the world, the movement has been toward a personalistic interpretation of faith, of dogma, and the Christian life.

Let us turn to the question of Christology. The interpretation of the incarnation in the categories of Greek metaphysics culminated in the decree of Chalcedon which has been the norm of orthodox Christianity for all these centuries. But dogmas have to be interpreted, and there has been a restlessness in Christian theology about the Chalcedonian formula from the beginning. Today such theologians as William Temple, Paul Tillich, Reinhold Niebuhr, John and Donald Baillie have raised serious questions about its adequacy. The direction of modern Biblical interpretation and theological doctrine is clear. It moves toward the full recognition of the humanity of Jesus, a man of his time, living a human life with a fully human experience of the world and of God. The question of what it means to believe that God has made himself a person for love of us (phrase is Martin Buber's) remains the central task of Christian theology.[13] Once we take the view that traditional dogmas are way stations for the faith of the believing community and not final and infallible oracles, we are free to try to say again what our faith means.

In this movement toward a deeper realization of personal faith, and the recognition of the ultimate personal context of liturgy and sacraments, dogma and authority, we can see many tendencies at work. Some grow, as we have said, out of modern Biblical scholarship; some result from the recognition of the transitory character of the world-view of the Biblical writers, and the new sense of the limitations of knowledge which has come with modern science. Some come directly from the influence of Martin

[13] Martin Buber, *Eclipse of God*. New York, Harper & Bros., 1952, p. 127.

Buber and other personalistic existentialists who have had a liberating influence on Christian thought. For all this, every seeker of truth should be grateful.

Without trying to defend any particular faith, we may say that the whole discussion shows how the issues of human freedom versus a false objectivism, and of how faith can be free from bondage to external human authority, are not simply issues between Judaism and Christianity but are perennial issues in religion and all human experience. I can accept Buber's characterization of Christianity as applying to much of what has been present in it. I cannot accept it as an adequate statement of the essence of Christianity. Every responsible seeker for the truth has a stake in the criticism of depersonalized religion and arbitrary authority. We all are involved in the question of how the personal recognition of the presence of God is possible for man. It may be that where we need to begin to talk with one another is in the re-examination of what did happen in the first century of the present era, on the assumption that none of us has a full understanding of it.

I take an example from a relevant current source, Mr. Robert Alter's able article in *Commentary* on apocalyptic in contemporary literature. He is concerned with the tendency in much contemporary literature to accept the determinism, the dualism, and the despair of an apocalyptic outlook. Alter appeals directly to Martin Buber's critique of apocalypticism, and then comments concerning Christianity:

> It is a historical commonplace that Christianity was born out of the apocalyptic side of Judaism.[14]

Now, surely, like all commonplaces, this one ought to be subjected to examination. It is much too simple. It is not precisely Buber's own teaching, for he sees Jesus in the prophetic rather than the apocalyptic vein. There is the further fact that much of Christian theology developed as an adjustment to the Hellenistic, not the apocalyptic world view. And finally, it is surely not a closed question as to why apocalyptic arises and whether it may throw light upon the human situation. We ought not to settle that question arbitrarily. We need to re-enter the discussion of the Biblical faiths in human history not with pre-conceived categories but with the recognition that we are the heirs of a complex tradition which must be appropriated and criticized in ever new situations. As I have thought of the possibilities of such discussion, there has come to me the phrase used by another great interpreter of religion, William Ernest Hocking, whose death occurred almost one year to the day after Martin Buber's. Hocking said that in the meeting of the world religions we should keep open the possibility of *Reconception* as each faith, maintaining its own integrity, seeks to grasp more deeply the truth from which it lives.[15]

[14] Robert Alter, "The Apocalyptic Temper," *Commentary*, Vol. 41, no. 6, p. 62.
[15] William Ernest Hocking, *Living Religions and a World Faith*, New York, Macmillan, 1940.

Something like this Martin Buber himself was calling for as he wrote at the close of *Two Types of Faith:*

> An Israel striving after the renewal of its faith through a rebirth of the person and a Christianity striving for the renewal of its faith through the rebirth of nations would have something as yet unsaid to say to each other and a help to give one another — hardly to be conceived at the present time.[16]

We have been speaking of the humanizing and personalizing of our conception of faith and dogma. Let us come to the question which is at the heart of all religion, the problem of evil and its redemption. One aspect of Buber's greatness is the tenacity and courage with which he has kept this question at the center of his thought throughout his life. Here lies the seriousness of life in the reality of evil, the evil in the self, and the evil in what men do. For Buber all evil is rooted in man, his directionlessness when he turns away from singleminded obedience to God, and the subsequent elaboration in imagination and fantasy of his pride, his self-glorification.

Buber sees in Christianity not a denial of evil, but a shifting of the source of evil from man and his responsibility to the realm of evil powers which rule man, and ultimately to the decrees of God. Redemption from evil, Christianity finds in a transaction wrought by God himself in Christ which becomes the means of a grace which descends upon man from beyond himself. Man's responsibility, his spontaneous freedom to seize the task at hand as the servant of God and to make the world good, is thus lost. For Buber, it is Judaism alone which understands the final seriousness of the call to be a nation wholly obedient to God's command and purpose. The redemption of the world lies in the people's acceptance of their calling to be the people of God. Buber is opposed to all views of redemption which move from time to eternity, from history to a consummation beyond this life and this earth. His well-known statement must be quoted again here:

> Now to the Christian the Jew is the incomprehensibly obdurate man, who declines to see what has happened; and to the Jew the Christian is the incomprehensibly daring man, who affirms in an unredeemed world that its redemption has been accomplished.[17]

We might say that here we have reached the final boundary between the faiths and there is no more movement which can take place. Or we can say that the question of redemption from evil is the final human question which we all must ask again, trying to see whether we may have missed some depth of the problem in all our formulations. Just here Martin Buber made his most direct challenge to Christianity, for he declared that Christianity has never understood the significance of the nation for redemption, and it does not really know therefore how re-

[16] *Two Types of Faith*, p. 174.
[17] *Israel and the World*, page 40.

demption is possible. But as he says this, he opens the way to the most critical questions which Christian theologians raise with him. For Buber's picture of redemption in history through the absoluteness of devotion of the single hallowed nation is filled with puzzling elements. He insists that he is not a utopian, but a meliorist, and I take this to mean that he believes evil is not to be completely eliminated but is to be overcome in specific acts of historical social righteousness. Yet this leaves us in a history where the full obedience of the nation, the achievement of the righteous people, is always ahead of us, always a demand; but is it a fulfillment?

When we ask how Buber conceives the movement of redemption in history, his most puzzling statements appear. He sometimes speaks as if redemption were going on all the time in a continual working of God which is present in every moment, in every history, in spite of tragedy and evil. Here Buber seems, in his own way, and in spite of his strictures against Paul, a kind of determinist. In *At the Turning* he says:

> Postbiblical thinkers have pondered how the freedom of the human will and the resultant indetermination of the future can be reconciled with divine foresight and predetermination. Outstanding among all that has been said in the effort to overcome this contradiction is the well-known saying of Akiba's ("All is surveyed, and the power is given"), whose meaning is that to God, Who sees them together, the times do not appear in succession but in progress-less eternity, while in the progression of times, in which man lives, freedom reigns, at any given time, in the concrete moment of decision; beyond that, human wisdom has not attained.[18]

Is this Buber's solution, or does he disavow it when he says that in the Bible itself there is no pondering; the Bible does not deal with the essence of God, but with his manifestation to mankind? I am unsure. The same theme of a redemption everywhere at all times appears again when Buber says:

> There are no knots in the cable of our Messianic belief, which, fastened to a rock on Sinai, stretches to a still invisible peg anchored in the foundations of the world. In our view redemption occurs forever, and none has yet occurred. Standing bound and shackled in the pillory of mankind, we demonstrate with the bloody body of our people the unredeemedness of the world.[19]

And again:

> From the point of view of the Bible, revelation is, as it were, focussed in the "middle," creation in the "beginning" and redemption in the "end." But the living truth is that they actually coincide. . . . if I did

[18] *At the Turning*, p. 55.

[19] Quoted in Ernst Simon, "Martin Buber: His Way between Thought and Deed," *Jewish Frontier*, XV (Feb. 1948), p. 26.

> not feel creation as well as redemption happening to myself, I could never understand what creation and redemption are.[20]

I do not really see how to bring this side of Buber's teaching together with his view of a melioristic attack on evil in history. Are there real new acts of God in history, or is there only one act which is at once the acknowledgement of the world's evil and its redemption?

We cannot avoid asking whether Buber's concrete social philosophy does not in fact hold a utopian element. He is not unmindful of the ambiguities of ethical choice and the tragic element in social reconstruction. But he seems to believe that one can find a pure program of social reconstruction, and he tends to disparage political structure in seeking a just social order. He says: "Political methods at their height mean the effective abolition of the human factor."[21]

It is on this issue of the nature and possibilities of ethical action in history where Christian moralists like Reinhold Niebuhr and Paul Tillich say that the question of evil in history drives us to see the significance of the doctrine of God's mercy beyond the structures of history, his grace manifest in suffering love which gives a standing ground in the midst of an ethically ambiguous history, and where political action and structure are indispensable for man's attempt to create a viable order in spite of human fallibilities.

We see at once that the issue is not simply one of political and social ethics, but the ultimate theological issue of the nature of God, his action in history, the meaning of the divine suffering for and with man. The theme of the suffering God which is so close to the figure of the Servant in Deutero-Isaiah here becomes a clue to history itself and the divine strategy of redemption. Without defending any historical formulation of the Christian doctrine of redemption, I would say that the discussion with Buber must begin here.

That such a discussion is possible at all is a great new fact about our existence in this present world history with its encounter of the faiths of mankind. Martin Buber has been one of the major influences in making this new fact possible. He has helped to create a new space for human meeting where we can bring our faiths and our questions without undue polemics into a genuine searching for the truth which may lie deeper than any of us have ever seen. I regard Buber's work in creating this new space for meeting as more important than the technical aspects of his dialogical philosophy. By his stature as man and teacher, by the depth of his grasp of his faith, and by his spirit as brother, he has given us all a new hope for some correction of ancient wrong and modern illusions. I am glad as a Christian and as a man to try to walk in that new space and to acknowledge Martin Buber's help in walking.

[20] *Israel and the World*, p. 96.
[21] Martin Buber, *The Knowledge of Man*, London, Allen and Unwin, 1965, p. 83.

Paul Tillich's Doctrine of Forgiveness 18

DANIEL DAY WILLIAMS
Professor of
Systematic Theology
Union Theological Seminary

FORGIVENESS is interpreted by Paul Tillich in the context of his analysis of the separation between man and God, between man and man, and of the cleft in every man. Salvation is the overcoming of separation in all these aspects. Forgiveness of sin, man's self-imposed separation from God, is an inseparable part of salvation; but it must be grasped in relation to other dimensions of man's existence. Reconciliation requires forgiveness, yet it requires more. In establishing this doctrine Tillich gives a searching analysis of the existential situation, and he affirms the answer of the Christian Gospel to man's ultimate questions. Tillich is sometimes charged with having an impersonal view of God, and of losing the personal center of the evangelical faith, but a careful analysis of his doctrine of forgiveness shows why he will not put the doctrine of salvation exclusively in terms of forgiveness of sin. Whatever one thinks of Tillich's doctrine he illuminates many aspects of forgiveness precisely because he sees it in relation to man's total situation and seeks to understand the experience in which contemporary men sometimes appear neither to understand nor to seek forgiveness.

In exploring Tillich's doctrine of forgiveness I shall begin with his analysis of the historical problem, that is, the relation of our spiritual situation to that of the Reformation. We move on to his analysis of the three-fold structure of anxiety and its implications for the meaning of salvation, and come to his account of forgiveness in relation to acceptance.

The Historical Problem

The problem of interpreting forgiveness in the twentieth century situation is posed by Tillich in the first volume of the systematic theology published in 1950. I mention the date, because there are some hints of a shift of emphasis in the later writings.

In the introduction to *Systematic Theology* Tillich is discussing the question of the theological norm, and the impossibility of a simple formulation of it. The Reformers affirmed the doctrine of justification by faith as material norm and the authority of Scripture as formal norm. But the norm has to be an expression of the encounter of the church with the Christian message. A theological norm which does not appear within the correlation of Gospel and human question will be irrelevant. Just here we come upon a critical problem concerning justification by faith and forgiveness. Tillich says:

> It is not an exaggeration to say that today man experiences his present situation in terms of disruption, conflict, self-destruction, meaninglessness, and despair in all realms of life. . . . The question arising out of this experience is not, as in the Reformation, the question of a merciful God and the forgiveness of sins; nor is it, as in the early Greek church, the question of finitude, of death, and error, nor is it the question of the personal religious life or of the Christianization of culture and society. It is the question of a reality in which the self-estrangement of our existence is overcome, a reality of reconciliation and reunion, of creativity, meaning, and hope.[1]

This would seem to push forgiveness to the periphery of contemporary concern. I suggest this is not Tillich's intent though his language is somewhat unguarded. In *The Courage to Be*, published in 1952, Tillich develops his analysis of three types of anxiety. Here forgiveness is not pushed to the background but appears as one of the three dimensions of man's need.

The analysis of ontological anxiety is well known. Man is estranged from being-itself, from God, the reality which determines the being or non-being of all creatures. Awareness of the threat of non-being is ontological anxiety. But now Tillich distinguishes three ways in which the threat of non-being threatens man's self affirmation: first, it threatens his ontic self-affirmation relatively in terms of fate, absolutely in terms of death; second, it threatens his spiritual self-affirmation relatively in terms of emptiness, absolutely in terms of meaninglessness; and third, it threatens his moral self-affirmation relatively in terms of guilt, absolutely in terms of condemnation.[2]

We note especially how Tillich identifies the forms of self-affirmation which correspond to each threat. We see that for the third self-affirmation, that connected with guilt, he uses the term "moral." Some of the special aspects of Tillich's view of forgiveness have to do with his use of this word. Here it implies that man is a responsible being who experiences the unconditional demand of God and who can reject this demand. It is an ultimate dimension of personal existence. The "moral" is not restricted here to the realm of particular moral commands or principles. When Tillich later speaks of "the transmoral personality" he does not reject this dimension of responsibility at the core of man's being. This is a critical point for understanding the significance of forgiveness in Tillich's doctrine.

We see that guilt which can only be overcome by forgiveness is one of the three structures of man's alienation. Tillich now says that the differences among the types of anxiety does not mean that they are mutually exclusive, in fact they are "immanent in each other."[3] It is true however that "normally" one or the other is "dominant." The word normally here must mean "in most cases." One may remark in passing that Tillich does not explore very fully the *interrelations* of the three anxieties. He does illuminate them profoundly at some points, but it would be instructive to inquire how the anxiety of death is related to guilt, and how the experience of meaninglessness is related to anxiety about fate and death. May not the experience of unlimited possibilities also

---

[1] Paul Tillich, *Systematic Theology*, Vol. I, (Chicago: University of Chicago Press, 1950), p. 49.

[2] Paul Tillich, *The Courage to Be* (New Haven: Yale University Press), 1952, p. 41.

[3] *Ibid*, p. 41.

produce its kind of meaninglessness?

What Tillich has offered so far is the insight that if we are to understand forgiveness in our time we must be ready to look at the question of estrangement and salvation in something more than "moral" terms. He has not discarded the issues of forgiveness but he interprets it in the setting of the contemporary spiritual situation.

Reconciliation, Salvation, and Acceptance

Man's condition is estrangement or separation. Salvation is reconciliation, healing, the bestowal of wholeness. As Tillich interprets salvation he finds a radical tension at the very center between that understanding of the relationship of man and God which is a "participation in being" and that aspect which is a personal reconciliation. He relates these two aspects to two of the ontological elements, participation and individualization. Where participation is dominant the relation to being-itself has a mystical character, where individualization is dominant, the relationship has a personal character.[4]

Since ontological elements are all inescapable structures in every experience, we may be a little puzzled to know how one can be "dominant"; but Tillich is talking about the way we experience our being, and in this existential situation it may be proper to speak of the dominance of an ontological element *as we experience it*. In any case what he points to here is fundamental for his interpretation of forgiveness in the Protestant tradition. Tillich recognizes that the Reformers, and especially Luther, affirmed personal communion over against the mystical type:

> In comparison with the mystical form of courageous self-affirmation the Protestant courage of confidence affirms the individual self in its encounter with God as a Person.[5]

This Protestant courage, which is Tillich's expression for faith, has the courage to accept acceptance in spite of guilt at its center. Forgiveness is the center of reconciliation in this form of the courage to be. Tillich makes the significant remark, "There is belief in forgiveness in all forms of man's courage to be, even in neocollectivism."[6] Here again we see that forgiveness is at the center of salvation even though it is not the exclusive meaning of salvation.

So far, then, we have a tension between salvation in the mystical type as participation in that which overcomes death and meaninglessness, and as acceptance of forgiveness which overcomes guilt and condemnation. But Tillich is driving the analysis toward what he now calls "absolute faith," and he says bluntly that he "does not think either mystical union or personal encounter fulfills the idea of faith."[7] The reason is that faith is the courage to be, and this must be an affirmation in which *all* the anxieties are overcome. Mystical experience and personal encounter must become one in the courage to be. Luther and the other Reformers saw *sin and death* as the twin marks of separation from God.

Luther knows the anxiety of meaninglessness in a profound way. Luther and also the pietists had to draw upon elements from the courage to be which is based on mystical union. In our time when the anxiety of meaninglessness is dominant, the radical question is whether the two dimensions of the courage to be can be united. Tillich gives one forceful argument to show why the interpreta-

[4] *Ibid*, p. 146.

[5] *Ibid*, p. 163.

[6] *Ibid*, p. 64.

[7] *Ibid*, p. 172.

tion of forgiveness today must be put in the context of the anxiety of meaninglessness. This anxiety can undercut every possibility of affirming the very basis of guilt and forgiveness. It is the radical skeptical position which must be met and overcome. If guilt is meaningless then there is no sense talking about forgiveness. Hence the faith which can be open to salvation must in some way overcome this radical doubt. Tillich insists that salvation means the overcoming of doubt and despair, not their elimination.

It is at this point that Tillich's doctrine of the "God beyond God" as the ultimate ground of faith appears. There have been many questions about his language and intent here. Some have held that the personal communion of man and God disappears and something alien to the Christian outlook is put in its place. Tillich holds that the Bible understands this situation of radical doubt and that we cannot escape it. But what becomes of the experience of sin, guilt, and grace as forgiveness if faith thus transcends the knowledge of personal relationship to God?

It is important to recall that *The Courage to Be* is an essay in apologetics. Tillich is meeting contemporary man in the extreme situation and pointing to the possibility of faith at the boundary of all meaning. But it is also necessary to recognize that when Tillich speaks of faith transcending personal communion and mystical experience he does not mean supplanting them. To show this it is necessary to turn to two essays which are fundamental for Tillich's theology and his view of forgiveness. These are the essays on "The Idea and the Ideal of Personality" and "The Transmoral Conscience" in *The Protestant Era*.[8]

Tillich considers the paradox of a "conscience" which transcends the moral category. This is crucial for his understanding of the anxiety of guilt. *Conscience* does not disappear from man. The "moral" dimension which conscience transcends is not that of responsibility and obligation, but it is here the sphere of *morality*, that is, of ethical principles and laws which enjoin particular kinds of rules upon behavior. Morality thus understood is man's search for integrity and relatedness through principles of right action, that is, through the "law."

Now Tillich belongs with those thinkers, some theologians and some antitheological, who have declared that the integrity and creativity of life cannot be confined to the sphere of morality thus understood. But Tillich rejects any view of the transmoral which makes it a reduction of man's responsibility. Those who dissolve responsibility into the instinctual drives below the conscious and responsible self are called primitivists by Tillich. The transmoral in the sense in which we are now using the term must be *above* the ethical sphere and it must constitute the ethical from beyond itself.[9]

The importance of this position for Tillich's view of forgiveness becomes clear. Forgiveness has meaning only in relation to man's misuse of his responsibility. Unless man is guilty, forgiveness is irrelevant. But Tillich sees in the transmoral dimension of existence the unconditioned obligation of man which goes beyond the attempt to unite a sensitive and a good conscience viewed from the standpoint of moral principles.

---

[8] *The Protestant Era* (Chicago: The University of Chicago Press, 1948). "The Transmoral Conscience" is reprinted in *Morality and Beyond* (New York: Harper & Row, 1963).

[9] "Transmoral can mean the re-establishment of morality from a point above morality, or it can mean the destruction of morality from a point below morality." *The Protestant Era*, p. 148.

Without this ultimate dimension forgiveness tends to degenerate into a moralistic and legalistic calculation of praise and blame. It becomes a blocking, rather than a healing in the depths of alienation. Tillich here makes his settlement with the Pauline-Lutheran tradition in which forgiveness is central. He keeps this, but he unites it with the other dimensions of salvation which are not fully included in the relation of guilt and forgiveness. He finds this new concept of conscience anticipated in Luther. Justification by grace has this deepest power of overcoming everything which separates us from the divine.

Acceptance

Since the full problem of reconciliation cannot be confined within the structure of guilt and forgiveness, God's acceptance of man is both forgiveness and something which transcends forgiveness. Acceptance is the word Tillich uses to speak of the central experience of the healing power of God, overcoming the basic anxieties and our separation from him. In the great sermon, "You are Accepted" Tillich describes the experiences in which "Grace strikes us" and these include experiences of guilt, but also those when "we walk through the dark valley of a dark and meaningless and empty life." And he insists that no particular form or mode of the experience of acceptance can be prescribed. "Nothing is demanded of this experience, no religious, or moral, or intellectual presupposition."[10]

We can therefore speak of acceptance as forgiveness but we must know that no forms or qualifications can be imposed on the reality of the unconditional divine acceptance. When Tillich does speak directly of forgiveness in the sermons he can say "nothing greater can happen to a human being than that he is forgiven . . . that is the greatest experience anyone can have."[11] Of course, Tillich does not mean to oppose the knowledge of forgiveness to the other aspects of acceptance, but it is noteworthy that this evangelical and Lutheran view appears to him as the highest point of the human knowledge of grace when he speaks confessionally in the sermons.

Tillich insists upon the openness and passivity of the receiving of acceptance even though courage is required to accept acceptance. In the sermon on acceptance he says:

> *You are accepted*, accepted by that which is greater than you, and the name of which you do not know. Do not ask for the name now; perhaps you will find it later. Do not try to do anything now; perhaps later you will do much. Do not seek for anything; do not perform anything; do not intend anything. *Simply accept the fact that you are accepted.*[12]

This is thoroughly in accord with the deepest note in Lutheran piety. Faith is openness to God's grace, and from faith works can flow, but to make faith a work is to destroy it.

It may be observed that on the question of human freedom to accept acceptance Tillich is untroubled within the structure of his theology, for while he affirms human freedom he also affirms the paradox of absolute predestination. With many others in the classical tradition he is content to leave the issue of human freedom in a paradoxical formula. A different doctrine of God might lead to a somewhat different view of the

---

[10] Paul Tillich, "You are Accepted" in *The Shaking of the Foundations*, (New York: Charles Scribner's Sons, 1948), chap. 19.

[11] Paul Tillich, "To Whom Much is Forgiven" in *The New Being* (New York: Charles Scribner's Sons, 1955), chap. 1.

[12] Loc. cit. p. 162.

element of human freedom in the encounter.[13]

In his concentration on the ultimate question of salvation in man's relationship to God, Tillich may seem to ignore many concrete issues about forgiveness. One concerned about the reconciliation of persons or about today's collective strife may look for more specific guidance in dealing with human estrangement and the ways of overcoming it. We can certainly ask for an elaboration of the implications of Tillich's doctrine for therapy and social conflict and the life of the church.

It would be quite wrong however to think that his analysis of the ultimate dimensions of acceptance throws no light on practical issues of human reconciliation. His discussion of forgiveness is suggestive at many points, some of which are the following:

1. Every experience of forgiveness and every act of human forgiveness is sustained by and fulfilled in a creative movement of the power of being. To forgive is to participate in the New Being, and to share in the power of God.

The importance of this insight into forgiveness as participation in healing power is immeasurable.[14] One can only ask what suffering and misunderstanding might have been avoided in the history of the church if the moralistic calculating view of forgiveness as sheer cancellation of debts had been supplanted by this doctrine of its healing and creative function as Tillich sees it. Perhaps what Aulen calls the classi doctrine of atonement came closest appropriating this standpoint in understanding of the divine forgivene but none of the traditional doctrines l been adequate.

2. Tillich succeeds in keeping structure of sin and grace at the cen of man's relationship to God with excluding the experience of the threat meaninglessness as that which must overcome if even forgiveness is to understood. What Tillich does is open the way for the therapist and ev person to look not only at the need forgiveness but at the total context estrangement if the word of reconci tion is to be adequately communica Healing and wholeness always inclu forgiveness, but it always involves so thing more in the power which un man with the source of his being.

3. At the core of the human prob we come to a limit to what man can for himself. Tillich's doctrine of forg ness is through and through theistic by this we mean man's reliance upo grace which he cannot command or c trol. Tillich does not restrict our un standing of God to any human symb but there is no question as to where source of forgiveness and of its hea lies. It is in the power of God, no man. The therapist who communic acceptance is in that action represen an objective healing power which is his own, but in which he and anc participate.[15]

[13] I have explored this issue in "Tillich's Doctrine of God" *The Philosophical Forum*. Vol. XVIII (1960–1961).

[14] For a contemporary discussion which is in part related to Tillich's doctrine of acceptance see Don S. Browning, *Atonement and Psychotherapy* (Philadelphia: Westminster Press, 1966).

[15] *The Courage to Be*, p. 165.

I. Tillich synthesizes the mystical on-
ogical tradition with Biblical per-
alism and the radical personalism of
her. It should be remembered that
her drew upon the mystical tradition
late Medieval German piety. In in-
preting the meaning of reconciliation
ich is driven beyond the moral
ere, and even beyond the structure
guilt and forgiveness as these can be
ectively identified, to an "absolute
h" which grasps the power of being
it overcomes meaninglessness. Yet in
depth where all forms seem to disappear Tillich preserves the sacramental reality of immediate experience. The estrangement and salvation which are at the center of life are known under many forms and potentially in any circumstance and experience of life. By thus uniting the interpretation of forgiveness with the radical forms of alienation of contemporary man, Tillich shows the way to the recovery of the meaning of forgiveness just where those traditions which have given it a more exclusive emphasis have tended to lose their hold upon it.

THE CONCEPT OF TRUTH IN KARL BARTH'S THEOLOGY

19

I

In this paper on Karl Barth's conception of truth I shall try to state his position regarding the nature of truth and the criterion of truth, and secondly I shall draw from his position some propositions which I believe exhibit a pattern in his theology which brings it into close relationship to a philosophical tradition.

In seeking to give a philosophical analysis of Barth's conception of truth I am doing what he regarded as impossible, or at least irrelevant, since he tries to separate theological truth and the method of theology completely from science and from philosophy. My thesis is that Barth's theology is not really exempt from questions about its relation to the general human inquiry after truth. There are presuppositions in his position which not only can receive philosophical statement, but which, I hope to show, have a definite philosophical ancestry. If this thesis is sound we may be able to show that Barth's discussion of truth can be suggestive in the realm of philosophical inquiry. In any case such an analysis may be one way of illuminating Karl Barth's theology.

Put in broad terms my thesis is that Barth began with a Kantian view of reason and its limits, and moved to a Platonic-Hegelian view which is the structural foundation of his *Church Dogmatics*. I am mainly concerned with the later phase, but some note must be taken of the earlier position.

Barth's earlier philosophical orientation was neo-Kantian. He saw no answer to Feuerbach in any God-idea which is derived from human reflection, that is from metaphysical analysis. The bias against metaphysics was reinforced by Barth's deep commitment to Wilhelm Herrmann's theology. Speech about God is possible only through elaboration of the structures implicit in the religious experience which the Gospel creates in us. Barth develops a doctrine of the majesty and sublimity of God. 'God confronts it (the mind) again and again as the pure negativity of everything finite, as the supreme one who lives in a light which no man can approach unto.'[1]

This restriction of knowledge of God to the relation between the religious attitude and its 'object' is a kind of ground-clearing for Barth when he makes his break-through to radical transcendance in the *Commentary on Romans*, the

[1] From an article by Barth published in 1914, 'Belief in the Personal God', quoted by Wilhelm Pauck in *Karl Barth: Prophet of a New Christianity* (New York: Harper & Brothers, 1931), p. 48.

B

first edition of which appeared in 1918. Barth interprets Paul's letter to the Romans in the light of Kierkegaard's doctrine of the infinite qualitative difference between time and eternity, and his view of man's radical guilt and self-alienation from God. All human self-knowledge is confined to the prison house of human effort and self-projection. Only the divine reality which comes to us from the other side, the reality of God's absolute judgment and mercy, can give us the truth about the human situation and our redemption.

'He who knows the world to be bounded by a truth that contradicts it; he who knows himself to be bounded by a will that contradicts him; he who, knowing too well that he must be satisfied to live with this contradiction and not attempt to escape from it, finds it hard to kick against the pricks (Overbeck); he who finally makes open confession of the contradiction and determines to base his life upon it—he it is that believes.'[1]

Thus only in the faith given by revelation straight from above can we know the 'incomprehensible, unpsychological, and unhistorical truth of God'.[2]

As is well known Barth moved away from this joining of existentialism and the biblical message as he began the writing of his systematic theology. He even re-wrote the entire first half volume in order to purge his method of all traces of existentialism, and to set his theology free from even auxiliary philosophical commitments. The main outlines of the conception of truth in the *Church Dogmatics* can be summarised as follows.

Christian theology is concerned with the truth which is known in the faith of the Christian people or the Church. Barth defines dogmatics as 'the scientific test to which the Christian church puts herself regarding the language about God which is peculiar to her'.[3] Thus even the language of theology lies within the closed theological circle.

In Barth's discussion of theology as science he is at pains to declare the independence of theology from any extra theological canons of inquiry. 'If theology allows itself to be called or calls itself a science, it cannot at the same time take over the obligation to submit to measurement by the canons valid for other sciences.'[4] Barth exempts theology from subservience to the law of contradiction so far as human statements of the truth held in faith are concerned. There is no contradiction in the truth ultimately in God, but for men there will be contradictions in its expression. Theology can assert a removeability in principle from contradiction but 'the propositions in which it asserts their removal will be propositions concerning the free action of God, and so not propositions that remove the contradictions from the world'.[5]

[1] Karl Barth, *The Epistle to the Romans*, English translation by Hoskyns, from the 6th ed. (London: Oxford Univ. Press, 1933), p. 39.

[2] Karl Barth, *The Word of God and the Word of Man*. English translation by Douglas Horton of early addresses. (Grand Rapids, Zandervan, 1935), p. 69.

[3] Karl Barth, *Church Dogmatics*. English Translation of the *Kirchliche Dogmatik*, Vol. I/1, page 1. Hereafter *C.D.* [4] *Ibid.*, p. 9. [5] *Ibid.*, p. 8.

We are already speaking of the subject matter of theology; God's free and saving action. The truth with which theology is concerned is solely the action of God in Jesus Christ. The following paragraph from Barth's *Dogmatics in Outline* gives the claim which underlies his theological method:

'And just because as Christians we may live in the truth of Jesus Christ and therefore in the light of the knowledge of God and therefore with an illumined reason, we shall also become sure of the meaning of our own existence and of the ground and goal of all that happens. Once more a quite tremendous extension of the field of vision is indicated by this; to know this object in its truth means in truth to know no more and no less than all things, even man, oneself, the cosmos, and the world. The truth of Jesus Christ is not one truth among others; it is *the* truth, the universal truth that creates all truth as surely as it is the truth of God, the *prima veritas* which is also the *ultima veritas*. For in Jesus Christ God has created all things, He has created all of us. We exist not apart from him, but in him, whether we are aware of it or not; and the whole cosmos exists not apart from him, but in him, borne by him, the Almighty Word. To know him is to know all.'[1]

For Barth faith is knowledge. The Church knows God and lives from this knowledge. Faith is the receiving and the beginning of understanding of the one absolute truth. This knowledge is revealed, it is not accessible to human effort. It does not arise from reflection upon experience. It is given from beyond man to man. Revelation is the Christian term for this givenness of the truth in Jesus Christ. Barth's doctrine of revelation is therefore at the centre of his doctrine of truth.

It is interesting that in his discussion of the knowability of God Barth slips into what appears to be a general definition of knowledge:

'By the knowledge of an object by men we understand the proof of their acquaintance with its reality in respect of its being there (or its existence) and in respect of its being thus and thus (or its nature). . . . As knowers they are got at by the known object. They exist no longer without it, but with it. . . . When faced with its trueness they can no longer withdraw into themselves in order from there to affirm, question or deny it. This event, this certification or proof we call, to distinguish it from mere knowings, knowledge. A knowing becomes knowledge when the man becomes a responsible witness to its content.'[2]

Here Barth seems to assimilate the theological definition of truth and knowledge to a humanly recognisable pattern. But alongside this he asserts that the knowledge which the church has comes by revelation alone, and revelation 'in fact does not differ from the person of Jesus Christ and again does not differ from the reconciliation that took place in him'.[3]

This truth then comes through the free action of God. It can only be received in faith. Christian knowing is a responsible witness to the truth which

[1] Karl Barth, *Dogmatics in Outline* (New York: Philosophical Library, 1969), p. 26.
[2] *C.D.* Vol. I/1, p. 214. [3] *Ibid.*, p. 134.

is the Word of God and which has been given, not as a human possibility, but as a divine gift.

Barth speaks of three forms of the Word of God; Jesus Christ who is the Word; Church proclamation, that is the announcement of the Word as an action within the community of faith, and the Bible which is the attestation of the revelation of the Word, and which the Church has received as the canon of its witness. Therefore Scripture becomes the concrete norm for theology.[1] Barth seeks to avoid the absolutising of human forms of the knowledge of the truth through his assertion that Church Proclamation and Scripture do not stand in quite the same relation to revelation as does Jesus Christ the Word himself. Scripture and Preaching 'from time to time become God's Word'. That is, they are dependent on God's present revealing action to become bearers of the truth. There is a sense then in which the truth theology is concerned with keeps coming into the world and human life through the new and free action of God, and a certain margin of openness to new knowledge is left for theology.

'This being true and coming true of revelation thus consists in the Church really recalling past revelation, receiving, grasping, and then genuinely proclaiming in faith the biblical witness to it, as the real promise of future revelation.'[2]

Thus Barth seeks to leave the way open for the corrigibility of all human expressions of the truth. In the last pages of the *Dogmatics* he returns to this theme in connection with the eschatological horizon and says:

'Nevertheless, he has not yet uttered his last Word in this matter. For he has not yet spoken universally of himself and the act of reconciliation accomplished in him. He has not yet spoken of it in such a way that the ears and reason and hearts of all must receive it. He has not yet spoken of it immediately, i.e. in such a way that even those who are awakened by him to faith and love can hear his voice in perfect purity and to the exclusion of every conceivable contradiction and opposition and above all participation in human falsehood.'[3]

Before we move to a discussion of the presuppositions of Barth's position it is well to look at his attempt to divorce theology entirely from philosophy. Certainly he recognises that philosophical terms will appear in theology. There will even be 'scraps' of philosophy, but the theologian is free from all philosophical commitments. Barth says at the opening of the *Dogmatics*, 'once and for all the Christian Church does not have Aristotle for its ancestor'.[4] He becomes even more polemical:

'Up to date, in practice—in each of the three departments of theological inquiry—philosophy, science of history, psychology, etc., have in a direct sense succeeded only in increasing the self-alienation of the Church, in degenerating and devastating her language about God.'[5]

[1] *C.D.* Vol. I/1, p. 47, cf. pp. 111–124. [2] *Ibid.*, p.135.
[3] *C.D.* Vol. IV/3, part 2, p. 903. [4] *C.D.* Vol. I/1, p. 11. [5] *Ibid.*, p. 5.

This 'up to now' might be taken as a call to a reconstruction of the language of the sciences in line with the theological requirement, but this is not Barth's intention. His reason is that all human reasoning is infected with man's alienation from God. This point must be kept in mind in all Barth's discussions of truth. All self-knowledge, even theological knowledge, stands in the uncertainty of human alienation and sin. The intractability of faith and its object should and will see to it that divine certainty cannot become human security.[1] This same structure applies to any claim to possess or to test knowledge of God in experience:

'What experienceable acknowledgment of the Word of God would not in the act of taking place be discovered and convicted by the Word of God itself—not of its undoubted imperfection and insufficiency, but of its utter perversion, and nullity; for as surely as all else we do, it is the work of the human heart, whose inventive efforts are bad from youth up and can only be helped by forgiveness.'[2]

Yet Barth can end this same paragraph on the 'bad heart' by a remark concerning the *finitum non capax dei*. He rejects this utterly as a philosophical statement available for theology. It is sinful man who is not capable of the Word of God. But he can know God's forgiveness. 'It is this real experience of the man claimed by the Word of God, which decides and proves that what makes it possible lies beyond it.'[3]

I can only reconcile Barth's statements here with the assumption that he sees the experience of God's forgiveness as being in no way subsumed under the general rubric of experience. It is *sui generis*.

II

The analysis I now propose of the structure of Barth's position is an attempt to grasp the inner movement of his thought and to ask whether it does not have an interest for philosophy which may not appear on the surface.

Barth writes about truth and theological science as a twentieth-century man fully aware of the modes of thought of modern man. His books are reasonable in temper and set forth in straightforward prose sentences which can be read by any literate person. Yet he rejects the theologies of Paul Tillich and Rudolph Bultmann who offer an explicit correlation between theology and contemporary man's self-understanding. Barth makes no appeal in his later work to a Kantian restriction on metaphysical knowledge. And he does not rely on the distinction between 'personal and impersonal truth' in the mode of Martin Buber's thought, although there are traces of that position throughout the *Church Dogmatics*. It is clear why Barth does not appeal

[1] *C.D.* Vol. I/1, p. 12. [2] *Ibid.*, p. 252 [3] *Ibid.*, p. 252.

to any general doctrine of 'types of truth' in order to find an autonomous place for theology. This would be to rely on a philosophical analysis, and would commit theology precisely where he does not want it committed.

Where Barth does turn for the structure of his conception of truth is all the more surprising. It is the move toward an ontological realism (in the scholastic sense). The move begins, as he himself has said, with his work on Anselm of Canterbury in 1931. What happens there is that Barth finds a way to return to the classical ontological mode of Christian theology and to keep his restriction of knowledge to faith at the same time. *Credo ut intelligam* is of course the Anselmian key.

It is God's being, that being than which nothing greater can be conceived, which is the object of theological thought, and of Anselm's prayerful search for understanding. It is God's being as love in act which is revealed in Jesus Christ, Barth says. Theology therefore is a reflection upon the being of God and an elaboration by reason within faith of the meaning of the divine perfection. As Barth later developed his doctrine in the great section on the Being of God in Volume II/1 all the classical attributes reappear. There is no doubt now about the pattern of truth which Barth's theology displays. It is the truth of being which is directly and finally disclosed to us in the event of Jesus Christ, and that truth can be given systematic rational exposition. This union of absolute being with the event in history constitutes the foundation of Barth's theological method. The universal truth is given in a single concrete history. The event of Jesus Christ constitutes the concrete universal. Hence for theology all that is can be seen and interpreted in the light of the one absolute truth.

To be sure we are not given an ontological system in the philosophic sense. But we are given a systematic rational reflection on what it means to be when that is understood from the standpoint of the faith of the Christian community that the answer is present in Jesus.

The centre of this truth is reconciliation. God's being cannot be known apart from metanoia. All human thought toward God is self-projection, idolatry, and yields only illusion. But there is a true understanding of being which sets human understanding on the right path.

We see that the book on Anselm has two important foci in Barth's quest for a valid theological method. The first has to do with the relationship of faith and reason. If Anselm's Proslogian is read as a philosophical proof of God's existence then it can be understood as appealing to a knowledge of God through natural reason. Barth rejects this as a right understanding of Anselm. The whole movement of Anselm's thought takes place within the structure of belief and prayer.[1] It is faith's understanding of God which he seeks. Barth sees Anselm as 'walking a very thin line' between the standpoint of faith and an appeal to natural human reason. Barth says:

[1] Karl Barth, Anselm, *Fides Quaerens Intellectum* (Richmond: John Knox Press, 1960), p. 150.

'Anselm's theology is simple. That is the plain secret of his "proving". Anselm is not in a position to treat Christian knowledge as an esoteric mystery, as a phenomenon that would have to shun the light of secular thinking.'[1]

The discussion does not take place on the unbeliever's ground. Anselm simply offers the unbeliever his own best reason functioning within the perspective of his faith. But the man of faith *can* reason, that is the clue.

The second focus of Barth's discussion of Anselm concerns the relation of reason and being. Barth shows himself in full sympathy with Anselm's conception of God as the being whose ontological status involves his necessary existence. Of course in this book Barth is expounding Anselm, not his own view systematically, but I think the key to his own doctrine is clearly given in what he sees in Anselm's argument. He seizes upon the Anselmian identification of God's being with the Truth which constitutes the *ultima ratio* of all thinking. He finds Anselm distinguishing between the reason which we possess as finite beings, our minds as reasoning subjects, and the *ratio* which is identical with God himself, the absolute being who is the source of all *ratio.*

'Fundamentally the *ratio* either as ontic or noetic is never higher than the truth, but truth is itself the master of all *rationes* beyond the contrast between ontic and noetic deciding for itself, now here, now there, what is *vera ratio*: in so far as the *ratio* of the object of faith and the use which man makes of his capacity to think and judge conform to Truth (by virtue of Truth's own decision) its true rationality is determined and the intellectus that is sought occurs.'[2]

We see then how theology can be rational discourse about the truth of God's being, but determined wholly from the side of God's being so far as its truth is concerned. Human rationality is not in itself ultimate but is only true rationality measured alongside the *summa veritas*. 'It is in the Truth and by the Truth, in God and by God that the basis is a basis and that rationality possesses rationality.'[3]

This confidence in reason as receiving Truth from beyond itself presupposes that being, that is, God, has revealed himself to us. The claim to revelation is all important for theology's claim to truth. We would still seem to understand theology as the explication of a truth given only to a few in one strand of history.

There is however in Barth's interpretation of revelation one theme which appears as his attempt to overcome the parochialism and arbitrariness of the dependence on a single revelation. It is Barth's insistence that the revelation in Jesus Christ is in principle available to all, and that therefore theology points to a truth which really does become available to all men everywhere. The view which in effect affirms Jesus Christ as the 'concrete universal' moves

[1] Karl Barth, Anselm, *Fides Quaerens Intellectum* (Richmond: John Knox Press, 1960), p. 68.
[2] *Ibid.*, p. 47. [3] *Ibid.*, p. 51.

the discussion from the level of a sectarian claim to the exposition of a universal truth which is open to all who will receive it. At least this seems to me Barth's intention. We have already seen that he understands Anselm as willing to expose his conception of God in the arena of secular thinking even though he in no way adopts the secular point of view.

The same point comes out clearly in an important essay of Barth's on *The Christian Understanding of Revelation* published in 1948. It is significant that Barth returns to the exposition of his concept of revelation fifteen years after the first volume of the *Dogmatics*. I do not believe there is new doctrine here, but there is an obvious concern to stress the public and universal character of revelation as Barth sees it. He affirms again the absolute uniqueness of the Christian revelation against all merely human knowledge.

> 'When the Christian language speaks of God it does so not on the basis of some speculation or other, but looking at this fact, this story, this person . . . it makes no presuppositions when it points to this event. Its sole concern is with the event itself.'[1]

But Barth is also careful to say that this revelation comes to all men with equal strangeness from outside and concerns all men with equal intimacy. It comes 'not as a special, but as a general revelation which concerns all and is meant for all'.[2] Here surely we are in the familiar Hegelian pattern of an event which embodies the concrete universal. Barth may say the Church makes no presuppositions in receiving revelation; but he certainly is making use of a general pattern of thought concerning truth in expounding it. Jesus Christ is the 'absolute event that is the goal of the Old Testament and the beginning of the New'.[3]

We take special note of the term 'absolute event'. It compresses in one phrase Barth's doctrine of truth. Revelation comes in event in history but it comes as absolute truth. To receive this event as the truth in faith is the beginning of all rationality, and all grasp of being. This view is clinched by Barth's statement in the same discussion that if a man does not submit to this word 'he chooses the impossible possibility, he chooses *nihil*'.[4]

This doctrine that all human self-understanding comes to nothing raises some interesting questions about Barth's attitude toward the truths of science and other human inquiries. He never says these truths are meaningless. He even expounds brilliantly his own doctrine of man's existence as existence for the other in community. Yet he remains certain that all human truth is in no way a step on the way to knowledge of *The Truth*; that is the truth of man's real being instead of nothingness.

[1] Karl Barth, 'The Christian Understanding of Revelation' in *Against the Stream* (New York: Philosophical Library, 1954), p. 211.
[2] *Ibid.*, pp. 203, 212–13.
[3] *Ibid.*, p. 220 (The phrase 'concrete universal' here is mine, not Barth's). [4] *Ibid.*, p. 215.

One really wonders why if the truth of faith is the universal truth about all things and every man it might not be possible to look for analogues, hints, clues to that truth in all human experience. If man's mind in order really to be a mind must be informed by the *ultima ratio* one is puzzled to know why all human self-understanding apart from the Gospel is relegated to sheer futility in the end.

But this is where Barth joins the issue with all humanistic doctrines. For him the biblical view of the real truth is that it can only be given from beyond man's self-understanding, and it comes as an event in history which breaks in upon all the human quests with the message of divine judgment and reconciliation. Certainly there is no philosophic way of refuting such a position or of showing that it is meaningless.

What I have tried to show however is that as Barth expounds his conception of truth he actually owes a very great deal to the philosophical tradition which stems from Plato. He may say that the truth he is talking about is utterly different from what any philosopher seeks. He may say that Plato's Form of the Good bears no resemblance whatever to the Christian idea of God, and certainly there is much room for discussion on that point. But to some theologians as well as philosophers, including the present writer, the claim that theology can exempt itself from laying its truth claim alongside others, and from inquiring about common patterns of thought, and the significance of theological and philosophical conceptions for one another is not convincing. Scientists, philosophers and plain men may also be humble before the given, and theologians do not really do their thinking apart from other human inquiries. The Christian Church may not have Aristotle for its ancestor; but Karl Barth's theology certainly has Plato, Anselm, Kierkegaard, and Hegel somewhere in its family tree.

Response to Wolfhart Pannenberg

20

DANIEL DAY WILLIAMS

Professor Pannenberg's theological work has been engaging the attention of many of us for some time, and it is a great privilege to have him in this place, to hear this wonderfully comprehensive paper, and to enter into discussion with him. I find his theological method and outlook very congenial. My questions are directed to his paper for clarification and for sharpening some issues which I believe are issues for all Christian thought, and certainly for my own.

To keep this paper brief I will confine myself to some remarks about his discussion of process theology. But I will first state where I find myself in strong agreement with him.

First, Professor Pannenberg recognizes Whitehead's doctrine of the entry of the future into every present. God's life has futurity within it for God himself embraces the realm of possibility in his being. I would only want to make even more emphatic the point that God not only holds future possibility before every actuality in the world, drawing it forward into the future; but that God in his being is Free Subject, responding to his world, making his free decisions with respect to that world, and sharing in the world's suffering and joy as he moves into his future. In Jesus Christ God has not only given us promises but has identified his life with us in love and thus created a new relationship which is the decisive content of hope and promise for all who respond to him in trust.

In the second place, Professor Pannenberg insists, quite rightly I believe, that Christian hope for the future always involves some recognition of the present love of God. There is no point in living by the promise if we have no idea of what the promise means. The kingdom is present now, though in a hidden way, and here Pannenberg does justice not only to the futurism in the New Testament but also to the theme of eternity penetrating time as it occurs in the Fourth Gospel and in many of the letters of Paul.

Third, I agree completely with his view that Christian hope does not permit us to have a purely optimistic view of the course of history. There is little evidence that the compacting of mankind leads in itself to an expanded consciousness. Go to Northern Ireland today, or any one of scores of communities within walking distance of us tonight, or let us look into our own consciences. Are we less parochial because we are more crowded in our cities? Process thought, and here I take it I am in agreement with Professor Pannenberg, holds that the question of the nature and limits of the possibilities of convergence toward a peaceful world community must be assessed empirically through historical experience. There is no inevitability about it.

Fourth, he pleads powerfully for a socialized world, a radical corrective of the individualism of Western culture. Here surely we must agree about the direction Christian action must take. I could only add that I believe theology should concern itself with the "middle range" problems of hope as well as with the ultimate and immediate problems. The life of nations, societies, communities needs the responsible criticism and direction which may come from religious thought. And surely we all hope for the ecumenical movement to have its impact on the world society, as far as we may still be from realizing full community even within the church itself.

Fifth, I accept fully Professor Pannenberg's view of the responsibility of theology to take account of the questions about what things are and how we know questions that philosophers discuss. Theology has its responsibility to appropriate philosophical insight and achieve clarity on ultimate philosophic issues.

I wish now to raise the single question which I find central to Professor Pannenberg's paper and tc his discussion of process theology. It is the question of the relation of hope to the unity of God, of the world, and of truth. Let me state first what I take to be this thesis, then note his criticism of process thought on this point, and then make some suggestions as to why I hold process theology to be a viable interpretation to the Bible and of man's situation. The point has to do with the "final event" which Pannenberg asserts must unify the whole of history and disclose its meaning.

Professor Pannenberg recognizes that Christian faith is through and through eschatological. This means for him that temporality is a characteristic of all reality and of God himself. History actually contributes to the identity or essence of things. He says: "The essence of things . . . depends on the temporal process and will be decided upon only by its outcome . . . eternity is not to be conceived as non-temporal, but constituted by the historical process and especially by its final outcome" (p. 72).

Now what does Professor Pannenberg see in process thought which differs from this position? This, I think: he sees process theology as having a more loosely organized universe in which there is an endless plurality of events; and therefore no final event which consummates or determines the unity of the whole. He does not state his position in exactly this way, but this is what I understand him to say. For example, he says that Whitehead splits creativity off from God so that it can, so to speak, "go its own way" and that therefore no unity is given for the whole, and therefore hope can never be directed toward one event in which the destiny of man is accomplished.

This is why when Professor Pannenberg says that the essence of things is temporal, and that eternity is constituted by the historical process, he remarks that Whiteheadians will find this statement strange. Surely this is what Whiteheadians have argued for, that being is temporal, that history contributes to the eternal life of God. But Professor Pannenberg is right: there is something different from process thought in what he is saying. He thinks that if we are to speak hopefully of the future, we must assert a final event which constitutes the unity of the whole or else we have no decisive standard of truth and no real fulfillment of man's destiny.

Parenthetically, I may comment on one of Pannenberg's characterizations of Whiteheadian cosmology. He suggests that Whitehead's world is composed of a stream of momentary events complemented by a realm of "mere possibilities" and this he sees as a kind of Platonism. But this is not an accurate characterization of Whitehead's view in which there are no mere possibilities. All possibilities are related to the concrete action of God and the real events in the world. They are possibilities of value and structure which may be exemplified in the ongoing of events. No event is merely momentary. It grasps possibility as an element in its becoming, but it also grasps its past and the other actual entities which become data for it. Further every event is experienced by God in his everlasting life and power. It lives on in its function of objective immortality for other events and for God.

I return to the Pannenberg thesis that there must be a final event which constitutes the meaning of the whole. Two points here can help to clear some ground.

First, Whiteheadians do not split creativity off from God. The creativity is nothing by itself. It is simply a name for the fact that all things participate in a dynamic interaction. But this does mean that the notion of a "final event" becomes a contradiction for this metaphysical view because God's creative action does not end.

Second, Pannenberg believes that Whiteheadians deny an essence for the whole of things. There is some terminological difficulty here because Pannenberg uses essence for reality itself. The essence of things as he sees it is the whole concrete process from beginning to end including the final event which constitutes the identity or at least the manifestation of the identity in the whole. Now Whiteheadians do not deny the concept of essence. For them the essence of anything is an abstract structure which characterizes it. God has an essence. It is the formal structure of his being which includes the structures of possibility. This essence has identity. It does not change. It is not modified. But God's concrete temporal life is more than his essence. It is the reality of his creative responsible action, moving in communion, judgment and redemption in relation to his world. What Whiteheadians do say is that the unity of the creative process is to be found in the community of God's being with his creatures, not in absolute unity which is summed up in a final event. Pannenberg is quite right in saying that process thought sees a certain inevitable plurality in being. The reason for this from the process point of view is that if God is love he must have a world to love, to act upon, and respond to. The creatures in that world must have their measure of freedom, creativity, and unique value if they are real things and not just mechanical expression of a prearranged plan.

Pannenberg does indeed say that the future will not be "simply identical" with the essence it determines (p. 73). It is in that little but mighty word "simply" that the whole issue lies. If the future is not *simply* identical with the essence, then what does it add? And if it really adds something, are we not really accepting the process view that in place of identity we have community between past and present and future.

My reasons for holding to the process view rather than accepting this single event constituting the unity of history can be stated both biblically and ethically.

As to the Scripture, the New Testament gives us at least two eschatological pictures of the end and not one. In one there is universal salvation. All things are made new. God's life embraces the whole, and all is redeemed. In the other, God divides the good from the evil in judgment. Some are lost. We should not be diverted by pathological conceptions of hell with God willing the eternal torment of his creature. The question is whether there is a real risk of lostness in being. I do not see that Professor Pannenberg's paper quite deals with this question. His final event seems to require the first option, an absolutely universal consummation which is the essence of every event, no matter what relation to good and evil it may sustain.

But I must ask, how can life be serious if in a final event it will all be one absolute good, no matter what has happened?

We can put the same point ethically in relation to the nature of love. Pannenberg speaks of the intrinsic logic of love. But surely this intrinsic logic includes the acceptance of the risk of creative freedom. Love is not the demand for the conformity of the other to an ideal; but the acceptance of the adventure of life into an unknown future. Love does not ask for guarantees. Why should love demand final completion when its very joy is participation in the task yet to be done, the anticipation of the community yet to be created? Of course there is rest, rest in every glimpse of fulfillment and every moment of communion. The intrinsic logic of love is not that of identity but that of creative community in which real suffering and loss are risked.

To open the discussion then with Professor Pannenberg where I believe we must take it, I suggest the following thesis: it is he who is the Platonist, or rather the Neo-Platonist who demands that the essence of things be identical with the transcendent One. Perhaps I misunderstand what he means by the final event which is identical with the beginning; but his view seems to be to take real hope away, for how can we hope if what things are and are becoming is really nothing more than what they have always been?

Hope and the Future of Man: A Reflection

DANIEL DAY WILLIAMS

Each person brought to the conference on hope his conception of the meaning of the gospel message, and his own perspective on hope. Each left the conference with some questions sharpened, some new perspectives, and probably with a conviction about where the theologies of promise and fulfillment for mankind must do further work. What I can do here is to give some reflections of one participant about what we were hearing from one another, and where we seemed to be moving.

We knew from the outset that Teilhardians, theologians of hope in the recent style of Continental theology, and process theologians have a common concern to bring to the world with its aspirations, its agonies, and its despair the gospel of hope based upon what God has done and will do in Jesus Christ. All three schools see the meaning of the Christian faith as eschatologically determined. Life is understood through what we shall be.

We discovered that we approach this search for a doctrine of hope in rather different ways. While the word "approach" is vague, we really need to speak of three approaches to the expression of Christian hope. We were already aware of some differences in theological method, and on the whole they were represented as might have been expected, but there were some surprises. The theology of hope as developed by the Continental theologians and represented also by Carl Braaten may be described as confessional in method. The theologians work from within the biblical message as they interpret it, and move out to conclusions about the meaning of the eschatological structure of faith. However, Pannenberg incorporates a metaphysical element derived from a philosophical interpretation of the unity of history, and he comes even closer than one might have expected to the method of the process theologians. Moltmann's book, *Theology of Hope*, is developed in a biblical confessional exegetical style; but his paper in the conference argues for the theologians' entering into an analysis of immediate human problems and letting that analysis reflect back on the ethical convictions underlying the Christian life.

Process theologians are frankly concerned with a metaphysical structure as one indispensable context for interpreting the word of God in Jesus Christ. They develop a metaphysical view of God, time and history and appeal for its validity to concrete experience informed by the light of the gospel. This does not prevent them from speculative ventures concerning the future and the meaning of life beyond death, as John Cobb's paper shows. Process theologians take the issue of hope to refer both to present expectations and to future possibilities within the divine redemptive action.

The Teilhardian perspective, like that of process theology, draws upon a general scheme of understanding the world as described by science and interpreted in a cosmic development toward final unity. In Philip Hefner's paper and in the discussion generally the Teilhardians put less emphasis upon the details of the cosmological scheme and more upon the spiritual vision which makes it possible for persons here and now to live religiously by participating in the slow, painful growth of humanity toward unity. To this participant this mystical and moral passion for sharing the creative action which is God's work in the world was the most impressive feature of the Teilhardian optimism, not the affirmation of a final success at Omega point, but the hopefulness about a significant ethical and religious life in the present age.

Of the many issues opened up by these approaches I mention three.

First, there is the question of how to relate the eschatological structure of hope with its vision of the "last things" to present problems of social and political history. Death is conquered by resurrection. But what does this mean for millions dying of starvation, or the millions of people dying at the hands of other men? All the contributions to the conference had this reality of the human condition explicitly in view. Every theological point of view was stated with awareness of the need for relating ultimate hope to immediate human problems. But I believe it is fair to say that the connection was not clearly made. What is different about the way one meets the present fulfillments and frustrations of life in the light of eschatology and what is different about a Christian theory of social causes because of the eschatological outlook?

There is for example the issue of utopianism, sharply raised by Carl Braaten at the beginning of the conference and penetratingly dealt with by Johannes Metz at the end. We are forced to ask: What kind of concrete involvement in present causes, actions, and commitments can we reasonably, faithfully, and fruitfully assert when we live by the ultimate promise of the kingdom? Johannes Metz' moving plea for a politics rooted in the memory of suffering aims to set us free from utopianism; but how do we then move to guidance about what causes are worth pursuing in the present history of suffering? Jürgen Moltmann's insightful analysis of biomedical problems leaves him open to the question Ogden asks about the bearing of this mode of analysis on the eschatological faith rooted in the cross and the resurrection of Jesus Christ.

The planners of this conference had in mind a succeeding conference in which the bearing of the Christian faith on such specific and critical issues could be explored by theologians with people from other disciplines. The present conference certainly led up to and pointed to the need for such a further exploration.

The second question concerns the truth of what we say and how we say it when we speak of hope and particularly of the final hope for victory over sin and death. The credibility gap between traditional theology and contemporary modes of thought informed by science, philosophy, and political outlooks is very great. That gap is likely to appear even larger when we speak of the future for then we speak of that realm where we have no present experience, and where we live by the promise, not the immediate reality. Here is need for further clarification of the relation between biblical exegesis and philosophic structure; between the standpoint of faith and a critical reflection on experience. Metz says there is "no mediation between nature and man." Teilhardians and process theologians hold that man is unintelligible except as participant in an evolving nature which sustains him. The relation between Moltmann's confessional standpoint in *Theology of Hope* and his exploration of the present issues involved in new medical techniques raises important methodological questions. Does the Christian have special insight into these issues and if so where is its source and how is it related to the insight which comes from secular work with such problems?

Finally there appears to run through the discussions an issue about the form and substance of Christian eschatology. It is the question whether Christian hope must be expressed in the affirmation of one final event which constitutes the absolute reversal of all the unresolved problems of human existence, or whether the Christian hope can be expressed in the form of a confidence in God in the midst of a creative adventure which need have no end, but which is open for the creative work of God forever. The theological perspectives here represented except that of the process theologians appear to move in the first pattern. For the former views the eschaton is the contradiction or complete reversal of the risk, suffering, and uncertainty of the present. The process theologians, on the other hand, regard creativity and the freedom to participate in it as one aspect of the perfection of love.

The issue is not whether there is hope for a meaningful life and participation in God's life after death. John Cobb shows that this is within the outlook of process thought. The issue is the subtle one of whether meaningful life here and now requires hope in an absolute end point such as the Omega point of the Teilhardians, or the final event of which Pannenberg speaks. The process view seems to sacrifice absolute victory for absolute openness to creativity. Is such an eschatology biblical and meaningful?

In all three views there is the conviction that everything in nature and history is subject to the redemptive work of God. There is a consensus that God is at work in time, bearing with his world, and going before it, making present life intelligible, and filling with hope our present work, suffering, and dying through the future which he holds before us. Christians understand that hope as it is given in the story of God's covenant with Israel and its climax in the life, death, and resurrection of Jesus. The hope there released into the world is for the whole creation and every creature.

The issues dealt with in the conference require the concentrated and critical attention not only of theologians but of every person who is seeking faith for the times in which we now live. The coming together of people of these different outlooks and their holding such conversation was itself a contribution to the spirit of hopefulness among us. Theological work can be done today not out of an assumption that any one school possesses all truth, but out of the hope born of the gospel message that the Spirit which binds us together will guide us into the Truth.

Daniel Day Williams, 1910-1973: A Bibliography

21

Jean C. Lambert

Those who know Daniel Day Williams through his books and essays in learned journals may be unaware of the literature he provided diverse audiences outside the professional ministry of the Christian church.

Exploring it the reader may gain fuller appreciation of Dr. Williams interests and convictions, though such exploration is unlikely to yield fundamental surprises. Whatever his audience, Dr. Williams' writing manifests his conviction that truth is served less by rhetorical decoration than by clear exposition; it likewise reflects the intellectual rigor, fairness to his sources, and deep spiritual insight his readers have come to expect.

My task as bibliographer was lightened by Dr. Williams himself. Among his personal papers he saved tear-sheets and lists of many of his articles and reviews. As I traced additional references to his published works, the personnel of the Union Theological Seminary Library answered scores of questions. Queried about Dr. Williams' publications in the un-indexed *Chicago Theological Seminary Register* Perry Le Fevre, academic dean of CTS, contributed a list of articles he personally culled from back issues. I am awaiting correspondence about several references to Dr. Williams' publications, so despite the efforts of many this listing is incomplete.

Users will notice that I have marked several items with an asterisk (*). These are mimeographed papers. They are available through the Union Theological Seminary Library, and I believe some of them may have been published elsewhere.

I invite readers who locate additional publications of Daniel Day Williams to send the information to me, % Union Theological Seminary; and to Mr. Tony Wolfe, % the Center for Process Studies, Claremont, California 91711. There the Williams papers are being prepared for scholarly use under the direction of Professor John B. Cobb and Eulalia (Mrs. Daniel Day) Williams.

As in water face answers to face,
So the mind of man reflects the man.
Proverbs 27:19

THE DEMONIC AND THE DIVINE (PUBL 1996)

Bibliography

I. Books by Daniel Day Williams

The Andover Liberals, a Study in American Theology. New York: King's Crown Press, 1941.

God's Grace and Man's Hope. New York: Harper Brothers, 1949.

What Present Day Theologians Are Thinking. New York: Harper and Row Publishers, 1952. Also published in England as *Interpreting Theology, 1918-1952*. London: SCM Press, 1953.

The Minister and the Care of Souls. New York: Harper and Row Publishers, 1961.

The Spirit and The Forms of Love. New York: Harper and Row Publishers, 1968. Also published in England with same title. London: J. Nisbet and Co. Ltd., 1969.

II. Articles and Sermons by Daniel Day Williams

"Belief and Behavior," *Chicago Theological Seminary Register*** (March 1934), Vol. XXIV, No. 2, pp. 22-24.

1940-1949

"Our Shared Vocation," *CTSR* (November 1940), Vol. XXX, No. 4, pp. 4-8.

"Worship Plus Action," *CTSR* (January 1941), Vol. XXXI, No. 1, pp. 11-13.

Question to Charles Clayton Morrison in his "What Is Christianity?" *The Christian Century* (April 16, 1941), Vol. LVIII, No. 16, p. 528.

"The Power of Faith," undated sermon, mimeographed, Union Theological Seminary Library.*

"Seminary Worship and the Christian Church," *Open Door* (January 26, 1942).*

"Theology and Truth," *The Journal of Religion* (October 1942), Vol. XXII, No. 4, pp. 382-97.

"The Victory of the Good," *The Journal of Liberal Religion* (Spring 1942), Vol. III, No. 4, pp. 171-85.

"Prayer and Action," *The Christian Century* (December 23, 1942), Vol. LIX, No. 51, pp. 1587-88.

"Prayer and Its Answer," pamphlet. Glen Ellyn: Friends for Victory Committee, First Congregational Church, 1943.

"Kindled Affections," *CTSR* (January 1943), Vol. XXXIII, No. 1, pp. 3-6.

"The Consequences of Believing in God," undated address.*

"Relation of Christian Living to Participation in War," *Open Door* (April 1943).*

"What Religious Freedom Means," *The Churchman* (September 1, 1943).

"Being a Christian in Wartime," *The Intercollegian* (October 1943), Vol. LXI, No. 2, pp. 4-5, 10.

"I Believe in Christ," *CTSR* (November 1943), Vol. XXXIII, No. 4, pp. 12-13. Reprinted with revisions in *The Intercollegian* (March 1944), Vol. LXI, No. 7.

"Christian Faith and Human Hopes," *CTSR* (November 1944), Vol. XXXIV, No. 4, pp. 11-15.

"Ten Years Out," *CTSR* (March 3, 1944), Vol. XXXIV, No. 2, pp. 29-30.

"Progress," *An Encyclopedia of Religion*, ed. Vergilius Ferm. New York: The Philosophical Library, 1945. pp. 611-12.

"Progressive orthodoxy," *An Encyclopedia of Religion*, ed. Vergilius Ferm. New York: Philosophical Library, 1945, p. 612.

"Evolution," *An Encyclopedia of Religion*, ed. Vergilius Ferm. New York: Philosophical Library, 1945. p. 265. Also, "Evolution, controversy over," pp. 265-66.

"Lewis Mumford and Christian Faith," *The Woman's Press* (May 1945), Vol. XLVI, No. 47, pp. 27-29.

"The Perplexity and the Opportunity of the Liberal Theology in America," *The Journal of Religion* (July

**Hereinafter *CTSR*.

1945), Vol. XXV, No. 3, pp. 168-78.
"Tradition and the Good," *Open Door* (1946) [unnumbered], p. 2.*
Untitled review of George Bellows exhibit at Chicago's Art Institute, *Open Door* (March 8, 1946), No. 583, p. 1.*
Letter to the Editor responding to student critique of his Bellows review, *Open Door* (undated), un-numbered, p. 3.*
"On Christian Love," *CTSR* (January 1946), Vol. XXXVI, No. 1, pp. 17-21.
"Democracy's Greatest Need," *Golden Jubilee Convention Digest* (1947), [no city]: National Congress of Parents and Teachers, p. 2.
"Brunner and Barth on Philosophy," *Journal of Religion* (October 1947), Vol. XXVII, No. 4, pp. 241-54.
"Truth in the Theological Perspective," *Journal of Religion* (October 1948), Vol. XXVIII, No. 4, pp. 242-54.
"The New Curriculum for the B. D. Degree," *CTSR* (November 1949), Vol. XXXIX, No. 4, pp. 6-10.
"What Religion Means to Me," *Pasadena Star News* (December 17, 1949), p. 6.

1950-1959

"Brother Lawrence," *The Intercollegian* (April 1950), Vol. LXVII, pp. 19-20.
"The Unity and Diversity of the Students," undated address.*
"The Gospel Is Greater Than We Think," *Advance* (December 24, 1951), pp. 9-10.
"The Meaning of Our Faith and the Life of the Church Today," *Divinity School News* (November 1, 1952), Vol. XIX, No. 4, pp. 1-9.
"Love in the Christian Faith [series of three lectures]": "The Form of the Gospel," *The Christian Sun* (July 10, 1952), p. 16: "The Cross and the Self," *The Christian Sun* (July 17, 1952), p. 16: "Christian Love and Social Justice," *The Christian Sun* (July 24, 1952), p. 16. [Bibliographer's note: these appear to be summaries of lectures given at the 1952 General Council of the South East Conference of Congregational Christian Churches at Claremont, California.]
"Faith and Order at Lund," *CTSR* (November 1952), Vol. XLII, No. 4, pp. 1-7.
"Christian Freedom and Academic Freedom," *The Christian Scholar* (March 1953), Vol. XXXVI, No. 1, pp. 11-22. [Bibliographer's note: an abridged version was printed in the *YWCA Magazine* (July 1953) as "Man's Freedom and the Christian Faith."]
"Christian Faith and Social Action," *Christianity and Society* (Spring 1953), Vol. XVIII, No. 2, pp. 7-13.
"Intercommunion at Lund, A Comment and a Proposal," *Ecumenical Review* (July 1953), Vol. V, No. 4, pp. 369-81.
"Basic Christian Affirmations [summaries of four addresses at the first national conference of the Faculty Christian Fellowship: Biblical Faith and Scientific Knowledge, Man in the Light of Christ, The Basis of Christian Ethics, History and Human Destiny]," *The Christian Scholar* (September 1953), Vol. XXXVI, No. 3, pp. 189-202.
"Christo-Centric Piety and Worship," undated, part of working papers of World Council of Churches' Commission of Faith and Order's Committee on 'An Enquiry on Worship for North America.'*
"Hope and Mystery in the Christian Faith," *Christian Century* (February 3, 1954), Vol. LXXI, No. 5, pp. 138-40.
"Christian Teaching and Christian Beliefs [pamphlet]," Boston, Chicago: Division of Christian Education, Congregational Christian Churches, 1955. Reprinted from six articles in *Children's Religion*; "God," November 1954, Vol. XV, No. 11; "Jesus Christ," December 1954, Vol. XV No. 12; "The Bible," January 1955 Vol. XVI, No. 1; "Man in the Christian Faith," February 1955, Vol XVI, No. 2; "The Church," March

1955, Vol. XVI, No. 3; "Death, Immortality, and Eternal Life," April 1955, Vol. XVI, No. 4.
"Christian Theology Today," *The YWCA Magazine* (May 1954), pp. 12-13, 32.
"The Significance of St. Augustine Today," *A Companion to the Study of St. Augustine,* ed. Roy Wesley Battenhouse. New York: Oxford University Press, 1955. pp. 3-14.
"The New Spirit in Theological Education," *Union Seminary Quarterly Review*† (November 1955), Vol. XI, No. 1, pp. 33-38.
"Andover Controversy," *Twentieth Century Enclopedia of Religious Knowledge,* ed. Lefferts A. Loetscher. Grand Rapids: Baker, 1955. pp. 41-42.
"The Form of Christian Freedom," *Advance* (January 25, 1956), Vol. CXLVIII, No. 2, pp. 11-12, 25-26.
"Niebuhr and Liberalism," *Reinhold Niebuhr: his religious, social, and political thought,* ed. Charles W. Kegley and Robert W. Bretall. New York: Macmillan, 1956. pp. 193-213.
Introduction to *The Ministry in Historical Perspectives* co-authored with H. Richard Niebuhr. New York: Harper and Brothers, 1956.
"Ministry under Tension," *Christianity and Crisis* (December 10, 1956), Vol. XVI, No. 21, pp. 169-70.
"Ministry of Reconciliation in an Unreconciled Age," *Alumni Bulletin* [Bangor Theological Seminary] (July 1956), Vol. XXXII, No. 3, pp. 1-5.
"The United Church of Christ," *Christianity and Crisis* (July 22, 1957), Vol. XVII, No. 13, p. 98. Reprinted in *The Guardian* [Madras] (September 12, 1957), p. 369(9)-370(10).
"Ethical Foundations of the Law: A New Interpretation," *Christianity and Crisis* (July 22, 1957), Vol. XVII, No. 13, pp. 99-101.
"American Theology Responds to New Interests," *Perspective* (October 1957). [Bibliographer's note: this is a condensation of the opening convocation address of the Southern California School of Theology.]
Letter to the editor re: article "Why Ministers Break Down," *Christianity and Crisis* (December 10, 1956), Vol. XVI, No. 21, pp. 169-70.
"Christianity and Naturalism: An Informal Statement," *USQR* (May 12, 1957), Vol. XII, No. 4, pp. 47-53.
"Pilgrimage and Promised Land," *Advance* (June 14, 1957), Vol. CXLIX, No. 12, pp. 10-11, 26.
"The Love of God," *Great Phrases of the Christian Language; a devotional book,* Roger L. Shinn, et al. Philadelphia: United Church Press, 1958. pp. 37-51.
"Professor's Column," *Union Theological Seminary Tower* (January 1958), Vol. IV, No. 3, p. 1. [Bibliographer's note: first line begins, "There is a widespread movement toward integration of the theological curriculum. . . ."]
"The Mystery of the Baptists," *Foundations* (January 1958), Vol. I, No. 1, pp. 7-9. Reprinted in *The Baptist Review* (May-June 1958), p. 12.
Definition essays, *A Handbook of Christian Theology,* ed. Marvin Halverson and Arthur A. Cohen. New York: Meridian Books, 1958. "Liberalism," pp. 207-10. "Love," pp. 216-20. "Modernism," pp. 233-35.
"Authority and Ministry," *USQR* (November 1958), Vol. XIV, No. 1, pp. 17-23. Abridged version, "What Is A Minister's Authority," *The New Christian Advocate* (July 1959), Vol. III, No. 7, pp. 69-73. Article reprinted in *Pastoral Preaching,* ed. Charles F. Kemp. St. Louis: Bethany Press, 1963.
Letter to the editor, fiftieth anniversary congratulations, *Christian Century* (April 2, 1958), Vol. LXXV, No. 13, p. 413.
"Fathers Reveal Reactions to Strindberg's Play . . . ["Road to Damascus"]," *The Vassar Chronicle* (April 12, 1958), Vol. XIV, No. 22, pp. 2, 4.

†Hereinafter *USQR*

"Man and Human Nature," undated.*
"Christological Distance: An Exploration in Ethics," undated.*
"Main Issues in Contemporary Theology," *The Future Course of Christian Adult Education . . .*, ed. Lawrence C. Little. Pittsburgh; University of Pittsburgh Press, 1959. p. 155-75.
"Education for the Christian Ministry," *Pulpit Digest* (January 1959), Vol. XXXIX, No. 249, pp. 22-26.
"Views of revelation," letter to the editors, re: whether theology is "scientific," *Christianity Today* (February 2, 1959), Vol. III, No. 9, p. 26.
"Moral Obligation in Process Philosophy," *Journal of Philosophy* (March 12, 1959), Vol. LVI, No. 6, pp. 263-70. Reprinted in *Alfred North Whitehead: Essays in His Philosophy*, ed. George L. Kline. Englewood Cliffs: Prentice Hall, 1963. pp. 189-95.
"The Incarnation," *Children's Religion* (December 1959), Vol. XX, No. 12, pp. 3-4.
"The Resurrection," *Children's Religion* (March 1960), Vol. XXI, No. 3, pp. 3-4.
[Bibliographer's note: the articles "The Incarnation," and "The Ressurection," were included with two by S. MacLean Gilmour in *Christmas and Easter, Message and Meaning*, pamphlet (1960). Boston, Chicago, Philadelphia: Division of Christian Education of the Board of Home Missions of the Congregational and Christian Churches, and Board of Christian Education and Publication of the Evangelical and Reformed Church.]

1960-1969

"What Are Theological Seminaries Doing to Enable Ministers to Cope With the Cultural Forces Today?" *New Dimensions in Lutheran Higher Education*. Papers presented at the Golden Anniversary Convention of the National Lutheran Educational Conference, Boston, January 10-12, 1960. pp. 137-41.
"Current Theological Developments and Religious Education," *Religious Education, A Comprehensive Survey of Background, Theory, Methods, Administration, and Agencies*, ed. Marvin J. Taylor. New York: Abingdon Press, 1960. pp. 44-53.
"Jesus Christ the Beginning," *Christianity and Crisis* (April 4, 1960), Vol. XX, No. 5, pp. 35-39. Reprinted in *Encounter* (Summer 1961), Vol. XXII, pp. 32-35.
"Therapy and Salvation, The Dimensions of Human Need," *USQR* (May 1960), Vol. XV, No. 4, pp. 303-17.
"Prayer Is the Soul's Venture in Honesty before God," *United Church Herald* (June 9, 1960), Vol. III, No. 12, pp. 10-11.
"Deity, Monarchy and Metaphysics: Whitehead's Critique of the Theological Tradition," *The Relevance of Whitehead*, ed. Ivor Leclerc. London, New York: The Macmillan Company, 1961. pp. 353-72.
"Tillich's Doctrine of God," *The Philosophical Forum* (1960-1961), Vol. XVIII, pp. 40-51.
"Tradition and Experience in American Theology," in *The Shaping of American Religion*, Volume I in *Religion in American Life* (series), ed. James Ward Smith and A. Leland Jamison. Princeton: Princeton University Press, 1961. pp. 443-95.
"The Life and Mission of the Church," *Encounter* (Summer 1961), Vol. XXII, No. 3, pp. 329-35.
"Vocation in the Christian Ministry," *The Minister's Own Mental Health*, ed. Wayne E. Oates. Great Neck: Channel Press, 1961. pp. 43-50. Reprinted from *Pastoral Psychology* (March 1961), Vol. XII, No. 112, pp. 8-12.
"God and Time," *The South East Asia Journal of Theology* (January 1961), Vol. II, No. 3, pp. 7-19.
"The True Measure of the Victory of God's Grace and Power, Message for Pentecost," *United Church Herald* (May 18, 1961), Vol. IV, No. 10, pp. 4-5, 31.
"Religious Issues in Twentieth Century Culture," in *Trends in Modern American Society*, ed. Clarence Mor-

ris. Philadelphia: University Press, 1962.

"What I Believe about Life after Death," *USQR* (May 1962), Vol. XVII, No. 4, pp. 315-20.

"The Philosophy of Henry Nelson Wieman," undated.*

"What I Believe about Christ," one of 1963 January Lectures at Union Theological Seminary, mimeographed.*

"The Vulnerable and the Invulnerable God," *USQR* (March 1962), Vol. XVII, No. 3, pp. 223-29. Also in *Christianity and Crisis* (March 5, 1962), Vol. XXII, No. 3, pp. 27-30.

"Love and Being," Duodecim (November 1963), mimeographed.*

"Changing Philosophical and Theological Concepts of Nature," undated.*

Definition articles, *Dictionary of the Bible*, ed. James Hastings; revised edition F. C. Grant and H. H. Rowley. New York: Charles Scribner's Sons, 1963. "Assurance," p. 65. "Doctrine," p. 219. "Heresy," p. 378.

"Wieman as a Christian Theologian," *The Empirical Theology of Henry Nelson Wieman*, ed. Robert W. Bretall. New York: The Macmillan Company, 1963. pp. 73-79.

"H. Richard Niebuhr (1894-1962), A Personal and Theological Memoir," *Christianity and Crisis* (November 25, 1963), Vol. XXIII, No. 20, pp. 209-13.

"Tragedy and the Christian Eschatology," *Encounter* (Winter 1963), Vol. XXIV, No. 1, pp. 61-76.

"What Is Systematic Theology?" in *A Report on an Invitational Conference on the Study of Religion in the State University*. New Haven: Society for Religion in Higher Education, 1964. pp. 24-49.

"How Does God Act? An essay in Whitehead's metaphysics," in *Process and Divinity*, Hartshorne-Festschrift, ed. Eugene Freeman and William L. Reese. LaSalle: Open Court, 1964. pp. 161-80.

"Disciplines of Participation," *Social Action* (May 1964), Vol. XXX, No. 9, pp. 23-70.

"Bibliography of Writings by Paul Tillich on Theology Related to Pastoral Care," mimeographed, 1964.*

"What Psychiatry Means to Theological Education," *USQR* (January 1964), Vol. XIX, No. 2, pp. 141-44. Reprinted in *The Journal of Pastoral Care* (Fall 1964), Vol. XVIII, No. 3, pp. 129-31, and in *Pastoral Psychology* (October 1965), Vol. XVI, No. 157, pp. 48-50.

"The Theology of Bernard E. Meland," *Criterion* (Summer 1964), Vol. III, No. 3, pp. 3-9. Reprinted in *Christian Century* (December 2, 1964), Vol. LXXXI, No. 49, pp. 1494-96, as "Liberal Theology Reconstructed, The Career of Bernard E. Meland."

"Some Queries to Professor Meland on His Paper: How is Culture a Source of Theology?" *Criterion* (Summer 1964), Vol. III, No. 3, pp. 28-33.

"Reflections on Thirty Years of Social Action," *Social Action* (December 1964), Vol. XXXI, No. 4, pp. 26-32.

"The Christian Mission and Higher Education," pamphlet. New York: Commission on Higher Education, National Council of Churches of Christ, 1964.

"A Christmas Message to Us," *YWCA Magazine* (December 1964), Vol. LVIII, No. 9, p. 2.

"The New Life in Christ: The Meaning and Experience of Continuing Redemption," address to a Methodist Conference on Christian Education November 11, 1965, mimeographed. [Bibliographer's note: this item is held at the library of Garret Theological Seminary, Evanston, Illinois.]

"The Being of God," one of 1965 January Lectures at Union Theological Seminary, mimeographed.*

"Christian Faith and the Human Community," *YWCA Magazine* (April 1965), Vol. LIX, No. 4, pp. 6, 34.

"The Grace of God and Secular Man," *United Church of Christ—Council for Higher Education Journal* (December 1965), Vol. IV, No. 3, pp. 1, 3-5, 8.

"St. Paul and Tillich," *USQR* (November 1965), Vol. XXI, No. 1, pp. 27-29.

Aphorism on "death of God theologians," *Time* (October 22, 1965), Vol. LXXXVI, No. 17, p. 62.

Comment on "Theological Reflections on the Gospel Accounts of Jesus' Death and Resurrection," by Hans W. Frei, *The Christian Scholar* (Winter 1966), Vol. XLIX, No. 4, pp. 310-12.

"Ministerial Responsibility and Tension Reduction," *The Journal of Pastoral Care* (June 1966), Vol. XX, No. 2, pp. 97-98.

Untitled essay on the question of truth and Martin Buber's philosophy, October 24, 1966, mimeographed.*

"John Knox's Conception of History," in *Christian History and Interpretation: Studies presented to John Knox,* ed. W. R. Farmer, C. D. F. Moule and R. R. Niebuhr, Cambridge: University Press, 1967. pp. 17-34.

"Martin Buber and Christian Thought," *The Central Conference of American Rabbis Yearbook, Vol.* LXXVI, 1966. Philadelphia: Central Conference of American Rabbis, 1967.

"A Comment on M. M. Thomas' Article ("Some Crucial Issues in Christian Social Ethics Today")," *Social Action* (January 1967), Vol. XXXIII, No. 5, pp. 16-20.

"Do You Believe in the Lord Jesus Christ?" Radio broadcast #146, WRVR (December 3, 1967), mimeographed.*

"The Disciplines of the New Freedom," *YWCA Magazine* (November 1967), Vol. LXI, No. 8, pp. 6-8, 28.

"Grace," in *A Dictionary of Christian Ethics,* ed. John Macquarrie. London: SCM Press Ltd., 1967. pp. 139-41.

"Tillich, Paul Johannes (1886-1965)," *Encyclopaedia Britannica,* 1967. p. 1156.

"Brunner, Heinrich Emil (1889-1966)," *Encyclopaedia Britannica,* 1967. p. 307.

"Priests, Prophets, and the Establishment," *Zygon, Journal of Religion and Science* (December 1967), Vol. II, No. 4, pp. 309-26.

"The New Theological Situation," *Theology Today* (January 1968), Vol. XXIV, No. 4, pp. 444-63,

"What Is Keeping the Churches Apart Today: Theological and Other Issues," Arden House Conference for Laymen, 1968, mimeographed.*

"The Prophetic Dimension," in *The Uniqueness of Man: A Discussion at the Nobel Conference,* ed. John D. Roslansky. Amsterdam, London: North Holland Publishing Co., 1968. pp. 139-63.

"Paul Tillich's Doctrine of Forgiveness," *Pastoral Psychology* (February 1968), Vol. XIX, No. 181, pp. 17-23.

"The Morphology of Commitment in Theological Education," *Theological Education* (Autumn 1968), Vol. V, No. 1, pp. 23-40.

"In Theological Explorations: The Roots of Hope," one of 1969 January Lectures at Union Theological Seminary, mimeographed.*

"The Next Step in Theology," *Union Theological Seminary Tower* (Spring 1969).

"Suffering and Being in Empirical Theology," in *The Future of Empirical Theology,* ed. Bernard E. Meland. Chicago: University of Chicago Press, 1969. pp. 175-94.

"A Theological View of Identity," in *The New Shape of Pastoral Theology, Essays in Honor of Seward Hiltner,* ed. William B. Oglesby, Jr. Nashville, New York: Abingdon Press, 1969. pp. 74-88.

"Law and Disorder: Some Reflections on the Political Philosophy of Edmond Cahn," *USQR* (Fall 1969), Vol. XXV, No. 1, pp. 19-36. Reprinted in *Social Responsibility in an Age of Revolution,* ed. Louis Finkelstein. New York: Jewish Theological Seminary of America, 1971. pp. 129-53.

"The Family Learns About Jesus" (pamphlet). Philadelphia: The Christian Education Press; Boston: The Pilgrim Press, 1960.

1970-1972

"Old Faiths and the New Humanity: A

View From Asia," opening convocation address, Union Theological Seminary, September 22, 1970, mimeographed.*
Pastoral Psychology, The Next 20 Years: In Relation to Theology," *Pastoral Psychology* (February 1970), Vol. XXI, No. 201, pp. 80-82.
Prozess-Theologie: Eine Neue Möglichkeit für die Kirche," tr. Helga Krüger, *Evangelische Theologie* (November 1970), Vol. XXX, No. 1.
The Concept of Truth in Karl Barth's Theology" *Religious Studies 6* (June 1970), pp. 137-145.
The Advancement of Theological Education in Asia," *The South East Asia Journal of Theology* (Autumn 1970), Vol. XII, p. 52-64.
Knowing and Hoping in the Christian Faith," in *The God Experience, Essays in Hope*, ed. Joseph P. Whelan, S. J., New York: Newman Press, 1971. pp. 168-89.
Time, Progress, and the Kingdom of God," in *Process Philosophy and Christian Thought*, ed. Delwin Brown, Ralph E. James, Jr., Gene Reeves. Indianapolis, New York: Bobbs-Merrill Company, Inc., 1971. pp. 441-63.
Theological Reflections on New Modes of Pastoral Care," in *Explorations in Ministry*, A Report on the Ministry in the '70s Project, ed. G. Douglass Lewis. New York: IDOC Dossier, 1971. pp. 240-56.
Response to Wolfhart Pannenberg," in *Hope and the Future of Man*, ed. Ewart H. Cousins. Philadelphia: Fortress Press, 1972. pp. 83-88.
Hope and the Future of Man: A Reflection," in *Hope and the Future of Man*, ed. Ewart H. Cousins. Philadelphia: Fortress Press, 1972. pp. 142-46.
The Logic of Theological Education," Willson Lectures, Wesley Theological Seminary, October 17-19, 1972, privately bound.
Seeming and Being [A series of lectures comprising: "The Being of God as Seen in Process Theology," The God of the Bible and Process Metaphysics," and "God and Demonic Evil."]," Truro: Nova Scotia Agricultural College, 1972.
"Response [to Committee on Collegiality]," *USQR* (Summer 1973), Vol. XXVIII, No. 4, pp. 293-96.
"A Philosophical Outlook," *Contemporary American Philosophy*, 2nd series, ed. John E. Smith. London: George Allen and Unwin, 1970, pp. 229-247.

III. Book Reviews
by Daniel Day Williams

1930-1939

Erasmus of Rotterdam, Stafan Zweig. *CTSR* (November 1934), Vol. XXIV, No. 4, pp. 26-27.
Science and Religion, N. Bishop Harman. *CTSR* (November 1935), Vol. XXV, No. 4, p. 31.
Towards the Christian Revolution, ed. R. B. Y. Scott and Gregory Vlastos. *CTSR* (March 1937), Vol. XXVII, No. 2, pp. 34-35.
The Study of Theology, ed. Kenneth E. Scott Kirk. *CTSR* (November 1939), Vol. XXIX, No. 4, pp. 29-30.
The Clue to History, John Macmurray. *CTSR* (November 1939), Vol. XXIX, No. 4, pp. 13-15. [Bibliographer's note: published as article, with title "Don't Despair."]

1940-49

Living the Christian Faith, Edwin Ewart Aubrey. *CTSR* (January 1940), Vol. XXX, No. 1, p. 23.
Man's Search for Himself, Edwin Ewart Aubrey. *CTSR* (November 1940, Vol. XXX, No. 4, pp. 27-28.
Our Knowledge of God, John Baillie. *CTSR* (November 1940), Vol. XXX, No. 4, 28-29.
The Human Meaning of Science, Arthur H. Compton. *The Journal of Religion* (July 1940), Vol. XX, No. 3, pp. 304-306.
Can Christianity Save Civilization? Walker Marshall Horton. *CTSR* (November 1940), Vol. XXX No. 4, pp. 26-27.

The Flowering of Mysticism, Rufus M. Jones. *CTSR* (March 1940), Vol. XXX, No. 2, p. 25.

A Philosophy of the Christian Revelation, Edwin Lewis. *The Christian Century* (December 4, 1940), Vol. LVII, No. 49, p. 153. [Bibliographer's note: published as article with title "All or Nothing."]

Swedish Contributions to Modern Theology, Nels F. S. Ferré. *CTSR* (January 1940), Vol. 30, No. 1, pp. 23-24.

The Presbyterian Doctrine of Children in the Covenant, Lewis Bevans Schenck. *Christendom* (Autumn 1940), Vol. V, No. 4, pp. 605-08. [Bibliographer's note: published as article with title "Infant Baptism and Church Membership."]

Theology and Modern Life: Essays in Honor of Harris Franklin Rall, ed. P. A. Schilpp. *CTSR* (November 1940), Vol. XXX, No. 4, pp. 25-26.

The Spiritual Aspects of the New Poetry, Amos N. Wilder. *CTSR* (November 1940), Vol. XXX, No. 4, p. 27.

Christian Faith and Democracy, Gregory Vlastos. *CTSR* (March 1940), Vol. XXX, No., 2, pp. 25-26.

The Problem of Religious Knowledge, Douglas Clyde MacIntosh. *CTSR* (January 1941), Vol. XXXI, No. 1, pp. 29-30.

The Christian's Knowledge of God, W. W. Bryden. *The Christian Century* (February 5, 1941), Vol. LVIII, No. 6, pp. 185-86. [Bibliographer's note: published as article with title "Misunderstanding Liberalism."]

The Christian Fellowship, Nels F. S. Ferré. *CTSR* (March 1941), Vol. XXXI, No. 2, pp. 23-24.

A Preface to Christian Theology, John A. Mackay. *CTSR* (March 1941,), Vol. XXXI, No. 2, pp. 22-23.

Can We Keep the Faith? James Bissett Pratt. *The Christian Century* (August 20, 1941), Vol. LVIII, No. 34, pp. 1030-31. [Bibliographer's note: published as article with title "Yes, But Will We?"]

Christianity: An Inquiry into Its Nature and Truth, Harris Franklin Rall. *CTSR* (November 1941), Vol. XXXI, No. 4, p. 22.

The Knowledge of God, D. Elton Trueblood. *CTSR* (November 1941), Vol. XXXI, No. 4, p. 21.

The Meaning of Revelation, H. Richard Niebuhr. *CTSR* (November 1941), Vol. XXXI, No. 4, pp. 20-21.

The Nature and Destiny of Man, Vol. I, Reinhold Niebuhr. *CTSR* (November 1941), Vol. XXXI, No. 4, pp. 19-20.

Wisdom and Folly in Religion, Joseph R. Haroutunian. *CTSR* (November 1941), Vol. XXXI, No. 4, p. 22.

The Christian Criticism of Life, Lynn Harold Hough. *The Christian Century* (December 3, 1941), Vol. LVII, No. 49, pp. 1505-06. [Bibliographer's note: published as article with title "Humanism and Christianity."]

Is God Emeritus? Shailer Mathews. *CTSR* (January 1942), Vol. XXXII, No. 1, pp. 26-27.

Man's Vision of God, Charles Hartshorne. *CTSR* (January 1942), Vol. XXXII, No. 1, pp. 25-26.

Suffering: Human and Divine, H. Wheeler Robinson. *CTSR* (January 1942), Vol. XXXII, No. 1, p. 26.

Christian Realism, John Bennett. *CTSR* (March 1942), Vol. XXXII, No. 2, p. 40.

Christian Doctrine, J. S. Whale. *The Christian Century* (April 1, 1942), Vol. LIX, No. 13, pp. 428-29. [Bibliographer's note: published as article with title "Preachable Theology."]

A Christian Faith, Nels F. S. Ferré. *The Christian Century* (September 2, 1942), Vol. LIX, No. 35, pp. 1058-59. [Bibliographer's note: published as article, with title "A Faith Necessary, Adequate and Final."]

Experience and the Christian Faith, Howard B. Jefferson. *CTSR* (November 1942), Vol. XXXII, No. 4, p. 23.

Prayer, George A. Buttrick. *CTSR* (November 1942), Vol. XXXII, No. 4, pp. 22-23.

A Realistic Philosophy of Religion, A. Campbell Garnett. *The Christian Century* (January 20, 1943), Vol. LX,

No. 3, pp. 80-81. [Bibliographer's note: published as article with title "The Mind of Liberal Religion."]

The Making of the Modern Mind, John Herman Randall, Jr. (revised edition). *CTSR* (January 1943), Vol. XXXIII, No. 1, pp. 18-19.

Philosophy in a New Key, Susanne K. Langer. *CTSR* (January 1943), Vol. XXXIII, No. 1, pp. 18-19. [Bibliographer's note: reviewed jointly with *The Making of the Modern Mind.*]

Our Eternal Contemporary, Walter Marshall Horton. *CTSR* (January 1943), Vol. XXXIII, No. 1, pp. 26-27.

God and Evil, C. E. M. Joad. *CTSR* (November 1943), Vol. XXXIII, No. 4, p. 28.

The Inner World, John Wright Buckham. *CTSR* (November 1943), Vol. XXXIII, No. 4, pp. 30-31.

The Nature and Destiny of Man, Vol. II, Reinhold Niebuhr. *CTSR* (November 1943), Vol. XXXIII, No. 4, pp. 26-27.

Redemption and Revelation, H. Wheeler Robinson. *CTSR* (November 1943), Vol. XXXIII, No. 4, pp. 29-30.

The Root and Flower of Prayer, Roger Hazelton. *CTSR* (November 1943), Vol. XXXIII, No. 4, pp. 27-28.

The Divine-Human Encounter, Emil Brunner, tr. Amandus W. Loos. *CTSR* (March 1944), Vol. XXXIV, No. 2, pp. 34-35.

The Healing of the Waters, Amos Wilder. *CTSR* (March 1944), Vol. XXXIV, No. 2, p. 34.

We Stand with Christ: An Essay in Catholic Apologetics, Joseph Clifford Fenton. *The Journal of Religion* (April 1944), Vol. XXIV, No. 2, p. 150.

The Path to Perfection, W. E. Sangster. *Christendom* (Summer 1944), Vol. IX, No. 3, pp. 386-88. [Bibliographer's note: published as article, with title "Perfect Love."]

Return to Christianity, Nels F. S. Ferré. *The Journal of Religion* (July 1944), Vol. XXIV, No. 3, pp. 227-29.

Slavery and Freedom, Nicholas Berdyaev, tr. R. M. French. *The Christian Century* (September 6, 1944), Vol. LXI, No. 36, pp. 1024-25. [Bibliographer's note: published as article with title "Is This a Phantom Freedom?"]

Religion Today and Tomorrow, "Social Religion," Vol. I; "Personal Religion," Vol. II; Douglas Clyde MacIntosh. *CTSR* (November 1944), Vol. XXXIV, No. 4, pp. 28-29.

A Man's Monument, Fred Eastman. *CTSR* (January 1945), Vol. XXXV, No. 1, p. 46.

The Christian Philosophy of History, Shirley Jackson Case. *Ethics* (April 1945), Vol. LV, No. 3, pp. 230-32.

Science and the Idea of God, William Ernest Hocking. *The Journal of Religion* (April 1945), Vol. XXV, No. 2, pp. 149-50.

The Vitality of Christian Tradition, ed. George F. Thomas. *The Journal of Religion* (July 1945), Vol. XXV, No. 2, pp. 218-219.

The Moral Theory of Evolutionary Naturalism, William S. Quillian, Jr. *The Christian Century* (December 5, 1945), Vol. LXII, No. 49, pp. 1354-55. [Bibliographer's note: published as article, with title "Naturalism, Old and New."]

The Christian Answer, ed. H. P. Van Dusen. *CTSR* (March 1946), Vol. XXXVI, No. 2, pp. 42-43.

Narrow Is the Way, William E. Park. *CTSR* (March 1946), Vol. XXXVI, No. 2, p. 44.

The Will To Be Christian, Jacob Spoolman. *CTSR* (March 1946), Vol. XXXVI, No. 2, p. 44.

Theology in an Age of Science, Leonard Hodgson. *The Journal of Religion* (July 1946), Vol. XXVI, No. 3, p. 231.

Faith and Reason, Nels F. S. Ferré. *CTSR* (March 1947), Vol. XXXVII, No. 2, pp. 42-43.

Foundations for Reconstruction, Elton Trueblood. *CTSR* (March 1947), Vol. XXXVII, No. 2, p. 44.

The Divine Imperative, Emil Brunner, tr. Olive Wyon. *The Christian Century* (December 3, 1947), Vol. LXIV, No. 49, pp. 1487-88.

Man in Revolt, Emil Brunner, tr. Olive Wyon. *The Christian Century*, (December 3, 1947), Vol. LXIV, No. 49, pp. 1487-88.

The Mediator, Emil Brunner, tr. Olive Wyon. *The Christian Century*, (December 3, 1947), Vol. LXIV, No. 49, pp. 1487-88. [Bibliographer's note: published with *The Divine Imperative* and *Man in Revolt*, as one review article, with title "Man Encounters God."]

Christian Apologetics, Alan Richardson. *CTSR* (November 1948), Vol. XXXVIII, No. 4, pp. 36-37.

The Reconstruction of Humanity, Pitrim Sorokin. *CTSR* (November 1948), Vol. XXXVIII, No. 4, pp. 37-38.

The Emotions, Outline of a Theory, Jean-Paul Sartre, tr. Bernard Frechtman. *The Christian Century* (December 1, 1948), Vol. LXV, No. 49, pp. 1304-05. [Bibliographer's note: published as article with title "Insights of an Existentialist."]

Evil and the Christian Faith, Nels F. S. Ferré. *CTSR* (January 1949), Vol. XXXIX, No. 1, pp. 29-30.

God Was in Christ: An Essay on Incarnation and Atonement, D. M. Baillie. *CTSR* (January 1949), Vol. XXXIX, No. 1, p. 29.

Skeptic's Search for God, Barbara Spofford Morgan. *CTSR* (January 1949), Vol. XXXIX, No. 1, p. 30.

The Philosophy of Decadentism, A Study of Existentialism, Norberto Bobbio, tr. David Moore. *The Christian Century* (January 5, 1949), Vol. LXVI, No. 1, p. 18.

The Doctrine of Our Redemption, Nathaniel Miklem. *Crozer Quarterly* (April 1949), Vol. XXVI, No. 2, pp. 161-62.

Commentary on Romans, Anders Nygren, tr. Carl C. Rasmussen. *The Christian Century* (September 14, 1949), Vol. LXVI, No. 37, p. 1073. [Bibliographer's note: published as article with title "Nygren's Paul."]

1950-59

The Reawakening of Christian Faith, Bernard E. Meland. *CTSR* (March 1950), Vol. XL, No. 2, p. 27.

Renewing the Mind, Roger Hazelton. *CTSR* (November 1950), Vol. XL, No. 4, pp. 34-35.

Psychotherapy and a Christian View of Man, David M. Roberts. *The Intercollegian* (March 1951), Vol. LXVIII, No. 7, pp. 13-14 [Bibliographer's note: published as an article, with title "Toward the Healing of Man."]

Systematic Theology, Volume I, Paul Tillich. *The Christian Century* (August 1, 1951), Vol. LXVIII, No. 31, p. 893. [Bibliographer's note: published as article, with title "High Peak of Theology."]

Preachers of Power, Paul Lembourne Higgins. *CTSR* (November 1951), Vol. XLI, No. 4, p. 30.

The Christian Understanding of God, Nels F. S. Ferré. *The Pastor* (July 1952), Vol. XV, No. 11, p. 33. [Bibliographer's note: published as article, with title "New Ground in Theology."]

Intercommunion, ed. Donald Baillie and John Marsh. *CTSR* (January 1953), Vol. XLIII, No. 1, pp. 42-43.

The Christian Doctrine of Creation and Redemption, Dogmatics, Vol. II, Emil Brunner, tr. Olive Wyon. *The Pastor* (May 1953), Vol. XVI, No. 9, p. 39. [Bibliographer's note: published as article, with title "Personal Character of Revelation."]

The Theology of Paul Tillich, ed. Charles W. Kegley and Robert W. Bretall *(The Library of Living Theology, Volume 1)*. *CTSR* (November 1953), Vol. XLIII, No. 4, pp. 31-32.

The Universal God, ed. Carl Herman Voss. *CTSR* (March 1954), Vol. XLIV, No. 2, p. 56.

Congregationalism: A Restatement, Daniel Jenkins. *Advance* (October 18, 1954), Vol. CXLVI No. 19, p. 10.

The Self and the Dramas of History, Reinhold Niebuhr. *USQR* (November 1955), Vol. XI, No. 1, pp. 56-57.

The Idea of Revelation in Recent Thought, John Baillie. *USQR* (May 1956), Vol. XI, No. 4, p. 81.

Changing Conceptions of Original Sin, Shelton Smith. *Review of Religion* (March 1958), Vol. XXII, Nos. 3-4, pp. 189-90.

Systematic Theology, Volume II, Paul Tillich. *Review of Religion* (March 1958), Vol. XXII, Nos. 3-4, pp. 194-200. [Bibliographer's note: published as article with title "Existence and the Christian Faith."]

Theology in Conflict: Nygren, Barth, Bultmann, Gustaf Wingren, tr. Eric H. Wahlstrom. *USQR* (November 1958), Vol. XIV, No. 1, pp. 73-74.

1960-69

Christ and Selfhood, Wayne E. Oates. *Pastoral Psychology* (September 1960), Vol. XII, No. 116, pp. 62-65.

Systematic Theology, Volume III, Paul Tillich. *The Christian Century* (April 22, 1964), Vol. LXXXI, No. 17, pp. 518-22. [Bibliographer's note: published as article with title "God's Grace and Human Estrangement."]

The Communion of Saints, Dietrich Bonhoeffer, tr. R. Gregor Smith. *The Alumni Bulletin* (Bangor Theological Seminary) (July 1964), Vol. XXXIX, p. 23.

The Voice of Illness, Aarne Siirala. *USQR* (November 1964), Vol. XX, No. 1, pp. 95-96.

Atonement and Psychotherapy, Don S. Browning. *The Christian Century* (June 14, 1967), Vol. LXXXIV, No. 24, pp. 784-85.

Christ and the Homosexual (Some Observations), Robert T. W. Wood. *Social Action* (December 1967), Vol. XXXIV, No. 4, pp. 30-37.

The Ethics of Sex, Helmut Thielicke, tr. John W. Doberstein. *Social Action* (December 1967), Vol. XXXIV, No. 4, pp. 30-37.

Toward a Christian Understanding of the Homosexual, H. Kimball Jones. *Social Action* (December 1967), Vol. XXXIV, No. 4, pp. 30-37. [Bibliographer's note: published with *Christ and the Homosexual* and *Ethics of Sex* in joint review, titled "Three Studies of Homosexuality."]

1970-1972

Existence and Love: A New Approach to Existential Phenomenology, William A. Sadler, Jr. *The Christian Century* (January 7, 1970), Vol. LXXXVIII, No. 1, pp. 21-22. [Bibliographer's note: published as article, with title "Humane and Hopeful."]

God and Rationality, Thomas F. Torrance, *USQR* (Winter 1972), Vol. XXVII, No. 2, p. 125.

Theological Dynamics, Seward Hiltner. *Theology Today* (October 1972), Vol. XXIX, No. 3, pp. 326-30.

IV. Publications Co-Authored by Daniel Day Williams

"Report of the Committee on 'An Enquiry on Worship for North America'," with other committee members, Williams being secretary. *Minutes* [of] *Commission on Faith and Order of the World Council of Churches and* [its] *Working Committees*, FOC Papers #21. Evanston, Chicago: World Council of Churches, 1954. pp. 22-24.

The Purpose of the Church and Its Ministry; reflections on the aims of theological education, H. Richard Niebuhr in collaboration with D. D. Williams and James M. Gustafson. New York: Harper and Brothers, 1956.

The Advancement of Theological Education, with James M. Gustafson and H. Richard Niebuhr. New York: Harper and Brothers, 1957.

We Believe: An Interpretation of the United Church Statement of Faith, with Roger L. Shinn. Philadelphia: United Church Press, 1966.

"Main Issues in Theological Education," with Helmut Richard Niebuhr and James Moody Gustafson. *Theology Today* (January 1955), Vol. XI, p. 512-517.

V. PUBLICATIONS CO-EDITED BY DANIEL DAY WILLIAMS

"Alumni Notes," with Eulalia Williams, *CTSR* (November 1942-March 1954). Vol. XXXII, No. 4—Vol. XLIV, No. 2.

Theological Education in America, Bulletin Nos. 1,2,3,4,5, with H. Richard Niebuhr. New Haven: April, September, 1954; January, September 1955; April 1956. [Bibliographer's note: D. D. Williams was associate director of the study project issuing these bulletins. No editors as such are listed.]

√*The Ministry in Historical Perspectives,* with H. Richard Niebuhr. New York: Harper and Brothers, 1956.

ADDENDA

To the published materials:

"Philosophy and Faith: A Study in Hegel and Whitehead," in *Our Common History as Christians: Essays in Honor of Albert C. Outler,* edited by John Deschner, Leroy T. Howe and Klaus Penzel. New York: Oxford University Press, 1975. pp. 157–174.

To the unpublished materials:

"A Critical Study of the Idea of God in E. S. Brightman and W. R. Sorley," A.M. thesis, University of Chicago, 76 pp. Typewritten, 1933.

"A Study of the Northwest Sector of Chicago." By G. K. Robinson, J. D. Noble, J. Mixon, D. D. Williams, and J. Berry. Typewritten, 1934.

"The Function of Theology in the Church," B.D. thesis. The Chicago Theological Seminary. Typewritten, 1934.

"Constructive Theology Class Notes 1949–1957. 3 Volumes, Autumn, Winter, and Spring Quarters. Recorded by students. Mimeographed.

"A Protestant View of the Bible Today." Undated.

"Dying and Living in the Spirit." Undated.

"Evil, Freedom and Hope." Undated.

"Current Theological Trends in America," 1970.

There are additional published items (book reviews, interviews, and letters) and additional unpublished materials (lectures, papers, drafts of encyclopedia articles, etc.) held in the Williams collection at the Center for Process Studies in Claremont, Ca.

Sources and Acknowledgements

The editor wishes to express his gratitude to Eulalia Williams for her encouragement and support for the project of reprinting many of her husband's papers and to Professor John Cobb and Tony Wolfe for their assistance along the way. He wishes to acknowledge the sources of the material reprinted in the previous pages and to thank the copyright holders who have given permission to reprint individual essays.

1. "A Philosophical Outlook," from *Contemporary American Philosophy*, edited by J. E. Smith. Reprinted by permission of Humanities Press, Atlantic Highlands, NJ, 07716.
2. "Theology and Truth," *The Journal of Religion* (October 1942), Vol. xxii, No. 4, pp. 382–97.
3. "Christian Faith and Social Action," *Christianity and Society*, (Spring, 1953) Vol. xviii, No. 2, pp. 7–13.
4. "Moral Obligation in Process Philosophy," *The Journal of Philosophy*, Vol. 56, No. 6, March 12, 1959, pp. 263–70. Used by permission.
5. "Deity, Monarchy and Metaphysics," from *The Relevance of Whitehead*, edited by Ivor Leclerc. 1961 George Allen and Unwin (Publishers) Ltd. Used by permission.
6. "Religious Issues in Twentieth Century Culture," from *Trends in Modern American Society*, edited by Clarence Morris, Philadelphia: University of Pennsylvania Press, 1962. Used by permission.
7. "How Does God Act? An Essay in Whitehead's Metaphysics," from *Process and Divinity*, edited by Eugene Freeman and William L. Reese, LaSalle: Open Court Publishing Co. 1964. Used by permission.
8. "A Theological View of Identity" by Daniel D. Williams excerpted from *The New Shape of Pastoral Theology* edited by William Oglesby. Copyright © by Abingdon Press. Used by permission.
9. "The Prophetic Dimension," from *The Uniqueness of Man: A Discussion of the Nobel Conference* edited by John D. Rolansky 1969, Amsterdam: North Holland Publishing Co. Used by permission.
10. "Knowing and Hoping in the Christian Faith," from *The God Experience* edited by Joseph P. Whelan, S.J. Copyright © by Newman Press, 1971. Used by permission of Paulist Press.
11. "Philosophy and Faith: A Study in Hegel and Whitehead," from *Our Common History as Christians: Essays in Honor of Albert C. Outler* by John Deschner et al. Copyright © by Oxford University Press, Inc. Reprinted by permission.
12. "Barth and Brunner on Philosophy," *Journal of Religion*, (October 1948), Vol. xxvii, No. 4, pp. 241–54.
13. "Niebuhr and Liberalism," from *Reinhold Niebuhr: his religious, social, and political thought* edited by Charles W. Kegley and Robert W. Bretall. New York: Macmillan, 1956, pp. 193–213. Used by permission of Dr. Charles Kegley and Mrs. Robert Bretall.

14. "Tillich's Doctrine of God," *The Philosophical Forum* (1960–61), Vol. XVIII, pp. 40–51.
15. "Wieman as a Christian Theologian," *The Empirical Theology of Henry Nelson Wieman*, edited by Robert Bretall. New York: Macmillan, 1963. pp. 73–79. Used by permission of Mrs. Robert Bretall.
16. "The Theology of Bernard Meland," *Criterion* (Summer 1964) Vol. III, No. 3, pp. 3–9 and "Some Queries to Professor Meland on His Paper: How is Culture a Source of Theology," *Criterion*, (Summer 1964), Vol. III, No. 3. pp. 28–33.
17. "Martin Buber and Christian Thought," from *The Central Conference of American Rabbis Yearbook* Vol. LXXVI, 1966. Copyright © Central Conference of American Rabbis. Used by permission.
18. "Paul Tillich's Doctrine of Forgiveness," *Pastoral Psychology* (February 1968), Vol. XIX, No. 181, pp. 17–23. Used by permission.
19. "The Concept of Truth in Karl Barth's Theology," *Religious Studies* 6, June 1970, pp. 137–145. Used by permission of Cambridge University Press.
20. "Response to Wolfhart Pannenberg" from *Hope and the Future of Man* edited by Ewart H. Cousins. Copyright © 1972 by Fortress Press. Used by permission.
21. Bibliography of Daniel D. Williams. Compiled by Jean C. Lambert. *Union Seminary Quarterly Review* (Winter–Summer, 1975) Vol. XXX, Nos. 2–4, pp. 217–229. Reprinted by permission.